NAPOLEON
1813

NAPOLEON
1813

Yehezkel Shelah

JANUS PUBLISHING COMPANY
London, England

Translated from the Hebrew
by Fred Skolnik

First published in Great Britain 2000
by Janus Publishing Company Limited,
76 Great Titchfield Street,
London W1P 7AF

Reprinted 2001

www.januspublishing.co.uk

Copyright © 2000 by Yehezkel Shelah
The author has asserted his moral rights

**A CIP catalogue record for this book
is available from the British Library.**

ISBN 1 85756 496 0

Typeset in 10pt Times New Roman
By Chris Cowlin

Cover design Peter Clarke

Front cover: Acknowledgement to John Schneider for use of
'The French Army Leaving Leipsic' from the aquarelle by
F. De Myrbach, from *Life of Napoleon Bonaparte*, New York,
The Century Company, 1896

Printed and bound in Great Britain

TO ASA

whose memory is always with me

CONTENTS

PREFACE

The story told in this book is first and foremost an exciting one that deserves to be told. Its hero is one of the most compelling figures in history – unusually talented, an inspiring adventurer, a commander of incredible charisma with a touch of charlatanism, a leader who repelled and attracted, a combination of generalissimo and führer. So many books have been written about him mainly because it is a pleasure to write about him. And this impossible without reading about him, which is an even greater pleasure. Liddell-Hart has said that history is the story of man's marchings and stumblings. Napoleon Bonaparte was indeed a man who marched and stumbled, marched and stumbled.

The year that this book deals with has certainly been studied, but other years in Napoleon's career have been studied even more. The year 1813 was an important and decisive one, but it has been treated generally as an intermezzo between the terrible Russian campaign and the inevitable end at Waterloo. It is curious that no one has taken cognizance of the fact that the characteristics of the 1813 campaign were substantially different from those of its predecessors. These differences have had an enormous effect on people's lives – to this very day. Whoever wishes to understand the events of the first half of the twentieth century would do well to turn back and explore the history of those times. There it can be seen that whosoever stirs up the whole world against him is fated to start a world war.

Wars represent a contradiction in terms. Its makers and heroes aspire to perfection, with everything unfolding in accordance with a precisely laid out scheme of solutions for every foreseeable possibility and ending in clearcut victory, pure and simple. In practice it diverges almost from the first minute from everything that was predicted. War is a chain of errors resulting mainly from the inability to foresee the effect of human weakness on events. It is easier to predict the final outcome of a war than what will happen until that result is achieved. Napoleon, mostly in the last years of his rule, is an ideal subject for the study of the connection between personal weaknesses, the design of policy and the way such policy is implemented militarily.

I was attracted to the subject of this book because the Second World War has been my interest for many years and I am still trying to discover its roots in the distant past. This was a truly great war, vast in scope and still unimaginable in its horror. The war of 1813 reveals the same characteristics and broad lines. In this war, too, a single individual imposed on the entire world, and on his own army, a total, all-encompassing war – which represented the only way to get rid of him. In both instances the world rebelled against the killing and destruction to mobilise all its resources – human, material, intellectual for the purpose of liberating itself from the evil genius that would stop at nothing to fulfil its designs.

I have tended to use books and studies written in the nineteenth century and early part of the twentieth, for the balance between the collection and study of facts and the wisdom of hindsight favours nineteenth century authors. This is not to say that in the literature produced before then there was no personal bias in regard to Napoleon, but this lack of objectivity serves in a way as an advantage to the modern writer: he must scrupulously re-examine the important facts, which is in itself something of an adventure. The number of versions, the different representations of the facts, the amount of errors – innocent but also intentional – is amazing and the whole process of nitpicking and sidestepping goes a long way towards sharpening one's focus.

This book is devoid of academic baggage, eschewing footnotes and other appurtenances of the researcher for the sake of easier reading. On the other hand, the process of research and writing involved the collation of sources and comparison of versions to ascertain the facts and clarify questions on which there is no general agreement. Whatever is still not clear is pointed out. When I adopt the opinion or view of any writer I acknowledge this and cite his name. When a judgement is unattributed it is my own.

It is customary to conclude a preface with acknowledgements, perhaps because the writer feels that his fixation has to some extent upset the lives of whomever helped him. My wife, Aviva, and my sons, Amir and Ofer, had to read almost every draft and will perhaps be consoled by the fact that I gave much weight to their comments, especially in relation to the structure of the book, its style and its omissions. Mrs Bina Pe'er edited the book with great skill and dedication and I thank her mainly for occasionally overlooking my pet quirks as well as for eliminating a good many of them. I will always be grateful to my good friend Shai Linn, who already knew years ago that the day would come when I would tear myself away from worldly concerns to write this book, and who obtained for me one of the most helpful – and rare – basic books on the 1813 campaign. Also deserving of warm thanks is the village schoolteacher from Gross Görschen – though there is almost no chance that he will read these words – who has been studying the battle of Lützen for many years, for the simple reason that his house borders the battlefield. I ran into him by chance when I was wandering around the village fields and he guessed why I was there and pointed out a few things that I have not found in any book.

Yehezkel Shelah

Tel Aviv 1999

INTRODUCTION

Napoleon Bonaparte was a product of the French Revolution. He was not drawn to the Revolution because its ideals inflamed his senses but as a young professional soldier called to the colours. The road he travelled from his position in the Republican regime to his coronation as emperor – his rapid advancement in the Republican army, first as a reward but later to get him out of France, his election as first consul and then the coronation – is part of an amazing story that seems to belong to the realm of historical fiction. At the same time, it should be emphasised that from the beginning Napoleon absorbed the ideas of the Revolution and his participation in the processes it engendered was not artificial or opportunistic. At a certain early albeit short-lived stage, he was even considered a Jacobin ('Marat and Robespierre are my saints,' he said). Indeed, only by looking into the depths of his soul and painstakingly tracing out the development of his personality may we find the dividing line between his ambition and his desire to contribute to the great social and political changes taking place in France. It was the British prime minister, Canning, who said that Napoleon was dangerous because of his character and not because of his policies.

This fascinating and unique individual has been written about endlessly. Only Hitler can compete with him in this respect and he as yet trails considerably behind him. This extraordinary interest in Napoleon derives from the fact that he is one of the greatest figures in human history, great because of being one of those very few individuals who have shaped the world and determined its destiny. One of the characteristics common to such individuals is their fatalistic concept of themselves as 'agents of destiny'. This idea, whether as a rationalisation for frightening acts or as a reflection of sincere belief, is certainly not naïve and underscores the need to understand the phenomenon of personal ambition insofar as it sets universal goals for itself. Napoleon himself said that it was hard for him to determine sincerely what his real and whole-hearted intentions were.

Napoleon emerged and rose out of the ceaseless turmoil that the Revolution created. There is no need for recourse to a deterministic view of history to see

1

that a radical process of change producing social and political anarchy will give rise to groups, and sometimes to individuals, who will exploit a chaotic and seemingly hopeless reality to seize power. Their chances of winning support are great and it is therefore easy for them to strengthen and legitimise their leadership by seeming to play according the rules laid down by the people, even if they have no intention of observing these rules once their regimes are recognised. It is therefore no wonder that one way or another these regimes are despotic in character, since tyranny is either inherent in them or required to achieve their goals. Probably both are the case. The need for a leader to restore order and bring peace makes for the acceptance of a tyranny that is seen as temporary, until the chaos is quelled. Napoleon said that as soon as he completed the consolidation of the Empire and brought peace he would institute democracy, freedom and prosperity. It was not only the masses who believed him. Goethe, for example, was one of Napoleon's admirers, saying that his personality was among the greatest in history and embodied everything that is logical, legitimate and European in the revolutionary movement. Beethoven too admired him, though he struck out his dedication to Napoleon of his Third Symphony – the 'Eroica' – after Napoleon crowned himself emperor. Beethoven saw this as foreboding evil.

Even if we call Napoleon a tyrannical dictator and voracious conqueror, we still have to admit that his regime in France was far from being one of fear and despotism. It was certainly authoritarian, reflecting the autocratic rule of a single individual, but the element of terror was not present. The background to his rise to power was indeed a reign of terror and disorder, but Napoleon had no need for his predecessors' methods and his authority replaced fear as an instrument of rule.

He was a conqueror, but he inherited the policy of conquest from his revolutionary predecessors, who wished to protect France from the conservative Europe that rose against it, as well as to export the French Revolution to other countries. His autocratic rule should thus be seen as growing out of the situation in France and his conquests as a direct continuation of previous policy. Certainly he seized upon both these cornerstones of his regime with considerable willingness – they were right for him and he was right for them – but he did not invent them.

Generally speaking, it may be said that Napoleon was not an original innovator in any field, including the military, where he won most of his fame. His strength lay in putting into practice the ideas he inherited, and as such it is hard to find anyone more successful. The mission he took upon himself –

either through personal force or destiny – and in whose name he justified all his acts, amounted to a natural process of carrying out the tasks he inherited. There is thus nothing in his personal rise to contradict the argument that he was a creature of the Revolution – 'the Revolution Incarnate', as Metternich put it. He was its direct continuation, and it is only because of his personality that the path he chose seems unique. The only creation of Bonaparte is Bonapartism, which is only the placement of his personal and very distinctive stamp on ideas, concepts and actions imagined by others.

This book deals with one year in the sixteen that Napoleon ruled. Its principal aim is to demonstrate that it was the first year in the modern history of mankind where war was fought as total war. The war of 1813 was the first world war. A hundred years would pass before the world once again saw total war, whose 'world' dimension requires no corroboration. The claim of the war of 1914 as a world war derives mainly from the differences in scope, numbers and intensity: the enormous size of the theatres of operation, the weapons technology, whose tremendous changes increased fire power and mobility, and the participation of the United States of America. Our emphasis on the close tie of Napoleon, the initiator of the first total war, to the revolution that preceded his regime is meant to help show that the gradual change that took place in the European regimes, starting with the French Revolution, led to a new kind of military conflict calling into play all the human and material resources of nations. Napoleon was an efficient and powerful instrument for the implementation of the first phase of this process of change. He inherited from the Revolution the fervour of the masses and their willingness to sacrifice themselves and he exploited them to the full. Without them the concept of total war would not have been realised. As Count Yorck said: 'Napoleon paved the way for wars in which whole nations take part, for the formation of armies based upon universal military service.'

Napoleon was born on the island of Corsica in 1769. He was educated in France from the age of nine, first in a military boarding school and afterwards at the Military School in Paris. From the time of his youth he had been a patriot – a Corsican patriot. Even when he was swept up in the republican enthusiasm that began with the Revolution of 1789 and continued with the riots that led to the temporary flight of Louis XVI two years later, it was because he believed that the changes taking place in France would be good for his Corsican homeland as well. From the beginning of the

Revolution up to the middle of 1793 Napoleon spent most of his time in Corsica getting involved in the local imbroglios and intrigues. When he was forced to flee to France he joined the artillery, for which he had been intended in the days of his military training, with the rank of captain. At this time he was identified with the Jacobins, who headed the Republican regime, and it was in their service that he suppressed the monarchist insurrection in Toulon at the end of 1793. As a reward he was placed at the head of artillery in the army earmarked to campaign in Italy and given the rank of brigadier-general. In July 1794 his benefactor Robespierre was deposed and executed. Napoleon himself was imprisoned and barely escaped a similar fate. The riots and anarchy that had marked the year repelled him and would not be forgotten when he came to power. In October 1795, when he was weighing his resignation from the French army and the possibility of offering his services to some other country, Barras, a member of the ruling Directory, called upon him to suppress another mass monarchist insurrection, this time in Paris. For his good work Napoleon was named commander of the Army of the Interior, a position that enabled him to put his ideas about law and order into practice.

The revolutionary wars that began in 1792 marked the beginning of modern wars resulting from political struggles and involving the clash of opposing social principles. They were still mainly related to the upsetting of the traditional balance of power but now took on added and previously unknown dimensions. For the first time dynastic rule was being challenged, opposed now by the rights of the individual and of the people, after being the basic principle among the major European powers for so long. From the beginning the ideas and events of the Revolution aroused much interest throughout Europe, soon leading to agitation that threatened the very foundations of the European regimes. The rulers – emperors, kings and princes – understood that what had begun as an internal affair of France might spread like wildfire throughout the Continent. At the beginning of 1791 the sovereigns of conservative Europe declared that, if the revolutionary government of France did not act with greater moderation, they would be forced to intervene to restore order and re-establish the authority of the French monarchy. France's reaction was sharp – the unequivocal rejection of their demands and the accusation that Louis betrayed his country and instigated its enemies. War was now only a matter of time, and it was France itself which declared it, in April 1792, at the height of the conflict between the revolutionary authorities and the king. The enemy was the Austrian emperor but, in fact, war was being declared against all of Europe, accompanied by a declaration that the French army was going to liberate all the peoples of the Continent. For their part, the members of the anti-French coalition (Austria, the German principalities that were part of the Holy Roman Empire, including military units made up of anti-revolutionary French emigrés, Prussia and Sardinia) affirmed their commitment to the principle of monarchy and the defence of European culture and began to march on France.

The French army was not in the best shape. It was made up of veteran units and the newly mobilised volunteers of the revolutionary National Guard. Many officers and soldiers had emigrated to Germany and the army itself was disorganised, lacking in discipline, deficient in training and wanting in equipment. Under these circumstances a declaration of war seemed rash, and indeed the first clashes added little to France's honour. Coalition forces arrayed themselves along the Rhine and invaded France in August and, after overrunning the border outposts, marched on Paris. The Austro-Prussian operations under Brunswick were carried out in the traditional cumbersome way, which enabled the startled French to bring up reinforcements and drive the enemy back to the Rhine after a battle in September near the village of Valmy, about 100 kilometres west of Metz. It was in fact the French artillery that won the battle, which in effect saved the Revolution. Though the battle could not be called a great military exploit, its moral effect on the army and the nation was enormous. On the other fronts as well, in northern and southern France, the revolutionary forces succeeded in expelling the enemy across the country's borders thus establishing, for the first time since the Revolution, boundary lines recognised as natural even by the belligerent powers. Dumouriez, the victor of Valmy, knew how to exploit his success and penetrated into the Low Countries, gaining control of most of Belgium, including Brussels, by the end of the year.

In France it was understood that military thinking would have to be changed before the next stage of the conflict with the hostile coalition. The shock of being invaded gave way to a kind of patriotic fervour which government leaders exploited to try to get the country on a war footing, with all its resources mobilised and universal conscription. But organisation was still faulty as was the concentration of material resources. Many soldiers deserted and despite improvements training was still far from satisfactory. On the other hand, the seeds of national mobilisation had been sown and the foundation laid for the changes demanded in fighting methods and logistics. A process of getting the best men into the army now commenced, facilitated by the improved conditions and status and the hope of an escape from the citizen's exposure to the depredations of the Revolution. The lack of transport facilities and equipment was compensated by the resourcefulness and the enthusiasm of the troops. The European armies were surprised by the new look of the French army: its speed and mobility and its ability to live off the land.

At the start of 1793, France's offensive in Belgium and the Rhineland was in full swing. The vested interest that King Louis had in the failure of the revolutionary army did not escape the eyes of the revolutionary government, which accused him of subversion even before the declaration of war. In December 1792 it was decided to put him on trial. He was convicted and executed in January, an act that shocked Europe and deepened the hostility to France. The military coalition was now broadened to include Great Britain, Holland and Spain. Thus a large-scale anti-French alliance took shape that lacked only the active participation of Russia. The British role was principally one of encouragement and financial support.

In March the Austrians crushed Dumouriez at Neerwinden in eastern Belgium and he himself went over to the enemy. France again faced the danger of invasion, but the sluggishness of its enemies and the involvement of some of them in other conflicts, in some cases among themselves, saved France from any immediate threat. Prussia and Austria were busy in Poland and Britain was engaged in its naval conquests all over the globe. France's new hero was Carnot, an engineer with military training who joined the Revolution two years after its start. It was he who determined the military targets and strategy, the training regime and the equipment programme. Large-scale conscription was instituted which succeeded despite the occasional opposition of royalists (it will be remembered that one such uprising had been put down by artillery captain Bonaparte). Everything proceeded at a snail's pace with senior officers replaced in regular succession. None the less the large size of the army and its improved methods of fighting and administration were beginning to give France an edge and, by the end of 1794, it controlled all of Belgium and a large part of Holland, had cleared the Rhineland, driven the Spanish across the Pyrenèes and occupied the Alpine passes leading to northern Italy. Thus came to an end the First Coalition against France and in the middle of 1795 two of its member – first Prussia and then Spain – made peace with the hated revolutionary land.

France now sat within its natural borders, but instead of living in peace it found itself being dragged into a new stage of military expansion by its big, war-hungry army. Though the army was not yet fully equipped, it was full of enthusiasm and officers at all levels showed great resourcefulness despite having been too quickly promoted, and without proper training. Forces were now organised into regiments, divisions and field armies. Battlefield strategy struck original notes: intelligent use of topographical data, high mobility enabling rapid advances, rapid concentration creating superiority at vital points, and more modest living conditions in the field obviating the need for permanent supply lines. Carnot pushed the army to attack wherever it had superior forces and to aim at destroying the enemy. All this would light the way for General Bonaparte when he came to take an active part in the Revolution.

Napoleon was now commander of the Army of the Interior and found enough to occupy him. He cleansed the police of its royalist base and now fought against subversive elements among the Jacobins. But, more than anything else, he wanted to return to the army of Italy, where he had been posted two years before – only this time as its head. The expansionist policy of the Directory, which began to take wing with the crumbling of the First Coalition, suited Napoleon's temperament and ambition perfectly. In February 1796, not yet 27, he got the appointment he coveted. It was said that Napoleon's bene-factor Barras gave it as a kind of dowry to his former mistress Josephine Beauharnais on her marriage to Napoleon in March. If this is so – and there is much evidence that it is – then of all the men who leaped to high position from their lovers' balconies no military figure was as gifted as Napoleon. The Italian campaign began immediately after the marriage ceremony and continued through to October of the following year. In conducting it, General Bonaparte was transformed from a wunderkind, regarded by his subordinates and staff officers with suspicion and scorn, to a successful and beloved general. It was this campaign that brought to light his extraordinary military talents and saw the formation of the strategic concepts that would guide him in the future. It also elevated his self-confidence to heights that would serve as a springboard in his meteoric rise to power. During the campaign Napoleon was not only the head of an army, he was also a first-rate politician and diplomat converting military victory into political agreements that gave his country highly significant advantages.

Napoleon's orders were to attack in northern Italy through the Alps and to pin down the Austrians while the main army of the Rhine made its way to Vienna. His adversaries, the armies of Austria and Sardinia (the House of

Savoy in northern Italy, with its capital at Turin), numbered over 70,000 men, giving them an advantage of almost two to one over his own. Napoleon crossed the Alps and struck the enemy a series of lightning blows that left his own and the enemy's forces speechless with wonder. Never having commanded so much as a large formation in battle, he eliminated the Sardinian army as a fighting force within a month. The Austrians were the next objective. At Lodi he defeated them in the fight for the bridge (May 1796) and the way to Milan was open. Here Napoleon demonstrated for the first time the supreme personal example that would guide him in the future – he placed himself at the head of his troops in the assault. At the end of the month he was in Milan. His front, which was intended to be secondary, now became the main theatre of operations. The great French offensive against Austria had been stopped cold and the Austrians under Archduke Charles defeated the army of the Rhine on German soil. Napoleon, on the other hand, fought off a series of Austrian counter-offensives that continued from July to the end of the year and in the end made his way to Vienna via the Tyrol. Austria sued for peace and Napoleon acceded at Campo Formio in October. The treaty gave France much more than the victory in Italy justified. It gave France Belgium and recognised its conquest of the Rhineland as well as of a number of islands in the Mediterranean and the Lombardy region in northern Italy, which became the Cisalpine Republic.

Already, at the beginning of the Italian campaign, Napoleon demonstrated one of the important foundations of his special brand of leadership – his ability to speak directly to his soldiers in order to persuade and inspire them. These orations, made in various campaigns, under different circumstances and quoted abundantly, serve as a model for leaders addressing troops and reveal a particular facet of all-conquering charisma. The commander of the army, barely 27, had declared in his order of the day before the campaign started: 'Soldiers! You are naked and starving. I will lead you into the most fertile plains of the earth. Great cities, opulent provinces, will be in your power; and there await you honour, glory and wealth.'

After Campo Formio, Napoleon returned to France and received a hero's welcome. The Directory was concerned. A mere boy springs from the ranks, captures the imagination of the masses, shows an independence that perhaps bodes ill and knows how to publish his glory. However, he is also an extremely capable general. The combination of this concern and esteem inspired the Directory to use the young general as its main instrument of foreign policy.

After the coalition dissolved, Great Britain remained France's only active open enemy. Napoleon was given the task of crossing the English Channel and invading its territory. But after studying conditions and analysing his chances, he came to the conclusion that the campaign was hopeless as long as the Channel could not be isolated in terms of naval control. The area of future operations against Britain and its imperial interests was then transferred to the Middle East and Napoleon was ordered to take Malta, Egypt and Syria. He was the main contributor to the strategic planning whose aim was the defeat of Britain and saw in it the means of gaining control of the sea lanes to India. Now, for the first time, the talents of Napoleon the Great Conqueror came to the fore.

His first land battles were successful but his fleet suffered defeat at the hands of Admiral Nelson (Battle of the Nile, August 1798). He conquered Malta and expelled its knights and then invaded Egypt, crushing the Mamelukes in a great battle that took place not far from the Pyramids in July. ('Soldiers! From the summits of the Pyramids, forty centuries behold you'). With lower Egypt now under French control, Napoleon turned to Syria, but was stopped at the gates of Acre and held up for three months (March–May 1799). At Acre Napoleon learned a number of lessons: that sieges are difficult and protracted affairs, that sojourns in distant lands expose an army to 'non-military' but debilitating nemeses like plague and harsh climate, and that a well-trained sea force can be a serious factor (the besieged of Acre received significant aid from the British fleet). Napoleon withdrew to Egypt again and found himself on the horns of a dilemma: on the one hand he could not move eastward and in the Mediterranean the British were in full control; on the other hand, he received information from home that the rule of the Directory was beginning to come apart. Given the circumstances, the commander of the Army of the East left his troops behind and, in October, after an exhausting and danger-fraught sea journey of six weeks, arrived in Paris. (Thirteen years later he would face a similar problem and abandon his army a second time.) The men he left behind remained in Egypt for two years and in the end were forced to withdraw from the country in an agreement that amounted to surrender.

At the time of Napoleon's return to France, the situation was extremely complex. France now faced the Second Coalition, almost identical in composition to the first, but this time with Russia far more active. Large portions of the land France had conquered in Italy, Switzerland and Germany had been lost and it was now being threatened from the Low Countries. Though there had been some improvement in the military situation from June 1799 the coalition was still a threat. The economy too was shaky: the Treasury was empty, unemployment and inflation were rampant and the nation was fed up with war and the corruption in government. Napoleon was again received with enthusiasm, even though he had abandoned his army without permission, and the Directory offered him any command he wished. But General Bonaparte now aspired to much more than army command. He preferred to enter the corridors of power. Two members of the Directory enlisted him in a plot against their colleagues 'for the salvation of the Republic'. The man who knew how to take brilliant advantage of changing circumstance was this time at his best and, in the coup d'état of 18 Brumaire (9–10 November 1799), he played a central role. He was the 'sword of the coup', as one of the conspirators put it. At the end of the day power was in the hands of three consuls, one of them being Napoleon. Soon enough, just 30 years of age, he became first consul with almost unlimited authority, the real ruler of France.

Napoleon, the strategist and leader, now aspired to peace, which he required to deal with the shaky situation in the country. It was clear to him that the road to peace would necessarily take him through another military campaign in order to break up the Second Coalition once and for all, to consolidate gains and to recoup losses. (More than ten years later he would also seek a general peace to consolidate gains and recover lost territory, but the scenario would be completely different and he would fail to understand the new rules, acting according to the old ones.) In the spring he attacked on two well-trod fronts: General Moreau penetrated the Rhineland and he himself crossed the Alps again through the St Bernard Pass and rolled south to the Po Valley. On 14 June, he met the Austrians at Marengo after they had come up from the coast. The Austrians seized the initiative and, by virtue of hard fighting, were on the verge of handing Napoleon a defeat that could have destroyed his military reputation. But the timely arrival of reinforcements and the perfect execution of a lightning counter-attack with the deadly support of artillery, turned defeat into an important victory. In the battle of Marengo, Napoleon made the right tactical move by trying to get into the enemy's rear but was foiled by the Austrian initiative, which took him by surprise. He also displayed presence of mind at a critical moment. In this battle Napoleon also learned to appreciate the element of luck in fighting. He knew how to turn Marengo into an important chapter in the Napoleonic legend, distorting the facts and playing down the role of other officers.

Thus French rule was re-established in northern Italy. In the other theatre, Moreau continued his advance into Bavaria and in December crushed the Austrians in the battle of Hohenlinden. Austria lost its thirst for battle and sought a cessation of hostilities. In February 1801 a peace treaty was signed at Lunéville ratifying the Campo Formio accords and putting an end to the Second Coalition. Great Britain was left alone against France. But it too now wanted peace, because of economic problems and fear of French invasion. The Peace of Amiens, signed in March 1802, satisfied British inclinations but did not last long. Napoleon was now the absolute ruler of France and in an August referendum won lifelong appointment. Meanwhile as first consul, his self-confidence soared and his determination to establish a Bonapartist dynasty hardened. In May 1804 the empire was proclaimed and in December, in the presence of the pope, who was a guest of honour at the coronation ceremony, Napoleon himself – he and not the head of the Church – placed the imperial crown on his own head and then on Josephine's.

France needed the peace to deal with its vital concerns at home: to establish law and order, to put into practice the social and constitutional changes brought about by the Revolution and make them a part of daily life, and to revive the economy. Napoleon was seen by the people as the right man to head the state at this opportune hour. He was seen as a product of the Revolution, loyal to its principles, young, heroic and supremely talented. And his achievements in the civil realm during the first years of his rule were in fact quite impressive. He completed the Civil Code, which had begun to be drafted in the second year of the Revolution, and established its basic principles in law: the freedom of the individual, equality before the law, separation of Church and State, freedom of expression, etc. It is not by chance that the Code bears his name – Code Napoleon – despite the fact that he was not the one to initiate it or formulate its basic principles. He also made important changes in public administration, many of which are still operative today both in and outside France. Similarly he brought about important reforms in the economy, particular in public financing and the currency.

The peace on the Continent was stable, though hostilities with Great Britain quickly erupted again as the British government found France's enormous influence on the Continent hard to swallow. The specific bone of contention was Malta, and Britain declared war on France in May 1803. But, since the war was conducted at sea and not on land, it in no way diminished the sense of peace and stability that reigned in Europe. It had turned out that Napoleon was an efficient and able ruler and now, with France secure within natural and recognised borders, as well as beyond them, he could devote himself to the satisfying personal goal of preserving peace and stability. Napoleon's inclination was certainly to act as a sole and all-powerful ruler and his style of governing was in the best tradition of time-hallowed enlightened absolutism, which the public accepted and grew accustomed to. The trouble was that the man who had crowned himself emperor intended to be what his title implied – a conqueror in the grand style. The fledgeling revolutionary legacy did in fact have this imperial element, as a means both of defence and of spreading the revolutionary idea, but with Napoleon it was a matter of temperament and ambition: to be a conqueror imposing his own and France's rule on all of Europe. His ambitions created the basis of opposition among the other regimes, as had been the case after the Revolution, but now the process was going to be more comprehensive and the conflict far more violent. The circumstances, interests and the personalities would broaden considerably the arena of political and military action. This expansion would necessitate enormous resources, to an extent never before seen in history, and would require military concepts suited to these new orders of magnitude. In less than ten years, Napoleon would drag Europe into a new kind of war – total war – and a new kind of mobilisation, powered by unconscious drives of nationalism and sacrifice 'for the Homeland'. The new anti-French alliance that would be forged – anti-Napoleonic more than anti-French – would paper over for a long time the divisions between the Powers that might have resulted in military conflicts ultimately beneficial to France. The alliance would also give birth to the idea of European co-operation – mainly to preserve the balance of power – as would happen 100 years later at the end of another world war, infinitely larger than its predecessor.

Anglo-French relations became *the* central problem in the tangled web of European affairs. Napoleon, of course, inherited these complicated relations with his neighbour across the Channel, but it was Napoleon's thinking about the future of France and the Continent as a whole that determined his attitude to each of the European powers. His strategy for destroying Britain – and it was precisely in these terms that he put it – was primarily economic insofar as it concerned Britain directly, with military implications for those countries required to join the French effort. All thoughts of military action against Britain at sea and on land were put off in the course of time. Napoleon believed that direct or indirect (via Ireland) invasion of Britain by land forces first demanded supremacy at sea, at least in the Channel during the invasion, and this he could not achieve. The crushing defeat suffered by the French fleet in October 1805 at the hands of his old rival Admiral Nelson off Cape Trafalgar in southern Spain dampened all thoughts in Napoleon's mind of another sea battle, of which in any case he knew next to nothing. Rather he sought to inflict a mortal wound in the soft underbelly of his sworn enemy, the world's greatest economic power.

The Continental System that he developed, which required the total adherence of all nations trading with Great Britain, was not Napoleon's original idea. The term became almost synonymous with Napoleon but was in fact coined in 1793. The desire to bring Britain down by hitting it economically had been part of French thinking ever since then, mainly in the Directory, but only in 1806 did it take on a solid shape. The Continental System was essentially a complex economic boycott (*Blocus Continental*) that included a naval blockade and a ban on British trade. The System was not only anti-British; it was also intended to give artificial protection to French industry, agriculture and commerce. An imperial edict of November 1806 banned all trade with Britain, set up mechanisms of inspection at sea and threatened punishment for violations, including confiscation of the goods discovered. The edict was made stronger by subsequent amendments, even more severe in nature, which took into account the lessons learned when attempting to put into force its complicated and problematic procedures. The continental blockade was not only the heart of Napoleon's policy ('the sea must be subdued by the land,' he said), it became an obsession that distorted his overall strategy, involved him in hopeless military adventures and, in the end, was one of the major factors in his downfall.

Another matter that preoccupied Europe, for ever threatening the balance of power and breeding conflict and suspicion, was the Polish question. Europe had known many wars against the background of the instability that had characterised Polish rule for generations. In the absence of a stable royal dynasty the appointment of a king would become an excuse for outside intervention and military struggles between various blocs of nations. In the eighteenth century, no fewer than five kings – two of them Saxons – were deposed as a result of pressures and interventions that at one time or another involved almost all the nations of Europe. The eighteenth century saw the Northern War (Sweden versus Russia and Saxony) and the War of the Polish Succession (France and Spain versus Russia and Austria) and many other military conflicts as well as insurrections within the country. Understandably, given the geographical and military circumstances, Russia had always been the power with the greatest influence on this source of tension, though other interested parties also exerted much pressure as they went about settling territorial questions among themselves. The effort to settle these disputes peaceably led to the Partitions of Poland, the First in 1772 on the basis of an agreement between Russia, Austria and Prussia. The Partition sliced off considerable portions of the country and in the parts that remained internal struggle continued, even being influenced at a certain stage by the spirit of revolutionary France. This was how the Second (1792) and Third (1795) Partitions came about, when Polish rebels were defeated by the Russians. With the Third Partition, Poland ceased to exist as a state, having been swallowed up by its three traditional predators, and first and foremost Russia. It will be seen below that even when the three co-operated fully to defeat the French emperor, mutual suspicions concerning Poland disturbed the seeming harmony between them.

After the Third Partition many Polish emigrés linked their fortunes to France. They were attracted by its revolutionary spirit and afterwards by the figure of Napoleon, in whom they expected to find a sympathetic ear and perhaps salvation. Thus were born the Polish legions which attached themselves to the French army to share a few campaigns. Napoleon knew how to exploit the Polish question, which pre-occupied the East European powers, for his own ends, using Poland as a pawn, particularly in his relations with Russia. He created the Grand Duchy of Warsaw as a territorial and political entity and, while it was a thorn in the side of the surrounding powers, it offered hope for their homeland to his Polish allies.

As mentioned, Napoleon did not delude himself as to his chances of defeating Great Britain in a land operation, though a state of war still existed between the two countries. Britain tried to put together a Third Coalition against him whose chief members would be Austria and Russia. But Prussia too gave him no rest. Thus it devolved upon him to go to war in order to demonstrate France's power and bring its enemies 'to their knees', as he put it. He now had a powerful army at his disposal, the Grand Army (*Grande Armée*), and with it he raced into Germany in an exceptionally rapid march, reaching the Danube from the Rhine and defeating an Austrian force at Ulm in an impressive exhibition of generalship. Making a wide flanking movement, he got into the enemy's rear, brought to bear decisively superior numbers and, while still engaged, sent another large force to meet the Russians nearby (October 1805). This was an early version of the lightning brand of warfare that sought to surround and destroy the enemy. In this case the destruction of the enemy was only foiled because the Austrians laid down their arms. Before long Napoleon was in Vienna and continued to move north towards the Russians, who had slipped away in October. He succeeded in drawing the Russians and Austrians into battle on 2 December at Austerlitz, not far from Brünn in Moravia. The battle is known to history as the Battle of the Three Emperors because of the presence of Tsar Alexander, Kaiser Francis and Napoleon. The Russian commander was Kutusov. At Austerlitz Napoleon won a great victory, perhaps his greatest, applying to perfection a broad array of principles of war: surprise, intelligent use of terrain, determined attack with the full use of cavalry and artillery, accurate reading of the unfolding of the battle.

The Third Coalition thus did not last long. At the end of December a treaty was signed at Pressburg with Austria, which gave up to France its possessions in Italy and Germany. The latter concession emptied of all meaning the title of Austrian emperor as head of the Holy Roman Empire and accordingly changed it from Francis II, the Roman emperor, to Francis I, the first kaiser of Austria. Napoleon hastened to create a new political entity in Germany in place of the meaningless old one, founding in July 1806 the Confederation of the Rhine (*Rheinbund*) under his leadership and protection. The Confederation included Bavaria and Wurtemberg along with 15 other principalities, all of whom put around 70,000 soldiers at the disposal of France. Thus Napoleon created a territorial wedge between France and the Eastern powers, tightened the economic boycott against Britain by closing still more markets to it and created a threat against Prussia, whom he had not yet met on the battlefield. He also added Holland and the Kingdom of Naples to his dynasty, naming two of his brothers as their kings.

Britain undertook to provide financial assistance to its partners, Russia and Prussia, in a Fourth Coalition. As far as Napoleon was concerned it was now Prussia's turn, with its military reputation going back to Frederick the Great. He left Paris at the end of September, joined his army in Germany and marched eastward to join battle with the Prussians near Leipzig. The movement of almost 200,000 troops demonstrated Napoleon's ability to control large forces moving rapidly over wide areas and to bring them to the attack instantly. Each column could attack in any desired formation or go to the assistance of another column and attack the enemy on its flank or in its rear. The battles of Jena and nearby Auerstädt are classic examples of holding and attacking an enemy in his front while carrying out a wide-flanking, pincer movement and encirclement from an entirely unexpected direction. The movements on the battlefield were carried out with great speed while amassing numerical superiority in the field (October 1806). At Jena, Napoleon achieved the decisive result he had always wanted – he destroyed most of the opposing army, pursued its fragments while marching on the capital and forced the enemy to seek terms in desperation amounting to unconditional surrender. Two weeks later Napoleon entered Berlin in a victory march and Prussia was left at his mercy.

Napoleon did not return to Paris, continuing to move east to crush the Russian army in Poland and eastern Prussia. In February 1807, a new phase began in his struggle against Russia. It started with a bloody, drawn battle at Eylau, where Napoleon was a step away from defeat, and continued a few months later in a victory that brought on a honeymoon in the relations between the two powers, a honeymoon that would end in a bitter and uncompromising war.

Between the battles of Jena and Eylau, Napoleon spent about a month in Berlin, drunk with victory and bursting with an enormous sense of power. He now controlled the greater part of Europe, aside from Russia. This was the period in which he elaborated the Continental System and published the edicts to put it into effect. His desire to continue fighting in the eastern theatre to cripple the Russians did not diminish his will to break the backs of the British, and in this lay the origin of his ill-considered idea to open immediately a new front far to the west, on the Iberian Peninsula. This was also the beginning of the end. Napoleon did not give enough the time to consolidating his gains and strengthening his grip on the Continent while the enthusiasm of the populace, which saw him as a great reformer and saviour, was at a peak there.

As noted, the origin of the Peninsular campaign, which dragged on for eight years, lay in Napoleon's anti-British strategy, which aimed at total French control of the European coast. The campaign opened in October 1807 with the invasion of Portugal, which had maintained its traditional close friendly relations with Britain. The invasion involved crossing Spain and was carried out not only with its agreement but with its participation. Relations between France and Spain since the Revolution had had their ups and downs and now they underwent a rapid change. Napoleon intervened in internal disputes of the royal family, occupied the capital, Madrid, in March 1808 and placed his brother Joseph on the throne. The removal of the Spanish king was greeted by a massive popular uprising which spread across the country and took on the form of a successful and nettlesome guerrilla war. The French were pulled in further and further under increasing military pressure, which grew even stronger with the intervention of Great Britain and the landing of an expeditionary force in Portugal in August. Under General Wellesley, the future Duke of Wellington, the French were bested in a series of clashes and in October the fighting was carried over into Spain. Napoleon was forced to send large contingents of the Grand Army from Germany and he himself left for Spain at the end of 1808 to take personal charge of operations. However, he had to leave after just three months to deal with the crisis with Austria. The French were not able to gain a significant victory despite their overwhelming numerical superiority, being forced to divide their forces and their command in the face of local guerrilla attacks and British pressure. Their losses were tremendous, as was the humiliation. The war in Spain was one of those poorly thought out wars whose ends are unforeseeable.

Austria saw in the Spanish war an opportunity to pay France back for the débâcle of 1805, get it out of Italy and Germany and stop the spread of the Revolution and Bonapartism into conservative Europe. In April 1809 a new agreement was reached between Austria and Britain and the Danube campaign commenced with the entry of Austria into Bavaria, which was allied with France. The offensive was carried out by the kaiser's brother, Archduke Charles, who headed a large army trained in accordance with the lessons learned from the Napoleonic wars of recent years. Charles hoped to divide the French army in Germany and defeat it in detail. Napoleon, who took personal command of the army, drove the Austrians back on the Danube and, on 10 May reached the gates of Vienna, receiving the city's surrender three days later. Desirous of destroying the remains of the still formidable Austrian army, Napoleon won an overwhelming victory at Wagram after gaining the north bank of the Danube in a fierce struggle. In the fight on the river the Austrians had the advantage at first but could not exploit it and Napoleon was able to make meticulous preparations for a decisive battle. He spent a few weeks reinforcing his troops and planned the crossing down to the last detail, with the men supporting each other during the crossing over an impressive engineering effort. He operated out of a big bridgehead, warded off a spirited Austrian counter-attack, brought his heavy artillery to bear wherever his line was broken and continuously stepped up his attack. Wagram (July 1809) was Napoleon's last decisive victory as emperor, gained at a tremendous cost in blood. A few days later an armistice agreement was signed which evolved into a peace treaty and apparent alliance between the two powers. Here was perhaps the chance to dismantle the Austrian empire into its component parts – Austria itself, Bohemia and Hungary, with Italy in any case under French control. But Napoleon erred in believing that he could bring the Austrian emperor over to his side and lost a golden opportunity.

At the end of the 1809 campaign the French empire reached its greatest extent, but it was already past the peak of its power. The chinks in its armour were both apparent and concealed. The signs were many: certain aberrations in Napoleon's political and military judgement, characterised by hopeless fixations (the struggle with Britain, the war in Spain, his thinking about a Russian campaign); the tremendous euphoria that led the emperor to believe he could achieve anything; the stirrings of national awakening in the imperial lands, brought on by France's prolonged and unwelcome presence there; changes in the opposing armies, stemming from the lessons learned in the recent campaigns that led to an attempt to adapt themselves to the new art of warfare demonstrated by Napoleon and his army and the growing fatigue of the French people, fed up with war and feeling that the hoped-for peace was not in sight.

It has already been remarked that in war as in everything else Napoleon was no great innovator, being basically conservative in his outlook. This outlook derived from the principles of war taught by the theoreticians of the eighteenth century, the adoption of principles that appealed to him and proved themselves valid in his own experience, and his own original thinking and the search for new solutions to every problem he faced. He read not a little about the great battles of the past and his heroes were Alexander the Great, Hannibal and Frederick the Great. He also read De Saxe, Guibert, De Bourcet and Du Taille and took over many of their ideas, such as the right combination of firepower and the element of shock, with the artillery supplying the main firepower and the cavalry the shock. It should be remembered that Napoleon was at heart an artillerist who believed in the superiority of cannon, so that he gladly subscribed to the school of thought that promoted the massive use of artillery and greater independence of its units. He also subscribed to the view that manoeuvre and mobility were important as well as the use of formations in movement and attack that make them possible. Consequently, he preferred to move in columns and not frontally, despite the fact that a frontal format allowed him to react more quickly and perhaps even more efficiently. His first aim was to get his troops where he wanted them at the right time and it was the business of tactics to serve this aim. He said that a commander must concentrate on the main objective: 'I only see one thing and that is the main body of the enemy's army, and I try to smash it.'

Many before him had utilised the principles he observed, but in modern times no one had used them all together and so brilliantly. In the past, too, few had reached his level. He believed in striking the flank and rear and cutting lines of communications. Attack in the centre was meant to break the enemy at its strongpoint and to decide the battle. He tried to operate as much as possible on interior lines to save on movement to vital areas and to avoid dependence on permanent supply bases by living off the land wherever he was fighting, while establishing bases during his advance. Whenever possible he tried to encircle the enemy with wide pincer movements. He aimed to penetrate the seams between the enemy formations, particularly between those of different nationalities in order to exploit the difficulties of communication between them. He preached unrelenting pursuit of a defeated enemy in order to seal the rout and reap as many political benefits as possible. He gave a great deal of independence to the corps and even divisions and built up the engineering units, which he considered of prime importance. He emphasised the importance of strategic and operational intelligence – he himself was an excellent map reader – and adapted De Saxe's view that 'the ground frequently would give one opportunities which the enemy had overlooked until it was too late and which would change a given situation.' Special emphasis was laid on field security in order to conceal his intentions and forces were often shifted from sector to sector, being placed under different commands thereby achieving flexibility and mutual support. He placed great emphasis on the morale of his troops and kept it up with an uncommon ability. He believed in the importance of maintaining tactical and strategic reserves. All in all, Napoleon demonstrated that the principle of generalship lies in the correct application of effective principles while exhibiting superior leadership. All this was more important than creating new military doctrines. He said that in war there are no predetermined rules and, of course, no absolutes. Everything is learned from experience – your own and others'. Leadership and practical application are all.

The post-revolutionary French army was the first in Europe to break the mould of eighteenth-century dynastic war. Frederick the Great, king of Prussia, was the last to fight this kind of war, whose aim was to wear down the enemy until he tossed in the towel rather than to destroy him. Armies were small and the resources available limited in national terms. The objectives which the French Revolution set for its army, first defensive, then expansionist, necessitated a much larger army and far greater resources. Compulsory universal conscription was meant to supply these needs and Napoleon inherited new forms of mobilisation. It was up to him to improve the army and mould it into the instrument of his aims and military principles.

The most important change was in taking the fragmented revolutionary army and turning it into a unified force under single command. In 1805 he stood at the head of 400,000 troops which, by 1812, had grown to nearly 700,000 soldiers recognising his authority as supreme commander in both the military and sovereign sense. The undisputed unity of command which the army now knew made it necessary to upgrade significantly its main means of command – the general staff. Napoleon worked with a personal staff where political and military business was done and also had a general staff to translate his ideas and instructions into detailed operational and administrative orders. He defined the assignments and procedures of headquarters at both army and corps levels. Other armies copied these patterns of command and they served as a model in the great wars to come (Hitler used the system of double headquarters and improved on it). But Napoleon himself found it difficult to delegate the authority required by the general staff because of his dominant and centralising character.

Napoleon made the infantry corps (*Corps d'Armée*) the basic formation of the army. The corps was made up of two to four infantry divisions according to needs and objectives, with the addition of cavalry brigades and some artillery, engineering and supply units. A full corps might number over 40,000 men and was a small army in itself, a force intended to operate independently. The corps as Napoleon designed it was a powerful assault force through which he could gain the advantages he sought, such as mobility, flexibility and the ability to decide battles. He saw numerical superiority as a decisive factor in the closing stages of a fight, even if the troops were not of top quality, though he had also fought successful battles at a numerical disadvantage. Therefore he had little patience for protracted training and shortened it for officer candidates, including those in engineering and artillery units. He maintained that 'there is no need to know everything about ballistics and construction. It's enough to receive training in fieldcraft and entrenchment.' Regular soldiers received very basic training lasting a week and were hardened on the march to the front. Discipline was not too strong among

French soldiers on garrison duty or while marching. On the other hand, their discipline in battle and willingness to fight were strong. Napoleon made it a habit to express his appreciation of entire units, officers and soldiers. Their rewards were decorations and medals of honour.

Napoleon did not dwell on tactical questions. Almost the only point about which he hesitated was whether to fire from a two- or three-row formation. He was afraid that the third row, though it would seemingly serve to intensify fire, would interfere with the first two rows when they had to reload and even cause them losses. On the other hand, artillery tactics were of great interest to him and he liked to position batteries on the battlefield himself. 'Fire is everything,' he said. 'All the rest is of no importance.' He also gave much attention to the cavalry for their contribution to intelligence and in deciding battles.

The pampering of the elite unit of the Grand Army, the Imperial Guard, was intended to serve two basic principles in Napoleon's military thinking: the aim of bringing battles to a decision and the wish to have a reserve for critical moments. The existence of this kind of Guard served as an example to the whole army, turning itself into a kind of inspirational legend. In its first years the Guard reached the size of a division, later growing to the proportions of a corps (more than 55,000 men). It was made up of the Old and Middle Guard and the Young Guard, which was established in 1809 and included mainly light infantry drawn from the outstanding recruits in every draft. In addition to infantry and cavalry, the Guard had artillery and engineering units. Though Napoleon determined their objectives, which were strictly defined, in many instances he hesitated to use them at the right time lest they suffer too many losses and not be available when he really needed them. For this reason the military value of the Imperial Guard is a subject of debate, as is the case with elite units in all armies to this very day. They attract the best men, who will then be lacking in the regular units that bear the brunt of the fighting. However, it cannot be denied that the Guard played a decisive part in a number of battles. Napoleon felt a special closeness to his elite corps, liked to quarter among its soldiers, ate and drank with them and shared experiences with them.

Napoleon's scenario for the destruction of an enemy was as follows: infantry corps advance in the theatre of operations along different axes, separated as required for rapid engagement and mutual support. With the opening of the battle, light units move out in a forward position to interfere with the enemy's deployment; artillery softens up and does great damage to the enemy; massed ranks of infantry advance in battle formation to within light weapons range and charge with the bayonet; when a weak point is discovered in the enemy line the reserve is rushed in, foot and mounted and, with artillery brought to bear, crushes the enemy. This is the harbinger of the lightning war, the blitzkrieg.

Until 1805 the great European powers warring against Napoleon clung to the old concepts and failed to understand the new military reality. Austerlitz and Jena taught them once and for all that the rules of the game had changed and that the process of reform and adjustment, which had begun at the end of the eighteenth century, would have to be completed as quickly as possible to achieve the desired superiority. Napoleon's victories meant for them that great battles were still to be fought, but with themselves as the aggressors. This future war would have one aim and one aim only – to demolish the French empire – which meant demolishing the French army, whose enormous size was in itself reason enough for reorganisation and new strategic and tactical concepts.

The changes in the Russian army began with the rise of Tsar Alexander to power in 1801 and mainly involved increasing its size and setting up a kind of ministry of war with limited, mainly administrative, authority. In 1810, General Barclay de Tolly was appointed minister and speeded up the process of reform. His fighting tactic was built around a three-brigade division, with one of the brigades deploying and moving to the attack behind a screen of light infantry while the other two stood ready to attack from the rear. The cavalry units of the division were kept in reserve in the rear in two lines stretched across the front. The main element in the reform concerned the artillery, in expanding and improving it technically, including an increased range. The artillery was to be placed on the flanks and in the centre and pour down concentrated fire to soften up and destroy the enemy. By 1812, Barclay organised the forces in Russia itself into two armies consisting of a number of corps. But while there was improvement in training soldiers and officers, the new tactics were beyond their understanding. Much time would be required to introduce them and time was not available. Fortunately for the Russians their major assets – their enormous strategic depth and the devotion of their troops – did not depend on any minister and would serve them in good stead in the great war to come.

In Prussia, which since the defeats at Jena and Auerstädt no longer existed as an independent political entity and was severely limited in its ability to raise another real army, there was a tremendous revolution in military thinking and patterns of military organisation. As we shall see, this was a process that embraced all of Prussian society, its education and its willingness to sacrifice human and material resources to recapture its past glory. Prussia was right behind France in its evolution towards total war. France, however, had been pushed into the idea as a result of the radical change in government caused by the Revolution of 1789. For Prussia it was a matter of life or death.

In Austria, not even the defeat of 1805 changed the thinking of the head of its army, Archduke Charles. Destroying and living off a country in order to maintain an army was an alien idea to him. His tactical approach was conservative to a fault and, even after Austerlitz, he held to the old scheme of frontal advance to contact and approach march to small arms range, quickening the pace and then the bayonet charge. The Austrian empire was multinational and therefore always plagued by national upheaval, which was an obstacle in the way of the large-scale conscription needed to create a national army – the burning need of the day – for fear of uprisings within the army. This approach changed before the 1809 campaign, but not drastically. The major change was in the size of the army, but the Austrian army did not adopt the advanced concepts of fighting and administration. However, as it was disciplined and professional, these deficiencies were not so telling and the quality of its officers won it a certain respect among other armies.

Thus, in an amazingly short time, enormous changes had taken place in the strategic and tactical thinking of the major armies of Europe as well as in their consequent organisation. These changes were far more marked than the improvements in weapons technology. There was also a lack of development in the different auxiliary services that were vital to the kind of large-scale fighting that evolved after the 1809 campaign. These were dependent on scientific and technological progress, which lagged behind needs. In a word, thinking outpaced means. The most important consequence of all this was that the size of the battlefield was constricted relative to the number of men fighting on it, because the limitations of weapons did not allow a broader spread and deployment of forces. The basic infantry weapon in all the armies was the musket, which weighed 13 lbs and was 1.25–1.50 metres long. Two or three rounds a minute could ordinarily be fired, the effective range was about 150 metres, accuracy was poor and misfiring was common. Parallel firing lines (two or three deep) were intended to assure overlapping fire during loading. The artillery included several kinds of guns differing in details. The salient point is that the mostly flat trajectory field pieces had a range of 400 to 1,200 metres, depending on calibre and the weight of the shells. This kind of weaponry dictated the compactness of forces in the field and the ranges of assault and contact. The large numbers of losses were a function of these basic conditions.

Medical services, too, lagged far behind the growing needs. It was the sick more than the wounded who required these services, as their number was far larger. Most of the wounded had to lie on the battlefield until the fighting was over and many died from infection and gangrene. Those with light wounds dragged themselves to the hospitals where operations were performed under intolerable conditions. Mortality among the wounded was extremely high. Medical disposition and the idea of saving lives were poorly developed concepts in all the armies, though slightly less so in Napoleon's army.

Administration – supply and ordnance – were much improved, together with the staff work necessary for the planning and supervision of administration. The staff planned logistic needs, set up storage sites and mapped out transport routes. Transport was by a large variety of wagons with the supply and maintenance of horses a key element in the management of the army. Here too the French army was ahead of the others, with improved staff and administrative procedures.

Observation and communications methods also failed to meet requirements and to a large extent determined the character of battle. Senior officers could see what was happening on the battlefield with their own eyes but, as the battle progressed, visibility became severely reduced in the surrounding smoke and fire. Orders were sent through couriers, who were junior officers. More detailed reports, on the situation of forces and the plans of their commanders, also relied on the courier system. Consequently, it took at least two hours to get orders or reports through on the battlefield, and in the case of distant troops, even in the same theatre of operations, sometimes days.

The first condition of total war is the participation of the entire nation in the war effort – large-scale conscription and the enlistment of the entire national economy. The French Revolution 'set free the strength of the people', in the words of General Ludendorff, one of the heads of the German army in the First World War. The entire populace was dragged into the revolutionary wars, which aspired to total victory. The limited engagement of professional armies came to an end. The home front became actively involved and, for the first time, rulers felt the need to win its support for their policies and the war that came as a consequence. Thus propaganda and information were and are a very important feature of waging total war.

Total war becomes world war when most major countries become involved in it. King Louis Philippe of France expressed this well when he said in 1835: 'Who cares if Africa fires a thousand shots if Europe doesn't hear them?' In the beginning of the nineteenth century the influential countries included most of Europe and to a certain extent the United States. Another main feature of this kind of war is that it takes place in more than one theatre and that each warring country has a grand strategy that embraces all the theatres. If a group of countries is fighting against a great power, or against another group of countries, strategy still has to be unified and all tendencies pulling in diverse directions eliminated so that one goal alone can be kept in sight. All this has a number of organisational implications deriving from the new military reality. The civilian authorities have to be more involved in the conduct and support of the war at the international political level, in mobilising resources and supplying the army's needs while keeping close watch on the progress of the war. No longer will it suffice to send an expeditionary force on a mission of conquest or defence and then sit back and wait for the results. Here lies the origin of war ministries, originally set up for purposes of administration and co-ordination but coming to shape strategy, including the means necessary to carry it through. The army had to go over to a system of decentralised command, deriving its authority from a high command drawing up general and discretionary orders from an operational point of view. This is how general staffs came into existence in the various armies along with large formations capable of operating independently in defined sectors of the theatre of operations.

The most important feature of total world war is that it contains within itself the code and formula for determining its outcome at an early stage. In previous wars, the decisive factor determining results was the quality of the armies and the resources invested in them as decided by the sovereign ruler. Thus an ambitious country could make gains through military victory even when factors such as size and population, natural resources and culture, left it at a disadvantage vis-à-vis its rivals. While such gains would not be lasting if these same basic factors were not augmented (through military conquest and enduring territorial annexations), the ability to prevail in a military campaign was in its own hands, particularly if it had an outstanding leader at the head of its army and the state. However, in wars that assume the dimensions of total war with numerous participants, the multiple of quantity and quality predominates, and if everything is calculated properly beforehand it is possible to predict the result. The total picture, the sigma, is what will prove decisive and it will not matter who stands at the head of the power or coalition that goes to war. If leadership is not at a high level on the winning side, the price of victory will be more costly because of blunders and mishaps, but the end is none the less inevitable.

Thus the first world war of 1813 followed from the wars that preceded it and pursued an inevitable course whose end was determined by the 'sigma equation'. In the hands of the coalition of enemies of the Revolution lay the clear-cut potential for decisive victory, even against a foe with the powers of Napoleon Bonaparte, whose leadership was superior to that of anyone who opposed him. But for more than a dozen years these countries did not succeed in forging a common strategy untainted by conflicting interests, which would enable them to realise their potential and convert it into decisive victory. The price they paid was painful, involving enslavement and humiliation. When they recovered and arrived at an agreed formulation of their aims based on common interests, the war they were conducting took on the same colouring as the war that Napoleon was conducting and became a total war with the inevitable result not long in coming.

The deterministic nature of world war does not diminish the importance of the individual. The story of war is complex and cannot be thoroughly understood without understanding its human aspects, including the motives, actions and failures of the people who start them and the commanders of the armies who fight them. The increasing importance of general staffs and the broad discretion given to formations in the field, which become armies in themselves, increase the importance of generalship, which is not necessarily an ability that attaches itself to everyone who holds the rank of general. This too is a subject that should be considered in the study of war, if only because great wars strike down the young generation, whose fate, for better or for worse, depends on the wisdom – and too often the folly – of the generals who command them.

First we should acquaint ourselves with the masters of these generals, the rulers, the overlords, all in their forties and very different from one another. The well-known historian Herbert Fisher describes Napoleon in the following terms: '...the small, almost dwarfish figure, the rounded symmetry of the head, the pale olive cheek and massive brow, the deep-set eyes of lustrous grey, now flashing with electric fires, now veiled in impenetrable contemplation, the white teeth and delicate hands, the compact energy of his chest and shoulders...' (Fisher, H: Napoleon). It is amazing how young he was when he rose to power and how quickly he learned to play the part of the ruler and super-captain – an adjustment that is an essential feature in leadership. For he was of lowly origins and was not the confidant of a court like his rivals. His leadership was domineering, authoritarian, undisputed, overwhelming. 'His presence on a field of battle was worth 40,000 men,' said Wellington, one of his great rivals. He knew how to put his thoughts into words and was superior intellectually to all the rulers of his day. He was impatient, prone to outbursts, sometimes hysterical, and critical; he was also industrious, with an incredible capacity for work and an excellent memory; also cruel and inconsiderate, though at the same time sensitive to the point of tears, and given to wishful thinking that was unable to reconcile itself to failure or admit to it.

Tsar Alexander I – son of the half-mad Paul I, who was murdered by conspirators in 1801 – was eight years younger than Napoleon. Alexander's feelings about the French emperor ranged from hostility to shortlived admiration and subsequently to the determination to bring about his downfall. 'I shall not make peace with Napoleon!' he said. 'I have learnt to know him now. Napoleon or I, I or Napoleon; we cannot reign side by side.' Alexander was a strange and complex individual, inclined towards mysticism, suspicious, melancholy, indecisive and, at the same time, stubborn. He had a powerful sense of mission and formulated confused ideas about reforming Russian society and government. After the war of 1812 he believed that he had been chosen by providence to be Europe's peacemaker and this belief formed the basis of his policy and decisions. He was first and foremost the leader of the final coalition that fought against Napoleon and to all intents and purposes acted as supreme commander, surrounded by a handful of religious advisers and wrapped in an air of religious mystery.

The king of Prussia, Frederick William III, was a year younger than Napoleon and had been steered towards army life from childhood, serving in the 1792–4 campaigns as an officer. He was crowned in 1797 but it soon became apparent that he was weak and lacking in determination, though well intentioned. Both his character and the pitiful state of his country after the defeat at the hands of France assured him an inferior position among the leaders of the Allies and put him totally under the influence of his partners. Napoleon terrified him and it was only after much hesitation that he brought himself to join the final coalition. It is true that he was present at the great battles of 1813 and nominally participated in the high command, but his

influence was minimal and there was a great gap between his feeble leadership and the fighting spirit of his officers.

The 'old man' among Europe's major leaders was Emperor Francis I of
Austria, who was born in 1768 and had been ruling since 1792. He was conservative by nature and an unimaginative bureaucrat, but he was also patient
and kind. In international affairs he had been under Metternich's thumb in the
crucial years since 1809. Metternich, who served as both his prime minister
and foreign minister, confessed that, while he sometimes held all of Europe in
the palm of his hand, his influence on Austria's internal affairs was nonexistent.

As mentioned earlier, one of Napoleon's great achievements as a leader was
to institute a unified command while at the same time creating an order of
battle based on corps, which were expected to operate independently, at least
for a limited time. In truth, in most cases, his subordinates did not rise to the
occasion. This became a more and more important factor, and we shall see
that Napoleon misjudged his army from this point of view and failed time and
again when he tried to employ an independent army not under his direct
command. This was also true for the general staff of the army, which was
adequate until the time of the Fifth Coalition but wanting when the Grand
Army took on mammoth proportions from 1812 and confronted armies that
had begun to operate along the lines of modern total war. Out of fairness it
should be said that the transition from conservative, traditional warfare –
dynastic war – to total war had been sharp and rapid, even if we include the
years of its development between the French Revolution and the 1813
campaign. It was beyond the power of any nation to produce enough commanding generals in so short a time, even among a population of 30 million.

A commanding general is produced through a combination of experience
and theoretical knowledge. Practical experience alone is not enough – the
element of theoretical knowledge must be added. The military theoretician
Jomini, whom we shall encounter again later on in our story, said that a commanding general 'must realise that every war is a great drama where a
thousand things influence it one way or another.' It is desirable that he have
some kind of feeling for statesmanship. He should be familiar with the principles of war, grasp their overall significance, remain true to them and know
where and when to apply them. He should identify the centre of gravity of the
theatre of operations he is responsible for and do everything in his power to
reach a decision there (this is the advice of Clausewitz, whom we shall also

meet again, which holds true today). It is important that he should be clear thinking and articulate, know how to evaluate a military situation intelligently and produce resultingly clear and sharply defined orders. General Schlieffen, the Prussian chief of staff at the beginning of the twentieth century and author of the famous plan for the conquest of France, said a commanding general 'must even destroy a superior enemy, and even when he does not know exactly where he is, not to mention his direction of movement and intentions.' This is a bold demand but just and necessary and whoever is not prepared to do everything in his power to satisfy it had better not allow himself to be placed at the head of an army or even a corps. Liddell-Hart maintained that the qualities of generalship were talent, courage, fairness and integrity and a disinclination to deceive oneself and others (including superiors).

Napoleon was a first-rate commanding general. Many are convinced that he was a military genius but even if he was not, he was an extraordinarily talented commander. In his army he had about 30 senior generals who were supposed to meet the above criteria, or at least the most important of them. It may be said that all of them met one criterion, important but far from sufficient – the criterion of courage and personal example. Only one, Marshal Davout, was blessed with most of the qualities described. He was independent, broad in his strategic thinking, tough, unemotional, disciplined and efficient. He fought decisive actions in various battles and mostly was given independent missions, sometimes far from the main body of the army. But Davout was not the rule. Apparently it was enough for Napoleon that he himself should have the qualities required of a great general and that the others should be no more than experienced and brave, as long as they proved that they were capable of winning battles. The bravest of the brave among the figures we shall encounter in our story were Marshals Murat and Ney, both Napoleon's age. Murat is considered one of the greatest cavalry commanders of all time. One of Napoleon's veteran lieutenants, with outstanding service at Marengo, Austerlitz and Eylau, he was an extraordinary individual, selfish, comic in his primping and mannerisms and admired by his soldiers, as well as by the enemy but, in the end, he disappointed Napoleon, who was also his brother-in-law. Ney was perhaps the most promising of the marshals and, as far as his actions on the battlefield were concerned, he fulfilled this promise, but he was not able raise himself up to the level of independent command. He distinguished himself as a corps commander in many battles, particularly at Jena, Eylau and Friedland and was at his greatest in Russia. When Napoleon gave him more than corps command he disappointed, first and foremost himself. He was also admired by his soldiers, who called him Le Rougeaud (Redface).

Four marshals at the head of corps are considered superior to the others in tactical and operational ability. The young Marmont (born in 1774) was a talented artillerist, with great administrative ability and tactical understanding. He was also entrusted with independent tasks in military government. Soult, who was Napoleon's age, was greatly admired by his commander and distinguished himself in the battles he participated in. He fought six years in Spain and in the last year of the war there commanded all the French forces. Augereau, one of the oldest marshals in the 1813 campaign (born in 1757), was a difficult and critical individual, but an excellent tactician. He was at his best mainly during the Italian campaign and at Jena. Gouvion Saint-Cyr (born in 1764) was also outstanding as a tactician and commanding officer but Napoleon's attitude towards him changed frequently and was somewhat ambivalent.

Marshal Berthier, 16 years older than Napoleon, was his chief of staff from 1796 and minister of war for about seven years, until 1807. He was an extremely industrious officer, loyal and meticulous, particularly in writing up orders according to Napoleon's instructions – perhaps even overly meticulous, as we shall see. Sometimes he played an important role as an intermediary between Napoleon and his marshals. While he was an incomparable master of detail and knew and understood Napoleon well, this was not enough to make him a creative chief of staff who could fill in for the supreme commander when he was away from headquarters for any reason. Therefore, the more complex the wars became and the larger the Grand Army, the less valuable Berthier became in terms of command. Napoleon himself said of him: 'His character was undecided, not strong enough for a commander-in-chief, but he possessed all the qualities of a good chief of staff; a complete mastery of the map, great skill in reconnaissance, minute care in the dispatch of orders, magnificent aptitude for presenting with the greatest simplicity the most complicated situation of an army.'

In a word, a chief of staff after Napoleon's own heart, when Napoleon himself was incapable of understanding – in this preliminary stage of great wars – what a real chief of staff was able to and had to give him.

In May 1804 Napoleon promoted 18 generals to the rank of marshal of France. In the following years, until his downfall, eight others received this rank. The emperor was also in the habit of giving his subordinates titles. All his marshals were also princes, counts or dukes along with a few generals who did not reach the desired rank of marshal. The title was generally accompanied by mention of the battle where the officer had excelled. Thus Ney was the prince of Moscow, Augereau the duke of Castiglione, and so on. The attitude to titles was serious and strict. The recipients, mostly of lower-class origins, addressed one another by their titles and signed documents with them. Napoleon also rewarded them during their service with large sums of money and with grants of property. In the last years of the empire Napoleon claimed that his marshals 'waxed fat and kicked'.

The two senior officers in the Russian army before the 1813 campaign were Barclay de Tolly and Wittgenstein. Barclay, who was born into a family of Scottish origins in 1761, joined the Russian army at the age of 15. He distinguished himself in the battle of Eylau and attracted the attention of the Tsar, who appointed him minister of war three years later in addition to army commander. After the 1812 campaign, his position in the army became less secure but he continued to hold high command posts, including commander-in-chief of the army. He prepared the Russian army to the best of his ability for the two great campaigns that awaited it. Wittgenstein was born in 1769 and was the son of a Prussian general who had served in the Russian army. He too was a favourite of the Tsar and from an early age commanded large formations against Napoleon and in Finland.

The outstanding officer in the Prussian army was also the oldest to take part in the 1813 campaign, General (later Field Marshal) Blücher. He was born in Prussia in 1742 but at an early age joined the Swedish army and even fought against his native land in the time of Frederick the Great. After being taken prisoner by the Prussians he joined their army but left at the age of 32 and spent 13 years as a farmer. When he was again called to the colours, with the rank of major, he fought against the revolutionary army and developed great hostility towards the French. He fought at Auerstädt and led the remains of the Prussian army to a safe shore on the Baltic Sea. Napoleon did not allow him to go on active service in the army because he appreciated his abilities and knew of his hatred of France, but Blücher was able to take part in the rehabilitation of the army. Before the 1813 campaign he was promoted to general and became the senior field commander of the Prussian army.

Every war has its great hero, the man who inspires others and takes the lead at every stage and in every situation. In the war of 1813 this was Blücher, a high-spirited Prussian patriot, crude and fascinating and well beloved. At his side was Gneisenau, who at a certain stage in the war became his chief of staff. Gneisenau, a brilliant soldier and superior chief of staff, gave Prussian headquarters the thinking and co-ordination required by the army and complemented Blücher's constant urge to advance and attack.

The outstanding Prussian field commander was General Yorck, who was endowed with the qualities of a commanding general. He was born in 1759 and joined the army at the age of 13. Yorck played an important part in getting the Prussian king to enlist in the military struggle against Napoleon. As a corps commander he had his own tactical ideas and argued frequently but was disciplined and highly diligent.

The future Eisenhower of the armies that combined to fight Napoleon in 1813 was Field Marshal Schwarzenberg of Austria. He was two years younger than Napoleon and the first wars he had fought in were against the Turks and the French in the Low Countries during the revolutionary wars. He survived by the skin of his teeth at Ulm in 1805 where he commanded a division, held diplomatic posts in Russia and France and distinguished himself in the fighting of 1809. His end, if we may jump ahead, came on 15 October 1820, when he returned to the battlefield of Leipzig for the ceremony commemorating the 1813 campaign and suffered a stroke.

Chapter 1 - THE NIGHTMARE OF 1812

On 5 December 1812, the French emperor Napoleon Bonaparte and his entourage were staying at the village of Smorgoni, about 70 kilometres east of Vilna, near the remains of his Grand Army who were strung out along the road from Smolensk to Vilna – sick, exhausted, starving, ragged and desperate. Left behind were hundreds of thousands of the men who had gone with Napoleon to this most terrible of wars, unrivalled perhaps in its cruelty.

In the evening Napoleon gathered together a few of his intimates and told them that in a few hours he would be leaving for Paris, the capital of his torn empire. He had been absent from Paris for seven months. It was true that what had befallen Napoleon and his army in the Russian campaign was not generally known there, but the bits of information that were beginning to filter through were not encouraging. No one, however, imagined the extent of the disaster. It was not yet known that the glorious Grand Army had in fact ceased to exist as a fighting force and that its men were desperately trying to save themselves and retreat in as orderly a fashion as possible while the Cossacks struck at them and the terrible cold went through their bones.

Bulletin No. 29, which Napoleon wrote on 3 December, gave an inkling of what was going on for the first time. The bulletin was sent on to Paris. While it admitted to the destruction of the army in a roundabout way, mostly the early harsh weather was blamed. Napoleon could imagine the shock the bulletin would cause in Paris and felt that only his presence there might calm things down.

There had been previous signs of unrest in Paris. In October, Malet – a retired general who had been involved in a republican conspiracy against the emperor as early as 1808 – had again plotted against Napoleon. The first conspiracy had been foiled and Malet imprisoned. This time he linked his fortunes to young Republicans and a group of Royalists whose common denominator was the powerful wish to depose the emperor. Malet spread the rumour that Napoleon had died in Moscow and tried to seize power but failed this time as well and the minister of police and internal security had him executed. Napoleon was informed of the plot but kept it from his circle. However, it caused him much concern and played a large part in his decision to hasten back to France and strengthen his rule.

On that same evening in Smorgoni, Napoleon and his companions knew that his leaving his army would make a bad impression and be regarded by many as desertion. Some believed that in his absence the army would fall apart. However, he was the emperor, and rulers could not be expected to stay with their armies in every stage of a campaign, and certainly not on its return. None the less the army was in the midst of a difficult retreat and in all of Napoleon's wars his soldiers were used to seeing their supreme commander every day with their own eyes. Many knew that he was sick and weak, that he was having trouble riding and taking command because of urinary problems and general physical weakness – but to leave the army to its fate and return to the fleshpots of Paris? That was not the commander they knew.

Napoleon felt that he had to be at the centre of things – only that way could he systematically plan his moves, test his grand strategy, reorganise and rebuild an army to replace the one he had lost. He also knew that he had to repair France's relations with its two nominal allies – Austria and Prussia. His troops had already been through the worst and were on their way to Vilna and its big supply base. There they could rest and get their strength back.

Thus with many misgivings Napoleon decided to return to Paris. Before he left on the long and perilous journey through hostile lands he appointed Marshal Murat to replace him as commander of the army. He chose a few intimates to accompany him and set out on the 2,300-kilometre journey in a convoy of three sleighs. With him in the same sleigh was General Caulaincourt, formerly the French ambassador to Russia and now serving on Napoleon's personal staff with the title Master of the Horse (in charge of stables, messengers and runners and the emperor's escort). It was Caulaincourt who had warned Napoleon time and again not to get involved in the Russian adventure. During the two weeks they were on the road, there was time enough for Napoleon to unburden himself to the man who had given him such sound advice. And indeed Napoleon talked and talked.

Napoleon's expansionist policy and the diplomatic efforts he undertook to advance his imperial interests in Europe had been aimed throughout his years of rule against his arch rivals Russia, Prussia and Austria. But his bitterest enemy was Britain. With the other three there had been ups and downs but with Britain relations were always the same, marked by bitter and unremitting rivalry. Though Britain had hardly sullied itself in the wars between Napoleon and the powers, it had given its support and material resources to the various coalitions that had risen against him. Napoleon was in no hurry to cross the Channel and invade the island, having been stung by the British fleet more than once. Therefore, as has already been mentioned, he did everything in his power to destroy Britain economically, mainly through the Continental System, aiming to enlist all the nations of Europe, an obsession that had a decisive influence on his political, and consequently military, moves.

Napoleon's campaigns of 1806 and 1807 had been directed against Prussia and Russia. Prussia, which had suffered a crushing defeat and was at Napoleon's mercy, lost its independence and most of its army in the fields of Jena and Auerstädt. At the end of 1806 the war between Russia and France on east Prussian soil was extended. The last battle in this war, after the bloody, indecisive battle of Eylau, was fought at Friedland in June 1807. Napoleon struck the Russians and hit General Bennigsen's forces hard. The Russian general, desperately in need of a respite to reorganise his troops, implored the tsar to arrange a ceasefire, and quickly.

The tsar met the French ruler at Tilsit on the Niemen River on June 25 1807, with the talks continuing for a few days. Napoleon exercised all of his charm on the young tsar. Alexander was well acquainted with Napoleon's demands in relation to Britain, which were the *sine qua non* of any agreement. Though good relations with Britain were vital to Russian economic interests, as it was Russia's biggest commercial customer, the disaster at Friedland convinced the tsar that it was best to make peace with France, even at the price of these relations.

Alexander resolved not only to make peace with France but to enter into an alliance with it. He saw no purpose in further debilitating his army to serve Prussian interests. This way of looking at things clearly revealed the influence of the French emperor, who asked his colleague again and again what was moving him to give Prussia his support when he was getting nothing in return for it. Out of a sense of obligation the tsar asked Napoleon to offer the Prussians an armistice without asking them to surrender its fortresses. The Prussian king, Frederick William, waited for his fate to be decided walking back and forth on the banks of the river in pouring rain.

At Tilsit, Alexander recognised Napoleon's conquests in Europe and committed himself to participate fully in the economic blockade of Britain and even exercise his influence on other countries on the Continent to join in. All this was laid out in a secret provision in the agreement which stated that if Britain did not agree to Russian mediation between itself and France, Russia would join the blockade and co-operate with France in tightening it. It is just this condition of Russian submission that demonstrates the fact that the agreement contained the seeds of its own rapid dissolution. The spirit of Tilsit did not in fact last very long. Alexander was awestruck by Napoleon and admired his military genius, especially his organisational ability, showering Alexander with praise, even saying to his companions that the tsar was handsome and 'has an intellect above what is commonly attributed to him'. The tsar, who wanted to turn the Russian autocracy into a modern monarchy on the French model, felt that his colleague the emperor could be of great help to him. He was interested in reforming many important areas of Russian life: the constitution, property laws, local self-government in his vast land. Napoleon's influence was indeed not to the liking of the conservative Russian nobility. Furthermore, Alexander's ambitions in the international arena did not accord with French interests.

One of the examples of the conflict of interests between the two powers was the Polish question, which was also discussed at Tilsit. The tsar wanted to create a pan-Slavic framework in which the Polish question might find a Slavic solution. After defeating Prussia in 1806, Napoleon had stripped it of the Polish territories it had annexed and created the Grand Duchy of Warsaw. After the victory over Austria in 1809, Napoleon annexed to the duchy Polish territories that had been taken by Austria in the partitions. He made his ally King Frederick August of Saxony grand duke of Warsaw, which nettled all the courts of Europe, including St Petersburg. The duchy's constitution was a copy of Napoleon's French constitution. The Poles hoped that Napoleon would give them what the Russians had no intentions of giving them. While the Tilsit accord saw agreement between the two rulers on the creation of the Grand Duchy of Warsaw, Alexander was concerned that in the end he would be forced to return former Polish territory in Russia's possession. Despite his pro-Polish stance, Napoleon made certain that the kingdom of Poland was not set up; none the less, Russia saw in France's growing influence in Poland an invasion of its front yard.

Another example of the conflict of interests between the two concerns the tsar's ambition to tear off large chunks of the Ottoman empire for himself, which even won Napoleon's support in the beginning. He promised the tsar, among other things, that he would co-operate with him in redividing the

Ottoman empire to Russia's satisfaction. This was a shrewd idea, satisfying Russia's ambition – going far back in time and tinged with religious overtones – to see the old Byzantine empire wrenched away from the sultan. In another secret provision in the Treaty of Tilsit it was stipulated that if the sultan did not agree to French mediation between himself and the Russian tsar, France would help the Russians gain control of Ottoman provinces in Europe. The Russian interests focused mainly on the Danube provinces of Walachia and Moldavia but they also set their sights on the Bosporus Strait and the Dardanelles. Napoleon did not respond favourably, fearing that the realisation of these ambitions would give Russia an outlet to the Mediterranean.

The next meeting between the two leaders began at Erfurt on 27 September 1808, and lasted around two weeks, with the spirit of Tilsit quickly evaporating. It was Napoleon who initiated the summit meeting. Since Tilsit he had been occupied with Spain, where increasing numbers of French troops were pinned down, and felt that he had to secure his eastern flank, which was now his rear. Austria worried him and he made no secret of the fact that he wanted Alexander to agree that an attack by Austria on France would be regarded as an attack on Russia. Other issues too were discussed that demonstrated the growing conflict of interests between the two supposedly friendly powers. Napoleon was dissatisfied with Russia's increasing influence in Finland, to the point that the tsar was now its grand duke. The French emperor was also not pleased with military developments in the Ottoman empire. The tsar suspected that Napoleon was planning to expand the area of the Grand Duchy of Warsaw and even establish a Polish kingdom. For his part, Napoleon believed that it was the tsar who was planning to annex large parts of Poland.

Thus, all the cats were out of the bag and mutual suspicion overshadowed their deliberations. The eyes of all of Europe were on Erfurt with the feeling that the fate of the Continent was about to be decided. Despite the splendour of the occasion it was entirely different from its predecessor in Tilsit. Alexander, sensing the approaching crisis, wanted to buy time and make his preparations. Important people in Paris who were opposed to Napoleon had hinted to him that there was no justification for displaying weakness in dealing with Napoleon, whose situation was extremely delicate. Though Alexander gave his consent to the agreement Napoleon sought on Austria, he left Erfurt feeling that he was an equal partner with Napoleon and would find it easier in the future to go back on his Tilsit commitments. When Napoleon left Erfurt he was convinced that the tsar had become his sworn enemy, and from this time on relations between France and Russia as well as between Napoleon and Alexander deteriorated.

Napoleon was disappointed with the extent of Russia's co-operation in the Continental System. He made this clear at Erfurt and afterwards as well. The System raised the hackles of all of Europe, since it hurt not only Britain but all the countries on the Continent. The damage was that much more serious because Britain blockaded the ports that had closed themselves to its ships as well as taking other measures. Russia was undoubtedly one of the principal victims. Its foreign trade was cut back and income from customs duties fell. In 1810 Alexander took steps to diminish Russia's active participation in the economic alliance against Britain. He allowed neutral ships to carry on part of Russia's foreign trade and restricted the importation of certain items from France. Liddell-Hart is convinced that Russia's efforts to throw off the shackles of the Continental System strengthened Britain's resolve not to negotiate with Napoleon.

Another affair that strained the supposedly good relations between Alexander and Napoleon was rooted in Napoleon's powerful desire to marry into one of Europe's important royal houses. The emperor wanted a wife who would give him an heir, which Josephine had failed to do. In 1809 Napoleon asked Alexander for the hand of his younger sister, the grand duchess Anna. Their mother the tsarina strongly opposed the match, giving vent to the Romanov hostility to the French emperor, and Napoleon went away empty-handed and deeply hurt.

There was more to come. At the beginning of 1811 Alexander resuscitated the idea of a Polish kingdom. He promised the Poles that he would help them if he was allowed to bear the title of king of Poland. Napoleon quickly got wind of what was afoot and immediately stopped co-operating with the tsar in everything that concerned the Polish question.

As the friction between the two continued it became settled in Napoleon's mind that he would go to war against Russia. There is much logic in the view of many historians that the main reason for this decision is linked to the question of the Continental System. Napoleon was convinced that war was unavoidable. The two rulers hurled serious accusations at one another and showed warlike intentions. At the beginning of 1812 Napoleon stepped up his pressure on the tsar to rejoin him in the struggle against Great Britain. Alexander, for his part, demanded that the French get out of Prussia and withdraw westward to the Oder River. Napoleon was convinced that war against Russia would help him bring the struggle with Britain to a quick and honourable conclusion. He would bring Great Britain to its knees. To this end he took further steps to tighten the blockade, particularly in the northern ports. Already in January 1811 he gained control of the duchy of Oldenburg, located on the shore of the North Sea and a member of the Confederation of the Rhine, deposing the tsar's brother-in-law Duke Peter Frederick. Needless to say, this move did little to improve relations between France and Russia. One good battle, thought Napoleon, would solve all his problems. Europe would become convinced that there was no sense in opposing him.

A wise ruler, even if he is sure of the justice of his ways and deeds, feels the need to discuss his ideas and plans and get the views of his subordinates. Napoleon, who set little store by the opinions of his advisers and intimates, liked to hold forth on his political ideas but generally ignored their views and comments. At the end of December 1812, when he was making his way back to Paris with his crippled army far behind, he might have remembered his conversations with Caulaincourt, sitting beside him now, in June of the previous year, before it had all begun.

Caulaincourt was the scion of an aristocratic French family. He joined the army at an early age. Already in 1801 he was sent to Russia on a diplomatic mission on Napoleon's behalf. Afterwards he was appointed the first consul's aide-de-camp. In 1807 he was appointed ambassador to St Petersburg. Caulaincourt was convinced that his chief task was to make sure that the Treaty of Tilsit was carried out and that the prevailing spirit of friendship was preserved. He established excellent personal relations with the tsar and the members of his court and did everything in his power to bring about a relaxation of tensions between Napoleon and Alexander. In May 1811 he completed his tour of duty and returned to Paris. In conversations with the emperor he tried to allay Napoleon's anger at the Russians and to explain to him that what looked like war preparations were in fact a natural and necessary reaction to his own preparations, which the Russians saw as a clear military threat, and justifiably so. 'I'm telling you,' Napoleon insisted, 'they're getting ready to fight me and humiliate France.'

Caulaincourt implored the emperor to observe the Treaty of Tilsit and refrain from any declaration in regard to the establishment of the Polish kingdom, thus keeping Russia as an ally and making it possible to conclude a peace agreement with Great Britain. He described the thinking of the tsar when he weighed the possibility of war against France. The tsar was putting his faith in the enormous size of his country and the long road the French army would have to travel under difficult conditions. Napoleon's superior military talents, which the tsar recognised and appreciated, would be set off by the given conditions. The hard, cruel Russian winter would be another obstacle in the path of the French and a faithful ally of their enemies. Therefore, Caulaincourt concluded, Alexander is confident of his ability to meet the French threat and has no intentions of giving in. The emperor dismissed these tidings with a shrug of his shoulders and self-confident assertions, sure that the tsar was afraid of him, and stepped up his preparations. First he went about putting together his armed forces, including those of his supposed and actual allies, and securing his flanks and lines of advance through both diplomatic and military activity.

Seemingly, Prussia and Austria supported France. Alexander had been wooing them, mainly with promises, while Napoleon relied on threats. In February 1812 he signed a military pact with Prussia. Prussia promised 20,000 men under General Yorck for the campaign in Russia, however, at the same time, it gave the tsar its word that it would not take an active part in the war. In March 1812 a similar pact was signed with Austria, which promised 30,000 men under Schwarzenberg, but, like Prussia, reassured the tsar of its unwarlike intentions. Austria and Prussia co-ordinated their positions. Not only did they promise not to help France in the war against Russia, they reminded the tsar of their common interest in not having the kingdom of Poland brought back to life and in opposing an increase in French power. Prussia was at the height of a process of reform in different areas and was secretly laying the foundations of a new army.

Napoleon was counting on his marital ties to Kaiser Francis I of Austria, whose daughter Marie Louise he married in April 1810. In March 1811 a son was born to the couple, given the title of king of Rome and earmarked as the next emperor of France. But Metternich, who had persuaded Francis that Austria had no choice but to accede to the pact with France, also assured the tsar that Austria did not take it seriously.

Thus, despite the commitments of Tilsit and the pacts of early 1812 and Napoleon's marriage to the daughter of the Austrian emperor, he did not succeed in driving a wedge between the three great powers who had been defeated by him on the battlefield. Their major concern was still to stop the spread of the ideas of the French Revolution in Europe. The Polish question was less important, all four of the powers regarding it with not a little political cynicism.

On the northern flank of the theatre of war was Sweden. The king of Sweden was Charles XIII and the crown prince none other than Jean Bernadotte, formerly a marshal in the French army. Bernadotte's relations with the emperor in the past had been complex and marked by almost continuous strain. In 1810 he had accepted the invitation of the Swedish parliament to become crown prince to the king, who had no male heirs (Bernadotte in fact became king in 1818). Napoleon angered Bernadotte when he gained control of Swedish Pomerania in January 1812 and threatened to annex Norway. Napoleon's efforts to enlist Sweden in the cause came to nothing and Sweden declared its neutrality, though it was clear that Bernadotte leaned towards Russia. The northern flank was therefore more secure for Alexander than it was for his rival.

The securing of the southern flank was tied to the relations of France and Russia with the Ottoman empire. Russia had been involved in a war with the sultan since 1806, whose aims, as mentioned, were the Danube lands and the Straits. In 1811 the Russian general Kutusov defeated the Ottomans on the northern bank of the Danube. Alexander, who could see the war with Napoleon coming, contented himself with the annexation of Bessarabia and signed a peace treaty with the Ottomans in Bucharest in May 1812. Russia thus received an accession of battle-hardened forces now released from their previous assignment and ready for the new war. Thus, too, the neutrality of the Ottoman empire also became a doubtful factor for Napoleon.

Attempts to make peace with Britain came to nothing and Napoleon was forced to reconcile himself to being faced with an enemy who would not hesitate, and would in fact rush, to aid his other adversaries. Alexander, on the other hand, made overtures to Britain to enlist its support. Few problems were encountered in these contacts and an agreement was signed in July 1812. The agreement put an end to the strain that had been growing in the relations between the two powers since Erfurt. Great Britain was eager to reach accommodations with the countries of Europe – and certainly with a power like Russian – both because of its bitter rivalry with France and because of its problems around the world. Simultaneously, similar understandings were reached with Sweden and, once and for all, the sting went out of the Continental System.

Thus the tsar secured his flanks with no little success while Napoleon foundered in uncertainty as to the responses of the different countries to a military move against Russia. This uncertainty interfered with the completion of his preparations, so vital to such a huge campaign, but more troubling than this was the Iberian adventure. The Spanish war drained the blood of his soldiers, pinned down large forces and occupied some of his best commanding officers, needed for the great war in the east. He thus had to pull out some of his forces on the Peninsula – some 200,000 still remained – and consequently made things worse there.

These were the relations between the main countries of Europe that were connected directly or indirectly to the growing conflict between France and Russia in 1812. Russia's flanks were well secured. It had extracted itself from the military conflicts it had been engaged in until then and had Europe behind it. Napoleon, on the other hand, could not count on the political and military arrangements he had made through his complicated diplomacy, since it is difficult to place credence on agreements with hostile nations who are potential enemies. A large part of his army was spread out on the Continent on garrison duty and in Spain he was involved in a bitter, humiliating and pointless war whose end was not in sight. The tsar's feeling of self-confidence was mounting. In April he presented Napoleon, through his ambassador in Paris, with a number of conditions that amounted to an ultimatum: evacuation of Prussia and compensation to the duke of Oldenburg. Napoleon considered these demands insolent.

The Grand Army that was going to take part either directly or indirectly in the Russian campaign numbered around 650,000 men in May 1812, divided into 12 infantry corps (including two as a general reserve of the army), three cavalry corps, the Imperial Guard, artillery units and engineering and administrative and auxiliary forces. This was the largest regular army ever brought together for a single campaign. Napoleon now stood at the head of an army of more than a million men if we take into account the troops in Spain as well as others. Less than half the force allocated for Russia was French; the others represented various countries in the empire or under its influence. These included Prussians, Austrians, Poles, Dutch, Swiss, Germans, Italians and Croatians – a mix of peoples called the Army of Twenty Nations. Of this huge force, 450,000 were intended to cross the Niemen.

The opposing Russian army numbered a little more than 200,000 men. Two armies defended the western border of Russia: the larger one, under Barclay de Tolly, was deployed along the Niemen up to the area south of Lithuania; the other one, much smaller, was deployed south of the Pripet swamps under the command of the young General Bagration, a nobleman of Armenian descent and very well liked in the army.

Napoleon did not have a comprehensive plan for the campaign. He determined its general course and did not go into details until the battle was joined. The army would invade Russia in three separate columns in the general direction of Moscow. He was to make his breakthrough on the right or northern wing of the Russians and afterwards attack the operational and supply lines of the left wing and centre in order to drive a wedge between the two parts of Barclay's army while isolating Bagration's army and then defeating each in detail. He thus hoped to destroy the larger part of the army opposing him before moving into the interior of the country. To achieve this aim he needed a large concentration of reliable troops and to this end he delegated to a certain extent his two strategic wings. On his northern wing he had Yorck's Prussian expeditionary force, on the southern wing Schwarzenberg's Austrians. For obvious reasons, the loyalty of both was questionable.

Of the possibilities open to the Russians, given Napoleon's general plan, he envisaged a slow and steady retreat by Barclay and a counter-offensive by Bagration in the direction of Warsaw. He believed that if such an eventuality materialised, it would play into his hands as the two parts of the Russian army would move apart and the way into the interior of the country would lie open before him.

The campaign started off in an atmosphere of high spirits. On 9 May 1812, the emperor left Paris in a huge royal convoy accompanied by his wife and many members of the court. Wherever he stopped he was received magnificently. At Dresden, the last stop in this nonmilitary procession, he was greeted by kings and princes, the most prominent being Frederick William of Prussia and his father-in-law Kaiser Francis of Austria. At the end of the month the ambassadors of the two belligerent countries, Prince Kourakin and General Lauriston, received their passports, one of the established signs of a state of war.

The first hostile act in the 1812 campaign was the attack on a Russian outpost near Kovno. On 13 June Alexander, who was in Vilna at the time, published a proclamation accusing Napoleon of aggression and calling on his army to resist the invasion with all its strength and to expel the enemy. The declaration concluded with the cry: 'You are the protectors of our religion, our Motherland and our freedom! God fights against the aggressor.' In his imperial proclamation of 22 June, Napoleon declared that the second Polish war had commenced (the first had ended at Friedland and Tilsit): 'At Tilsit, Russia swore eternal alliance with France and war against England. She has violated her oath... Should we be no longer the soldiers of Austerlitz? She has placed us between disgrace and war; the choice cannot for an instant be doubtful! Let us then cross the Niemen and carry the war into her territories.' The French crossed the Niemen on 24 June in the Kovno area and began to advance towards Vilna.

It is not difficult to imagine the cumbersome manner in which the campaign got under way. First there was the demonstrative splendour of the movement east. Beyond this, already in Saxony and Silesia tens of thousands of soldiers dropped out of the ranks owing to disease and desertion. On the left bank of the Niemen, the operational start line, there was a long delay and, after the crossing, another one of more than 10 days – first at Vilna and then at Vitebsk.

Marshal Davout advanced from Minsk and tried to make contact with Bagration, but the latter slipped away to Bobruisk. The Russians retreated without stopping, fighting only limited actions. The First Army, the northern one, retreated to Vitebsk while Bagration crossed the Dnieper and withdrew towards Smolensk. At this stage, with the two armies joining at Smolensk, Napoleon had already lost over 100,000 men, without his Grand Army making real contact with the enemy. Napoleon had not yet understood that the enormous distances of Russia were a huge trap negating his offensive strategy even before Russian forces had to be committed to great battles. At French headquarters there was already talk about postponing the campaign to 1813, but the emperor would hear nothing of it, fearing the effect on the countries of Europe and the French people. He was still hoping to strike one decisive blow and bring the war – which did not look too good at this point – to a victorious conclusion. He therefore had to take Smolensk, which lay on the main road to Moscow, hoping to advance rapidly eastwards from there along the expected Russian line of retreat towards Moscow.

Napoleon decided to attack Smolensk from the south, but he was unable to bring on a real battle, as most of the Russian army began to retreat in the direction of Moscow and just 20,000 men under Dokhturov remained behind to defend the city. None the less the fighting was hard (17–19 August). Three French corps advanced side by side, took the suburbs, but failed to penetrate the city itself. Napoleon did not demonstrate the determination that his sub-ordinates were used to seeing in him. In the end, Smolensk was occupied but Murat and Ney could not prevent the Russians from retreating or block their main axis of movement. A force under the command of Victor was brought up to Smolensk to secure a supply base for the advancing Grand Army. Victor arrived at the end of September, but Napoleon was already hastening towards Moscow by the end of August. Had he remained in Smolensk, getting organised and sparing himself and his army the rigours of winter, he would have had a better chance of victory when he renewed his campaign in the spring of 1813. But the urge to win a quick, decisive victory and impose peace on the tsar with Moscow in his hands overcame him. Immediately after occupying Smolensk he declared that in another month Moscow would be his and in another six weeks he would have a peace treaty. Now he moved east on the Smolensk–Moscow highway, his frustrated, hungry soldiers burning and pillaging everything that came to hand.

The tsar now decided to replace the head of his Army, Barclay, with Kutusov, 67 years old, sick and indecisive, who was clearly no match for Napoleon. But Barclay was of foreign origin, he was not the figure to inspire the patriotism needed at this time and he was identified with the strategy of continuous retreat. His replacement accorded with the mood of the country. The general feeling among the Russians was that battle should be joined, and immediately.

Kutusov retreated to Borodino and deployed his forces there. This was a rel-atively strong position, around 80 kilometres from Moscow, with consider-able engineering works. The fighting began on 5 September and the main battle, bloody, shifting in fortunes but finally indecisive, took place two days later. The Russians dug in along the Moscow highway, behind a water line and fortified positions. Their weak point was on the left wing, which Napoleon could not have failed to see. None the less he chose to attack the enemy frontally with the aid of heavy artillery fire but without any manoeuvring of troops. Losses on both sides amounted to 80,000 men, the Russians losing nearly twice as many as the French. Though the battle was undecided, both sides claimed victory. To his intimates Napoleon confessed that the results of the battle did not justify the losses. Kutusov began to withdraw his forces and, despite his heavy losses, the retreat was carried out in good order. On the 12th he held a council of war with the discussion revolving around the question of whether to attack or retreat. Kutusov decided in favour of continuing the retreat, which was now resumed – towards Moscow. Reaching the city, the

Russians passed right through it and continued on their way, with most of the population on their heels.

Napoleon entered the abandoned, burning city on 14 September. The French army, whose discipline had begun to melt away, occupied itself in pillage and destruction. Churches were converted to stables and altars to mess tables. Again doubts were raised about continuing the campaign. Winter was approaching and conditions were becoming more and more difficult, but Napoleon knew that retreat would be an admission of failure, which he could not permit himself. He knew he had to do something and, if not for the opposition of his officers, would have sent a large force towards the capital, St Petersburg. He would remain in Moscow as long as there was a chance of achieving peace. On 5 October he sent General Lauriston to Russian headquarters to open negotiations on whatever basis possible. The Russians refused as long as French soldiers were on Russian soil. Napoleon then decided to retreat. His total force numbered just 100,000 men.

The Russian army concentrated along the old Kaluga axis in the Tarotino area, where it was relieved and reinforced with large quantities of men and equipment. Napoleon, who could have retreated to the west, towards Vitebsk, and thus avoid the main French force of the enemy, was afraid that such a course of action would show that he was afraid of the Russians and he therefore decided to turn south, towards Kaluga, and from there to Smolensk. The retreat began on 18 October and on the 24th he ran into the Russians at Maloyaroslavetz. Dokhturov attacked first. The fighting was fierce and lasted all day, until the two sides broke off contact. Napoleon marched toward Mojaisk, which shows how unnecessary the last battle had been and how meaningless the losses, since if in the end he had to get back on the direct route to the west, what was the point of the southern detour? All indications suggest that Dokhturov would have avoided a pitched battle at Kaluga if the French had got there.

Winter came early and the cold struck the troops and prevented regular supply. Bands of Russian partisans soon appeared and began to hit the supply convoys, the bases in the rear and the garrisons in the occupied cities. Cossack raids emanating from the main Russian army became bolder and more frequent. At the beginning of November, Kutusov too began to increase the pressure under the urging of his advisers and subordinates. On 3 November the French, freezing and fleeing pursuit, passed through Viasma. Their suffering was at its peak. The soldiers ate horse flesh and cannibalised the dead. Soldiers froze to death in the deep snow. On the 9th the French arrived at Smolensk, where Napoleon learned that the Russians had retaken Vitebsk to the northwest. He put together a force of 50,000 men and moved towards Krasnoi, in the direction of the Dnieper River. As the Russians had occupied Vitebsk he gave up the idea of going into winter quarters along the Dwina River. The battles around Krasnoi ended in French defeat. Ney, who commanded the rear guard, retreated towards the Dnieper and crossed the river with fewer than a thousand men. On the 16th the rest of the French crossed the Dnieper at Orsha, now moving towards the Berezina River. Three days previously the Russians had occupied Minsk on the southern flank of the French line of retreat and west of the Berezina.

The Russians now had more than 60,000 men on Napoleon's two wings. Half the force, under Wittgenstein, was arrayed north of the Smolensk axis and moving southwest towards the river. The other half, under Tchitchagov, was coming up from the Danube, since the fighting with Ottomans had ended, and was moving from Minsk toward Borissov. The situation of the French was becoming desperate. They were now being pursued by an enemy that smelled victory and was at a numerical advantage. Napoleon, who had first planned to cross the river at Borissov, understood that under the new circumstances he would have to make the crossing farther north and get on to the Vilna road somewhere around Zembin and between the two Russian forces. He ordered Oudinot to construct a bridge at Vesselovo and Victor to secure the crossing point against Wittgenstein's force. Oudinot covered the engineering operation with the artillery at Studianka but was surprised to discover that no enemy forces were in the area of the crossing point. The Russians, believing that the crossing would be made farther south, at Borissov, had advanced slowly. The engineering work began on 25 November and was a brilliant chapter in the campaign. Napoleon himself crossed the river on the 27th. Only then was real contact made with the Russians, who surrounded the French from every side and outnumbered them significantly. Half the French force was lost – partly shot, partly drowned – but the rest reached safety at Berezina. They still had a long way to go, but the Russian pressure now fell off. Napoleon began to consider leaving his army and returning home. 'In the existing state of affairs,' he told Caulaincourt, 'I can only hold my grip on Europe from the Tuileries.'

Now Napoleon was on the long road to Paris. On the stops along the way – Vilna, Warsaw, Dresden – there was not a trace of the enthusiastic welcome he had received just half a year ago. Accompanied by Caulaincourt, he stayed at wretched inns, shivering with the cold and not even recognised by anyone. As mentioned, he did a lot of talking on the journey, analysing the campaign from every point of view and expanding on his plans for the near future. He pointed to the strategically weak point of the Russian war, and seems to have hit upon the truth: 'I wanted to do in one year what should have taken two.' He should not have left Smolensk for Moscow when he did. He should have brought on a decisive battle at the early stage of the campaign despite the slippery tactics of the Russians, but he was not his old determined self. He also understood that he had remained in Moscow two weeks too long to his own detriment, in the hope of receiving peace overtures from the tsar.

Napoleon blamed the British for the campaign. He claimed that they had persecuted him, not leaving him in peace. 'If England had let me,' he insisted, 'I would have lived in peace.' But Napoleon had stubbornly sought to bring Great Britain down with economic measures, doomed to failure by their very nature, as they hurt the rest of Europe as well. If not for this economic warfare he could not have tied the war in Russia to the need to tighten the continental blockade and, what he proclaimed on the eve of the war to be one of its most important reasons, would have been absent. But even if he was 'forced' to embark on this war to step up the economic war against Britain, the irony was that one of the results of the campaign was to strengthen the British position as a world power.

If Napoleon had had strategic aims like 'peace and security for all', as he argued at the end of his life, he could have achieved them without embarking on this impossible campaign. He could have reached accommodations over Prussia and Poland and concentrated on disentangling himself from Spain, afterwards strengthening his wide-ranging empire and avoiding the terrible bloodshed of 1812. There is no question that making war on Russia before finishing the one in Spain was a serious mistake, for conducting two wars of such proportions simultaneously was beyond his powers.

As mentioned, in the message sent to France on 3 December, Napoleon put the blame on the hard winter, which had arrived early. This excuse, which in the course of time became the standard one, was exaggerated. Unquestionably the weather conditions contributed significantly to the defeat of the French, but as the Grand Army was not equipped properly to begin with, it would not have been able to withstand the Russian winter even if it come 'on time'. The French emperor had arrived in Moscow with just 100,000 men, about a fifth of the number that had crossed the Niemen at the end of June. Most of the soldiers who did not reach Moscow had in fact fallen victim to the summer. On the whole, until the crossing of the Berezina, there was nothing out of the ordinary about the winter weather and it could have been withstood if the men had been properly equipped for it. It became unbearable when contact with the Russian army had pretty much been broken off. The organisation of French supplies throughout the campaign failed completely and the argument that winter came early strikes one as baseless, like saying, 'It was cold in the winter and hot in the summer and that's why we lost.'

Napoleon's main problem in Russia was thus logistic. The supply of such a big army in a vast and hostile country where supply lines kept getting longer and longer was an impossible task given the technical means available at the time. Add to this the insufficiencies of the Grand Army general staff, inexperienced in controlling such large forces at such great distances, and the reason for the administrative failure is plain to see. The planning of transport was poor throughout the campaign, even if we take into account natural obstacles and the scorched-earth policy of the Russians. Supply bases were too far from the fighting forces. The fact that the remains of the army found large quantities of food in the rear bases proves that the failure in organisation was greater than the lack of means.

Napoleon was convinced that if he made war against the tsar and struck him one decisive blow he could bring him to terms. As mentioned above, in their conversations months before the start of the campaign, the returning ambassador, Caulaincourt, had warned Napoleon that he was mistaken. In truth, the determination of the tsar was even greater than the ambassador had supposed. His domineering mother and religious circles urged him on and planted the mystic idea in his head that it was incumbent on him to repudiate the French Antichrist. Another factor was the behaviour of the Russian people during the war. They demonstrated fervent and unforeseen patriotism, despite the harsh treatment they received at the hands of the tsar. The peasants fought a fierce guerrilla war, striking lines of communication that got farther and farther away from the main bases as the French army moved east. These partisans killed large numbers of stragglers and weakened the will and endurance of the French troops, who had to stay on constant alert.

Finally there was Napoleon himself. The emperor was not at his best during the campaign. He put on weight and was sick most of the time, making riding difficult. His military genius was affected as well as his fighting spirit. He did not demonstrate his characteristic perfect sense of timing and his orchestration of operations was uninspired. If one examines the course and timetable of events in the war one gets the feeling that Napoleon did not go into it wholeheartedly, though the decision not to get involved would have been entirely his. Nevertheless he did not modify in the least the centralisation of command that was his hallmark. Caulaincourt commented on this: 'The staff foresaw nothing, but on the other hand, as the emperor wanted to do everything himself, and to give every order, no one, not even the general staff, dared to assume the responsibility for giving the most trifling order.'

Another consequence of the war was the explosion of the myth of Napoleon as unvanquished. Occasionally, it is true, at the most critical times Napoleon showed the old spark, the high point being the crossing of the Berezina, considered one of the great exploits in military history. Clausewitz said that 'on the banks of the Berezina Napoleon won new glory'. This ability to get back on his feet after suffering such punishment was indeed an omen of things to come.

Napoleon told Caulaincourt a great deal about his plans for the coming year. He would hold on to the reins in Germany and even tighten them, and he would dictate terms to Russia. On reaching Warsaw he told the French ambassador there: 'It is but one step from the sublime to the ridiculous,' meaning that there was a very thin line between his getting to Moscow and holding it and being disgracefully driven out. Because the line was so thin he did not see any reason not to believe that his fortunes would be reversed, already in the coming year. The idea of 'a hair's breadth', incidentally, recurs throughout his career as a general and a ruler. As early as 1797 the young General Bonaparte wrote to the French foreign minister that all great events hang by a thin thread and the wise man does not neglect anything that can give him a second chance. Now too he was convinced that when he got to Paris he would be able to take things in hand and achieve his aims. He told Caulaincourt: 'Our disasters will cause a great sensation, but my arrival will counterbalance the distressing effects.' He was going to call the youth of France to the flag, create a new army and strike the Russians a lethal blow, strengthen his regime and his hold on the country and persuade the French people, through the force of his leadership, to gird their loins again.

On 18 December, in the night, the emperor reached Paris, battered but full of spirit. The palace guards at the Tuileries hardly recognised him, but when they identified him their joy knew no bounds. He said to Caulaincourt, 'Goodnight, my friend, you need some rest too,' and hastened to his wife.

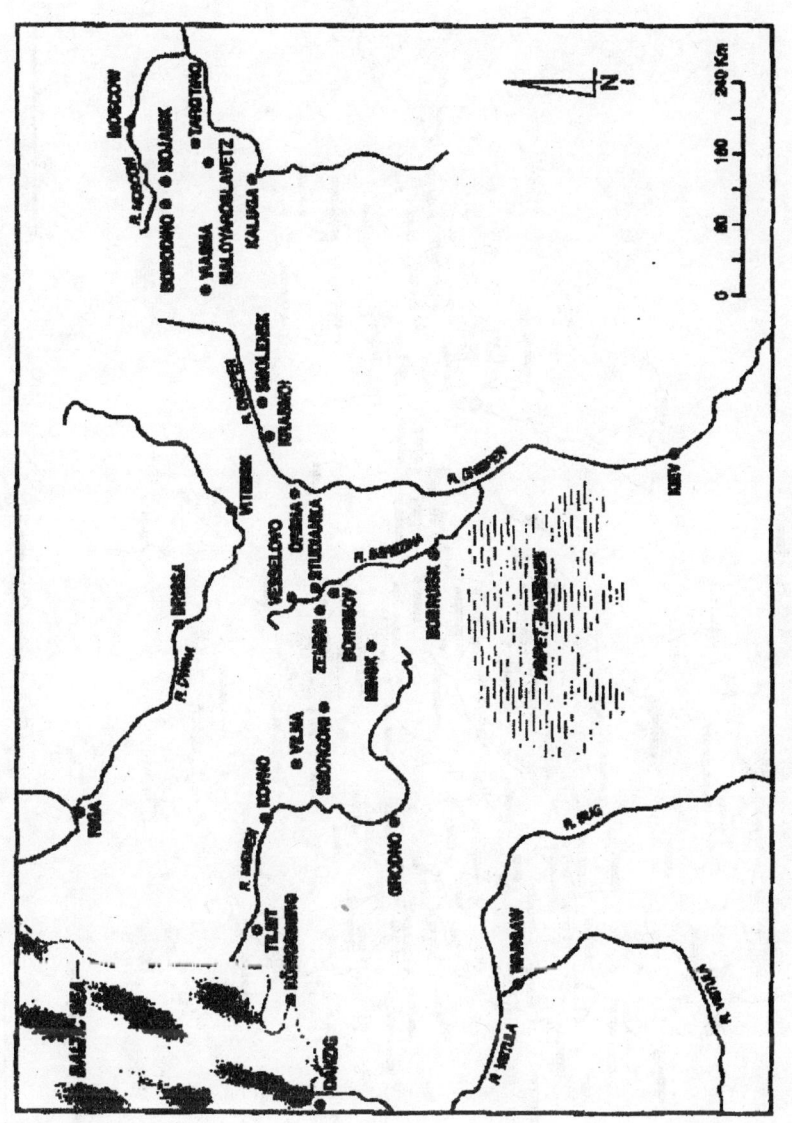

Map 1   Russian Campaign – 1812

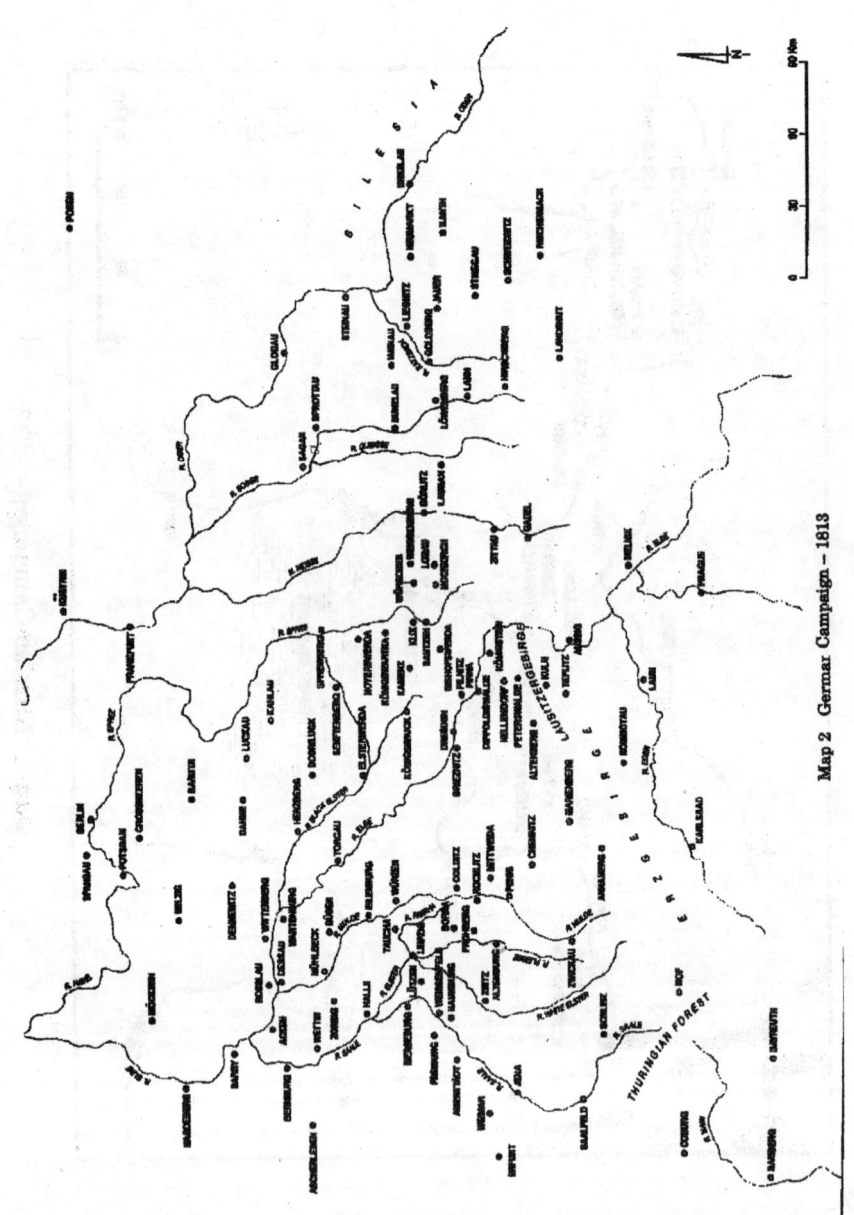

Map 2 German Campaign – 1813

Chapter 2 - PREPARATIONS FOR TOTAL WAR

Napoleon did not need much rest. Already on his first day back in Paris he worked 15 hours and within a week had the affairs of the empire under control – from Dresden to Madrid. He promulgated decrees, instructions and letters on a wide range of topics: the capacity of supply wagons in the light of the Russian experience, steps to be taken against the press in Westphalia, aid to Polish and Lithuanian refugees, organisational measures for the fleet, instructions for preparing the national budget for 1813 – all these being random examples of his numerous decisions and actions. Though he knew that people had physical limitations, he thought of himself as a workhorse and his capacity for work was indeed seemingly limitless. He displayed great self-confidence and radiated uplifting optimism, as if untouched by the Russian disaster. The Imperial Bulletin of 3 December, which could only have sent shock waves through France, had indeed done so, but these were quickly replaced by wonder at Napoleon's journey from Russia to Paris. From Dresden to Paris in four days – who would have believed it? People buzzed in the salons of the capital.

Napoleon was well aware that his plans demanded a form of organisation entirely different in nature and scope from what he and the French nation had known in the past. It was true that the basis of total war, mobilising manpower and economic resources at the national level, had been laid in the first years of the French Revolution, but Napoleon's first campaigns were conducted more along the lines of traditional warfare. The Revolution had demanded such a great concentration of resources because of the collapse of existing institutions and the creation of a multinational anti-French coalition that went to war against France. Napoleon, on the other hand, had conducted his first campaigns, up to 1806, not far from France and against relatively small armies, while local populations were as yet not really a hostile factor. When he went to war against Russia in 1812, he knew that the old ground rules would not work. He was far from France and faced a large army. During the campaign itself he ran into the serious problem of the hostility of the populace, which he had not foreseen, together with its consequences. Now, back from Russia and planning his moves for 1813, he knew that the theatre of operations would be Eastern Europe and that he might have to fight a coalition wider than the ones he had fought in the past. There was no reason not to be able to assess correctly the scope of popular resistance either. There were many signs to be seen. His brother Jerome, who was king of Westphalia, had already warned him at the end of 1811 that if there was a new war in Europe it would be accompanied by popular uprisings 'in all the provinces between the Rhine and the Oder'. However, Napoleon did not set much store by such predictions. In fact, he did not foresee that the factors affecting his going into total war would assume the proportions that they actually did in 1813. But even what he did foresee led him to base his war preparations on the fullest mobilisation possible of French and client-state resources.

The emperor saw the support of the French establishment and the entire population as an essential condition for the realisation of his plans and felt it necessary to make certain that he had this support. France was clearly tired of war and incessant strife. As long as it was successful and did not demand intolerable sacrifices there had been no negative reverberations in the public, but the failures in Spain and Russia eroded bourgeois support, which Napoleon needed more and more. The bourgeoisie had reconciled itself to his system of government in the hope that it would inaugurate an era of tranquillity at home and abroad and allow it to reap the rewards of the Revolution.

This tranquillity was not achieved. The emperor's struggles assumed a dimension that the French commercial class had to contend with at the same time as they were forced to accept it, a dimension that sprang to life from the economic boycott Napoleon was attempting to impose on Britain. Although the blockade protected the various sectors of the French economy, it also deprived the French of the free access to raw materials that they required as well as to numerous markets. Many manufacturers benefited from the Continental System – in the cotton, silk, metal and coal industries – but many also suffered from it, such as shipowners and winemakers. Thus the public had mixed feelings about Napoleon's policy towards Britain and this too had to be dealt with by Napoleon. His attitude towards the commercial class was characterised by suspicion and the belief that commerce and industry must serve the state and its needs, but he knew that if he wished to enlist them in his political and military efforts he must win their support and reassure them.

The erosion of public support derived in part from the public's understanding that the burden on the nation, in manpower and resources, were going to assume unheard-of proportions. Napoleon dealt with the national mood with the same thoroughness with which he dealt with everything else. From the beginning of his rule he had used propaganda as a means for improving his image and furthering his goals. He stole a march on the dictators of the twentieth century in its use, knowing that a nation perpetually at war requires information and reassurance. The means for raising morale were, among other things, the publication of imperial manifestos, the playing down of bad news and the launching of slogans and ideas promoting identification and unity.

A few days after returning Napoleon acted quickly to quell any thoughts about rebellion and deposition. In a speech before the Senate in December he made reference to Malet's conspiracy and to the odour of treason that emanated from it. 'Feeble-hearted and treacherous soldiers are liable to cost the nation its independence,' he said, 'but feeble-hearted office-holders trample on the majesty of the law, the prerogatives of the crown and the social order.' In all his public references to that failed rebellion he emphasised his own authority and noted that he had already saved the country from anarchy once, allowing it to raise its head again, and therefore it owed him its full allegiance.

We may now follow the final stages of the retreat from Russia. What happened to the army after Napoleon left it and its deployment before they met again was an important starting point for the preparations for the 1813 campaign. The retreat and the look of the army at the time were the visible sign in Europe's eyes of the failure of the French invasion and the last image they had of it before the fighting was renewed. It was this sight that fed the flames of nationalism spreading through the Continent and gave the war of 1813 still another multinational facet. Here the myth of the invincible French army was shattered.

It will be remembered that Napoleon gave Murat temporary command of the Grand Army. For all his courage on the battlefield, Murat was not suited in any way to lead an army facing such difficult conditions and whose aim was not to fight but to save itself. The cruelty of the Russian winter was at its peak at just this stage, the final one, taking the army from the Berezina to the Niemen. The cold reached –40°C. The depleted units moved in total disarray.

Whoever stopped to rest could not summon the strength to get up again and froze to death. A long line of corpses marked the route. A horse collapsing from fatigue was immediately pounced upon for its flesh by the men as though by ravenous bloodhounds. Nights were unbearable. Soldiers were afraid to sleep and remained standing lest they die in the snow. Whoever succeeded in lighting a fire chased everyone away to keep it for himself.

Between Smorgoni and Vilna the French lost another 20,000 men. The rest reached the town on 9 December. Vilna had been turned into a big supply depot that was supposed to have enough food to feed an army of 100,000 for 40 days. But the supply in the city had no intention of being on hand to greet the mob that was descending on it. No one had bothered to inform them of the condition of the approaching forces. The mad dash for the food supplies made it impossible to maintain orderly distribution. Ney, in command of the rear guard, defended the eastern approaches to the city against Cossack attack and Murat, who realised that things were out of control, continued the retreat the next day despite Napoleon's orders to remain in the city for ten days.

On 12 December the army reached Kovno on the Niemen and the next day it crossed the river. Ney was the hero of this phase of the retreat. He had commanded the rear guard since Viasma, marching to the Niemen in 37 days with his force changed four times, not by the book but because each time his troops melted away. In the first stage the rear guard numbered about 5,000 men and now just a few hundred. At Kovno, Ney covered the crossing of the Niemen with 700 men and 24 guns. In the final stages of rearguard fighting the force was further reduced and Ney found himself with only a few dozen soldiers around him. Ney was the last soldier in the Grand Army to leave Russia.

Murat called the marshals together for a council at Gumbinnen, east of Königsberg. He called the emperor insane and caused a uproar. Davout accused him of ingratitude and pointed out that everything he had he owed to Napoleon. The rift subsided for a while and the retreat was continued to Warsaw on the Vistula and from there to Posen. In this stage, from the end of December to January, the Prussian and Austrian forces, which had been operating on Napoleon's flanks and had separated themselves from the French army, deserted (as will be related later). Murat, whose command was now at Posen, decided to abandon the army and, on 16 January, returned to Naples. The truth is that when he was given command, the army was no longer an army and that Count Yorck was right when he asserted that 'after the crossing of the Berezina there were no further operations of a military nature'.

Napoleon transferred the command to his stepson, Eugene Beauharnais, who was Josephine's son and who had been with him in Russia where he had commanded a large formation. On 22 January Napoleon wrote to him: 'My son, take command of the Grand Army. I am sorry I did not entrust the army to you when I left ... I believe Murat's conduct is most untoward and I am considering imprisoning him as an example. He is a brave man on the battlefield, but he is deficient in moral courage.' Eugene's main mission was to block the advance of the enemy as much as possible and pin him down in the eastern part of the theatre in order to give Napoleon the time and space needed to complete his preparations.

The Poles and Prussians, observing the remnants of the Grand Army returning to their land, regarded them with a combination of hostility and pity. Eugene conducted the retreat in a reasonably orderly manner and divided his troops among different cities while still fighting rear-guard actions against the pursuing Russian forces. During the pursuit the Russians gained control of parts of Poland. On 13 January, Wittgenstein crossed the Vistula and sent troops towards Danzig, where a big French garrison was stationed. Tchitchagov advanced to Thorn, Kutusov to Plock and Miloradowitz towards Warsaw.

Eugene sent forces to Stettin, Küstrin, Glogau and Spandau to serve on garrison duty. A fresh division up from Italy was sent to Berlin, as Eugene understood that Prussia was no longer loyal to France, though the emperor still refused to admit it. A new threat materialised on the northern flank – Cossack units sent out by Wittgenstein arrived in the lower Oder region and worried the French there. On 18 February, Eugene arrived in Frankfort on the Oder and Reynier retreated from Kalisch to Glogau with his corps.

Eugene's holding line on 20 February therefore rested primarily on the Oder. He had 17,000 men in the fortified garrison towns on the river and 3,000 at Spandau near Berlin. All in all, Eugene had 80,000 men. Poniatowski with 8,000 Poles was in Galicia under the command of the Austrian Schwarzenberg but the force was in fact cut off from the French army.

On his return to Paris, Napoleon's main efforts were concentrated on one aim over which he wasted little time: the raising and arming of a new army. The emphasis was on the word 'new', as the army of 1812 no longer existed. In a document dated 27 January, Napoleon requested reports on his forces in Eastern Europe from army headquarters there. What he received was enough to make his head spin, reporting, among other things, that of the 107,000

French soldiers belonging to the I, II, III and IV Infantry Corps, just 6, 436 remained. The average infantry company, which before the campaign had numbered 115 men, now had seven. Even after seeing these disturbing figures, Napoleon spent little time thinking about making immediate peace with Europe, though many around him felt that the Russian campaign spelled the beginning of the end of the French empire. He was confident of his ability to build an army almost from the ground. This ability of his would serve as a striking demonstration of his spirit and iron will.

Already in 1812, through an imperial edict published in March, a kind of national guard called the Cohorts was created. This force was meant to defend the French homeland and serve as a reserve for the regular army if required. Each cohort numbered six companies of 140 men, a headquarters company and an artillery company. Officers were taken from the regular army and from among soldiers who had been demobilised in the course of time. By the end of the year the Cohorts numbered 80,000 men. On 11 January 1813, a new imperial edict was published attaching the Cohorts to the regular army. The edict applied to 100,000 new recruits from the 1809–12 drafts and 150,000 from the 1814 roll whose conscription was pushed up. The French provinces were required to furnish 20,000 trained and equipped men to the regular army. Around 10,000 naval artillery men, who had been unemployed because of British naval supremacy and the limited activity of the French fleet, were also transferred to the growing army. Thus, by the beginning of the year, 360,000 men had been enlisted in the army and were being equipped and trained.

The rebuilding of the army demanded huge outlays of public funds. The campaigns in Russia and Spain had also swallowed up enormous amounts of money and the budget presented to Napoleon on his return from Russia showed a very large deficit. He was not inclined to burden the public with direct taxes, understanding the damage they do to economic growth as well as the undesirable resentments that accompany them. In all of 1813, direct taxes amounted to less than 30 per cent of total government income. Napoleon preferred indirect taxes because of the ease with which they could be collected, the possibility of keeping the rates low and changing them at will, as well as because they could be spread around. The main commodities that delivered the goods were tobacco, alcoholic beverages and salt, yielding around a quarter of the government's income in 1813. The rest came from customs duties and stamp taxes. This method of financing did not affect the commercial and industrial sectors, which Napoleon correctly understood would have to be co-opted to the national effort, so unlike any the nation had known in the past. This can be seen from the fact that the 1805 campaign had cost around 60 million francs, while military requirements for 1813 were estimated at over 800 million francs (in fact they came to 817 million francs).

The cost of the coming campaign along with the outlay on the Russian campaign involved a planned deficit of 200 million francs. Napoleon, whose economic thinking was logical and advanced, did not consent to covering the deficit by printing money, preferring to force local authorities to sell the government many of their assets against income-bearing bonds. This arrangement guaranteed the authorities a yearly income to meet expenses, while the sale of the assets generated abundant sources of public funding which allowed the effort to mobilise the resources required for the war to continue.

In accordance with the imperial edict of 3 April, 170,000 new recruits were enlisted from the 1807–14 rolls (the 18–26 age group). In addition, 10,000 trained cavalrymen were called up from the provinces. Another 120,000 were added from the 1813 conscription, who were already drafted in September 1812 and were now completing their training. Napoleon also ordered the concentration of battalions stationed in France, Holland, Italy, Germany and Illyria which were inactive and not contributing to the renewed war effort. Thus a total of 650,000 men came to be placed at the emperor's disposal, from which the order of battle required for the 1813 campaign could be drawn.

Thousands of veteran soldiers and officers were among the new forces, but most of them were young men inexperienced in warfare. NCOs with combat experience were made junior officers. 'Compulsory conscription,' the emperor told the people, 'is the nation's eternal root. It cleanses its morals and shapes its habits.' This approach with its 'moral' underpinning is necessary for a leader preparing his people for total war based on an all-out effort, but Napoleon would yet experience the unavoidable defects of this kind of accelerated organisation, particularly at the command level throughout the entire army.

The national effort demanded to create such a large army so quickly was enormous and unprecedented. The population of France at the time was 36 million. The organisation of such a great mass of people as well as the means of war for a campaign in distant lands was something any modern leader could be proud of. The mobilisation was accompanied by a no less impressive effort on the part of industry, which was responsible for supplying the new forces, particularly in regard to ordnance. 'France became one big workshop,' Caulaincourt noted. 'The entire French nation overlooked the emperor's reverse and men vied with one another in showing their zeal and devotion. It was as glorious an example of the French character as it was a personal triumph for the emperor, who, with amazing energy, directed all of his genius into the organisation and guidance of this great national endeavour.' Napoleon has often been called the father of French industry, though the economic boycott against England kept technological innovations from reaching French shores, particularly in the realm of mechanisation. None the less, the growth of France's military industry at the beginning of the second decade of the century was particularly striking. Despite everything, the level of mechanisation rose and the number of workers grew significantly. Not only military needs drew so much manpower to this industry but also the fact that its workers were exempt from military service.

Alongside the extraordinary achievements it is also necessary to describe the weak points in the purely military sense that could be discerned at the end of this process of national organisation. These weaknesses were bound to have a significant effect on the nature of the coming war and its outcome. While conscription statistics were impressive, drilling in shooting and marching was deficient and the pressure to attach the new conscripts to their units affected training at the most basic level. Marching drill was mainly carried out en route to the home bases of the corps in Germany, where the conscripts were sent shortly after induction. The shortage of muskets was also a cause of concern and the emperor urged his war ministry to increase factory orders and push for increased production to make up the shortage quickly. Some of the conscripts received foreign-made arms. Unlike the inexperienced and undertrained conscripts, the senior officers – from regiment commanders up and including most battalion commanders – had combat experience, under Napoleon's leadership.

The new infantry units were almost up to standard, though Caulaincourt called them 'but an organised mob'. J. F. C. Fuller preferred the view of Baron von Odeleben, a Saxon officer attached to Napoleon's staff and in Fuller's opinion an unprejudiced observer: 'It would be almost impossible to find elsewhere soldiers who braved death with so much integrity and courage and who, in the midst of all difficulties and dangers, could have shown themselves more devoted to their chief and their service.' (Fuller, J.F.C.: The Decisive Battles of the Western World). None the less, it would seem that Caulaincourt, even if he went overboard, was more accurate in his assessment of things and there is no doubt that the fault lay more with the officers – mostly at the junior command level – than with the rank and file. In a famous letter to his minister of war, Napoleon described a visit to one of the regiments on 27 April, just before the opening of the 1813 campaign: 'It is impossible to encounter better soldiers, but it is equally impossible to encounter worse officers.' The decline in the quality of the infantryman in the Grand Army had its effect on Napoleon's basic military thinking and he now set more store by superior numbers on the battlefield than by his old principles of mobility and intelligent tactical movement.

The Achilles heel of the new army was its cavalry units – specifically its crying need for more men and horses. Its veterans were too old and the quality and training of the new recruits was insufficient. Losses among soldiers and officers in Russia had been enormous, but the losses in horses had been even more serious. Most of the horses who had left on the campaign – more than 175,000 – did not return and the French army had never recovered from this blow. The suppliers of quality horses were located in Prussia and Germany, and the Prussians as well as many of the Germans were not being co-operative. Thus the French were cut off from their traditional supply. In addition, care of the horses was poor. Still another problem was the length of time required to train a cavalryman – much more than an infantryman. This was bound to have an effect on the operational ability of the army, mainly for the gathering of intelligence and the possibility of rapid and immediate pursuit to exploit success.

On the other hand, the artillery was in a satisfactory state. Though 900 of the 1,300 guns taken to Russia had been lost, French industry was able to meet the army's needs and the accelerated conscription supplied enough artillerymen. The artillery was considered an elite unit and service there was much coveted by the young conscripts. Because of the drop in quality in the infantry and cavalry, more was expected of the artillery than in the past. F. N. Maude said that it had to 'learn to co-operate and not lose sight of the general overview in its pursuit of glory'. Napoleon gave the infantry divisions more guns to make up for their poorer fighting quality. The shortage of horses was also felt in the artillery units, in relation to transport and haulage as well as maintenance, but mostly to bringing up ammunition.

Let us return to the defection of the Prussian and Austrian troops under Yorck and Schwarzenberg from the Grand Army. This marks the beginning of the grand coalition that fought against Napoleon in 1813 and, while at the time it was just another symptom of the disintegration of the Russian campaign, the results would have a much more far-reaching effect. These forces had indeed fought alongside Napoleon in Russia, but it will be remembered that Prussia and Austria had given the Russians their word that their participation in the war would not be particularly active. Yorck had commanded the Prussian expeditionary force attached to the French Marshal Macdonald's corps. This corps also included Polish, Bavarian and Westphalian regiments with only the staff being French. Macdonald was responsible for securing the left flank of the Grand Army, operating in the area of Riga and the Baltic provinces. Before crossing the Niemen he received a message from the Prussian king urging him 'to take care of his men'. The corps carried out its limited duties and suffered few losses in the campaign.

Macdonald noted that Yorck was in no hurry to operate against the Russians, though his objectives were quite modest. In the second half of December, Macdonald completed his withdrawal from the Riga area to Tilsit and Königsberg in obedience to Murat's orders and in co-ordination with the retreat of the main body of the army. During the retreat the Russians surrounded Macdonald's rearguard, commanded by Yorck. It turned out that a few months previously Yorck had received a communication from the Russians vowing that Russia would not lay down its arms until Prussia was restored to her situation before the defeat of 1806. The Russian commander of the troops surrounding Yorck now reaffirmed this guarantee. If we take into account Prussia's lack of enthusiasm to begin with and the rumours of the destruction of the Grand Army, it is not difficult to see that conditions were ripe for defection. The stunned Macdonald referred to it in his memoirs as the greatest betrayal in history.

Yorck and the Russians met at Tauroggen in the vicinity of the recent movements and, on 30 December, signed a military pact according to which the Prussian corps would maintain neutrality and the Russians would be allowed to move freely in areas bordering on Prussia. Yorck found a common language with the Russians not only because of the identity of interests but because Clausewitz appeared during negotiations on the Russian side. He had joined them before the beginning of the war, determined to fight against Napoleon. The Tauroggen pact was to remain in force for two months, until new instructions were received from the Prussian king. Frederick William instructed Yorck to break off contact with the French when his retreat took him into Prussia and to request Russian protection if necessary. At the same time he also sought to appease the French. He told the French ambassador in Berlin that Yorck's actions had taken him by surprise and even sent a delegation to Paris to mollify Napoleon and assure him of Prussian loyalty. For

France still maintained control over Prussia and Frederick William was fearful of Napoleon's anger. The immediate military effect of Yorck's defection was the withdrawal of Macdonald from Königsberg to Danzig, since the Russians now appeared before him. Yorck's actions were received with great sympathy in Prussia and strengthened anti-French sentiment there, which would soon have its effect on the king's thinking and course of action.

As mentioned earlier, Prince Schwarzenberg, commanding the Austrian corps fighting alongside Napoleon in 1812, had been placed on his southern flank with Minsk as its general objective. Its part in the campaign was marginal, as expected, since Austria had committed itself only to provide auxiliary forces and not to take part in the main effort. Schwarzenberg mainly maintained contact with the enemy on his flank and did not do any real fighting. The corps of Reynier and Poniatowski operated alongside his. In November he retreated from the Minsk area to Warsaw, thus allowing Tchitchagov to move up to the area of the Berezina crossing and press the French from the south. When Eugene assumed command, in January, Schwarzenberg evacuated Warsaw without fighting and moved south towards Cracow. His excuse was that he had to secure Galicia, but the move was co-ordinated with Miloradowitz, the Russian commander facing him. At the end of January, Schwarzenberg reached an agreement with the Russians similar to the one with Yorck. He moved into Galicia together with Poniatowski (the Polish officer rejoined Napoleon only in the summer) and left Reynier to his own devices. The move angered Napoleon more than the Prussian actions, as it was carried out with the express consent of the Austrian government in defiance of its contractual obligations. There was a good deal of shrewdness in the Austrian move, as Schwarzenberg's presence in Bohemia posed a veiled threat to the Russians as much as to the French flank. This deployment laid the foundation of the special position Austria achieved for itself. The threat to the flanks of both warring parties could be converted into support for one of them. In practice, the pact between Austria and Russia forced the French right wing to withdraw into Saxony.

On his return from Russia, Napoleon still hoped, given French relations with the other countries of Europe, to maintain his supremacy on the Continent. The Low Countries, the Apennine peninsula, Illyria (the Balkan provinces which became modern Yugoslavia) and Germany were all under his thumb. He had alliances with Prussia and Austria. The Austrian emperor was his father-in-law and Francis's grandson was the French crown prince. Only

Britain and Russia were his declared enemies. British forces were indeed giving him problems in Spain but they were also pinned down there and Russia was exhausted by the war.

Napoleon was still thinking in terms of conflicts between rulers. In analysing the state of affairs he measured the interests of the sovereigns, making them the decisive factor in his considerations. In December, when he was hurrying home, he had said to Caulaincourt that the rulers of Europe were afraid of the tsar and that he would be stopped on the Niemen, mainly because of the Polish awakening. The shrewd, sensible Caulaincourt had replied that he was mistaken: 'They are in fear of you, of your great empire, of the dynasty you are establishing, of the taxes you impose. Enmity towards you has become a national force.' This statement is the key to understanding the special nature of the year 1813 and the decisive events that occurred in the context of relations between the powers. Napoleon's successes and the disappointments that had sown the seeds of rebellion now saw his enemies becoming peoples and nations. He was slow to grasp this profound transformation. On the contrary, on 21 January, when he was feeling that his military preparations were going well and his recovery was coming along with a rapidity that surprised perhaps even himself, he wrote to his ally, the king of Saxony: 'The events that overtook my army after my leavetaking of it, and General Yorck's betrayal, greatly harmed my cause in the north; but I shall soon have at my disposal such forces that when the opportune moment arrives, I shall contrive to drive back the enemy more swiftly than his rate of advance.'

When the remnants of the Grand Army were moving toward the Vistula, Napoleon was already in Paris and could not have known the effect of his army's condition on the populace that saw it in such a sorry state. Among the soldiers returning from Russia, many were from the countries that had contributed troops to the French army and their reports also played a part in the general atmosphere that was being created. A Westphalian officer writes to his father on 18 February, for example: 'I remember the day the troops marched to Russia, polished and confident of victory... And now they return dressed and bandaged in rags. It is said that only a few thousand remain of the 23,000 Westphalians who set out on the campaign.' Documents like these are countless. All through Europe there was the feeling that a new day was dawning. Napoleon had not been the liberator people had hoped for. He was a conqueror and oppressor. He was no longer perceived as an emancipator of serfs and patron of national uprisings against tyrannical rulers. The opposite was true: his actions and the conduct of his conquering armies encouraged uprisings against him and created a general feeling that said: 'The time has come to act.'

The Germans led the popular awakening in Europe. One language, one history, one spirit – these were what united the people of Austria, Prussia and the many German principalities. All eyes were first raised towards the Austrian emperor, who symbolised the unifying slogan Kaiser and Reich, but the Austrian ruler, Francis, disappointed with his indecision and inconsistency. He wavered between one political position and another. The truth was that the unification of Germany was not in Austria's interests. While it was interested in expelling France – preferably without bloodshed – and creating a federation of German states under its aegis, it was very far from wishing to bring about a full unification of all the German political entities.

Prussia's defeat in 1806, which for all intents and purposes put an end to its independence, also eliminated it as a leader in the movement towards unification. The defeat had an enormous impact on Prussian society and of course on its army. Its territory and population were reduced and the financial burden of the war was tremendous. The desire of its leadership – political and spiritual – to regain Prussian independence at some future date demanded social and miliary reforms. Under the existing circumstances, it was Prussia that led the way towards the national conscription which was to characterise the coming war and could already be seen as a tendency among the partners in the multinational coalition that would fight against France.

Prussia after its defeat thus became a focal point of national aspirations and reform. The first to promote these feelings were the intellectuals. The leading figures were Herder and Fichte. Though Herder had died in 1803, before the débâcle, his social philosophy laid the foundations of the patriotic and nationalistic sentiments that flowered afterwards. Following Rousseau, who argued that the individual will best develop the powers lodged within him by giving expression to his personal values, Herder expanded the concept to include national life as a whole. Nationalism, in his view, was a product of nature. Fichte concurred with Herder and emphasised the patriotic element of his philosophy. He argued that philosophy is not only correct as a system of knowledge but as an active way of life. This approach encouraged professors and students alike to look at abstract theoretical discussion as having pragmatic value. Fichte attributed the military failures to moral and educational decline and demanded changes in the educational system that would

65

transform subjects into real citizens. His students at the University of Berlin were the first to enlist in the 1813 campaign. One day, in February, Fichte concluded his lecture by saying: 'Studies in this department are now suspended and will resume only at the end of the battle, when we are living in a free Fatherland or have sacrificed our lives for freedom.'

Alongside these ideas and the enthusiastic burst of volunteering 'for the Fatherland', there developed strategic and organisational concepts whose aim was to build a real military force despite political and economic restrictions. Napoleon had severely limited the size of the Prussian army. In an edict promulgated on 1 January 1809, he fixed the size of the army for the next ten years: ten regiments of infantry and eight of cavalry, 6,000 artillerymen and engineers and 6,000 royal guards – in all, 42,000 men. The Prussian solution to this problem of size was to create an army of reservists, which by its very nature has a broad popular base, unlike a permanent professional army. Fuller wrote with a certain show of warmth: 'At Jena, Napoleon destroyed not only a feudal army but the last vestiges of the feudal idea, and out of the ashes arose a national army.'

The organisers and architects of this army, Scharnhorst and Gneisenau, were not only professional soldiers but also military thinkers. Scharnhorst was perhaps the first Prussian to understand the need to change patterns of thought in the wake of the French Revolution. He argued that the Revolution had introduced a new factor that had to be recognised – 'the arms-bearing nation' – and that if one wished to maintain the strength of the nation and even increase it, one had to satisfy the spirit of the people in the manner of the Jacobins. In the same spirit Gneisenau said: 'The people have to be given a Fatherland, so as to defend it properly.' The débâcle of 1806 gave both of them the opportunity to apply their ideas with the blessing of the royal house, though at the same time they had to overcome the natural resistance of the conservative establishment and, of course, the sharp eye of the hostile French.

The main device that the two men used was abbreviated military service, which created an army that at any given moment was small but whose accelerated cycles consistently expanded its base without violating the quotas laid down by the French emperor. Whoever completed his regular service was attached to the guard units (*Landsturm*). Even the terminology of command was changed to fit the new popular spirit: officers became 'leaders' and instead of an army there was an 'armed nation'. The command structure was expanded to include as officers not only the nobility but the middle class as well. The principle was that the positions of command would be open to all on the basis of education and other qualities. There was a general house-cleaning among the officers associated with the humiliation of 1806. Of the more than 140 generals who had served in that campaign, just 22 remained. Corporeal punishment, which had been a regular feature of the Prussian army, was abolished.

The British historian A. J. P. Taylor warned against arriving at far-reaching conclusions on the basis of these changes. He argued that the new military system did not attest to 'liberalisation of the Prussian state, but militarisation of the Prussian people'. (Taylor, A. J. P.: The Course of German History). In other words, the main objective of throwing off the Napoleonic yoke and re-establishing an independent Prussia justified even such means as creating a mirage of illusory freedom.

Scharnhorst changed completely the mode of operation of the general staff, turning it into the principal command body, staffed by first-rate officers educated at staff officer schools. The general staff was meant to occupy itself permanently with strategic thinking and conduct the war. Alongside every corps commander a chief of staff was to be found. The military establishment had its opposite number in the ministry of war – a necessity given the com-prehensive scope of national mobilisation – which was responsible for the civilian apparatus supplying the human and material resources needed for the war. Industrial capacity was expanded and the factories were given the task of making up the enormous shortage of muskets and cannon that had resulted from the destruction of the army at Jena. Procurement was and remained the weak point in the big Prussian reorganisation of 1809–13 and only England's aid at the last moment prevented a problematic situation.

In organising the order of battle, the emphasis was placed on corps of equal strength acting according to clearly defined field regulations. The Prussian corps was not meant to be an independent force in the French manner. Moreover, owing mainly to the restrictions on recruitment, it was smaller than a French corps and based on brigades rather than divisions. The brigade consisted of two infantry regiments, a picked battalion of Grenadiers and cavalry and artillery units. A corps consisted of two brigades. Field regula-tions determined the battle formations and the speed of movement and fire. Much emphasis was placed on close co-operation between infantry and cavalry. Infantry assault tactics were complicated and required great co-ordi-nation between the units. Light units opened the attack and quickly made way for massed units advancing at different speeds depending on the proximity of the enemy. All this demanded hard training, strict discipline and a spirit of courage and self-sacrifice.

The entire country bristled with intensive organisational activity, carried out with a devotion fed by hostility to Napoleon and the French. Citizens shared the desire to restore the lost territories and their own human and national rights. Recruitment embraced all classes, both by force of law and through volunteering: Noblemen and peasants, lecturers and students, intellectuals and the common man. Women gave their jewellery and many gave money. In addition to the regular reserve units (Landwehr), there were also created volunteer units intended to defend the interior of the country and operate as partisans using sabotage and scorched-earth tactics. These units, however, did not really prove themselves when the time came as their quality was not particularly high, though much importance was attached to their creation to encourage the patriotic fervour that was sweeping the land.

At the head of these fervent people stood King Frederick William III, a limited man, hesitant and slow of thought and decision. Napoleon terrified and haunted him. He still did not understand that the destruction of the French army in Russia had given him new opportunities and increased his freedom of action. He was also afraid of the revolutionary tendencies inherent in the very nature of the popular movement that was developing, though he understood that the only way to throw off the French yoke was to copy its methods. In addition, he continued to be suspicious of Russia and the Russian tsar even when their common interests took on broader dimensions. The Prussian king was convinced that the ultimate goal of the Russians was to annex Poland and perhaps even Eastern Prussia. He also believed that the Austrians were in league with the French.

Alongside Frederick William stood the head of his government, Chancellor Hardenberg, who was returned to office in June 1810 after being dismissed at Napoleon's insistence immediately after Tilsit. Hardenberg directed Prussia's foreign relations throughout these complicated times, his policy being characterised by a clear-cut Russian orientation. He carried out financial and social reforms which, together with the army reforms described above, laid the broad, firm base for Prussian resistance to France.

Napoleon underestimated the process of change taking place in Prussia and was convinced that the awakening there was a passing phase that had to be dealt with harshly in order to make it to disappear as if it had never existed. Oddly, as a creature of revolution himself and witness to the far-reaching changes that had taken place in French society and the French army, he set no store by the similar changes occurring in Prussia. Apparently he felt that the condition for real change was anti-royalist civil insurrection, though he should have realised that he was the object of the Prussian awakening, not Frederick William III. On 5 March, Napoleon wrote to Eugene: 'Remain in Berlin as long as you can. Preserve discipline and insist on obedience. Handle these matters with the required severity. Respond to any insult. If anything happens in some village or town, set it ablaze.' Referring to the restrictions on the size of the Prussian army, he continued: 'Do not forget that the Prussian population numbers no more than four million souls, and at the best of times her military force numbered no more than 150,000 and nowadays cannot recruit more than 40,000.'

At the end of December 1812 the tsar established his headquarters at Kalisch, where he intended to complete his consultations with the Prussians, make political contact with the Austrians and try to swing the Poles over to his side also. At Kalisch he could also plan the continuation of the war. While maintaining contact with Yorck the Russians sent a written proposal to the king of Prussia whose principal feature was the restoration of Prussia to its pre-1806 status in exchange for an immediate break with France and enlistment in Russia's military struggle against the French. The proposal also contained a threat: if the king persisted in his alliance with Napoleon, Russia would see this as a declaration of war and would aim at the encirclement and partition of Prussia. In the weeks that followed Yorck's defection and the signing of the pact at Tauroggen, Prussia, as we have seen, played a double game, which Hardenberg was very good at. He had to mollify and deceive the French, to whom the Prussians were tied by a solemn and binding military pact, while at the same time advancing Prussia's interests through uninterrupted negotiations with the Russians. Napoleon, who saw in Yorck's defection 'the worst thing that could have happened', as he put it, still believed that the Prussian people would obey its king and that its king would obey him. The extent of Napoleon's misunderstanding of the situation can be gathered from a letter he wrote his foreign minister, Maret, who was one of his most intimate associates. The letter referred to a report he had received on the conduct of Prussian army units in Silesia: 'They act as if they are afraid of us, instead of aiding us for the benefit of their own country.'

Hardenberg persuaded the king to leave Berlin, because he would be more secure and free to act as he wished anywhere else, since Berlin still had a French garrison stationed there, making it difficult, if not impossible, to maintain the vital contacts with Russia and Austria. On 22 February, Frederick William transferred his seat to Breslau. He was under great pressure to shore up relations with the Russians still further, to the extent of entering into a military pact with them against France. It was perhaps at this point that he hardened his position and determined to do everything in his power to strengthen his standing. While still in Berlin he saw too that Russia was his best option. As mentioned, Austria acted with indecision, sitting on the fence. The Prussian king hoped that future events, henceforth co-ordinated with the Russians, would cause the Austrians to join them without any compunction.

Frederick William and his associates acted with great caution. The French were told that the king was co-operating with the Russians against his will, since Russian forces were stationed on Prussian soil, where they had arrived, it will be remembered, following the retreat of the Grand Army. The Prussian ambassador in Paris, who enlarged upon the difficulties the king was facing, made various demands that were clearly going to be rejected out of hand. Now, at the same time that the Prussians were engaged in their deceit of the French, contacts with the Russians entered a decisive phase. The Prussian general Knesebeck was sent to the tsar to conclude negotiations and arrive at an agreement. The talks were conducted in Kalisch.

At first Knesebeck departed from the policy dictated to him. Under the sway of the pan-German feeling prevailing in his country, he laid claims to territory in Saxony and even in Poland. The tsar responded positively to the claim on Saxony, which was allied with Napoleon, but would hear nothing of Prussian demands in regard to Polish territory, declaring that Russia would always maintain its presence on the Oder. The tsar carried on the talks with the advice of Stein who, until 1808, had been the Prussian prime minister but had also been dismissed on Napoleon's demand and had now been advising Alexander for a year. Stein, who said that he hated the French 'insofar as a Christian is permitted to hate', shored up the hostility of the tsar to the French emperor. He convinced Alexander that the only way to get Napoleon to be satisfied with a Greater France and give up the idea of a great empire was to carry on the war and push the French army across the Rhine. Frederick William believed that the battered Russians stood in great need of Prussian help and sought to exploit this to get the most he could for his country in exchange for co-operation. On Stein's advice, the tsar ignored Prussia's excessive demands, made first by Knesebeck and then by the king as well. In the end a compromise was reached and, on 26 February, the treaty of Kalisch was signed. The tsar agreed to honour Prussia's current borders and act to restore the territories lost in 1806, including regions that would safeguard the land link between Eastern Prussia and Silesia. Both sides signed a military defence-and-attack agreement. Russia undertook to provide an army of 150,000 men and Prussia 80,000. It was further agreed that the supreme commander would be Kutusov. The first and most important tier of the Allied alignment had come into being.

In the middle of March a conference was held at Breslau between Russia and Prussia that was meant to be continuation of the Kalisch process. The tsar was the king's guest. The conference reaffirmed the principle of restoration of Prussia's pre-1806 political and economic position. It was also agreed that after Napoleon's expected fall he would be stripped of his German possessions and the Confederation of the Rhine would be abrogated. Russia would recognise Prussian expansion into northern Germany, excluding Hannover, where Britain had traditional interests which Russia did not wish to prejudice. In addition, the German kings and princes, along with the entire German people, would be called upon to do their part in the anti-French alliance. Any ruler who failed to respond to the summons would lose his throne.

Frederick William did a great deal of complaining at Breslau about the French emperor and everything he had suffered at his hands. Once he even burst into tears. The tsar consoled him and assured him that these were the last tears he would ever have to shed because of Napoleon. On 17 March, the protocols of the conference were signed and the treaty of Kalisch was published. On the same day Hardenberg handed the French ambassador, Count St Martin, a note declaring war between Prussia and France. Napoleon took the declaration in his stride. 'Better a declared enemy,' he said, 'than a dubious ally.'

The conduct of Austria was more complicated. Despite the defeats and humiliations administered by Napoleon – almost from the outset of his career as conqueror and even before he became emperor – Austria had not lost its standing as a European power. As we have seen, it no longer represented the ideals of the German peoples nor their pan-Germanic nationalist aspirations. However, it remained an important factor on the Continent, courted by one and all. Though in fact tied down by an alliance to France, now more than ever it sought to throw off its shackles. It will be remembered that Schwarzenberg had separated himself from the Grand Army, an act amounting to defection that had disappointed Napoleon greatly. However, neither country saw this as constituting a political break.

The real wish of the Austrian emperor was to preserve the old order. Napoleon's victories had undermined his country's pretensions to be the leader of all of Germany and now all that was left to it was to maintain its own strength. This pretence to leadership had ended in 1806 when Napoleon terminated the Holy Roman Empire and Francis, who stood at its head as Emperor Francis II, had to satisfy himself with the title of Francis I of Austria. Taylor rightfully said the 'it was Napoleon who put an end to Medieval Germany, not the Allies'. (Taylor, A. J. P.: The Course of German History). The real meaning of the wish to preserve the old order was to break off physical contact, actual and potential, with the other powers and to live with them in accordance with permanent and convenient arrangements. For despite the collusion between Austria and Russia, which should not have surprised anyone – it will be remembered that according to the 1812 understanding with the tsar the Austrian army would only go through the motions of aiding Napoleon – Francis had no wish to see Russian soldiers running wild in his country, pillaging and gaining a foothold in it, which was his worst nightmare. Similarly, he wished to rid himself of the French yoke, even if it appeared much lighter.

These seemingly contradictory aspirations forced the Austrian emperor to play a double game and practise deceits. No one was more suited than Metternich, his chancellor and foreign minister, to conduct the labyrinthine and convoluted foreign policy necessary to achieve these aims. Francis and Metternich believed that it was best if Napoleon continued to rule in France, where he would put a stop to revolutionary ideas while opposing both Prussian pan-Germanism and Russian aspirations in Poland. It was Talleyrand of all people, Napoleon's foreign minister until 1807, who put it best. He said to the Austrian ambassador in Paris: 'The time has come for Emperor Napoleon to be king of France.' The shrewd and wily Talleyrand was among the first to detect, at an early stage, the signs of the emperor's decline and resigned his office so that in the future he would not bear the taint of being associated with him.

The path Austria chose was dictated by the realities and served its political ends in the best possible way. It carved out a position for itself as a peace-maker and mediator. Napoleon wanted war to recapture past glory, Frederick William wanted it to restore Prussia and Alexander saw it as a necessary means to rid Europe of the French heretic and expand Russian interests on the Continent. Austria, on the other hand, wanted peace in order to achieve its political and territorial aims without suffering the destructiveness of war, taking advantage of the opportunity to seduce the three other powers and to be courted by them. However, in its framework and conditions, the peace that Austria wanted served Napoleon's rivals more and had a clear-cut anti-French basis.

Austria's peace strategy included the decision to operate as a mediator out of a position of military strength, namely as an 'armed mediator'. It created an armed force of 200,000 men, which gave it the option of acting independently, of dissolving the alliance with France when the time came and offering its services for mediation and compromise in a manner that would be taken seriously by the other powers and satisfy Austria's aims without prejudice to their own interests. Metternich spoke of lasting peace and not 'Napoleon-style disguised armistices' – peace that would limit France's power and 'constitute a balance of power and equilibrium between the major powers'. In this way Austria could be a partner in the redivision of Europe dictated by the peace agreement without shedding its army's blood.

Napoleon knew that if Austria joined Russia and Prussia he would face war on two fronts, or on one front but with an overwhelming combination of enemy forces. It was therefore clear to him that he had to secure Austria's co-operation or at least its neutrality. In March he appointed a new ambassador to Vienna, Count Narbonne, and instructed him to represent to Metternich the possibility that Prussia would be divided again in such a way that Austria would get big pieces of Silesia, all this on the condition that Austria would take its place at his side and provide an army of 100,000 men. As expected, Metternich turned the new ambassador down. Narbonne also requested that the Austrian corps that had entered into a ceasefire agreement with the Russians in January – the work of Schwarzenberg – should now terminate it. Metternich informed him that the Russians themselves had already done this. This was true, but the foreign minister concealed the fact that it had been done at Austria's request in order to allow the Austrian corps to get to Bohemia, re-equip there and serve as the nucleus of the new Austrian army (on 25 February an armistice agreement was signed between Russia and Austria, putting an official seal on the termination of hostilities between the two powers). 'Is this corps about to act?' the ambassador asked, and the answer was: 'That depends on how Napoleon behaves; to what extent he ceases to exercise his enslaving supremacy in Europe.'

At the same time Metternich made great efforts to win over the rulers and princes of the Confederation of the Rhine, proposing a neutral alliance that would aspire to peace in order to guarantee their independence. These efforts came to nothing because of the Germans' fear of Napoleon. The king of Saxony was tempted for a short while but immediately caved in to the French, even mote so than in the past. The Bavarians too hesitated, still shocked by the fact that so many of their countrymen lay buried in the snows of Russia, but in the end contributed a division to the Grand Army. A similar course was adopted by the courts of the important princes of Germany, who still swore allegiance to the French emperor.

Vienna appointed a new ambassador to Paris, our old friend Prince Schwarzenberg. On 9 April he met the emperor, who ironically complimented him on the 'fine campaign' he had conducted in 1812. Swallowing hard, Schwarzenberg represented vigorously his country's desire to act as a mediator and prevent war, for France and its two rivals in the east were in fact already enmeshed in a state of belligerency. The emperor replied that he had absolutely no interest in war, which as a matter of course would be bloodier than the one he had broken off in Russia. He added that Great Britain was the principal obstacle to peace. All the ills and curses that plague mankind came from London. If Tsar Alexander really wanted peace he had to take the initiative. 'I cannot take the initiative, for any approach of mine would be considered capitulation, as though I am in hard straits.' He emphasised that whatever was proposed would have to be advantageous to himself, for 'if I consent to peace without honour I shall bring about my overthrow. This is a novel situation. I must take account of public opinion in France, for I am in need of that public. The French are a people of great imagination, avid of glory and devoid of patience.' Schwarzenberg's mission was therefore without result, increasing suspicion between the sides.

On 21 April, Metternich wrote to Nesselrode, a Russian diplomat of German origin: 'I beg you to continue to place your trust in me. If Napoleon is stupid enough to go to war, one battle wherein he is defeated will suffice for the whole of Germany to take up arms.' Ringing words and along with them a pledge. However, for Austria to fight alongside the allies – Russia and Prussia – they would have to demonstrate their fighting ability and Napoleon would have to be bested in at least one battle.

At this stage, Russia did not concern itself with entering into new alliances and securing flanks as it had before the French invasion in 1812. As noted previously, Russia had made great efforts at that time to extricate itself from military entanglements in the north and south in order to bring to bear most of its forces against the approaching invader. The war on its own soil was behind it, the enemy had been expelled and at this point was being pursued westward. The Russian commander-in-chief, Kutusov, maintained that the fighting should stop at the Prussian border and a peace be arranged. The tsar, on the other hand, wanted to avenge himself on Napoleon and destroy him militarily. At the same time, Alexander foresaw that the Russian army could not do this alone and would need additional allies. He was influenced in his thinking by his Prussian adviser, Stein, who argued that if the Russian army remained on the defensive along the Vistula, Napoleon would be tempted to mount another invasion in 1813 and that the security of Russia demanded relentless pursuit of the French across the Elbe and encouragement of a large-scale German uprising against the French. These words fell on eager ears. Not only would such aggressive action put an end to Napoleon's supremacy – the sacred goal – but it would also give Russia a free hand to impose a long-term solution to the Polish question. Alexander also adopted the view of the young Nesselrode that, while Russia did in fact need lasting peace, it would not be achieved until Napoleon was defeated decisively on the battlefield. In this way, at the end of the process, the old balance of power between the leading European nations would be reinstated. In essence, this was the Metternichian view, but by other means. If you want peace, the Russians said, go to war.

Another factor supporting the tsar's view – and the view of those who thought like him – that Napoleon had to be defeated before the old order could be re-established in Europe was the unlikelihood that France would conquer Russia, even if the approaching campaign was a failure. From this point of view, Russia occupied a unique position on the Continent, where France was a threat to every nation or political entity, if it had not already conquered it. Thus Russia could lead a European-wide struggle against Napoleon without having to mobilise all its resources. The 1812 campaign was its insurance policy. It could still rely on its untapped manpower resources, and this campaign had provided the most tangible evidence of this. Consequently there was no need for major reform of its conscription methods, which were the toughest in Europe.

The Russian soldier, drafted in accordance with regional quotas, left home for life, which in any event was not too long. Discipline was strict and cruel, with punishment including humiliation, flogging and execution. He was thus the end result of a formula that included lifetime service (in effect, since the law provided for 25 years) and iron discipline that had no rival, accompanied by the inculcation of values combining religious mysticism with unqualified allegiance to the sovereign. On these compulsory foundations was superimposed the tried and proven element of boundless devotion to Mother Russia. The British general Wilson, who was an observer for his country and part of the tsar's entourage, described the Russian soldier as fearless, disinclined to take advantage of the ground for cover and undaunted by casualties. Similar descriptions by military men from different countries abound in memoirs. Russian officers came from the upper classes, mainly the rural aristocracy, whose educational level was low and whose training was deficient. The army also employed foreign officers, mainly in staff appointments but also in senior command positions.

As already mentioned, the Russian army did not incorporate in 1812 most of the new tactical principles formulated in the two years preceding the campaign, principles that were too innovative and too strange to suit the character and experience of the Russian generals. However, the clash with the French army, mainly at Smolensk and Borodino, brought about a fusion of the tactical lessons learned and the more advanced thinking that Barclay had tried to introduce into the army. Add to this the morale of the victor and the almost mystical aspirations of the tsar and you have an army posing a threat that in no way could be overlooked.

Despite all this, Napoleon believed, or pretended to believe, that the Russian army was in dire straits and that things would get worse as long as it continued to advance and distance itself from the country's borders. He was convinced that its military operations were forcing it to spread itself very thin and concentrate large siege forces around the many strongholds between the Vistula and the Elbe. He assured one of his hesitant allies that 'the further they advance the more certain their downfall'.

As for Great Britain, it remained Napoleon's uncompromising foe. Its main concern was indeed the maintenance of naval supremacy, which France had not succeeded in overcoming, but Britain was not capable of putting an end to French supremacy on the Continent. This was an irksome state of affairs, mainly for economic reasons, but also in terms of prestige. The British remembered Napoleon's remark that Britain was destined to be a 'French island'. The Continental System was no longer effective at this point, but recent memories – piers piled up with goods that could not be shipped and mounting unemployment – still fanned the flames of Britain's deep-seated hostility to Napoleon. It had fought against him with no little success on the Iberian Peninsula. Britain's economic strength enabled it to offer financial support to any country ready to fight the French emperor, but it had neither the intention nor the ability to engage in another war on the Continent. During this period the British government was also involved in a dispute with the United States, which reached its climax in the three-year war of 1812. The dispute involved two bones of contention: British insistence on searching neutral ships for vital strategic materials earmarked for France, and America's territorial ambitions in Canada, which England opposed.

England gave its wholehearted support to the Russo-Prussian alliance of March 1813. The British ambassador to Russia, Lord Cathcart, affirmed this support to the tsar and his circle. At the same time, it did not encourage Austria's efforts at mediation. Already at the beginning of the year an emissary, Lord Walpole, had been sent clandestinely to Vienna to pledge England's support for the restoration to Austria of their lost provinces in the Tyrol, Illyria and Venice. However, Walpole had been forced to leave Vienna at Metternich's request when word of his mission reached the French. On 9 April the British foreign minister, Castlereagh, informed the Austrian ambassador in London that from England's point of view the hopes for peace had evaporated. As an example of Napoleon's intransigence, Castlereagh cited his declaration in the French Senate that a French dynasty ruled in Spain and would continue to rule in Spain. The British government would reject any effort of France to enter into negotiations so as not to undermine the war effort of Russia and Prussia. In practical terms, this rejection was also a final rejection of the idea of Austrian mediation.

Sweden constituted another tier in the coalition against Napoleon that was rapidly taking shape. Sweden had its eyes on Norway, which was under Danish rule. Napoleon did not agree to lend a hand to its covetousness and Bernadotte, the Swedish crown prince, decided to go over to his enemies. At the end of 1812 he broke off diplomatic relations with France and, on 13 March 1813, signed an agreement with Great Britain giving him a pledge of British support for Swedish interests in Norway. Immediately thereafter a Swedish force of 12,000 men landed in Pomerania; however, it remained there for the time being without advancing inland.

The French emperor also turned his attention to relations with Pope Pius VII – a subject that had not been dealt with in the tangled web of his foreign policy, though it also had domestic implications. Napoleon wished to normalise relations with Pius VII to mollify the millions of French Catholics, who at the same time as they were being asked to harness themselves to the national effort were highly critical of the emperor's relations with the Holy See. The dispute between Napoleon and Pius was at it peak in 1809. In that year the emperor declared the papal state a province of the empire and in July he exiled the head of the Church from the Quirinal Palace in Rome to Savona on the Mediterranean coast. In the following year Pius refused to recognise Napoleon's divorce from Josephine. On 18 January 1813, the two met on the emperor's initiative to discuss the outstanding issues between them and on the 25th they signed the Concordat of Fontainebleau. As much as Napoleon wanted to mollify the head of the Church, he still did not give him what he wanted more than anything else – restoration of the papal state to its past glory. The new Concordat satisfied the pope only in matters related to the authority of the Church, but not in that other highly charged political issue.

A glance at Spain will complete our picture of French deployment in Europe. At the end of July 1812 the northern part of Spain appeared to be at Wellington's mercy. But his siege of Burgos was unsuccessful. In the south, Soult evacuated Andalusia and withdrew to Valencia, moving from there towards Madrid. Wellington was forced to call off his offensive, break off contact and go into quarters on the Portuguese border. He preferred to pass the winter there and use the time to plan and build up his forces for a more deter-mined offensive. Consequently Napoleon's forces on the Iberian Peninsula were not under excessive military pressure when he was occupied with planning his East European campaign. Thus he could attach to himself as a corps commander Marshal Marmont, who had been seriously wounded in Spain and out of action for a number of months. Soult, whose movement toward Madrid from the south was largely responsible for Wellington's inac-tivity until the spring of 1813, was also recalled to France at the beginning of the year. Returning together with him and joining the new army were a number of generals, many junior officers, who were needed to train the recruits, and a few full infantry regiments.

Thus in April the main political moves were completed and a clear picture emerged of the political alignments arrayed to take part in the unavoidable war that was to come. On one side stood France and its tireless emperor together with their German allies, whose enthusiasm for the alliance was not what it had been in the past. France could also count on the sympathy and dependence of the Poles, which in practical terms added a Polish army corps, currently inactive, to the Grand Army. On the other side, a coalition had taken shape whose members were not yet equally committed to it: Russia and Prussia were bound in a firm political and military pact; Britain was a bona fide member in the alliance but mainly contributed economic support; Sweden was very close to becoming a full partner; and Austria was still straddling the fence, though its intentions were unmistakable.

The French emperor's main motivation was his view that it was incumbent upon him to preserve the empire – Greater France, with additions of territory and influence throughout Europe. He understood very well that the destruction of his army in Russia and the military failure there had set him back. He also understood that the alternative to the empire was at best a France within its traditional borders. Conservative Europe did in fact want France to exist – but without its revolutionary ideas and satisfied with its lot within the framework of an agreed European balance of power. From Napoleon's point of view, the first condition for the preservation of the empire was possession of Germany and unchallenged influence in Prussia. This condition also determined quite naturally the theatre of war in 1813: the eastern part of Germany, Prussia and part of Poland – as far removed as possible from France and close to the Russian army. It was also meant to be an opportunity to pay Russia back for 1812 and dictate terms. Another aim of the coming war was to link up with the French garrisons cut off throughout Eastern Europe in the wake of Eugene's retreat. Finally, it can be assumed that a sense of injury and tarnished prestige played no small part in Napoleon's strategic thinking.

In the middle of April, Napoleon was once again getting ready to leave Paris to take command of the army and conduct the major new campaign. We return to the second half of February 1813, to Eugene Beauharnais, commander of the army in Germany and deployed in a temporary holding line on the Oder. Opposite him are the advancing Russian forces, operating without any clear-cut strategic framework in regard to Russia's war aims. This strategy was due to take shape in just a few days, on completion of the feverish deliberations with the Prussians. The Russian army had one clear aim – to station itself on Prussian soil, between the Oder and the Elbe.

The Oder fortifications were held by fairly strong French forces. It was true that a few thousand Cossacks were operating in their rear and there was street fighting in Berlin and its environs, but these were just raids without the assistance of the main Russian army, which was still far to the east of the Oder. Wittgenstein was in Pomerania with 20,000 men and Kutusov was in Kalisch with 40,000. The Prussian army, which was still not officially involved in the war against France, was deployed from Eastern Prussia to Silesia. Accordingly, the Russian advance units withdrew northwards from Berlin. Under these circumstances Eugene should have stayed where he was, for there was no reason for him to abandon the positions he held. But Augereau, who throughout the campaign had commanded a reserve corps stationed on the Oder, put pressure on him from Berlin. Fearful of an uprising, he was overly anxious. Eugene gave in to his pleas and leaving a small force along the Oder set out for Berlin, arriving on 22 February. Angered by this step, Napoleon chastised Eugene severely: 'Had you concentrated at the Küstrin front, the enemy would have thought twice before crossing the river. You would have gained 20 days at least, and forces from the Elbe would have arrived to defend Berlin.' In Eugene's defence it may be said that his situation was fundamentally problematic. In effect, the advancing Russian forces encountered no real difficulties of terrain and the rivers, which were the main natural obstacle, were frozen and thus easy to cross.

In the meantime the treaty of Kalisch had been signed and though it had not yet been published Frederick William ordered his forces to move to the Oder in the wake of the Russians, though not to take part in the fighting. The Allies concluded that the French were now incapable of real resistance and decided to advance on the Elbe across a wide front. Wittgenstein, operating on the right wing with his Russian troops and an additional 30,000 Prussians under Yorck and Bülow, crossed the Oder between Küstrin and Stettin on 2 March and marched rapidly on Berlin. The Prussian General Blücher was on the left with 27,000 Prussian soldiers and another 14,000 Russians, mostly cavalry under the command of Winzingerode, and they advanced from Silesia to Dresden. Blücher was old but full of spirit and energy, a figure exercising much influence on the entire Prussian army. At his side were our old friends Scharnhorst as chief of staff and Gneisenau as quartermaster. Kutusov, the commander-in-chief of allied forces, was positioned in the centre with Miloradowitz's reserve and earmarked to move behind the left wing but at a considerable distance from it.

Eugene did not wait for the advancing Wittgenstein, immediately beginning to withdraw towards the Elbe. In truth, he evacuated the Prussian capital without a fight in the face of inferior enemy forces and again aroused the ire of his stepfather, who made the following edifying remarks in a dispatch to him on 9 March: 'Nothing could be more unmilitary than the position you took up to the rear of Berlin. Had you located yourself on its front, the enemy would have assumed that you were eager for a fight, and would not have crossed the Oder before he had contrived to mass 60,000 or 80,000 men... You abandoned a position that the substance of the art of war is its defence.'

Eugene moved towards Wittenberg and did not cease his retreat until his entire army was concentrated behind the Elbe. His troop dispositions embraced Wittenberg, the sector from Königstein to Torgau and a left wing whose centre was at Magdeburg. Headquarters were transferred to Leipzig and Victor with 12,000 men dug in behind the Saale River at Bernburg. On 12 March Eugene gave orders to abandon Hamburg because of the great distance separating his army from the French force occupying that northern city. The concentration of his forces along the upper Elbe had as a result the abandonment of a large part of Saxony, on the one hand, and the exposure of Hamburg and Holland in the north, on the other. Eugene held fast to his view that the principal aim of his dispositions was to throw up a forward security screen behind which, in the Main Valley, the new French army could organise. Thus he had to hold Dresden and secure the roads from the Main Valley to the Elbe. He had not yet received Napoleon's dispatches on the defence of the Oder and Berlin, and here too reverted to his principle of defence to the rear, along the Elbe. He made another mistake in deploying his troops along a 250-kilometre front without reserves. Napoleon felt that such deployment would suffice only against light troops and not against an enemy attacking in massed force against which bridgeheads across the river would have to be defended.

The military situation of the French indeed justified, and even dictated, a vigorous offensive by the Allies, and the Prussians in fact pushed for this. But the advance was slow, because of the slowness of the advance guard and of Kutusov, who was still in Kalisch. Reassessing the situation, Napoleon ordered Eugene to concentrate 65,000 men at Magdeburg and transfer the centre of his defensive alignment to the lower Elbe. As for Dresden, Napoleon authorised its evacuation if the enemy advanced on it in great strength; all in all, Eugene was not required to bring on a major battle but to confine himself to manoeuvring his forces.

Eugene began to redeploy around Magdeburg only on 18 March. On the 17th Davout left Dresden after blowing up the bridge on the river. Wittgenstein and Blücher advanced to the Elbe. Blücher occupied Dresden and Yorck's advance guard appeared opposite Magdeburg. Napoleon's orders in the event that the Elbe line and Dresden were lost was to avoid at all costs a retreat in the direction of the new army in the Main Valley and to continue to the northwest. In truth, Napoleon expected and hoped that Eugene would hold out longer on the Elbe and that the allies would hesitate to cross the river with Eugene threatening Berlin. As it turned out, heavy fighting broke out between Eugene and Wittgenstein on 2 April at Möckern in the Magdeburg area and lasted three days. The French scattered their forces to defend the routes to Magdeburg and were consequently hit hard on the battlefield. Wittgenstein crossed the Elbe without difficulty on 10 April. Yorck advanced upriver, to Rosslau and Dessau, and threw up a bridge. Eugene moved to the Saale in order to defend the area between the river and the Erz Mountains. The allies were now in a position to operate west of the Elbe under Wittgenstein and Blücher, but Blücher was careful to stay close to Bülow because of the large French force at Magdeburg.

At this point the allies gave up all intentions of advancing west, wishing now to concentrate their forces against Napoleon's new army, which was about to complete its final war preparations. Kutusov left Kalisch only on 7 April, Blücher arrived at Leipzig with Wittgenstein on his right and Barclay with 15,000 men besieged Thorn, which fell on 18 April. Thus the allies lost an opportunity to strike the French before fresh troops came up, with the emperor at their head. These troops began advancing from their staging area on 15 April.

On the same day, at dawn, Napoleon left Paris for Germany.

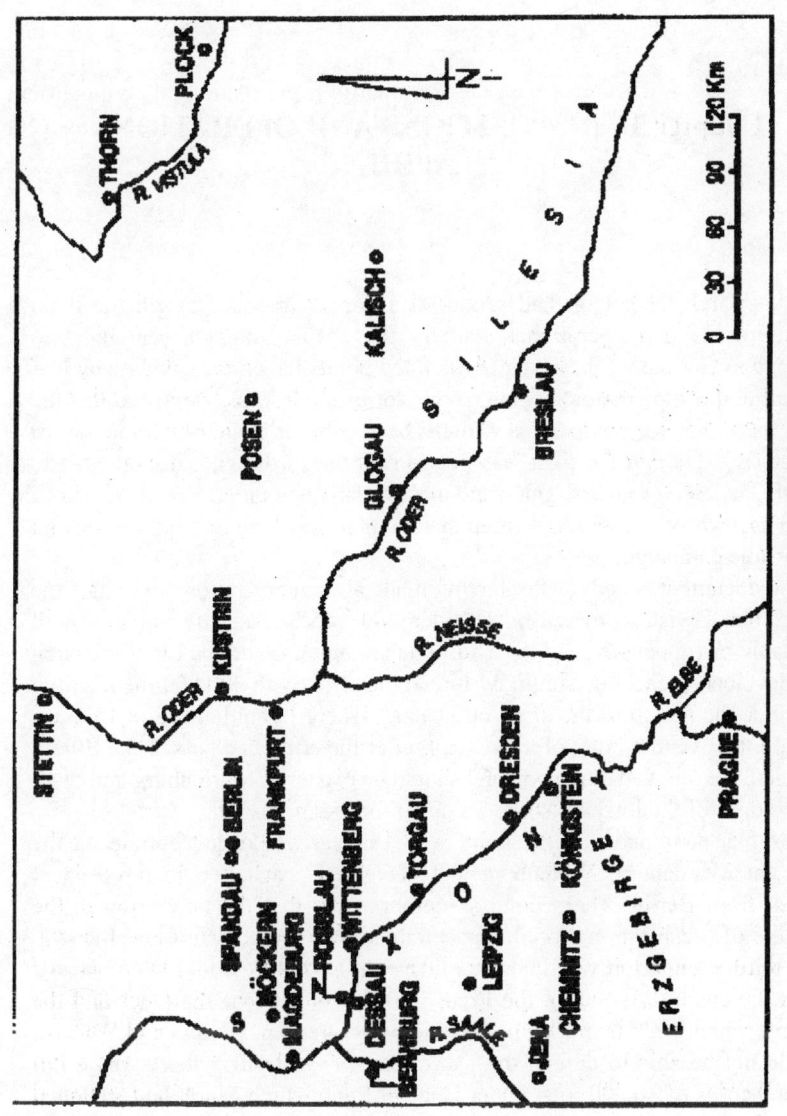

Map 3   Theatre of Operations: January–April

Chapter 3 - DISPOSITIONS AND OPERATIONS IN APRIL

On 11 March, Napoleon had produced a document setting forth the main points of his first operational plan for the 1813 campaign, sending it to Eugene in Germany. These sharply defined points have fascinated many historians and commentators. Count Yorck, for example, was convinced that the plan 'need not fear comparison with his best, either in point of boldness or of brilliancy'. Though the plan was not carried out in the end, it can serve to clarify Napoleon's clear-sighted and inspired strategic thinking and the war of 1813 as a whole. Fuller has written that the plan was kept in mind throughout the whole campaign.

The document stated: 'After having made all demonstrations to induce the belief that I wish to march on Dresden and into Silesia, my intention will probably be (under cover of the Thuringian mountains and the Elbe) to march by Havelberg, reaching Stettin by forced marches, with 300,000 men, and to continue the march of the army on Danzig, where I could arrive in 15 days; and on the twentieth day of movement, after the army had passed the Elbe, I should have relieved that town, and should be master of Marienburg and of all the bridges of the lower Vistula. So much for the offensive.'

The plan assumed that the army with Eugene would concentrate on the Elbe, at Magdeburg, Wittenberg and Havelberg, each two to three days' march from Berlin. The second assumption was that the new army in the process of organisation would concentrate at Würzburg, Erfurt and Leipzig. The third assumption was that the movement to Stettin would be concealed from the enemy. At Stettin the French army would cross the Oder and the enemy, which Napoleon assumed would be at Dresden, Glogau and Warsaw, would not be able to defend the Danzig sector. At Danzig there was a full French corps of 30,000 men under General Rapp which Murat had stationed there during the retreat from Russia before withdrawing from the Vistula.

Now the intention was to save Danzig and to append Rapp's corps to the Grand Army.

But there was much more to the plan. This move would have made the lower Vistula and the frontier area of Eastern Prussia and Poland the theatre of war, bringing it to the heart of the Prussian enemy. Fuller was right when he said that if the plan were implemented it would place Berlin at Napoleon's mercy. Prussia's war preparations would have been impeded, mainly in the conscription of troops. Napoleon's move would have constituted a clear threat to Russia's transportation lines in Poland and pinned down some of their forces far from Austria. And it was Napoleon's desire to create strategic conditions serving to isolate Austria from its potential allies, Russia and Prussia.

Opponents of the plan hid behind Napoleon's own strategic concepts, though it would have been simpler to say that the chances of implementing the plan were next to nil. They argued that Berlin, even if the fortifications of the Oder and the Vistula were taken into account, was not in itself a sufficient objective for an entire army, since the main goal, according to Napoleon himself, was the destruction of the enemy army. The plan lacked clear provision for a decisive battle, and the emperor himself taught that the decisive battle is the heart and soul of military strategy.

Maude, who stated that for years he was against the 11 March plan, for the reasons given above, also admits that he changed his mind when he understood that the march on Berlin, when it reached Königsberg, would not only bring about the collapse of the Prussian monarchy for the second time but would also clearly threaten the lines leading to St Petersburg. Napoleon certainly had a right to believe that the threat to Berlin, like the similar threat in the 1806 campaign, would force Russia and Prussia to realign and try to prevent it. Then Napoleon might find himself in the strategic concentrated-dispersed formation he so loved, over a wide area where it would not make any difference to him where and how the enemy chose to attack, as Maude concludes his intelligent review of the plan. It made no difference to Napoleon because one way or the other the political and territorial concept seemingly inherent in his plan would lead to a decisive and destructive battle. Thus, despite the impression that may be created, Napoleon was still faithful to his old ideas.

Count Yorck was convinced that the plan was bold and brilliant: bold in the idea of advancing from Stettin to Danzig along the sea while the right flank, farther inland, remained exposed; brilliant because the movement towards Havelberg was well thought out and the cover of the Thuringian forest and the

Elbe would create surprise and minimise the danger to the exposed flank. The appearance of the French on the Vistula would make a great impression on all of Europe, and Yorck of course remembered Napoleon's adage than 'in war prestige and morale effect are more than half a battle'.

It should be remembered that on 11 March, when he wrote the document, he had not yet been informed of the treaty of Kalisch and Prussia had not yet declared war against France. He also did not imagine that he would not be able to set his plan in motion until May because the forces he was counting on were not ready until then. In addition, he was lacking troops to pin down enemy forces in Saxony in the Dresden area while advancing north-east and east to the Vistula. There was also a very real danger to the vital line along the Saale. The plan diverged from the principle that almost always guided Napoleon: quick contact with enemy forces. Conceivably his apprehensions derived from the possibility that the enemy would retreat before him and force him to pursue before he had sufficient cavalry. Maude was convinced that the possible retreat of the enemy was a decisive factor in the thinking of the emperor, who tended to underestimate the military prowess of the Coalition that aligned itself against him and was concerned that it might escape battle, even abandoning Eastern Prussia and retreating into Russia if it had to, with everything that such a distant war entailed. See under: 1812. For since that time he had come to know the Russians well with their methods of evasion and attrition. But his plan also held the key to major and prestige-building gains in Poland and Napoleon needed such gains to repair his tarnished image. Fuller found much resemblance between the surprise move he now planned and his brilliant action at Jena. If he acted in accordance with these ideas and came upon his rivals from the north when he was facing west, he would have the chance to achieve a second Jena. Fuller developed this thesis winningly, but for our purposes the tale of Jena is only a fable, as Napoleon came up from the south and moved to the front with his left wing and not the right, as the plan indicates. But it is certainly possible to agree that the spirit of Jena informed the basic military idea of the move.

In any case, a few weeks after Napoleon revealed his plans to his stepson, he scrapped them, on account of the manpower limitations already mentioned but also because a number of basic political facts became apparent to him. Given the state of unrest among the members of the Confederation of the Rhine, he considered it best to remain close by. He was also afraid that he was about to lose Saxony as an ally and felt less and less certain about Austria's position. In the theatre of operations itself, there were signs of allied movement up the Saale towards Jena. In his report to Napoleon, Eugene noted that the enemy was concentrating his forces for a broad sweep to the Saale sector. Commentators who admire the 11 March plan say that it should not have been scrapped for these reasons, arguing that they were insufficient to justify giving up its advantages.

All the apprehensions and misgivings mentioned above were at the root of Napoleon's second plan, which was much simpler and less brilliant, suiting the conditions and circumstances prevailing in April 1813. Now his principal aim was to defeat the allies in the Elbe theatre, cross the river, mopping up the area on both sides by attacking to the north and south and gaining control of it in order to be near to Germany in his rear and Austria to the south as well as controlling Saxony. The rivers would help him overcome his lack of cavalry, which made it hard for him to defend long logistic lines and widely scattered supply bases. He always saw the solution to these problems in deployment along the river. Berlin would still be within reach, and we shall see that he would return to the idea of taking it more than once, but not before making gains on the southern flank of the theatre of war. The second plan could make these gains possible. He would advance directly to Leipzig and then to Dresden. His enemies would be forced to fight him there or withdraw behind the Elbe. Both these eventualities served his aims and each was a distinct possibility. He thus gave up on his idea of a strategic flanking movement and went back to his old principle of striking the enemy at its heart. He was indeed going to do this from lack of choice, owing to unfavourable military and political circumstances, but it gave him the opportunity to destroy his enemies by his favourite military tactics.

Napoleon's second operational plan was indeed limited in scope and aims in comparison with the first, though a very short time had passed between his unveiling the first and deciding on the second. It is doubtful if Napoleon really intended to carry out the wide, complex flanking movement that he had elaborated in the beginning of March, but he quickly adapted his aims to the new conditions already beginning to prevail in Europe at the end of 1812. His assessment of the new situation took into proper account each of the factors that was liable to affect, and in fact did affect, the achievement of his political aims: his falling prestige on the Continent and the weakening of his power to intimidate and, likewise, the throwing off of his political and military hold and the creation of effective alliances against him. The fact that the military force he had created – with incredible speed – was young and untested probably influenced his thinking as well, though to the outside world he displayed confidence in its ability and as always underestimated the strength of his enemies.

However, these basic conditions should have been sufficient to discourage Napoleon from taking military action to achieve political aims. Had they done so, his reign might have lasted longer and the history of the first half of the nineteenth century might have been completely different. But such a possibility never occurred to him, for to his mind it could have only one result – the end of the French empire and at best a return to the borders of 1792. Napoleon rejected such thoughts out of hand. He did not recall his troops from Spain at the beginning of the year, though they were quite numerous and he was in desperate need of all the experienced officers and men tied down there, because he felt it would be an admission of failure which would also have one result – the beginning of the end of his empire.

Other questions may be asked in this context: was Napoleon aware of the changes taking place in himself, in his personal capabilities, and did he take them into account when he assessed his situation and made his plans? The answer is of course no. On the one hand it was clear to him that under the new circumstances his personal military leadership – which in the past had been so important – was now even more vital. He had said that he would conduct the campaign as General Bonaparte and not as the emperor. On the other hand, it is doubtful if at this stage of his life he was capable of summoning the physical and inner strength to realise his intention. He should have taken account of this possibility when planning his moves.

When Napoleon left for Germany on 15 April, he was again accompanied by Caulaincourt, who described this journey as well in his memoirs: 'When the carriage started, the emperor, who had his eyes fixed on the castle of St Cloud, threw himself back, placed his hand on his forehead, and remained for some time in that meditative attitude. At length, rousing himself from his gloomy reverie, he began to trace in glowing colours his plans and projects.' For a moment he had been sad, finding it hard to leave behind him the pleasures of life to which he had again grown accustomed in his few months in Paris, but then went back to being the self-confident ruler. Which was the real Napoleon? Caulaincourt continues: 'Then he assumed his natural simplicity of manner, and spoke to me with emotion at the regret he felt in leaving his "bonne Louise" and his lovely child. I envy, said he, the lot of the meanest peasant in my empire. At my age he has discharged his debts to his country, and he may remain at home, enjoying the society of his wife and children; while I, I must fly to the camp and engage in the strife of war. Such is the mandate of my inexplicable destiny.' This is not the Napoleon of Italy and Austerlitz, where he had been at the peak of his glory, and apparently not of Eylau and Wagram either. He was now 44 years old, weary of battle and the life of action and more inclined than before towards the comforts of the hearth. He had become sickly and bloated and the impression of the rigours of Russia were still fresh and painful in his memory. His remark about 'the mandate of inexplicable destiny' was typical of another weary dictator, 130 years later, who complained about the bitterness of his fate in roughly the same terms.

Many historians deny totally that the deterioration of the emperor's health and his addiction so to speak to the pleasures of life diminished his will and self-confidence. Some of them admire him deeply and make no effort to hide it, so there is no point in quoting them. But Fuller is certainly not one of them and he too is convinced that Napoleon's self-confidence did not diminish; on the contrary, in his opinion self-confidence was the villain of the piece. Napoleon still believed that his unique personality would get him through everything, as a ruler and as a captain. He did not understand that conditions had changed and that the conduct of the war in 1813 would be different from what it had been just a few years before. In any event, even if signs of weakness were apparent that could effect both him and his ideas, there were also signs of fervour and self-mastery.

If we disregard the personal factor, it would not be incorrect to say that the second plan was certainly a realistic operational plan. It would give the Grand Army the edge in a theatre war of reasonable size. Napoleon himself could be present at any point he chose in order to control developments in accordance with his favoured method of centralised command. He would not be able to threaten actual or potential enemies strategically, but could initiate battles of destructive scope that might achieve the desired results.

The order of battle of the Grand Army of France planned to take part in the East European campaign was set forth in an imperial decree – the Trianon Decree – drafted on 12 March 1813, and amended in April. The decree concerns itself with the Imperial Guard, infantry corps, cavalry corps, artillery units, engineering units and auxiliary and administrative units.

Below are the infantry corps with their commanders and the number of divisions they contained (in parenthesis):

I	Corps – Davout (3)
II	Corps – Victor (3)
III	Corps – Ney (5)
IV	Corps – Bertrand (2)
V	Corps – Lauriston (3)
VI	Corps – Marmont (3)
VII	Corps – Reynier (3)
VIII	Corps – Poniatowski
IX	Corps – Augereau
X	Corps – Rapp
XI	Corps – Macdonald (3)
XII	Corps – Oudinot (3)

All the corps included a cavalry brigade, artillery and engineering units.

At the beginning of April, Napoleon had over 220,000 troops at his disposal in Germany, divided into two armies:

The Army of the Main – which Napoleon himself was to command. It included the III, IV, VI and XII Corps and most of the Imperial Guard (infantry and cavalry). The IV Corps had been formed in Italy under a compulsory draft by imperial decree. The XII Corps was also in the process of formation and included one French division and one Bavarian division.

The Army of the Elbe – under Eugene's command – included the V and XI Corps, parts of the I, II and VII Corps and the I Cavalry Corps under Latour-Maubourg. The II Corps still did not have a full complement of men. The VII Corps had just one division at this stage, but was scheduled to receive two more (from Saxony) shortly. The number of operable guns in the two armies stood at 450. Napoleon also had a reserve, created in the wake of his most recent conscription decrees, which numbered around a quarter of a million men. The reserve served as a source of manpower for those of the above corps that were still in the process of being formed. The VIII Corps, under Poniatowski, was still in Galicia because of Schwarzenberg's armistice. The IX Corps, which we last encountered in Berlin in February, was to become an active fighting body only in September. This was a new corps organised in Würzburg from recruitment in Germany, mainly in Bavaria. After completion, it was to control the approaches to Bohemia and keep an eye on Bavaria. The X Corps, it will be remembered, was garrisoning Danzig.

The Army of the Main made its preparations in the Main Valley and to the east of it, in the direction of Würzburg and Bamberg. At the beginning of

April it numbered about 150,000 men, including Bertrand's Corps, which had marched from the Tyrol to Bamberg. The northernmost forces of the army were at Schweinfurt, Coburg and Bayreuth. The deployment of the army was still not operational, but mainly administrative. The Army of the Elbe, which in the second half of March had marched and countermarched between the Elbe (north-west of Dresden) and the Saale, was stationed before the end of the month in the Halle-Magdeburg sector.

Thus two distinct concentrations of the French army were created. Their disposition, along with the progress of Eugene's fighting to that point, naturally created the impression that Napoleon's objective was Dresden ('After having made all demonstrations to induce the belief that I wish to march on Dresden and into Silesia...') and of course, but before that, Leipzig as well. And in fact the possibility of operating along the lines of the 11 March paper – the march north to Havelberg, bypassing Berlin to the west, and the movement north-east to Stettin – seemed logical now too, at least in terms of the disposition of forces, though quite daring and therefore also not practical.

The amount of information reaching Napoleon about the disposition and movements of the enemy was not great because of the weakness of his intelligence. He knew that he would not be able to deploy at full strength along the Saale until the end of April and assumed that the enemy too would not be able to reach the river until that time. The staging area of the army of the Main was fixed as the country around Erfurt, north of where the corps were then stationed. Napoleon hoped that if the enemy did manage to get an early start, Eugene would be able to hold on while Napoleon hastened with the main body of his forces to the front. He was convinced that in this case as well he would have a large numerical advantage over the enemy. He also believed that the advance of the allies across the Elbe would not take them north of Torgau, because they would not dare to distance themselves too much from the Austrians. As it turned out, he was right, though by the middle of the month Prussian troops (Yorck) did reach Dessau, north of Torgau; however, they arrived from the north. The main body of allied forces did not cross the line connecting Dresden and Leipzig.

The emperor's orders were therefore that the III and VI Corps as well as the Imperial Guard were to deploy along the routes to Erfurt by 18 April. The orders gave the German forces in the army of the Main the responsibility of securing the Franken Wald sector in the direction of Hof and Schleiz, thereby strengthening the adjoining Erz Mountain sector. Another German division would be responsible for the Saalfeld sector. Bertand's troops, which were now near Bamberg, would continue their movement toward Saalfeld and also serve as bait to draw the allies on towards the upper Saale. Bertrand would avoid, the order continued, being drawn into serious fighting. He was even authorised to turn back towards Coburg if necessary. With the completion of the entire movement, the army of the Main was to have established a continuous front west of the Saale with the Dresden and Leipzig option open to it.

A few dozen kilometres to the north of this front most of the army of the Elbe was holding a sector whose centre was at Aschersleben, securing the northern French flank as well as threatening Leipzig from the north-west. The Saxons too should be mentioned, still holding Torgau on the Elbe, about 60 kilometres north of Dresden, and if their loyalty to the French was not certain, neither could it be said that they were leaning toward the allies. The instructions of the Saxon king to the commander of this force, Thielmann, were to hold the place against both sides. We therefore see Napoleon carrying out the preparations for his second operational plan, which required that he shorten the distance separating his two armies along the slope of the Saale.

The allies were not doing much at this point and, as we have already mentioned, lost the opportunity to strike the enemy while he was still making his preparations. They engaged mainly in engineering work on the Elbe, around Dresden, and occasionally made nettlesome raids. Up to the middle of April the advance forces of the allies had completed the following dispositions: Wittgenstein, commanding the Prussian corps of Yorck and Bülow, from Magdeburg to the area north of Leipzig; Miloradowitz at Dresden; Blücher, whose command included the force of the Russian Winzingerode, from Leipzig south to Altenburg and resting on the Pleisse River and Winzingerode in the Dresden area.

This deployment gave the allies an almost continuous front opposite the Saale, running from Altenburg north – though in the southern sector about 40 kilometres from the river – and a strong striking force behind this front, at Dresden. Kutusov still tarried in the rear and Barclay only took Thorn on 18 April after completing his siege, but was not expected to join the army at the front for another few weeks.

Miloradowitz completed his crossing of the Elbe at Dresden on 19 April and moved toward Blücher in order to link up with him and create a strong front between Dresden and the Erz Mountains. Tsar Alexander with the Russian Guard as well as the king of Prussia arrived at Dresden on the 24th.

At this stage Russian general headquarters maintained the view that

Wittgenstein must join Blücher to occupy the solid Leipzig–Altenburg line. Miloradowitz would move farther south to the mountain area, reaching Zwickau, and Tormassow would occupy Chemnitz behind this front. This view was based on the assumption that Napoleon was still incapable of launching an offensive, and that if he attacked in May it would be with the army of the Main on his right wing. Wittgenstein and Blücher, it must be emphasised, believed that the French might be ready before and pressed for continuous, though cautious, movement towards the Saale. They were sure they could respond to Napoleon's movements in one of two ways: by retreating towards the Elbe or by concentrating against and destroying the advance units of the French while they were engaged in crossing the Saale, or at least isolating them. The first alternative was dangerous, as the French already occupied two strongholds on the Elbe, at Wittenberg and Magdeburg. The second possibility was not only bolder but had a chance of success because of allied superiority in cavalry. This superiority could be exploited given the type of terrain on the right bank of the Saale and the inferiority of French cavalry.

General Toll, of the tsar's senior advisers, urged an advance of the allies' left wing from Altenburg north-west to occupy Napoleon's vital axis from Naumburg on the Saale to Leipzig. The idea was based on information in Russian hands on 25 April that French movement was faster than anticipated and a decisive battle could take place sooner than expected. Convinced of the correctness of his view, Toll returned from the front to headquarters at Dresden but did not find the tsar there. Alexander was visiting his sister in Teplitz, about 50 kilometres from Dresden and a few hours away by coach. Toll gave his estimate of the situation at headquarters and the chief of staff, Wolkonski, decided not to wait for his master. He ordered Tormassow to move up from Dresden immediately without stopping at Chemnitz as planned but continuing west to Frohberg and Kohren behind Altenburg. Clearly this movement of Tormassow's would be a step in the direction of carrying out Toll's plan.

On 26 April allied forces were deployed as follows:

Wittgenstein's forces: Bülow in the northernmost sector, between Kothen and Rosslau, with advance units nearer to the Saale, opposite Eugene. Yorck at Zorbig, south of Kothen, with advance units at Halle and Wettin north of Halle, right up to the Saale. Berg in Wittgenstein's southern sector, at Landsberg.

Blücher's forces: Winzingerode between Leipzig and Borna. Prussian infantry filling out the sector to the south, between Borna and Altenburg, with units to the rear at Mittweida north of Chemnitz. Russian cavalry opposite the Saale at Weissenfels and Merseburg. As mentioned, Tormassow was moving towards Altenburg. Miloradowitz, who was at Chemnitz, was using cavalry units based in Zwickau.

This was the unbroken forward line along the Elbe in the north, with its centre at Leipzig and running south along the Pleisse with forces in the area between Dresden and Leipzig, mainly in the Chemnitz area. Advance units operated near the Saale, in a sector not yet held very strongly by the French, and downstream on the Saale opposite Eugene. It should be emphasised that these pre-battle dispositions were not rigidly defined. These were points in the line of possible forward movement in the future, with the troops kept in a state of alert for an immediate advance in accordance with military developments or the estimate of the situation made by headquarters and commanders.

A day later, on the 27th, Wittgenstein transferred Berg and Yorck along with his own headquarters to Leipzig and to the west of it. He was apparently afraid that when the French advanced north along the Saale, his dispositions north of Leipzig would no longer be effective. He set forth his intentions clearly in the orders he sent to his commanding officers on the 26th: 'I desire to assemble all available troops at Leipzig, so that, in union with the northern forces of Generals Blücher and Winzingerode, I may, if the enemy assumes the offensive from the Saale by Weissenfels, offer battle at Lützen.' The village of Lützen lay south-west of Leipzig. Its name was known to devotees of military history as the site of an important battle in 1632 between Gustavus Adolphus, king of Sweden, and imperial Catholic forces under Wallenstein. The battle was a turning point in the Thirty Years War. On 27 April Wittgenstein was due to be named commander-in-chief and, as we shall see, his prediction on 26 April of where the future battle would take place would bear fruit in just a short while.

All of Napoleon's orders were written in Paris by 15 April and dispatched to Germany. Leaving the capital, he hastened to Mainz, arriving there in two days, at midnight on the 16th. He stayed in Mainz a whole week, as he saw no need to intervene in the preparations being made and in the movement of the infantry along the routes prescribed in his detailed orders. He was disturbed by the fact that the Austrians showed no signs of responding to his overtures and its army could not be counted on. Saxony too was recalcitrant, refusing to give him the cavalry he requested. It should be remembered that the allies were now on Saxon territory and in the capital, so that even if the king had been very eager to help the French emperor, he would have been hard put to do so. And in any event he was not. On the other hand, the news about the enemy in the Elbe region and in Leipzig was better. The information in Napoleon's hands told him that the enemy was advancing slowly while his own were moving rapidly, in accordance with the timetable set forth in his operational plan. His main intention at this point was formulated at his headquarters on 22 April. Berthier, the chief of staff, wrote to Eugene: 'The intention of the emperor is to guard the whole of the Saale, in order to prevent the enemy from detaching any party on the left bank of that river.' Plain and simple, with additional emphasis on what should already have been clear: when the movement is completed the offensive phase of the plan will begin. At that point the river will provide security and also allow the French movements to be carried out in reasonable secrecy.

French orders for 25 April were as follows: the army of the Main to be on the Saale, in the Jena–Naumburg sector; the army of the Elbe to move south and deploy up to Merseburg; Bertrand, whose mountain route delayed him somewhat, to move north as far as Jena.

The emperor transferred his headquarters to Erfurt and busied himself with completing the organisation of supplies for the big advance army. He decided that Erfurt would be the main supply base and the road from Mainz to Erfurt the main supply axis. The following is the order he dictated: 'Everything must be done to turn Erfurt into a forward supply base containing, within four days, 200,000 rations of bread, two million rations of flour, large quantities of beef, cattle for slaughter, and as much brandy and oats as possible. To purchase all these things quickly, they should be paid for in cash.'

Napoleon reviewed the columns marching north through the Thuringian Valley and was impressed by their fervour and enthusiasm. He heard that veterans were telling the young soldiers about the days of Jena and Auerstädt. Though he did not have the 300,000 men he had counted on, and was well aware of his lack of cavalry, he believed that his enemies were timid and that at least on this front he enjoyed a definite edge in numbers. He showed confidence in his strength and in his ability to gain victory and proclaimed that all he had to do now was to act with speed and determination. In those waning days of April all his energies were devoted to linking together all the forward elements of his army. On 28 April he wrote to Ney: 'The great affair at this moment is the junction.' To Eugene he wrote: 'You know that my principle is to debouch en mass. It is then in mass that I wish to pass the Saale.' On the 27th he forwarded a manifesto to all his corps commanders: 'The campaign

ahead of us demands that you serve as an example to all officers and men...
The emperor believes that leadership will make up for our limitations.'

In the midst of this tense and hectic situation, Kutusov died, sick and weary
and ill disposed to accept the strategy dictated to him. He held on until 28
April and died at Bunzlau, almost 200 kilometres to the rear of his troops. The
tsar, who had the authority to appoint a new commander-in-chief according to
the terms of the Alliance, wanted Wittgenstein. The Prussians agreed they
were convinced that Wittgenstein was an active person who used his initiative. Blücher, who had no pretensions to the appointment for himself and
knew his limitations as a military strategist, gave it his support, though the
new commander-in-chief was much younger than him – only 44, which was
Napoleon's age. Everyone knew that Napoleon too had a high opinion of
Wittgenstein for his ability and courage. It was the Russians of all people, the
colleagues and comrades in arms of the tsar's candidate, who raised objections. Miloradowitz and Tormassow were senior to him and found it difficult
to accept the decision. The tsar had decided on the appointment a day before
Kutusov's death and the solution to the problem raised by the Russian
generals was mapped out in the letter of appointment of 27 April:
Wittgenstein would be commander-in-chief of the combined army of the
allied powers – those under his and under General Blücher's direct command;
the two problematic commanders, Miloradowitz and Tormassow, would
receive their orders directly from the tsar, over the head of the commander-in-
chief, and sometimes, as would become apparent, without his knowledge as
well. At this important juncture in time, with battle approaching, the allies
thus became enmeshed in an unresolved problem of command, inviting difficulties.

The last days of April 1813 witnessed feverish activity in the two armies.
Wittgenstein's orders of the 27th showed that the feeling for battle was
stirring in his blood. He felt that he had done all that was required to create
favourable conditions for the expected battle. Not everyone at allied headquarters agreed with him, or among themselves, as to what Napoleon's next
steps would be or how they should be met. Toll was convinced that the French
would come up between Leipzig and Altenburg and he therefore wanted to
strengthen the position at Altenburg and its environs. This, he believed, would
meet all the possibilities open to the French emperor: if he advanced on

Altenburg the allies would be in an excellent position, confronting him in great strength. From here they could also cover the general line of operations – Dresden–Chemnitz–Leipzig. If Napoleon advanced on Leipzig, Altenburg would effectively threaten his right flank and the forces at Leipzig would engage him up to the holding line on the Elbe, between Wittenberg and Magdeburg. At the heart of this concept was the assumption that the French would make a strategic movement aimed at Berlin and that Leipzig was a way station in this movement. And, in fact, we do know that Napoleon planned to turn his attention to Berlin, but only after reaching a decision in the southern sector of the Elbe.

The Prussian military experts did not go along with Toll's thinking. Scharnhorst advised that every formation remain where it was. If the French attacked on the left flank of the allies, the forces would move toward Pegau, which would solve the problem. If, on the other hand, the French advanced on Leipzig, the forces would retreat to Brandis north-east of Leipzig. Apparently he believed that, in such an eventuality, it was better to be near the Elbe than to fight a battle in the urban area of Leipzig or south-west of it. Clausewitz, now serving on the Prussian staff, made a radical suggestion – to retreat immediately and deploy defensively between the Freiberg Mulde and Elbe rivers. It would seem that the author of On War was quite afraid of the French emperor, or perhaps had far-reaching strategic aims that are hard to fathom.

In the face of the cautious and somewhat sophisticated Prussian views, the Russians put forward simple ideas whose end was offensive, including the reasonable concept of mutual operational support between the different sectors. The differences between Wittgenstein and Toll were not great, but Toll had justice on his side in emphasising the positions south of Leipzig.

In any event, the French in the meantime completed their deployment along the Saale. When their forces appeared at Weissenfels and Naumburg, all the debates about command ceased at once and everything was made ready for the coming events. It was now clear to Wittgenstein that he would have to adopt Toll's approach, which did not in fact override his own favourite idea – to concentrate forces in the Lützen area later on and strike the French there.

The last days of April also witnessed limited fighting between the two sides: at Halle, the Prussians beat back an attack by Lauriston; at Merseburg, a unit of Yorck's was defeated, forcing the Prussians to evacuate Halle as well; at Weissenfels, Ney defeated a Russian cavalry force. These encounters came about as a result of the process of French deployment along the Saale. And indeed, on 30 April, the deployment was almost complete. A division from the IV Corps and all of the XII Corps were still in the midst of their movement, about 100 kilometres from the main body. Napoleon was eager to fight and already had 150,000 men in the planned area of deployment. His picture of enemy dispositions was not complete, owing to his poor intelligence set-up. He was convinced that the enemy was widely scattered along the Dessau–Leipzig–Zwickau line and that a number of his units were concentrated at Altenburg. He believed that he outnumbered the enemy and must not lose time. If the enemy also became aware of this numerical superiority, he thought, he would lose his nerve and conceivably retreat across the Elbe and evade battle. Therefore Napoleon had no intention of waiting to complete the concentration of his forces. The French deployment along the Saale actually amounted to the juncture of two armies ready for battle under cover of the river.

The allied deployment was different, of course, from what Napoleon imagined. The allies were operating in accordance with the orders issued in the last few days: the Prussian generals under Wittgenstein were in the Leipzig area; Berg from Leipzig to Zwenkau on the Weisse Elster about 20 kilometres south of Leipzig; Yorck on a more westerly line from Schkeuditz to Zwenkau; Kleist from Schkeuditz to Lindenau, the western suburb of Leipzig; Blücher at Borna holding the sector running up to Altenburg; Tormassow at Frohberg and Kohren; Miloradowitz's force remaining in the distant southern sector and he himself in Penig behind the lines – apparently a violation of orders as, according to Toll, he should have been advancing on Altenburg.

The orders issued from Napoleon's headquarters for 30 April instructed the army of the Elbe to transfer forces from Merseburg to Schladebach, about 12 kilometres west of Leipzig; the III Corps and the cavalry of the Guard to advance from Weissenfels toward Lützen; the VI Corps to assist the III Corps; the IV and XII Corps to move as quickly as possible on Naumburg. It would seem that the emperor gave Ney an independent mission on the wing where he was advancing to cover the advance of Lauriston and Macdonald towards Leipzig and of Marmont towards Lützen. Were Ney to be attacked from the direction of Zwenkau his force would change from guarding the flank to comprising the advance guard of the entire army, enabling Eugene to attack the enemy from his left.

Ney's movement east brought him to an open plain advantageous to cavalry, which, as mentioned, happened to be what the French lacked. This forced Ney to march his troops in tight formations and not in columns, always on the alert against cavalry attack. And in Wittgenstein's operations log for 1 May he does in fact mention a clash between his cavalry and a French force that had crossed the Rippach creek, in which the French got the upper hand. It is doubtful if the Russian general knew what a heavy price the French paid for their victory in this minor skirmish. Marshal Bessières, commander of the cavalry of the Imperial Guard, was hit by a shell and killed. The same morning, during breakfast, he had told his companions that he was eating his fill even though he was not hungry because he wanted to die on a full stomach. Bessières was extremely well liked by Napoleon, who was inconsolable at the loss.

All the attempts made by the Russians on 1 May to stop or impede Ney's advance failed. Ney and the emperor – the emperor more so than Ney – were much pleased with the functioning of the young soldiers. Ney's report was enthusiastic and, given the insignificance of the clash, even somewhat exaggerated: 'I have never seen in any body of troops an enthusiasm equal to that of these battalions, finding themselves for the first time before the enemy ... this spectacle was worthy of His Majesty's eyes and must strengthen his opinion of these young soldiers who became veterans in a single day.' This response bears witness to the great nervousness among the French command about the quality of the troops.

The emperor spent the night in Lützen, in the house where Frederick the Great had stayed on the eve of the battle of Rossbach in 1757.

On the eve of the real beginning of the 1813 campaign it is edifying to read the words in praise of Napoleon by Count Yorck – a descendant of one of the outstanding officers in the campaign, General Yorck (the future von Wartenburg) – who was a staff officer on Prussian general staff: 'We cannot but admire the iron energy of the man and his high gifts as an organiser, when we see him a few months after the tremendous ruin of a whole army in Russia, standing again with so large a force.'

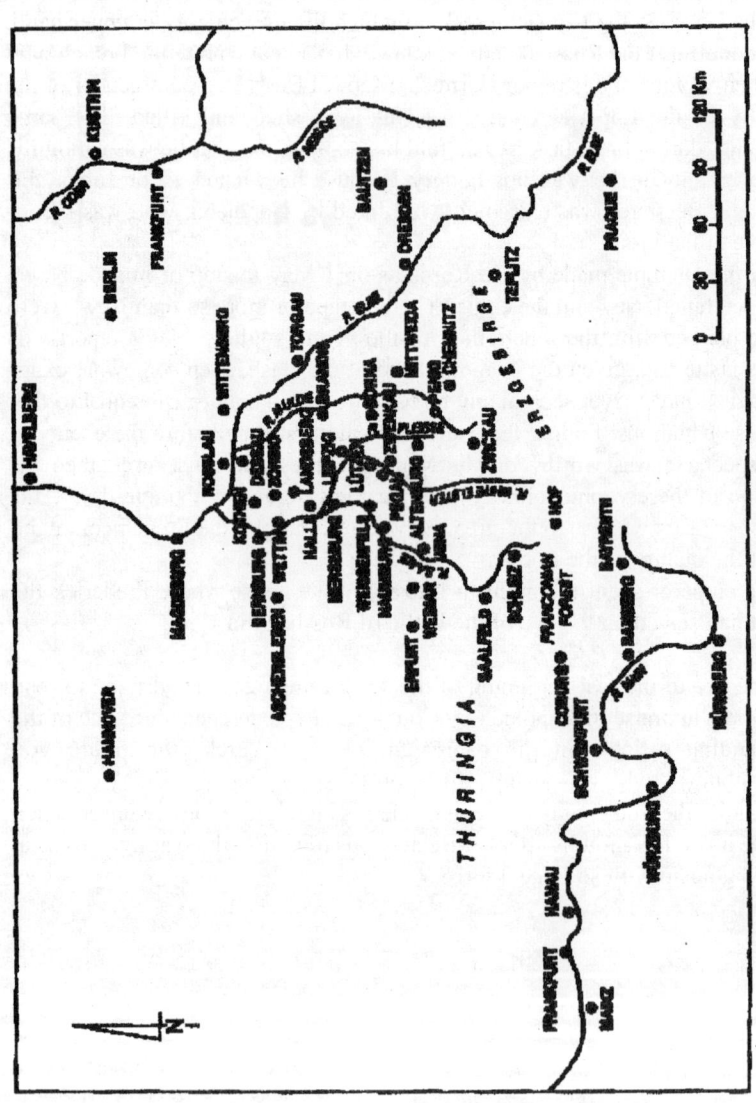

Map 4 April Operations

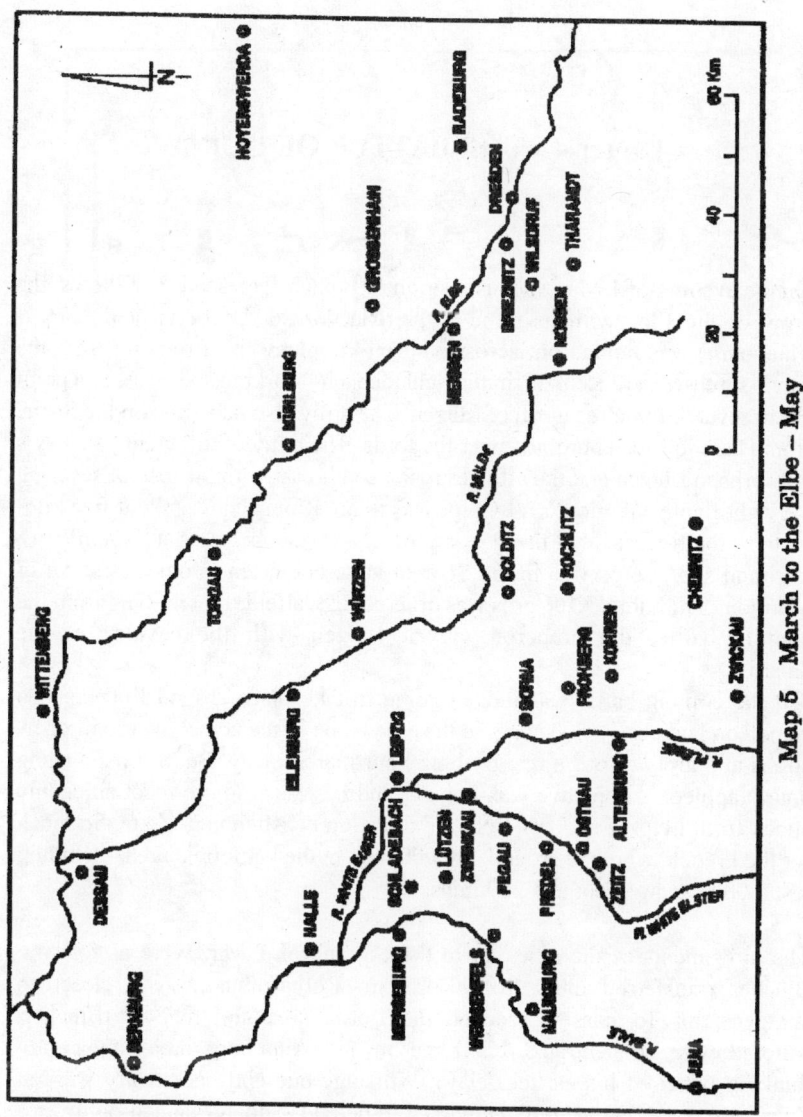

Map 5   March to the Elbe — May

Chapter 4 - THE BATTLE OF LÜTZEN

On the evening of 1 May, the disposition of French forces was as follows: the army of the Elbe with its three corps (Macdonald, Lauriston and Latour-Maubourg) was fanned out across a seven-kilometre front running from the south-south-west of Leipzig, in the Schladebach–Märkranstadt area, to a point about seven kilometres north of Lützen. The army also had units on the Saale, from Halle to Merseburg, to cover the fords. The army of the Main had Ney's III Corps in Lützen and the villages to the south-east with the task of securing the right flank; Marmont's VI Corps was in the Rippach area, about five kilometres south-west of Lützen (one of its divisions was at Naumburg); Bertrand's IV Corps was in the Stossen area, about ten kilometres south of Marmont; Oudinot's XII Corps was ordered to Saalfeld, far removed from the coming battle; the emperor was at Lützen with the cavalry of the Guard.

If the coming battle was indeed going to take place around Lützen, then Napoleon had nearly five corps in the area – one in the actual theatre of operations and around four a one-to-three-hour march away. But at this evening hour Napoleon's objective was Leipzig and he was ready to meet an enemy attack from Leipzig itself or from the direction of Altenburg–Zeitz. So much for the French, who had around 140,000 men in the battlefield area, including just 8,000 cavalrymen, and 380 guns.

The movements of the allies up to the evening of 1 May were as follows: Blücher transferred units from Borna to Rotha, thus getting closer to Wittgenstein; Tormassow reached the Borna area and relieved Blücher; Miloradowitz concentrated his force in the Altenburg area (apparently thinking better of his earlier delay); Winzingerode and his cavalry were at Zwenkau. The allies were thus massed to defend Leipzig, fanned out over a 15-kilometre area between Schkeuditz and Zwenkau with a force that 50,000

men – under Blücher, Tormassow and Miloradowitz – including 13,000 cavalrymen, were concentrated along the Pleisse from Altenburg to Rotha near
Zwenkau. Allied artillery numbered 550 guns.

We, of course, remember Wittgenstein's thoughts about the coming battle at
Lützen; however, reports coming in during the day turned eyes south.

When the night-time pickets went on duty on 1 May the overall picture around
Leipzig was as follows: the French were between the Saale and an imaginary
line connecting Jena to Leipzig. The army of the Elbe, on the left wing,
commanded the northern sector, near Leipzig. It held the axis along which the
army of the Main was intended to move – under the direct command of
Napoleon – straight towards Leipzig in a south-west to north-east direction.
On their right flank, allied forces were arrayed more or less from the Weisse
Elster to the imaginary line mentioned above (in the area of Leipzig itself and
even west of it). On this flank the armies were very close to one another, not
exceeding a few kilometres apart. On the left flank, allied forces were
deployed between the Pleisse and the Elster, with the juncture between the
two wings at Zwenkau. In the southern sector as well, allied forces were
around a three-hour march from any possible field of battle.

And, in fact, the battle took place on 2 May and was unpreventable. The
forces were too close together and clashes and skirmishes had already taken
place in the previous days. Napoleon was determined to fight a decisive battle
as soon as possible and we have already noted that Wittgenstein saw Lützen
as a potential battleground if the French emperor advanced to Leipzig, which
was precisely his intention.

In the war journal of history, which describes all wars as of a well-ordered
piece, devoting a few lines to each day of battle regardless of how complicated things became, the following would have been recorded: starting on 1
May Napoleon brought his main force up to the area east of the Saale and
began to march on Leipzig. In the absence of precise information on the
whereabouts of the enemy, he hoped that this movement would enable him to
flank the right wing under the Prussian generals, to attack the enemy centre in
great strength and to crush him with a series of powerful blows. He kept a
large force in the villages south-east of Lützen. While the main body of the
army marched on Leipzig, starting out in the early hours of 2 May, heavy
artillery fire was suddenly heard on the right. Wittgenstein, who had received

reports of the French movement, had decided to attack the forces guarding the French flank at Gross Görschen and Kaja immediately. General Blücher was given the task. Napoleon understood at once the meaning of the sound of the artillery and left immediately for the sector under fire, which was commanded by Ney. He arrived in the afternoon and learned that Ney was in serious trouble. He organised the troops, mounted a counter-attack with the support of artillery and pushed the enemy back in a fierce fight. Miloradowiz did not get very far past Zeitz in his advance. Had he reached the battlefield in the early evening hours, his presence might have changed the outcome completely. During the evening hours the French gained control of the battlefield and Napoleon ordered a general advance on the enemy's lines of retreat. Both sides suffered heavy losses. The allied retreat towards the Elbe was carried out in good order and the French did not succeed in organising an effective pursuit because of their lack of cavalry. Napoleon, who was personally involved in the battle to a greater extent than in previous battles, knew that although he had won, the victory in the battle of Lützen was not decisive.

We return to the camps of the armies. Most were the site of feverish activity before dawn on 2 May as the men got ready to move. Some of the allied forces had already begun to move at midnight in the wake of the alert for the following day. On the same day, Napoleon was scheduled to join his stepson, Eugene, whom he had not seen since December. This meant the juncture of the two French armies and future operations under unified command. When the troops moving up from the south arrived it would be an army with clearcut numerical superiority in its infantry.

On the same morning Napoleon was at Lützen with the cavalry of the Imperial Guard, not far from the monument to Gustavus Adolphus, king of Sweden, who had fought nearby in 1632, winning the victory but falling in the process. The Prussians and Russians were unleashed according to the mood of their commander-in-chief, Wittgenstein, under the influence of his masters and in keeping with the inclinations of the commander of the central sector, General Blücher.

The area south of Leipzig – forming a triangle with its apex at Leipzig, its base stretching from Altenburg to Naumburg on the Saale via Zeitz and its sides the Pleisse and the line connecting Leipzig to Naumburg whose southern half was the Saale – was a broad plain becoming more uniform in terrain as one moved east. The south-west part was more sectioned and ran down to the Saale. On the plain itself there were small villages and farmhouses a few kilometres from one another. Two rivers flowed from south to north – the Pleisse and Weisse Elster – and a third river, the Saale at the rim of the plain, carried their waters into the Elbe between Dessau and Magdeburg. The Pleisse was more of a creek, about ten metres wide with low banks and a surprisingly strong current. It emptied into the Weisse Elster near Leipzig. The Weisse Elster was broader than the Pleisse and had higher but not especially steep banks. The land around it soaked up its waters and was marshy. The Weisse Elster emptied into the Saale around Halle. The plain between these two bodies of water, the Pleisse and the Elster, was bisected by ravines and small creeks and dotted with woods and groves, mainly near the rivers themselves. We should also mention the Rippach, a creek draining a small area near the Saale and emptying into it.

The information the French had about the exact location of the allies and their intentions was vague. At allied headquarters, on the other hand, estimates were better, as cavalry patrols were frequent and the clashes of the last few days strengthened the feeling that Napoleon was heading for Leipzig. It has already mentioned that a number of reports diverted the attention of allied headquarters from the centre of gravity of French movement and deployment. According to one such report, numerous French forces were ten kilometres south-east of Stossen, but in fact Bertrand's IV Corps, which was in the area, did not get that far. Another report underestimated the size of French forces in the villages near Lützen. In actuality a full division under Souham was at Kaja and another under Girard at Starsiedel, about three kilometres farther west. Both divisions belonged to Ney's III Corps, whose headquarters were at Kaja. The rest of the corps was in the Lützen area, or on the way there.

The advancing columns of the French army stretched for dozens of kilometres, from Weissenfels to Leipzig. Intelligence reports on the advance forces of the French produced the feeling at allied headquarters that an attack might be launched on the southern flank as well, in the direction of Zeitz. Ney's two divisions, at Kaja and Starsiedel, whose size the patrols were unaware of, were thought at headquarters to be a small flank guard covering the marching columns.

In the late hours of the morning the picture would become clearer and it would be easier to pinpoint the centre of the conflagration that would break out on the Leipzig plains. It would become apparent to both sides that early assessments were not a simple matter in this developing battle, where many minds had joined together to evaluate the situation and plan moves.

At this point we would do well to familiarise ourselves with the terrain and first of all with the site on which the fighting of 2 May took place. The designated battlefield was part of the broad plain described above, stretching southwards from Leipzig. In its northern part there was a small stream, the Flossgraben, turning north around Kaja and constituting the eastern boundary of the battlefield. The stream, which flowed parallel to the Elster about five kilometres to the west, was not a real obstacle to infantry, but its banks were a problem for the passage of cavalry and artillery. The woods on both sides of the stream did not make things easier. The area east of the Flossgraben, from Stöntzsch north to Sitteln, comprised a blind spot when viewed from the west. The highest observation point was a low escarpment called Monarchs Hill (Monarchen Hügel). The escarpment rose just slightly above the plain. From this ridge a gentle slope descended toward the villages of Gross Görschen, Klein Görschen, Rahna and Kaja. These villages formed a rectangle, with narrow roads connecting them. In the western part of the area flowed the Grüna Creek, irrigating a level, cultivated valley and very convenient for the manoeuvring of cavalry. The Starsiedel area was somewhat lower than the Kaja–Gross Görschen area and looked out over blind ground. This was therefore the chosen battleground for the day's fighting – a square with sides less than ten kilometres long. The villages dotting the landscape were surrounded by dirt walls and embankments and the stone houses were highly flammable because of their thatched roofs.

At Wittgenstein's headquarters the following plan was formed: to launch a surprise attack against the French columns, in their rear, thereby throwing their advance on Leipzig into confusion; to destroy the flank guard at Kaja and Gross Görschen and to advance from there to Lützen; to drive back the forward columns already past Lützen and marching north to the Weisse Elster marshes, thus diverting them from their objective – Leipzig.

The plan designated the following forces and objectives: Blücher to move on the Elster in two columns – the right reaching the halfway point between Zwenkau and Pegau, opposite Werben, and the left reaching Pegau; the two columns to cross the Elster and reach the Flossgraben by 6 a.m., cross it and advance in attack formation to the Rippach by way of the villages south-east of Lützen; Yorck and Berg to follow Blücher, Yorck behind the left column, Berg behind the right; Winzingerode to cover the Zwenkau passages and the Elster in the direction of Leipzig as well as Blücher's right column; the

Russian guard to advance from its camp north of Altenburg to Pegau by 7 a.m. and act as a reserve; the main signal for the reserve would be a French attack on Blücher's left from the direction of Weissenfels; Kleist to remain where he was, at Leipzig and Lindenau; if attacked in superior numbers he would be authorised to retreat north-east to the Mulde in the area of Würzen; if not attacked and the sound of battle was heard to the south, he was to operate against the enemy in his front; Miloradowitz to move in the direction of Zeitz; the heavy artillery of the Russians to be attached to Blücher and to be under his command.

Napoleon, whose plan for 2 May was to continue to advance rapidly and link up with Eugene, took into account the possibility of a large-scale engagement on the same day. He knew that enemy forces were concentrating on the Elster near Ney and that there was a chance that his flank would be attacked at any moment. He was also convinced that such an eventuality would not mean that he would have to change his basic idea, for if attacked while on the move he would be able to strike back quickly enough and, if not attacked, it would be easier for him to deal with the enemy once he got to Leipzig and crossed the Elster at his convenience, on bridges. This line of thinking lay behind his orders for 2 May: Marmont, who had one division at Naumburg, to recall it to his corps, all of which would be located east of the Rippach creek; Bertrand to advance to Starsiedel and position himself there quickly, with at least one division; the Young Guard under Mortier to concentrate rapidly at Lützen; Lauriston to attack Kleist at Lindenau and Leipzig; Macdonald to fight his way towards Leipzig and Zwenkau; Ney to carry out aggressive action and patrols in the direction of Zwenkau and Pegau and concentrate his entire corps at Kaja; Oudinot to advance to Naumburg.

These orders bear witness to Napoleon's firm commitment to the principal objective he had defined for himself, while taking into account the latest information at his disposal, albeit in quite general terms. He advanced his southern forces to get them close to the area of operations, ordered an attack on the enemy in the area of the final objective, namely Leipzig, and strengthened himself in the area where the battle was planned to take place if the enemy crossed the Weisse Elster. Had he been certain that the enemy was going to cross the Elster, he would have strengthened the position of Ney's corps even more and taken more general preventative action in the Zwenkau–Pegau sector. It is generally difficult to choose from among the possibilities open to an enemy operating on one's flank, as these are quite numerous from the defender's point of view. Napoleon's orders stand out for their lack of a definite assignment for Latour-Maubourg's cavalry corps, which was with Macdonald in the Märkranstadt–Schladebach area. It is reasonable to assume that this was because of the weakness of the French in cavalry, so that Napoleon wished to save the corps for other eventualities, as much fighting still lay ahead.

Napoleon's plan was characterised by its simplicity and determination. He assumed that Ney's large force of nearly 50,000 men would succeed in stopping the enemy in his front while the other four corps moved against the flanks of the enemy, including his rear. If the enemy's main effort were to be directed against Ney, it would be no problem to reinforce him with another 50,000 men within a few hours. Till the end of the day it would thus be possible to concentrate around 140,000 men in the mooted area of battle – which meant clear-cut numerical superiority.

Much criticism has been directed against the allied plan, which bears the stamp of Wittgenstein's thinking as it took in the latter days of April. It is generally regarded as an unwieldy plan, requiring involved orders and creating tactical problems in its application which are not sufficiently resolved: the approach to the Elster on such a narrow front demanded meticulous planning of the order of march and the crossing, but the time available for planning and preparations had been very short; Blücher's assignment forced him to create an excessively wide corps front between the Flossgraben and the Rippach.

Conceivably the criticism is justified at the tactical level, given the problems that arose in the field. It is also conceivable that the orders bear witness to faulty staff work in terms of co-ordination and formulation. At the operational level, on the other hand, the plan demonstrates a determination to strike hard and perhaps decisively at the French under conditions favourable to the allies. Most of the French army was caught up in rapid movement and its lack of cavalry created not a few weak points along its entire route. The securing of the flank of this great advance did not appear very diligent and Wittgenstein hoped to complete it en route to destroying the French along their line of march. This hope is in keeping with the aggressive spirit of the entire plan. Miloradowitz's assignment appears somewhat unclear and this probably derives from the nature of the personal relations between the veteran general and his new chief. But it is also possible that the stationing of Miloradowitz so far south has its origins in the wish to maintain a strong reserve and meet a possible attack from the direction of Stossen, where Bertrand's corps was located.

Blücher's corps got on the road before midnight and would not attack for another 12 hours. His advance to the Elster, followed by Yorck and Berg, was carried out as planned, but with much delay. The delay was caused by the congestion at the fords of the river and the movement in long columns. Blücher crossed the river in the Pegau area, the last troops getting over around noon. Had Ney operated in the direction of Zwenkau and Pegau on the same morning and sent out patrols as ordered, he would have spotted Blücher's movement, since any patrol moving south-east along the Flossgraben would have avoided the blind spot vis-à-vis Gross Görschen and looked down from high land on the large-scale close-order advance of the enemy. But Ney did not send out patrols, nor did he recall his divisions at Lützen to his position within the four-village rectangle despite specific orders to do so.

As the sun rose Napoleon heard nothing from the direction of Ney, leading him to believe that there would be no enemy attack from the direction of the Weisse Elster. Therefore his morning orders did not change the disposition of his forces or their objectives but urged Lauriston to speed up his attack on Leipzig and Marmont to hasten east to Pegau. The rest of the forces were ordered to carry out their designated movements quickly. Macdonald was placed on the alert pending possible action at Leipzig or Zwenkau. At 10 a.m. Ney joined Napoleon at Lützen and the two of them had a conversation beside the Gustavus Adolphus monument and from there rode to Märkranstadt. There is no evidence that at this hour Napoleon was aware of Ney's negligence in carrying out his morning assignment. Ney reported to him that everything was quiet and enemy movement routine. It can be assumed that Napoleon relied on the marshal and did not go into details about Ney's own activities.

At the same hour a few allied advance units and staff officers arrived at Monarchs Hill. The Prussian General Muffling rode up to the edge of the village rectangle and came back to report that the French there were unaware of their precarious position and comporting themselves lackadaisically as they went about their morning routine. Wittgenstein arrived at Monarchs Hill at 11 a.m., observed the enemy and heard reports based on the interrogation of prisoners. Most of the troops of the Prussian generals were already on the plain and Winzingerode's reserve was also on the way. The men were worn out from marching and the river crossings, so it was decided to rest awhile before going into battle. Wittgenstein went down to the road linking Gross Görschen to Stöntzsch, in the blind area. An old general on horseback rode up to him, saluted and requested permission to attack. This was Blücher. 'God be with you,' Wittgenstein said in German. The Russian tsar arrived and the commander-in-chief brought him to the crest of the ridge. The monarch was impressed by the fact one could observe the enemy camps bustling with activity but uncovered by forward positions. He commented on this to his entourage. Wittgenstein hastened to assure him that within an hour the enemy units he saw would be at his feet. The Prussian king also joined them and they all stood beside a pile of rocks observing the scene. The presence of the two rulers on the low-lying hill was the reason for its name, recorded now in history.

Blücher ordered an immediate attack and his men began to come over the ridge and move rapidly on Gross Görschen. The French stationed there were completely surprised by the waves of Prussians pouring towards them and it can be assumed that some of them were caught with their pants down, as it were. Wittgenstein too was in for a surprise when the battlefield came to life – from his nearby observation post he could see that a much larger French force than had been reported to him only an hour before was present in the villages in front of him. Consequently he halted the infantry a few hundred metres from the village and let loose a heavy artillery barrage that lasted 40 minutes.

While all this was taking place Napoleon was in Märkranstadt. There he reviewed the XI Corps and observed through field glasses the battle Lauriston was conducting with the V Corps against Kleist at Lindenau, the western suburb of Leipzig. The French attacked in strength and drove Kleist back. Kleist had heard the sound of battle from the direction of Lützen but circumstances forced him to defend himself and operate in accordance with the first option mentioned in his orders. He moved to his rear, towards Würzen. Napoleon also heard what Kleist heard – heavy artillery fire – and understood immediately that his enemies were doing what he had expected them to do, though an hour or two later than anticipated: they had indeed crossed the Weisse Elster and were now attacking the III Corps. Ney, who had been with his commander, galloped off to join it in great haste. The emperor, clear of mind as usual when under pressure, dictated his orders and handed them to his couriers: III Corps to hold its positions to the last extremity; VI Corps to reinforce Ney's right, western, flank; IV Corps to operate against the enemy's left flank, the flank nearest to it; XI Corps and I Cavalry Corps to move rapidly to the south and operate against the right flank of the enemy; V Corps (fighting at Leipzig) to leave a division behind and move to Märkranstadt, standing ready to move to the battle area.

The emperor mounted his horse and rode to Lützen, where the Imperial Guard stood on the alert in accordance with its earlier orders. The hour was about 1 p.m. Couriers from the corps under attack were waiting for him there: Ney requested reinforcements – and quickly, if possible.

Wittgenstein's artillery pounding of Gross Görschen ended and a Prussian brigade assaulted the village and took it easily. Prussian and Russian cavalry came up from the left riding towards Starsiedel. There too the French were completely taken by surprise and there too the assault was called off in order to bombard the village, which held out until Marmont's reinforcements arrived. Girard, who had been in command, turned over the defence of the place to Marmont and went to the assistance of Souham. Blücher, who saw the Prussian attack on the left petering out, sent another brigade to the right to attack Klein Görschen. The two now attacked furiously. Their commanders, Generals Klüx and Ziethen, urged the troops on. The villages went up in flames and the French retreated from Klein Görschen and Rahna north to Kaja.

At this stage of the battle the breathless Ney had already reached his headquarters at Kaja. Passing through Lützen, he had corrected what needed correcting, though very late in the day, and ordered the division commanders still there to hasten to the battlefield: Marchand to Eisdorf to extend the French front eastwards; Brennier and Ricard to Kaja. Souham's men too had been pushed back to Kaja in the face of the Prussian assault. Now Ney made up for his sins of the morning. He placed himself at the head of Brennier's division, rallied the retreating and fleeing forces around himself and went out to meet the Prussians. The cannons on the left at Kaja pounded the area between the villages with heavy fire. Ney retook Rahna and Klein Görschen but was stopped in front of Gross Görschen by an artillery barrage. Now Blücher, who had the battle well in hand, sent in another brigade, under Röder, and the three Prussian brigades mounted a co-ordinated attack from the direction of Gross Görschen, which now became the solid centre of the Prussian position on the battlefield. They ploughed hotly into Ney's Frenchmen and the villages again fell into their hands. The French retreated to their stronghold at Kaja, which was also under heavy pressure. The clashes between the troops were violent and bloody.

Wittgenstein sent Berg towards Starsiedel to ease the pressure on Blücher, who was operating in a very small area. On the French side, Marmont attempted to follow orders and approach the village rectangle from the west, i.e. from Starsiedel. Berg, while on the march, saw Ney retake the villages, and Marmont was hit by the Prussian cavalry charge. The two rival commanders gave up their attempts: the Prussian halted where he was and the Frenchman sent his advance units back to Starsiedel.

It was now 2.30 in the afternoon and the turning point in the battle was close at hand. Napoleon, and with him the Imperial Guard, had arrived at Kaja. The appearance of the emperor, riding his horse, was as electrifying as always. The arrival of the Imperial Guard also had a considerable salutary effect on the men of the III Corps, who were engaged in a furious battle. The emperor immediately saw how serious the situation was, but still did not feel the time was ripe to strike the blow he reserved for such occasions. Consequently he halted the Guard outside Kaja. He believed that Ney would hold on, though on the way he had seen many French soldiers fleeing across the plain towards Lützen. Macdonald and Latour-Maubourg were coming down from the north and Bertrand was on his way from the south. They would close on the enemy from his flanks and rear and then the Imperial Guard at his side would be thrown in hard on the battlefront. In the meantime, he believed, the enemy would commit his last reserves and then the moment would come. At this stage of the battle Napoleon concentrated on what was going on around him and tried to exert an immediate influence. He told his staff: 'We have no cavalry. No matter, I commit myself, without fear, to the valour of our young conscripts. It will be a battle as in Egypt.' He was of course referring to the Battle of the Pyramids of July 1798, when Bonaparte's soldiers had closed ranks, blocked the Mameluke assault and then torn them to pieces. Now he galloped across the plain to the hot spots on the battlefield. He ordered one of the generals on his staff to rally those of Ney's men running around on the plain who were still capable of fighting and clear Kaja and its environs of the enemy. The villages of Klein Görschen and Rahna again fell to the French. A courier came up from the west with a request from Marmont for reinforcements. Napoleon replied: 'Tell your marshal he is mistaken; he has nothing against him, the battle turns about Kaja.'

The Russian reserves arrived in the area at around 4 p.m. and positioned themselves south of the village rectangle. Wittgenstein ordered Yorck to attack with two brigades. Klein Görschen and Rahna exchanged hands a third time and with them Kaja. Napoleon understood that the patience and cool-headedness he was exhibiting were liable to prove costly and decided to send in part of the Guard. The French soldiers charged with the bayonet and the villages were retaken. The slaughter was terrible, the two sides fighting furiously against each other. This phase of the battle was particularly costly: one French division commander was killed and another wounded along with many other officers. Ney's horse was shot from under him. Blücher and Scharnhorst, the father of the new Prussian army, were wounded, the latter mortally (he died in Prague on 28 June). Losses in men were heavy.

At 5.30 p.m. Klein Görschen and Rahna were again in Prussian hands and their front now extended from Flossgraben to the Lützen road. At this hour Macdonald and Bertrand were very close to the battlefield. Macdonald was approaching the right flank of the enemy, Bertrand the left. Morand, commanding Bertrand's lead division, passed Pobles, south of Starsiedel. Marchand also reached his objective, near the sharp bend in the Flossgraben on the right flank of the Prussians. Macdonald too was near the bend. Marchand and Macdonald arrived just in time, blocking the advance of units of Winzingerode's infantry sent to support the attack on Kaja. A new battle now began in the Eisdorf–Kitzen–Hohenlohe sector while the battle of the village rectangle entered its seventh hour.

Less than two hours of daylight remained and Napoleon knew that this was the time to strike if he wished to win the battle. At 5.30 he ordered the entire Guard to advance. In the official French report on the 2 May battle, it is noted that the emperor was aware that 'the critical moment which decides the gain or the loss of battles had arrived'. As they moved to their assault positions facing south, French artillery unleashed concentrated fire from 80 guns on the area between the four villages. The Young Guard led the assault, the left column moving toward Klein Görschen, the right toward Rahna. The Old Guard fell in behind it and the cavalry of the Guard brought up the rear. The movement was made in tight formation, all in the Napoleonic style of advance and fire. Those of Ney's men who could still fight joined in. Couriers from the emperor's headquarters co-ordinated the movement of the Guard with the flank movement from the east and west. Two of Marmont's divisions attacked Rahna from the direction of Starsiedel and the village, hit from the front and the left, fell to the French. Klein Görschen met the same fate, attacked in front by the Guard and from the right by one of Macdonald's divisions arriving from the direction of Eisdorf. The Prussians were pushed back beyond Gross

Görschen. Napoleon had torn apart the enemy facing him by throwing in relatively fresh reserves belonging to his elite force. He had mounted a coordinated attack by forces from different units and rained down deadly artillery fire. This action, together with the growing darkness, brought the fighting to a close.

The time was 7 p.m.

The villages had been burning all afternoon and the battlefield was lit up by the flames rising above it. It was a ghastly sight. The exact number of losses is a matter of dispute, but the approximate picture is clear. The French lost at least 20,000 men, most of them in Ney's reinforced corps. The allies lost around 12,000 men, approximately 8,000 of them Prussians belonging to the commands of Blücher and Yorck, who bore the brunt of the fighting. The spoils were negligible and few prisoners were taken.

After the fighting, the allied commanders concentrated their forces south of Gross Görschen and on the Pegau road. At this stage the French did not make any preparations for pursuit. They were tired and battered and had no cavalry reserve. Napoleon ordered his troops to bed down close together by division and during the evening made his rounds among the units to see that his orders were being carried out.

In the course of the day Napoleon could sense that a new spirit had been animating the enemy, whom he had seen in a different light in the past. He even said about the Prussians: 'These animals have learned something. They are no longer the wooden toys of Frederick the Great.' It is interesting that the Russian Nesselrode also mentioned the Prussian king when he wrote about the battle, but in the opposite context: 'The Prussian troops have covered themselves in glory; they have become once more the Prussians of Frederick.'

The four generals who had fought the battle for the allies – three Prussians and a Russian – kept to their objectives and acted energetically. On that same day their commander, Wittgenstein, did not show the same determination as his subordinates. He of all people, who had wanted to meet Napoleon in a lightning-quick, decisive battle and had even foreseen the site of the battle, had hesitated at a number of critical points and hindered the flow of the fighting when the initiative was entirely in his hands.

It is possible that if his staff had planned the crossing of the Elster better, his forces would have arrived in the area of the fighting a few hours earlier and he would have had more men there. The Prussian commentator, von Cäemmerer, was convinced that this advantage would have been attained if

Yorck and Berg had made the crossing on their own opposite Hohenlohe instead of crossing together with Blücher's columns. Had they done so they would have arrived at the village rectangle directly from the east and would not have had to make the flanking movement from the south imposed upon them by the plan. The forces assigned to cover the fords of the river were too large and it would have been better to send more men to the battlefield.

The allied staff should have given more thought to Miloradowitz's assignment. Many students are convinced that if he had taken an active part in the battle of Lützen the results would have been completely different. It is true that there was a justifiable fear of a French attack from the Stossen area, as Bertrand was there and Oudinot was moving up on the Jena–Naumburg road, but it would have been possible to position Miloradowitz between the Weisse Elster and the Rippach in the area of Predel, as the French commentator Lanrezac suggested. This would have made available a force of 8,000 men, a quarter of them cavalry, if the French did not attack from the south, which they did not. Not using Miloradowitz was Wittgenstein's big mistake. It should be mentioned that the French thought highly of Miloradowitz, considering him a brilliant commander; he was even given the flattering nickname of 'the Russian Murat'.

Among the French it was again made apparent that Napoleon's generals, operating in his shadow, showed no initiative, displaying indecision and weakness at critical moments. Ney was certainly a brave soldier and fierce fighter, but acted apathetically and without initiative before the battle. The marshals operating on the flanks demonstrated none of the valour of their comrade in arms. Marmont acted hesitantly on the right flank. Macdonald moved slowly east of him, though he claimed that this was because at a certain point he had to withstand a spirited attack by units of the tsar's and the Prussian king's guard. Bertrand delayed on the way to the battlefield 'waiting for orders' after he discovered that the advance guard of Miloradowitz was in the area. Neither does Lauriston come off any better in the criticism levelled at the French generals operating that day. He carried out his assignment and caught up with Kleist in Leipzig, but his orders directed him to leave just one division there and advance towards the battlefield with the rest of his corps. It is true that his orders only called on him to prepare for the movement, but as a corps commander he should have taken more initiative. An angry Napoleon asked the next day: 'What were you doing yesterday, when we were fighting here? You were warming your behinds in the sun!'

The emperor himself was at his best that day. His greatness and personal conduct are noted in all descriptions of the battle and no words of praise are spared. His brilliant grasp of what was happening on the field of battle again came to the fore, in the most striking way. From the moment he arrived on the battlefield at the head of the Guard his young soldiers took heart again. It is worth quoting the comments of at least one observer, the Saxon Odeleben, who describes the moment of Napoleon's arrival at Kaja: 'From all sides there rang out the cry of Vive l'Empereur! Hardly a wounded man passed before Bonaparte without saluting him with the accustomed "vivat". Even those who had lost a limb, who in a few hours would be the prey of death, rendered him this homage.' Napoleon encouraged the troops and led them forward. 'This is probably the one day in all his career,' writes Marmont, 'on which the emperor incurred the greatest personal danger on the battlefield.'

Surprised tactically, the emperor reversed his fortunes but did not succeed in creating the conditions required to turn the victory into strategic gain, namely decisive victory. During the night he said to Caulaincourt: 'My eagles triumphed again, but my star grew dim.'

Indeed, at Lützen, Napoleon did not achieve a decisive victory, as he had at Austerlitz and Jena. After the latter battles his foes had been incapable of any more real fighting. The triumphant emperor had pursued them until he destroyed them. He then dictated terms of surrender that had far-reaching political and military implications. This did not occur at Lützen. Napoleon indeed declared that 'this battle will rank higher than the battles of Austerlitz, of Jena, of Friedland and of the Moscowa' and even ordered couriers to be sent to loyal courts – including Constantinople – with the news, but all this was what the French called 'a manner of speaking' (*façon de parler*). In his heart Napoleon knew that the battle signalled a basic change, apparent to the enemy as well, in French fighting ability, a change that it was still difficult to define precisely but was most strikingly seen in the fact that despite an almost two to one advantage he did not succeed in bringing the battle to a clear-cut resolution.

It should not therefore be thought that Napoleon really attached such great weight to the victory. He had wanted to raise the spirits of the army, strengthen his political support and perhaps even raise his own spirits. He sent a letter to his wife, whom in his absence had been appointed regent, asking her to send a paper which he himself had composed to all the bishops in the empire. The paper declared that the victory at Lützen had been an act of Divine Providence. He also requested that the Te Deum and other hymns of praise to God be sung in all the churches. These requests too show how much

Napoleon craved the return of his past glory. They also evince his boundless industry: after the battle, having fought beside his men, he supervised every detail of propaganda and its dissemination throughout his realm.

The allies could not have looked for a decisive victory at Lützen. They were still at a numerical disadvantage and had not yet discovered the secret of defeating their great foe. Even if they had emerged victorious at Lützen the French would have extricated themselves and moved towards the north and west and still commanded a large enough army. At the same time, it should be emphasised that the young French recruits did not display a high level of fighting ability at Lützen and it was impossible to hide their lack of combat experience. Napoleon was aware of this, as evidenced by his 5 May letter to his minister of defence, Clarke: 'I find myself on the battlefield without officers... Many are required to replace them, but without promoting them too quickly, which in any case does not serve the purpose... If you need officers and NCOs, the army in Spain is an unexhausted source and I authorise you to transfer them from there.' On the same day, the 5th, Lauriston told Berthier that 'the information obtained from the inhabitants is that the Russian and Prussian officers feel humiliated and they say that it is dishonourable for them to be overpowered by children.'

There had indeed been moments in the course of the battle when it had seemed that allied forces were about to overwhelm the French. This occurred during Blücher's attack, which Wittgenstein had stopped in order to shell the villages. It occurred again during Blücher's first counter-attack, when he retook the villages. Lord Cathcart, who was attached to the allied general staff, claimed that this was also possible during the final stage of the fighting. As he wrote in his report on the French attack in the late afternoon: 'The vivacity of this movement of Bonaparte made it expedient to change the front of our nearest brigades on our right; and, as the whole cavalry from our left was ordered to the right to turn this attack, I was not without hopes of witnessing the destruction of Bonaparte and of all his army, but before the cavalry could arrive, it became so dark that nothing could be seen but the flashes of the guns.'

An incident that occurred at 9 p.m. perhaps symbolises the fact that the French were only a hair's breadth away from defeat at Lützen and that allied commanders might argue that the French had not won at all. At that hour Blücher led some cavalry lancers on a raid against the French. He created a fearful panic and almost captured Marshal Marmont, who had been tending his wounds and barely escaped being taken prisoner or struck down. The raiders almost got to the unit where Napoleon was camped. In the end, the French succeeded in driving off the attackers, thanks to having carried out Napoleon's orders for the night, which, as will be recalled, directed that the men camp close together in large formations. Odeleben, our Saxon observer, who was present at French headquarters reflecting on history, related that the emperor was stunned for a few minutes by the daring of the enemy but could not even dream of retaliating with a similar operation that night.

The Russian tsar and the Prussian king, who had followed the fighting the entire afternoon, did not have a feeling of having been defeated at the end of the battle and may even have felt that they had missed an opportunity. They descended from their hilltop observation post at 10 p.m. and rode to Pegau in the dark accompanied by Cossack guard units. During the night they learned that Kleist had been driven out of Leipzig, leaving them no choice but to withdraw their forces, lest their lines of retreat be cut off. The tsar was also swayed by the report of his artillery commander that all their ammunition had been used up during the day. The reserve ammunition was far to the rear and there was no chance of bringing it up before the following morning.

At first light Napoleon rode over to the previous day's battlefield. He saw the thousands of bodies covering the ground – most of them young recruits – and his face reflected great sadness. In one of the descriptions of this ride it is told that 'the emperor came across the dead body of a young Prussian, who in death seemed to press something closely against his bosom. The emperor approached and found that it was the Prussian flag which the soldier had grasped tenaciously. He stopped and gazed in silence upon the spectacle: "Brave lad," he said, "you were worthy to have been born a Frenchman. Gentlemen, I wish some of you to render funeral honours to this young man. I regret I do not know his name, that I might write to his family."'

The allies, who had decided during the night to break off contact with the French and withdraw behind the Elbe, wished to carry out their retreat in as orderly and calm a fashion as possible under close cavalry cover. The retreat was planned as follows: Miloradowitz to deploy and cover the retreat along its entire breadth (the distance to the Elbe was 80–100 kilometres); the Russian column to retreat to Dresden on the Frohberg–Rochlitz axis; the Prussian column and some of Winzingerode's cavalry to retreat to Meissen on the Borna–Colditz axis; Kleist, who had begun his withdrawal the previous day, to get to Mühlberg. At each of the three points designated for the Elbe crossing there were convenient means for bridging. The rearward movement began that same night and the forces marched east in accordance with the plan. Miloradowitz carried out his assignment by the book. He moved from place to place, taking up positions from time to time and forcing the French to deploy and move against him. This was an exemplary holding action that made it possible for the main body of the army to conduct an orderly retreat.

Our detailed description of the order of retreat is meant to underline the change that occurred in relation to the previous retreats of Napoleon's foes after defeat. The rearward movement was well co-ordinated, even if the 'national' colouring of each axis was preserved. A single delaying force was assigned to deal with any possible pursuit and keep the enemy from striking along the axes. Emphasis was placed on maximum evacuation of the wounded as well as arms and equipment. In short, the allies attached importance to the feeling of self-confidence of their troops even after defeat in a given battle, on the assumption that there were more to come. This was one more proof of the failure to reach a decision in the battle of Lützen on 2 May.

The Russian column on the southern line of retreat crossed the Mulde River and marched to Dresden via Wilsdruf, arriving there on 7 May. The Prussian column crossed the Mulde east of Colditz, reached Meissen and crossed the Elbe from there also on 7 May, as did Kleist from Mühlberg, as planned. Miloradowitz got across the Mulde at Nossen and the next day, 8 May, crossed the Elbe at Dresden. On that same day all allied forces were on the right bank of the Elbe.

While the withdrawal behind the Elbe was carried out calmly, such was not the atmosphere at general headquarters. During those same days, feverish discussions had been taking place as to what strategy to adopt once allied forces were on the right bank of the river. One plan followed another and disagreement grew sharper with accusations flying back and forth about events at Lützen as well. The stormy debates were a result of the conflict of interests between the Russians and Prussians. The Russians' chief concern was the safety of their main line of communications, reaching Warsaw by way of Bautzen, Görlitz and Breslau. Control of it would leave them close to Austria as well, whose full and open co-operation they desired. This aim demanded movement east of Dresden. The Prussians' main concern, on the other hand, was the defence of their homeland and capital and therefore they pressed for a northerly movement. On 8 May the matter was still not settled. In his orders, Wittgenstein disregarded the entire question as it were, focusing on the obstacle of the river as the problem that demanded immediate planning and decision. His orders called for a defensive alignment along the river from Dresden to Mühlberg. The main body of the Russians would be at Radeburg and the main body of the Prussians at Grossenhain, about ten kilometres past the river. The stone bridge at Dresden was blown up.

On 3 May, in the waning hours of the night after the battle of Lützen, orders were issued for the French pursuit in the wake of their victory. Ney's corps, which had borne the brunt of the fighting, had sustained heavy losses and was totally exhausted. The corps was given the day to get organised and lick its wounds. On 4 May it was to move out towards Wittenberg and from there to make for Berlin, proving that the idea of an advance on the Prussian capital, which was at the heart of the 11 March plan, was still alive. Now Napoleon set forth two goals: one, to get the Prussians to break off contact with the Russians and move north towards their capital and defend it; the other, to continue to stick to the master plan – the liberation of Danzig and the shifting of the war from Saxony towards Prussia and Poland. During the day the rest of the army would cross the Weisse Elster in the Zwenckau–Pegau sector on the heels of the retreating enemy, Macdonald's corps in the lead.

The great fatigue of the French and the effective delaying action carried out by Miloradowitz caused progress to be minimal on 3 May and contact with the enemy nonexistent.

On 4 May, Napoleon formulated his further plans: the main force, under his command, to advance to Dresden and a secondary force under Ney to occupy Wittenberg and Torgau. The emperor apparently gave up his idea of moving immediately on Berlin, laid out the previous day, though the general direction remained the same. For the principal effort Napoleon would have at his disposal over 130,000 men, including about 10,000 cavalry, and around 400 guns. Ney would command about 65,000 troops, including 4,000 cavalry, and 130 guns. In addition to his own corps, Ney had a division belonging to the VII Corps that had been in the process of formation and was due to be attached to Reynier's command upon completion. Two additional corps – Victor's II Corps, nearing completion, and Sebastiani's II Cavalry Corps, stationed in the lower Elbe area – were also expected to join Ney. There were also Saxon units at Torgau that Napoleon hoped to attach to his army. Ney's assignment and his detachment from the main body of the army was intended to secure the Elbe line, to get the Saxon units actually attached to the army and to make some kind of threat against Berlin.

Lauriston, who left Leipzig on the 3rd, was to move on the northern flank and hold himself ready to assist Ney. His corps would be the link between the two parts of the army.

On the evening of 5 May, Ney positioned himself in front of Torgau after driving the Prussians under Bülow away. Bülow had retreated towards Torgau from his designated sector on the Saale and had been ordered to reach Berlin and defend it with his small force. The army under Napoleon positioned itself opposite the Mulde. The allies were in its front at a distance of one day's march.

Napoleon's intelligence on the intentions of the enemy led him to believe that the allies, marching in national columns, were about to split apart: the Russians moving east along their main axis and the Prussians north. If that were the case, he would pin the Russians down with a relatively small force and attack and destroy the Prussians at a two to one advantage. As mentioned, he hoped that Ney's presence at Torgau would prompt the Prussians to make this movement.

The French advance was slow and the amount of stragglers a cause of concern. This phenomenon was a result of the great effort demanded of the troops and poor administration, which forced the men to fall out of the line of march to look for food. Napoleon dealt with the problem in his order of 6 May, where he required his commanding officers to establish rearguard units to gather up the stragglers and any other strays. The lack of discipline appalled him: 'His majesty orders that every soldier who fires a shot, while marauding, or to unload his weapon, will be punished by imprisonment and demoted. If the shot has wounded or killed someone, the soldier will be punished by death.'

On 8 May, with the allies across the Elbe, Napoleon entered Dresden with I Cavalry Corps and the VI and XI Infantry Corps. Bertrand and Oudinot were ten kilometres behind him in the Tharandt–Wilsdruf sector. Lauriston was at Meissen and Ney opposite Torgau. Thielmann, the Saxon commander at Torgau, refused to co-operate with Ney and hand over the city to him. He was awaiting instructions from his king, who had escaped from Dresden when the allies approached and was now in Prague.

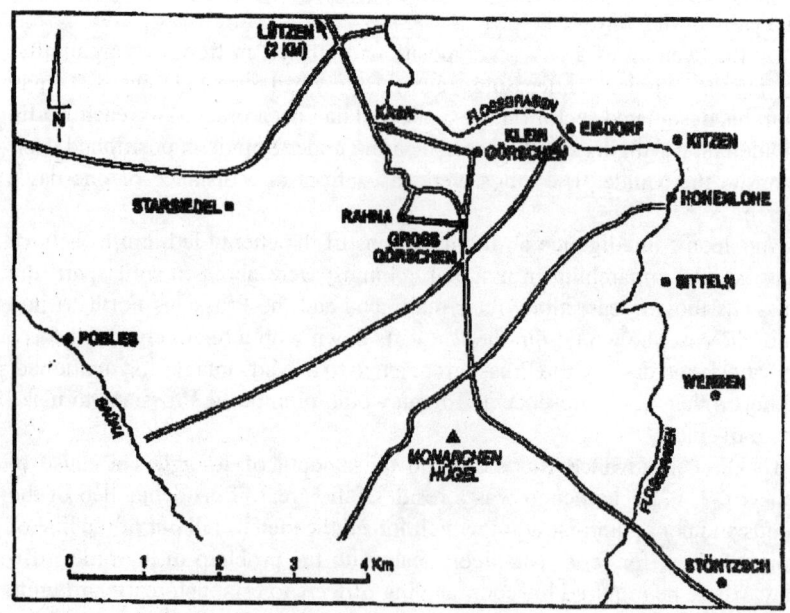

Map 6   Battle of Lützen

Chapter 5 - THE BATTLE OF BAUTZEN

The day the French entered Dresden, the capital of Saxony, was a fine spring day in May. The beautiful city, surrounded by green hills, was divided by the Elbe wending its long way from Bohemia to the North Sea. At this time of the year the Elbe flowed tranquilly, watering the city's gardens and fruit orchards. From the left bank of the river the glint of enemy bayonets could be seen in the sun. The city greeted the French emperor and his army with a chorus of bells, drowned out by the cannon fire of the pursuing French and of the rearguard delaying them in order to assure an orderly retreat. The city fathers, who a few days previously had greeted the Russians and Prussians, now opened their arms to their new guests, as did the common people cheering in the streets. Napoleon, who enjoyed the reception, was as practical minded and to the point as always, demanding that the fathers supply his army with meat, bread and wine. 'Are we friends or are we enemies?' he said. 'You richly deserve to be treated as a conquered people. But I forgive all, from regard to your king. He is the saviour of your country. You have already been punished by having had the Russians and Prussians among you.' He ordered Marmont to march through the streets of the city with his corps in the afternoon: 'The troops in parade uniforms and marching in the strictest order. Send the baggage and everything that does not look well around by the floating bridge.' Marmont and his VI Corps were scheduled to march through the city, as ordered, on 11 May, to impress the populace, as could be expected, and then continue marching east in accordance with the war plan.

Napoleon sent for King Frederick Augustus in Prague to discuss future relations between France and Saxony. The king arrived in Dresden on 12 May and the two rode side by side through the streets of the capital to the sound of marches played by the army band and a salute of cannon. This was the last royal ceremony that Napoleon attended as emperor of France. When they reached the royal palace they sat down to talk and Napoleon came straight to the point. He demanded an unequivocal declaration of the Saxon's loyalty. The king avowed his friendship, though in truth he had previously reached an agreement of neutrality with the Austrians. The emperor demanded that Torgau be handed over to Ney immediately and the Saxon troops there placed at Reynier's disposal. He also demanded that the Saxon cavalry be recalled to Dresden and attached to the French army. As a final sign of obeisance the king was requested to affirm to the emperor in writing his unequivocal agreement to fulfil all past obligations, for if he did not, 'I shall declare you a felon, outside my protection, and, in consequence, you will cease to reign.' Needless to say, couriers were sent out urgently and Thielmann was ordered to accede to the emperor's wishes. He obeyed but went over the allies, true to his heart. Ney breathed a sigh of relief.

Moving far to the north, we find ourselves with Davout's I Corps, which had been responsible from the outset for the lower Elbe region and making a show of French force in this part of Germany, which was not really involved in the war. As the French army reached Dresden, Davout attacked Hamburg. A Swedish force had been stationed for two months at Stralsund, about 200 kilometres north-east of Hamburg on the Baltic Sea. Bernadotte did not come to the assistance of the beleaguered city. He contended that if he came to an agreement with the allies, his army would take part in the larger conflict and therefore he was not willing to divide it. The king of Denmark, who despite his alliance with Napoleon sent a few gunboats to support Hamburg, was ready to help. He hoped to make a favourable impression on the allies and get them to back him up in Norway. But he was mistaken. Allied support went, as expected, to his rival Sweden and he recalled the gunboats immediately. Davout, who commenced his attack on 9 May, entered Hamburg on the 30th.

One incident turning attention from the main events was closely connected with them. On 12 May, Napoleon wrote to Eugene: 'My son: You must start tonight for Italy. I am ordering the minister of war to place under your command the troops that are in the Kingdom of Italy and the Illyrian provinces.' Eugene Beauharnais, senior commander in the French army, had been the viceroy of Italy since 1805. When not on active duty in his stepfather's wars he resided in Milan and was even held in high esteem by his subjects. Eugene had distinguished himself in a number of battles, in 1812 as well, but had caused Napoleon to swallow many a bitter pill after he had been given the privilege of conducting the last phase of the retreat from Russia and commanding the army of the Elbe. An incident on 5 May serves as an example of Napoleon's dissatisfaction with Eugene's conduct and was perhaps the straw that broke the camel's back. During the French pursuit after the battle of Lützen, Eugene had run into some Prussian units on the Mulde and fought quite indifferently. Napoleon, whose almost every response is documented in some way, wrote an enlightening note on the matter: 'My son: Yesterday would have been a beautiful day if you had brought me three thousand prisoners. Why, in a country where the enemy could not employ his cavalry to advantage, were you not able to send me anyone?' Now he sent Eugene to Italy with the assignment of concentrating troops there for the defence of northern Italy against the Austrians. Napoleon was afraid that the Austrians would send a strong force to Lombardy to get back territory taken from them in the past. In this way Napoleon could also pin down a large number of Austrian troops on their southern flank and keep them from taking part in the next phase of the war between France and the allies. Eugene was pleased. The truth was that after Lützen he was going to ask for leave in any event. He intended to rest up after his hard campaigning and still be of use. He would never see his stepfather again.

This episode was one among many that demonstrated the importance Napoleon attached to his relations with Austria at this stage. The anticipated decision of his father-in-law, the emperor of Austria, concerning his active participation in the war, could determine its result. Napoleon hoped that the news from Lützen would tip the scales in his favour when it arrived in Vienna.

Napoleon acted in accordance with the rules of diplomacy of the time and conducted himself as someone who had prevailed in battle and was now making a gesture of reconciliation and peace. His aim was to establish direct contacts with the Russians and create a network of common interests between the two powers without having to enter into additional arrangements. The latter would derive from the agreements between the French and the Russians, if attained. He hoped that understandings with Russia would relieve him somewhat of the need to court Austria.

Caulaincourt was ordered to request an interview with the Russian tsar, which naturally brought back pleasant memories of his days as ambassador in St Petersburg. Caulaincourt was supposed to tell the tsar that he had the opportunity 'to take a splendid revenge for Austria's foolish diversion in Russia', as Napoleon put it in his written instructions. He told Caulaincourt that 'my intention is to build him a golden bridge so as to deliver him from the intrigues of Metternich. If I must make sacrifices, I prefer to make them to a straightforward enemy than to the profit of Austria, which power has betrayed my alliance, and, under the guise of mediator, means to claim the right of arranging everything.'

The following is what Napoleon intended to propose to Alexander through the former ambassador: the territories of the Grand Duchy of Warsaw and the Republic of Danzig would be handed over to Prussia, which would cede its lands west of the Oder, namely Brandenburg (including Berlin), and part of Silesia. These territories would be divided between the king of Westphalia (Napoleon's brother Jerome) and the king of Saxony, vassals of the French emperor. In this way Prussia would be entirely under Russia's sway. Napoleon would agree to cancel the British provision in the Treaty of Tilsit, his only wish now being that a general peace should reign. Russia would be satisfied, as the Polish question and the matter of Russia's participation in the economic blockade of England were the reasons for the war the year before. Napoleon begged the tsar to meet him halfway and come to terms with him before he again would have to go to war against him and defeat him. He was offering him an honourable way out and suitable terms to Prussia, along with the neutralisation of Austria.

The tsar refused to see Caulaincourt. This was on 18 May. Already on the 7th Alexander had assured Cathcart, the British officer at his headquarters, that he was determined to carry on the war and that the game of mediation being played by Austria was only meant to buy time: 'Austria will wear the cloak of mediation till the time her immense force is ready to act, at the end of the month. An Austrian envoy is hourly expected here: he will bring proposals of terms of peace and similar ones will be sent to the French head-quarters. Receiving and refusing these proposals will occupy most of the time.'

The Austrian envoy was Stadion, the minister of war in 1809. He arrived at allied headquarters and met Nesselrode and Hardenberg. Stadion declared that Austria had the status of an armed mediator, meaning that it was still neutral and trying to bridge the gap between the parties but was itself liable to become a belligerent at some stage. Stadion laid out the terms he was going to propose to the rival parties: the Grand Duchy of Warsaw would be dismantled and Napoleon would cede the provinces beyond the Rhine (Holland, Oldenburg and the cities of the Hanseatic League) and give up his protection of the Confederation of the Rhine; Prussia would again be established as an independent state; Illyria would be ceded to Austria and boundary adjustments would be made between itself and Bavaria. The real meaning of these proposals was the end of the French empire, but they did not touch the boundaries of France itself. The deliberations were concluded on 16 May with a declaration by Stadion's opposite numbers that went even further than the Austrians themselves.

The envoy who presented himself at French headquarters to make known the peace terms was Count Bubna, an experienced Austrian diplomat who knew his hosts well. His task was far more difficult than his colleague Stadion's. The emperor spent many hours closeted in talks with him and Bubna spoke to him earnestly: a general peace will only be attained if France relinquishes the greater part of its empire. If Napoleon takes this step, England will join the process and compensate him for his loss of territory in Europe, because if it does not do so it will feel cut off and isolated from the Continent. When he laid out Austria's ideas he neglected to mention explicitly the matter of Bavaria's borders and the Confederation of the Rhine but was quite forthright in making it clear that Austria was prepared to go to war to realise its demands.

Napoleon concluded immediately that Austria was in league with his enemies. In a letter to the Austrian emperor he assured him that all he desired was peace and that he was all for convening a peace congress with the participation of Austria, Britain, Russia, Prussia and France. He wanted to strengthen the impression that he was seeking a general peace and thus added that he was even prepared to invite to this peace congress the Spanish rebels, though he was not prepared to be humiliated by the British: 'I am ready to die at the head of all high-spirited Frenchmen, rather than become the sport of England.'

The Austrians were quite take aback by Napoleon's harsh words but still did not completely rule out the possibility of acting as a mediator between the sides. They knew about Eugene's posting to Italy and of the French emperor's attempts to reach a separate arrangement with the Russian tsar. Austria's inclination to participate in the war on the side of the allies was strengthened. Now Napoleon too understood that there was no avoiding another battle.

The French crossed the Elbe on 11 May. Though the allies had destroyed Dresden's bridges they did nothing else to impede the crossing. The French laid a bridge at Brieznitz, at the southern end of the bend in the river that surrounded Dresden on three sides. Strong artillery covered the engineering work and when the bridge was up the troops began to cross the river. Ney too crossed the river on that same day, at the captured town of Torgau. The number of troops crossing on the 11th reached 115,000 – 70,000 at Dresden and 45,000 at Torgau.

On the day of the crossing Napoleon was quite tense. Even though he had not yet formulated his operational plans he felt he had to advance rapidly and urged his troops on. The allies mainly tried to delay the crossing with their cannon. Napoleon ordered the artillery of the Guard to deal with the problem, and its commander, Drouot, quick and efficient, hastened to open fire, but the hoped-for result did not come. The emperor instantly revealed two of his characteristics in such situations: impatience and tactical intervention in the placement of the batteries. Drouot insisted that there was no better position for his guns and in fact, after a short while, the problem was solved. The head of the French empire and supreme commander of the Grand Army had been trying to position batteries with his own hands!

The crossing of the Elbe at this point contributed to the indecision of the allies. Wittgenstein was convinced that the French were going to move on Berlin and that their activity in Dresden was only a diversion. The real story was Torgau. It should be recalled that Ney was in command of an army of three corps – the III, the V (which Napoleon had already ordered on 4 May to be ready to assist Ney and which had in fact reached him and crossed the river) and the VII, to which the Saxon division with its artillery had been attached as a consequence of the threats against the Saxon king. Therefore Wittgenstein believed that the proper response was to deploy on the Herzberg–Luckau line anchored on the Schwarze Elster and Spree rivers and blocking the way north to the Prussian capital. This deployment was also convenient for an attack against the French forces in the north during their river crossing or while they made their dispositions after the crossing.

The tsar wanted to hear nothing of this plan, which amounted to abandoning the main Russian line of communications and operations going through Bautzen. Wittgenstein made his dispositions in accordance with the tsar's wishes. He gave the Russians the principal axis, designating the Bishofswerda area for their deployment, and placed the Prussians in the sector around Königsbruck, some 25 kilometres north of the Russians. If his fears materialised and it turned out that the French were headed for Berlin, he could still attack the French flank under Ney's command, but if Napoleon's goal was Silesia he would retreat to Bautzen. Confronting the enemy in that region would naturally push neighbouring Austria into actively joining its natural allies.

Napoleon too tried to guess the intentions of the allies, mainly of the Prussians. For Berlin had fired his imagination from the beginning of the campaign. The division of his forces into two armies and the designation of their positions had been meant to create a serious dilemma for his enemies and heighten the conflict of interests among them. The emperor wrote to Ney: 'I do not see clearly what the Prussians have done; it is certain that the Russians are retiring on Breslau; but the Prussians, are they retiring on that town, as it is said, or have they thrown themselves towards Berlin to defend their capital, as seems natural? You must feel that, with the considerable forces you have, it is not a case for remaining quiet. To occupy Berlin (so as to put the prince of Eckmuhl [Davout] in a position to take Hamburg and advance into Pomerania) and to gain possession of Breslau myself, those are the three important projects which I propose to myself, and which I should wish to accomplish within the month. In the position which I am going to make you take, we shall always be united, able to move right or left with the maximum masses possible, according to information received.' Wittgenstein guessed well, but not everything. It was going to be Berlin and Silesia. In this concept of Napoleon's there can be seen both the intelligent exploitation of numerical superiority and a choice of objectives embracing clear-cut political aims. It would seem that the words 'we shall always be united' were somewhat exaggerated, as the distance between Napoleon and Ney was about 80 kilometres. However, the terrain was good and determined marching, if the need arose, could reduce the distance in a relatively short time.

The orders received by Ney before 16 May called for deployment from Dahme and Schönwald to Dobrilugk while Ney himself, with the III Corps, would be stationed at Luckau.

Already on 12 May Wittgenstein overcame his indecision and ordered a general retreat behind Bautzen. Miloradowitz was again assigned to the rearguard and fought holding actions against Macdonald in the Weissig–Schmiedelfeld sector. Kleist's Prussians clashed with Bertrand, who was advancing north-east towards Königsbruck, and retreated to Kamenz. Marmont advanced in the same direction and attacked along the Reichenberg–Radeburg–Marienstern line. Napoleon's army was now moving energetically along three lines of advance leading to Bautzen and the area north of it. On 15 May all allied forces were across the Spree. The holding actions were broken off and the French advance geared itself to the coming battle, which might prove decisive. Napoleon too was no longer in doubt – the enemy was retreating to Bautzen. Frederick William, who had had misgivings about the division of the army, gave up on the idea of a large-scale defence of Berlin and Brandenburg and gave the assignment to Bülow's corps, which numbered 30,000 men. With his forces spread out along part of the Elbe and a longer section of the Saale in the sector between Magdeburg and Halle, Bülow was ordered to concentrate in the Rosslau area and secure the routes to the Prussian capital.

Wittgenstein, after being out all day examining the ground, took part in a night-time council with the sovereigns. They were thinking in terms of a line extending from the wooded ridges south of Bautzen and near the Bohemian border to the Hoyerswerda road. The right flank would command the high open ground to the west, across the Spree, from Bautzen north. This line of thinking with regard to the right wing derived from the basic fact of relative strengths – allied superiority in cavalry. The left flank would take full advantage of the ground and not need a large number of forces. From the right flank it would be relatively easy to mount an attack. Allied forces in this sector numbered 105,000 men after Barclay de Tolly's corps linked up with them upon the surrender of Thorn. As mentioned, Bülow was at Berlin.

Napoleon was eager for battle. His objectives seemed clear and, more important, obtainable. The allies had not divided their forces as he had hoped they would, but he still had a clear-cut advantage in numbers. The corps in the process of formation had been completed and joined Ney and himself in accordance with the organisation of forces determined by him. On 15 May, his force numbered over 200,000 men and he had around 80 batteries of artillery. Ney's army stood at 85,000 and included the III, V, VII and II Corps (the latter joining Ney at Torgau after completion), one division from the I Cavalry Corps, which was attached to Lauriston, and Sebastiani's II Cavalry Corps. Napoleon's army numbered a little less than 120,000 men and included the IV, VI, XI and XII Corps along with the Guard divisions and the I Cavalry Corps (less one division) Davout's I Corps, it will be remembered, was fighting at Hamburg.

Logistically, the French army was organised as follows: a logistic centre at Dresden served Napoleon's southern army and a logistic centre at Torgau served Ney's northern army. Dresden was the advance administrative base for the whole army. The main line of supply ran from Mainz through Frankfort, Erfurt and Weimar and from there split into one leading to Dresden (via Jena and Altenburg) and one to Leipzig (via Naumburg). Leipzig was the logistic base for the cavalry units.

After two or three days of vacillation Napoleon understood that if he wished to bring on a decisive battle, which had been denied him at Lützen (and he had wanted it with all his heart), he would have to concentrate all his forces. His orders to the army under his direct command were clear and consistent. It was moving in three columns across a 25-kilometre front opposite the enemy at Bautzen: Macdonald on the right, Bertrand on the left and Marmont in the centre. At this stage Oudinot's XII Corps was in reserve at Bishofswerda with the assignment of cleaning out the wooded area south of the Dresden–Bautzen axis up to Austrian Bohemia less than 20 kilometres away. The I Cavalry Corps and a division of the Imperial Guard were to operate north of the army and secure communications with Ney's army. This force, under Mortier, was assigned among other things the task of dealing with the Cossack units operating in the Königsbruck–Grossenhain sector and in fact did clash with these raiders, driving them back to Elsterwerda on the Schwarze Elster. On 17 May it linked up with Lauriston, who was advancing on Ney's southern flank.

Napoleon's orders to Ney still did not reflect his policy of concentrating forces and he was now going to pay the price of his indecision of the past few days. The orders issued to Ney before the 16th called for deployment as far north as possible with a serious feint towards Berlin. Now his desire to concentrate caused him to change his orders from one extreme to the other within less than two days. Some students are convinced that Napoleon and his chief of staff, Berthier, simply forgot what they had ordered a short while back and no staff officer thought of adding a sentence to the new orders cancelling the previous ones. It would seem that we have before us a phenomenon typical of a staff overloaded with work and afraid of its supreme commander.

And this is what took place: the orders received by Ney in the evening hours of 16 May directed him to move from Herzberg to Spremberg on the Spree. But Ney had already acted on previous orders and was at Luckau, more than 50 kilometres from Spremberg. However, this was not the only change in Ney's orders that day. The movement south east to the Spree was longer than the one on the alternative route leading directly to Hoyerswerda. Napoleon's choice of the first derived from his fear that such a large-scale movement on the Bautzen highway via Hoyerswerda would frighten the allies into retreating farther into Silesia. If they did, Napoleon would miss his chance to join battle in the place he had chosen to fight a decisive action. French intelligence reported to the emperor during the day that there were growing signs that the enemy had decided to make his stand at Bautzen. Accordingly, new orders were issued in the afternoon hours of the 16th which directed Ney to get to Hoyerswerda as quickly as possible. The truth was that Ney had begun advancing on the Hoyerswerda axis even before he received the order to do so. He did so on the advice of his chief of staff, Jomini. The orders for Lauriston, also received during the evening, directed him to move his corps from Dobrilugk to Hoyerswerda. For a change, these orders were consistent, as Lauriston was indeed in Dobrilugk. In the end the French would concentrate two corps at Hoyerswerda in the space of two days.

The main and most serious confusion concerned the II and VII Corps under the command of Victor and Reynier. The emperor had intended to assign Victor the task of attacking Bülow at Brandenburg, including Berlin of course, with a force encompassing the corps of Reynier and Sebastiani in addition to his own. But the orders received by Ney in the evening of the 16th did not mention this. Moreover, the orders did not specify which units were to move to Spremberg. On the advice of his chief of staff, Ney decided to move all his corps there, with the exception of Lauriston's. The sensible Jomini seems to have believed that when all was said and done Bülow would not have to fight for Berlin and that what was required now was to adopt the principle of concentration of forces. However, in the afternoon orders of the 16th, which Ney received the next morning, Victor's corps was explicitly directed to march to Berlin, capture the city and destroy Bülow's force. In the part of the orders referring to Ney himself, his corps (in the singular) was spoken of and there seemed to be no reason for further misunderstandings. Ney halted Reynier at Luckau and ordered Victor to change direction and take Berlin, specifying his order of battle. Victor, who was in the rear, began moving rapidly towards Dahme. While Ney was writing out his orders, Napoleon reconsidered – he had bedded down for the night on the Bautzen highway and naturally reflected on the coming battle – and in the morning sent out new orders along the lines of Jomini's thinking: Victor and Reynier were also to arrive at Hoyerswerda and link up with Ney. Berthier, who drafted the orders, wrote: 'Everything leads to the belief that we are going to have a battle.' For the second time in two weeks the emperor awakened from his visions of Berlin, but this time the result was that one corps arrived in the area of the battle a day late and one did not get there at all. Thus 25,000 men were subtracted from Ney's army and did not take part in a battle that was meant to be decisive. Ney hastened to forward his new orders and directed the two corps to advance rapidly towards Bautzen by the Kahlau–Hoyerswerda route.

If Napoleon had had a general staff that was more independent, always developing ideas inspired by the strategy of the supreme commander, it is conceivable that the failure of command described above would have been avoided. This kind of general staff can be counted on to refrain from hastily sending out orders before the commander makes his final decisions. Berthier had been serving under Napoleon almost from the beginning of the emperor's military career. He had been appointed chief of staff during the Italian campaign of 1796, knew the emperor well and knew how to read his thoughts, but he never dared to make decisions himself. Caulaincourt criticised him harshly in his memoirs on this point, stating that though he always knew what his chief was thinking and knew his plans, he avoided making decisions. In 1806 Napoleon had told Berthier always to follow his orders: 'I alone know what I have to do.' In the same spirit Berthier told Ney that the emperor did not require advice and that 'our duty is to obey'. It is small wonder then that this is what the supreme commander got from his chief of staff. It should also be remembered that in the age of courier communication, orders would reach their destination hours after they were written and in the meanwhile forces would have changed position. Failures such as the one described are quite typical of overworked headquarters operating under pressure. Similar mix-ups have occurred in many wars and large forces have been moved great distances before having to be turned back without carrying out their main assignment. All commanding officers who have had this experience can console themselves with the thought that this also happened to a military genius like Napoleon.

On 18 May the French army was advancing along the routes leading to Bautzen in an impressive movement over the long distance from the west to the north. Lauriston arrived at Hoyerswerda with his advance units while the units closing up the rear were at Sorne and Senftenberg on the Schwarze Elster. The orders drafted for Ney in the morning already outlined Napoleon's battle plan and timetable. The orders made the basic assumption that Ney's corps would all be at Hoyerswerda on 19 May and move south, reaching the eastern side of the Spree in the Drehsa area on the 21st. The orders spoke explicitly of 'all your forces united', indicating that the lessons of the past few days had been learned. Nevertheless, as already mentioned, there was no chance that 'all the forces' would actually get there. The orders also indicated the general disposition of enemy forces at Bautzen – the Prussians on the right and the Russians on the left. They also said that, 'having passed the Spree you will find that you have turned the enemy's position; you will take up a good position there, which will either have the effect of making the enemy retire farther, or of putting you in a position to attack him with advantage.'

The staff officer sent to deliver Ney's orders of the 18th noticed on the morning of the 19th a large enemy force moving towards Hoyerswerda. He reported this to Lauriston, who decided to halt in the Maukendorf–Wittichenau sector south of Hoyerswerda and await Ney's orders. The day before Ney had ordered Lauriston to move south, west of the Schwarze Elster, in the area between Zerna and Neudorf. It is clear the Ney was convinced that the allies were deployed west of the Spree. He intended to reach Marienstern with Lauriston and then advance east to the Spree shoulder to shoulder with the emperor on both sides of Bautzen. The new orders made it clear that his assumption was incorrect and he therefore changed his previous orders immediately: Lauriston would advance to Opitz and Lipitsh on the eastern side of the Schwarze Elster in order to reach Drehsa. The III Corps would move south along the river towards Königswartha and Neudorf.

The force that Berthier's courier spotted in the morning was Barclay's corps just about to attack Lauriston on the march. From dispatches that had fallen into their hands the allies had learned of the French advance from the north. Allied headquarters had concluded that this force was aiming to link up with the emperor and together with him mount a broad frontal attack. Wittgenstein ordered Barclay to make the flank attack on the lead corps of the French and assured him that when he heard his gunfire the French on the Bautzen front to their left would be attacked. Cathcart, who was in a position to listen in on the table talk at allied headquarters, wrote that the whole idea was cooked up to make it possible for Barclay, who had spent so much time on the siege of Thorn, 'to do something'. Von Cäemmerer asserted that no preparations were made for the promised attack opposite Bautzen and that the idea was 'nonsense'.

Barclay, who had marched the whole night in two columns, happened to run into Bertrand's lead division in the Königswartha area and attacked it in the afternoon with very good results. The Italian troops of the French division were not noted for their fighting spirit and were roughly handled. The pursuit was also carried out energetically. The pursuers got as far north as Wartha but were somehow blocked there, allowing the Italians to escape. Barclay was convinced that the division he had attacked belonged to Lauriston's corps. Together with Yorck's Prussian force, which was under his command, he made dispositions to delay and block the French along their lines of advance in the sector running from the Spree to Weissig. These dispositions existed more in his mind than on the ground. Now the intentions of the French were clearer to Wittgenstein and his masters, and Barclay and Yorck were recalled to take their place in the main allied line.

This operation, which so fires the imagination, was quite hastily conceived and the expression 'more luck than sense' is appropriate here. Wittgenstein had sent a large part of the forces at his disposal against Ney and exposed his main position – especially his right wing – to Napoleon's main army. Allied forces were not only inferior in number but spread on a very wide front. Now there opened before the French emperor the possibility of a concentrated attack on a narrow front, which could have smashed the allies to pieces. All's well that ends well. The detached force quickly returned to the front to reinforce the thin line of defence.

On the same day, 19 May, there was little operational activity in Napoleon's sector. His forces were deployed along the entire breadth of the front and were just a few kilometres from the enemy at their centre. The emperor was in the Godau–Klein-Förstchen area with the Guard; the IV Corps, on the left flank, was advancing between the Schwarze Elster and the Spree; the VI Corps was moving between the IV Corps and the Dresden axis; the XI Corps was parallel to it, south of the Dresden axis; the XII Corps was advancing from still farther south. The assignments for the day were mostly to carry out reconnaissance to get a better picture of enemy positions and to complete dispositions for the coming battle.

The region between Dresden and Bautzen slopes down from the southern mountains – the ridges of the Lausitzer Mountains – bordering Bohemia. This is the south-eastern part of Saxony, draining the mountain region and dropping to the north. The land around Bautzen is hilly. The region where the events of the waning days of May 1813 took place is spread out between the Elbe and the Spree. The Schwarze Elster flows through its centre. The Spree flows from south to north, bypassing Berlin and uniting with the Havel River not far from it. The Schwarze Elster flows in a south–north direction up to Hoyerswerda and then in a west–north-west direction until it empties into the Elbe not far from Wittenberg. The area neighbouring Bautzen is flatter, and not for the most part hilly, becoming rutted and marshy as one goes north. Numerous streams flow through it on their way to the Spree.

On the eve of 20 May the two armies were arrayed on the two sides of the Spree from Doberschau, south of Bautzen, to Klix, along a front about 20 kilometres wide. In the southern sector, from Öenna to Bautzen, and from there to Doberschau, the banks of the river were fairly steep and therefore fording points had to be chosen carefully. In the sector starting at Doberschau the river was calmer and the banks were lower, but the many streams in the area were also a real obstacle to infantry. The high hills here, Gottlobsberg and Kiefernberg, rise south of Niedergurig. At their foot a road runs from Bautzen north, crossing the Spree via a bridge south of Niedergurig and linking up, much farther north, with the Hoyerswerda highway. Another waterway coming into play in the assessment of the terrain should be mentioned – the Blossauer-Wasser, running parallel to the Spree two or three kilometres away and emptying into it near Lomischau. Its importance in terms of terrain is connected with the marshy nature of the adjoining area, mainly to the east, more than with its mere presence as a body of water. The sector north of the Bautzen–Würschen axis is convenient for cavalry action but the streams are only passable for horses on bridges or at well-guarded fords.

In the centre of the area, above the plain, there rises a group of hills – the Kreckwitz Heights, north of the village of Kreckwitz. North of these heights the land is quite level, though here and there one can find knolls. The knolls worthy of note are located between the villages of Malschütz and Glein and the most prominent of them is the windmill knoll south-west of Glein.

Two roads lead from Bautzen to Görlitz and from there east into Silesia via Breslau. One is the highway running through Hochkirch and Lobau and the other is the road running through Würschen north of the highway. Another route worth mentioning leads from Bautzen to the north-east, passing through Drehsa and continuing in the same direction up to the Neisse River. The whole area is dotted with wooded land, especially on the banks of the river and streams and on the slopes of the hills and ridges.

A major landmark in the area is the Hochkirch church, rising above its surroundings and visible from almost anywhere in the neighbourhood. Here the Prussian army of Frederick the Great was defeated by the Austrians in October 1758 after being surrounded on all sides, only getting away by the skin of its teeth thanks to its cavalry. The town of Bautzen is surrounded by an ancient wall and is also protected on the west by the Spree, which is deep and steep-banked there. The course of the river to the foothills of the town forced the troops defending it to move a certain distance to the east of Bautzen. The town itself was well fortified. As it was surrounded by mountains on almost every side, it represented a problematic salient in the centre of the left-hand sector of the allies.

In the past week most of the allied army had been able to rest from marching and fighting. This was a chance to reorganise and to set up field-works. The engineering units utilised the earthen embankments remaining from the Seven Years War, adding ramparts, mainly for the artillery. An assessment of ground conditions led to the conclusion that it was best not to come up too close to the Spree. Around Bautzen this was because of advantages in terrain and the need to hold vital areas as well as because of the length of the line relative to the forces available, and to the north because of the flatness of the land and the many waterways. It was therefore decided to deploy in positions parallel to the river and three to four kilometres from it, behind the Blossauer-Wasser. This line extended across high ground falling off from the Lausitzer Mountains to the Bautzen–Würschen axis. From there, along level ground, the line of defence would be advanced to the river and occupy the commanding knolls and hills along with the villages and farm-houses in the plain.

The Russians were on the left flank. Their left extended to the Drohmberg and Schmoritzberg hills. This southern sector enjoyed a commanding height, about 350 metres above the river, and the advantage of concealment in the forests, groves and villages. To the north the Russian line was supported by embankments and fortifications from behind which artillery could do good work. The vital areas were at Melteuer, at Rabitz, between the Bautzen–Hochkirch axis (at Jenkwitz) and Baschütz, and from there to the south of Litten.

Miloradowitz with 15,000 troops was the forward element in the front and held the first line of defence, from Doberschau to Burk. He was ordered to impede the French crossing of the Spree as much as possible. Were the enemy to overpower him, he was authorised to withdraw to the left of the Russians, from the Görlitz road in the Klein Jenkwitz area to Auritz and the wooded area.

The main Russian position, under the command of Gortchakow, with strong artillery, was based on the Rieschen–Jenkwitz–Baschütz line. An infantry reserve was positioned about two kilometres to the rear, south of Canitz-Christina. This central position was manned by 35,000 men including the reserve. It was an extremely strong position, both because of the nature of the ground and the large number of defenders.

The right wing, mainly in the plain, was manned by the Prussians. Most of Blücher's 23,000 men occupied the low-lying hills in the Kreckwitz area, including the Kreckwitz Heights. The defence of his northern sector was made easier by the difficult terrain – the marshes and bodies of water. It included the villages of Plieskowitz and Malschütz. Barclay and Yorck, who had operated together in the northern expedition and had come back to be incorporated into the general line of defence, were deployed in a kind of reverse arc in the sector extending from Klix to Preititz. Yorck was ordered to defend the fords of the Blossauer-Wasser and the marshlands. Barclay, whose position was centred in Glein, was designated to support the two flanks as well as the point of contact between them. Kleist, whose corps was half Russian and half Prussian, about 5,500 men, was positioned to the left of Blücher, with the assignment of preventing the crossing of the Spree in his sector and authorisation to withdraw to the Basankwitz–Nieder Kaina sector. The Prussian Guard was designated as a reserve in the Drehsa area, in the northern sector. The headquarters of the Russian tsar were at Pürschwitz and the headquarters of Frederick William at Würschen.

Allied dispositions and the forecast of French operations were based on very reasonable expectations. The French were expected to attack from the Dresden line. Gneisenau also anticipated an attack from the north, but no one was listening as yet. The basic idea of the plan was to stop the French in their centre and on their right and to counter-attack on their left. The preliminary orders for the counter-attack were sent to Barclay and Kleist: if the enemy attacked in the centre he was to be attacked on the left; if he attacked the left flank he was to be driven towards the mountain region. No orders were issued taking into account a French attack from the north. The thinking of the general staff about this possibility was vague and unfocused: Blücher would extend his forces to Drehsa, the Russian lancers and the Prussian cavalry reserve would be put into action and Gortchakov would extend his forces to Kreckwitz.

It would not be correct to attribute the erroneous allied assessment of Napoleon's plan of attack to pigheadedness and a lack of military understanding. Unquestionably the disregard of the possibility of an attack along two axes, from the west and the north, shows a limited imagination, but Napoleon had made every effort to deceive his enemy into believing that his attack would be frontal, from west to east. In the orders of 18 May sent to Ney, where the movement of all his forces was spoken of – with the emphasis on 'all' – it was intended that the movement would indeed create a definite impression that the two armies were going to link up for an all-out frontal attack. The movement east to the Spree set forth in the orders was meant to occur in the final stage of the advance and lead to an attack from the north as well.

Napoleon's plan, excluding the brilliant two-pronged attack, was very simple. It was determined by ground conditions and relative strengths. It required one more day for Ney to reach his designated position north of the battlefield. Therefore Napoleon would attack with his army on the Bautzen front using his favourite tactic – attack at all points with effective artillery support, pushing back the enemy or at worst pinning him down until the decisive blow can be delivered. Ney's northern attack was founded on sound principles of aggressive warfare – a movement outflanking the entire front, assault from the rear, surprise and deception. It was also a suitable answer to the possibility that the operations on the right flank would play into the hands of the allies, who may have preferred that the French become engaged on the Spree in the initial stage, near Bautzen. Then the allied army would hit its flank from the direction of the Blossauer-Wasser. In that case, Ney's move would be a thing of beauty.

The forces and assignments in the 20 May battle were determined by the positions of the corps on the Spree front, which were a function of their lines of advance on either side of the road leading from Dresden. Bertrand and Latour-Maubourg were to attack Blücher in the sector opposite Niedergurig, Marmont and Macdonald from the two sides of Bautzen, Oudinot, who was south of the highway, in the Singwitz sector. Maude was convinced that Napoleon wanted his forces on the right flank to engage the Russians as quickly as possible in order to forestall their retreat. This conviction derived from Maude's experience in the Russian campaign of the previous year.

The orders Napoleon gave for the placement of his artillery in the first stages of the battle were typical of him. It would remain on the left bank of the Spree until the battle was decided so that not a single gun would be lost in a retreat back across the river if, God forbid, the French were bested. This cautionary note aside, he was bursting with self-confidence, to the point of arrogance. When he was told during a reconnaissance outing before the battle that Frederick the Great had taken the position they were looking at, he replied: 'That may be, but Frederick is not here now.'

The battle of Bautzen lasted two days, 20–21 May. And these are the few lines that might be written about it in the journal of war history: some time after noon on 20 May the French crossed the Spree and attacked the allies on both sides of Bautzen. At nightfall Bautzen and its environs were in French hands and the Russian left flank was in a perilous situation. On the 21st, Napoleon mounted a co-ordinated attack along two vertical axes. By evening the Russian left wing had been cleared out. On the allied right wing Ney came down from the north, bypassed Blücher and attacked Barclay, who had already arrived at Preititz shortly after noon. The town fell into Blücher's hands in the wake of his counter-attack. Napoleon unleashed his centre and attacked the Prussians in strength and at the same time Ney retook Preititz with the big force that had been gathering around him during the day and forced Blücher to retreat. Ney was unable to keep up the pressure and Blücher was saved from the predicament he found himself in. Towards evening the French were in the midst of a general advance and the allies had withdrawn from the entire battlefield and were arrayed on both sides of the Görlitz road, from the Spree to Weissenberg. The retreat was carried out in good order, leaving little booty for the French. Napoleon had again gained a victory but this time too it was not decisive.

On 20 May Ney was at Königswartha, at about 15 kilometres from the assembly areas near the area where the enemy was deployed – at Klix and Leichenam – on the northern edge of the mooted battlefield. Napoleon had defined the objectives of the 20th as follows: to pin down the enemy in his positions so that he would not be able to impede Ney's advance and to drive the enemy out of his forward positions in the sector opposite the main French force. At 8 a.m., on a hill opposite Bautzen, Napoleon ordered Oudinot to cross the river and attack the extreme left of the Russian left flank; Macdonald was ordered to take bridges north of Bautzen, and Marmont to take two bridges north of Macdonald.

At around noon the sign was given and the artillery opened fire. Within a few hours, with the Imperial Guard behind him, Macdonald occupied three bridges and ordered two more to be set up. Oudinot crossed the river on a bridge and at a ford at Singwitz and pushed back the Russian infantry until a Russian cavalry force came up and pushed him back. One of his divisions occupied the Drohmberg and Schmoritzberg ridges and thus commanded the area south of the battlefield. Another of his divisions took Doberschau and

Strehla. Marmont operated from the Öenna area, crossing the river under heavy artillery fire and penetrating into the city from the north-west at 3 p.m.

Miloradowitz, who had been attacked across his entire front, took stock of his situation: Oudinot on his left was threatening to cut him off from his main line of defence and Macdonald and Marmont were pouring into the city. He ordered a general withdrawal from his forward line to the positions prepared in advance three or four kilometres to the east. Even though his order was in line with the original plan there is evidence that the move did not please general headquarters.

Simultaneously Bertrand attacked Kleist at the juncture between the Russians and the Prussians. He crossed the Spree in the area of the Gottlobsberg hills and Niedergurig and paid a heavy price. Prussian resistance was stubborn and determined. Only a small number of French managed to get across the river by the early hours of evening. Kleist also stood firm against Marmont's left division, which attacked Burk Hill, but in the end could not withstand the superior French forces and when they crossed the Blossauer-Wasser at Basankwitz withdrew his troops to Litten as planned. None the less, the operations of Bertrand's corps had been greatly disrupted.

At the end of 20 May, the situation in the sector occupied by Napoleon's army was as follows: only part of the IV Corps was on the eastern side of the Spree, near the Bautzen–Gottau road. Napoleon had sent Soult to this sector before the battle began, authorising him to assume command over Bertrand (it will be remembered that Marshal Soult had fought in Spain from the end of 1808, joining the emperor after the death of Bessières; it was he whom the emperor after Austerlitz called the best tactician in Europe!) The VI Corps was deployed from the Hochkirch road (Nadelwitz had been captured in the afternoon) to the north-east up to Basankwitz via Nieder Kaina. The XI Corps had reached the Rabitz hills. The XII Corps, which had advanced the farthest on the right, southern flank of the French, had to fight the Russian reserve sent up against it and blocked its advance toward the vital Melteuer and Pielitz area. Oudinot passed the night on the Blossauer-Wasser. The Guard and Latour-Maubourg's corps camped east of Bautzen.

The commitment of the reserve in strength against Oudinot's corps at this early stage shows how jumpy the allies were with regard to Napoleon's intentions in the southern sector. It was the Russian tsar, afraid that Napoleon was aiming to cut the allied army off from the Austrians in Bohemia, who sent the reserve in. This was an overreaction, in view of the real plan of the emperor, whose every thought was turned to Ney and the possibility of finally achieving a decisive victory at Bautzen. However, it is possible to understand the tsar's strong reaction, given the importance attached to Austria by all of the belligerents and the reasonable assumption that Napoleon was aiming to strengthen his hold on the border area.

Ney's orders for the 20th instructed him to reach Klix and cross the Spree. During the day he advanced to Brehmen, skirmishing with Cossack units but not impeded by them. His III Corps went into camp along the Sdier road and his forward units made contact with Barclay's outposts at Klix; Lauriston was at Särchen, near Ney; Reynier was at Hoyerswerda, Victor far to the rear at Senftenberg. Reynier and Victor were too far away, to the emperor's disappointment, and we know the reasons for their delay.

During the day the allies acted in accordance with their original assessment of the situation: they stubbornly resisted the attack on their left and centre; their forward units withdrew to the agreed line extending Gortchakow's sector and Kleist extended Blücher's line. The only action that was out of the ordinary in terms of the overall fighting was the commitment of the Russian reserve on the slopes of the southern hills.

Napoleon achieved what he had set out do in the 20 May fighting. The Spree was behind him and the allied general staff had not been able to organise a counter-attack during the crossing; had it done so, it would have made things very difficult for him. It is conceivable that he chose to mount his attack late in the day expressly to prevent this, as such an operation requires daylight. The imperial bulletin of the same day was meant to emphasise that the battle of the 20th was a preliminary encounter, which could be called 'the battle of Bautzen', and was in fact the prelude to 'the battle of Würschen', which would take place the next day. During the night the last of the French troops crossed the Spree, aside from the IV Corps, which was still behind schedule. At 9 p.m. Napoleon returned to his headquarters at Bautzen in soaring spirits and spent the whole night with Berthier and other officers making preparations for the next day's fighting. At 11 p.m. he received a note from Bertrand confirming that contact had been made with Ney as desired.

At the headquarters of the tsar and the king of Prussia, at Pürschwitz and Würschen, councils of war were convened in a calm, confident atmosphere characterised by the feeling that everything was under control. According to battlefield reports, the enemy had suffered heavy losses, weakening him considerably for the next day's battle. It was still believed that the attack of the 20th had represented the main effort of the French, while too little importance was attached to the French effort in the northern sector.

Since history holds Marshal Ney responsible for the missed opportunity of the battle of 21 May, it is worth describing in some detail the orders and instructions Ney received and his response to them. In this way we shall be better able to judge the accepted view of the brave marshal's shortsightedness.

As mentioned, the orders of the 18th called for Ney to be on the eastern side of the Spree on the 21st, in the area of Drehsa. Berthier drafted another order on the 20th, which was sent off in the afternoon. Ney was ordered to drive the enemy out of Drehsa and advance toward Weissenberg. At the same hour the first troops of Ney's army were beginning to cross the Spree in the Klix area. Ney read: 'The emperor orders, Prince, that you should direct yourself on Drehsa near Gottamelde, driving the enemy from his position, getting into connection with us, and that from there you should direct yourself on Weissenberg in such a manner to turn the enemy.' This is the place to mention the fact that the name Drehsa appeared twice on the maps: next to Gottau ((i.e. Gottamelde) and south of Würschen. To which was the emperor referring when he dictated the order to Berthier? The emperor, who had studied the battles of Frederick the Great, should have known that Drehsa south was an important position that the Prussian king had been determined to hold when he was fighting in the area in order to cover his advance. It was also located between two roads that were a possible line of retreat for the allies to Görlitz. What is more, Drehsa north was very close to Klix and a self-evident reference point in Ney's line of advance and therefore its mention in Berthier's order strikes students as unlikely, as mentioning it explicitly would deceive Ney into believing that his line of advance was to run parallel to Napoleon's and not as stipulated. There is no question that this was not the intention.

Students are convinced that the emperor said 'Drehsa' and meant the south, expecting Ney to roll the enemy south towards Würschen and Hochkirch (we recall the 'prelude to the battle of Würschen'). Apparently Berthier remembered the northern village, or simply saw its name on the map in the area where Ney was positioned and added Weissenberg on his own to justify explicitly mentioning Drehsa. Jomini, Ney's chief of staff, wrote that Napoleon meant the Drehsa south of Würschen and told his superior that they should attack in the general direction of the Hochkirch spire, which was visible from the distance. The major weakness of this version of things is that to be at Drehsa on the 21st Ney had to fight his way there, which is not mentioned in the order. Incidentally, Count Yorck too wrote that Napoleon meant Drehsa 'in the rear of the allies'. Berthier's defenders, and they are not lacking, naturally point to Berthier's reluctance to interpret Napoleon's orders and instructions.

In any event, the order of the 20th caused Ney understandable bewilderment and was of course debated at headquarters. Ney deserves better: it is easy to peruse documents in a reading room and draw up historical analogies, giving convoluted meanings to an order that is meant to be clear and simple. At the same time, it is no simple thing to get to the bottom of an ambiguous order under field conditions after being in a hard saddle all day and with no way to clarify anything except through couriers bringing back answers hours later. Moreover, it is easy to be a chief of staff who is cleverer and more learned than a rough-hewn officer on whom all responsibility rests and who cares not a whit about the exploits of Frederick the Great. In the end, before dawn, the perplexed Ney chose the route of clarification, a courier, one of his officers, the 15 kilometres to Napoleon's headquarters, which he reached in three hours, arriving after 7 a.m. Ney wrote: 'The troops are ordered to be ready to march tomorrow morning by way of Baruth on Weissenberg. I desire to know the intention of Your Majesty, whether you approve my movement or prescribe me a new direction. As the cannonade and fusillade begin again in the direction of Hochkirch and Bautzen, I will not make the movement on Weissenberg until I receive the orders.' There can be no question that during the night Ney was torn between military logic and discipline. There can also be no question that Napoleon and his staff, or perhaps both, did not act in this matter in the spirit of the emperor's rule: 'Be clear and all the rest will follow.'

The emperor himself briefed Ney's officer. He pointed out the positions of the allied army and explained the disposition of forces. The courier was sent back to his superior with a note with the following clarification: 'The intention of the emperor is that you should follow constantly the movement of the enemy. His Majesty has shown your staff officer the positions of the enemy, which are defined by the redoubts which he has constructed and occupies. The intention of the emperor is that you should be this morning at 11 o'clock at the village of Preititz. You will be on the extreme right of the enemy. As soon as the emperor sees you engaged at Preititz we shall attack vigorously at all points. Cause General Lauriston to march on your left so as to be in a position to turn the enemy if your movement decides him to abandon his position.' A copy of this order was sent to Soult, who was with Bertrand, with the additional instruction 'to attack the enemy vigorously with three divisions advancing between Marmont and Ney'. At this point, Drehsa no longer interested Napoleon, who was apparently not aware of the confusion his previous order had caused.

The wait for new orders did not change Ney's morning timetable and the crossing of the Spree in his sector commenced before 5 a.m. Lauriston crossed at Klix, turning the Russian line in the direction of Leichenam and marching from there towards Drehsa and Gottau. Ney ordered him to continue advancing along the Baruth axis and to send one of Lauriston's divisions to Malschütz to cover his right. Ney himself, together with three divisions from his own III Corps, marched south-east towards the windmill near Glein. Barclay was pushed aside there with little resistance and withdrew to Preititz. It was 10 a.m. At that moment, beside the windmill, Ney received Berthier's note, which according to witnesses had been hastily scribbled. Jomini, who was convinced that his position in the night-time deliberations was being confirmed and naturally overjoyed that history was repeating itself, added in his own hand: 'Thereafter the march will be directed on the Hochkirch spire.'

Ney, who was accustomed to obeying the emperor's orders to the letter – and when he did not, did not fail to hear about it – was afraid that he was running ahead of schedule, since he was where he was supposed to be an hour later ('the intention of the Emperor is that you should be this morning at 11 o'clock at the village Preititz'). Therefore he did not heed his chief of staff, who urged him to continue at once to Preititz. It is hard to believe that the emperor intended in his note to fix a precise time for the co-ordinated attack to begin. Mentioning the hour of 11 o'clock was more in the way of a rough estimate and not an agreed hour. It is reasonable to assume that he gave Berthier an approximate hour and the latter quoted it in his note in a firmer way than the emperor intended. Ney also believed that waiting an hour would bring his forces into alignment – Malschütz would be in his hands by then, Lauriston would be at Buchwalde and Reynier with the VII Corps would cut down the distance between them. What is more, the note stated that the emperor would open a vigorous attack when Ney became engaged at Preititz and he expected this at 11 a.m. and not before. Ney therefore decided to wait, both to obey instructions and to get the most out of the vigorous display expected from Napoleon's wing.

The morning of 21 May greeted the emperor pleasantly. There was quiet all around and Napoleon felt that on this summer's day a decision was going to be reached. At 5 a.m. he was already riding towards the front, to a point near

Nieder Kaina in Marmont's sector from where it was possible to look out over the plain of Jenkwitz and Baschütz to the left of the Hochkirsch road. The other rulers too, his foes, were already in the field at that hour, in Gortchakow's sector, and were even observing Napoleon through Lord Cathcart's high-powered fieldglasses, which were better than theirs. According to Cathcart, Napoleon was within range of the Russian batteries and someone even suggested putting them to use, but 'we were too courteous to disturb his meditations by a shot'.

Napoleon's plan for this hour of the morning was to continue pinning down the enemy in his positions until Ney appeared in full strength in the centre of the rear of the battlefield. Then perhaps all forces, including the reserve, would be sent against the enemy, delivering the coup de grâce. Napoleon at his best. Now Oudinot mounted an attack towards Kunitz and Rachlau on one axis and Pielitz and Döhlen on another. On his third line of attack he succeeded in capturing Rieschen. The tsar, in the thrall of his fear of Napoleon's designs for the southern flank, again sent in the Russian reserve and Miloradowitz again pushed back Oudinot, to the Binnewitz hills.

Until 11 a.m. nothing of note occurred on the front and the main action was of the artillery. The French did not exert too much pressure on Blücher in the centre, who was already feeling the threat of Ney in his rear. He was in a strong position in the Kreckwitz sector and his orders were to defend it stubbornly and not give up ground. Marmont's left was exerting some pressure at Basankwitz, but Soult together with Bertrand's corps was still crossing the Spree and not in a position to carry out Napoleon's last order – to attack in strength in the sector between Ney and Marmont. Napoleon did not believe he would be called upon to make important decisions during these morning hours and sank into a deep sleep, a scene immortalised in one of the most famous paintings of his campaigns. Caulaincourt, who spoke of this nap in the field in his memoirs, says that Napoleon was capable of sleeping in any situation and at any time. Before going to sleep, Napoleon said: 'Things should be left to run their course; it will be another two hours before I can strike a blow.' (Abbott, John S.C.: The History of Napoleon Bonaparte, Vol. III, 1855). So he spoke and stretched out on his bearskin, leaning on his right elbow. Given what was happening at just that moment, it might have been a fatal sleep.

While Ney awaited his appointed hour, Blücher responded to Barclay's call for reinforcements and sent troops to Klein Bautzen and Preititz itself. Had

Ney attacked earlier, Blücher would have hesitated to reinforce Barclay with his lines of retreat threatened. At the appointed hour Ney attacked Preititz with just one division, under the command of Souham, and the reinforcements drove it back, though not before it momentarily took the town. Only then did Ney send in three full divisions to capture the position after some fierce, wild fighting.

Bertrand finally completed his crossing of the river early in the afternoon and began to attack the Kreckwitz Heights under a heavy cover of artillery. The strength of the attack caused Blücher to withdraw within this sector to the Doberschütz–Kreckwitz line. Oudinot, who was under considerable pressure from the Russians, got help in the end from Macdonald's right, which attacked opposite Grubditz and in the Binnewitz area. This enabled Oudinot to hold his ground. The clash with the enemy left, though not favoured with great success, did not especially worry Napoleon, who was glad that his right was pinning down the enemy and allowing Ney to fight in his sector against unaided forces. When he was requested to come to Oudinot's assistance he said that a decision was expected at 3 p.m. and until then Oudinot had to hold out as best as he could. To step up the pressure on Blücher, Napoleon sent in a unit of the Imperial Guard to co-operate with Marmont's left and occupied the gap between Nieder Kaina and Kreckwitz in Kleist's sector. He also advanced the rest of the Guard and the cavalry reserve to the rear of Basankwitz.

It was 3 p.m. The tsar had already become convinced that there was real danger on his right and that what was going on there was not a diversion. Now Blücher, who a few hours ago had been bold enough to help Barclay, found that he was being attacked on all sides. Ney was drawn to this sector of Blücher's while waiting for the hour of 11 to arrive and had time to observe the area. This was apparently why he attacked Preititz the first time with just one division. Now he too joined the push against Blücher. The latter was forced to abandon the vital Kreckwitz Heights before the ring closed completely around him. Yorck, who had been previously sent there by Wittgenstein to help, realised that the French had taken the position. The Prussian retreat was conducted in exemplary order and the men were redeployed across the Blossauer-Wasser in the Pürschwitz area.

An orderly retreat was the best thing the allies could hope for now given the overwhelming weight of French numbers on the battlefield. Blücher agreed to withdraw with great reluctance and suffered heavy losses in the retreat. The French poured across the plain. The Guard and Latour-Maubourg's cavalry, at

Nadelwitz, were ordered to move out and take Litten. These veteran soldiers advanced towards the hesitating Blücher's left flank in high spirits and perfect order. At 4 p.m. allied headquarters ordered a general retreat. The Prussian line of retreat was along the Würschen road and the Russian on the Hochkirch road. Barclay was ordered to cover the first stage of the retreat. From the hills of Klein Bautzen, Ney observed the enemy retreating to the rear with hungry eyes. Had he acted sooner he would now have been planted squarely across the enemy's line of retreat and blocked the escaping troops. In his report he wrote with something of self-criticism: 'It was essential to overturn everything in front of me, to touch my right to Your Majesty and to be able to enter into action.' The imperial bulletin of that day may have asserted that 'seeing his right turned, the enemy began his retreat and soon his retreat became a flight', but this was an inaccurate description of the situation. The French lacked cavalry, whose job it was to bring about just this kind of flight. The heavy rain which began to come down towards evening no doubt increased the frustration of the French. Count Yorck summed up the last phase of the battle well when he said that Napoleon was indeed keen on a spirited pursuit of the retreating enemy but the lack of cavalry again did him in and the allies, 'who after all had abandoned the battle before being entirely defeated, retained their good order'.

Losses on both sides in the two days of fighting reached around 35,000, two-thirds among the French. They took almost no prisoners and no field pieces at all. The Russians and Prussians camped overnight in the Weissenberg–Hochkirch–Lobau area and the French wherever they were at the end of the fighting. The next day Napoleon toured the battlefield, as was his custom, and again had a chance to bewail the results: 'What! after such butchery, no results? No trophies? No prisoners? These people will leave me no claws!' At that very same moment a shell fell in the vicinity of his entourage. General Duroc, one of Napoleon's favourites, was mortally wounded and the emperor's heart was broken. In the farmhouse where the dying man was brought, Napoleon sat at the bedside and held his hand. 'Duroc, there is another life,' he exclaimed, 'there you will await me. We shall one day meet again!' The next day an order was published cutting back considerably the number of people in the emperor's party – all the rest would travel far back in the rear. Two weeks later, in the manner of soldiers bemoaning fallen comrades, Napoleon was already able to express his feelings with black humour:

'Duroc's death made me very sad. It was the first time in twenty years that he failed to please me.'

For the second time in three weeks the emperor had prevailed in battle without achieving a decisive victory. He had won the bloody game of chess he had played with his rivals but they had left the table with their strength intact and the feeling that there would be another round. From this point of view, Bautzen was worse than Lützen. At Lützen the battle had developed in a situation where the French had been on the move and Napoleon had not chosen the ground. At Bautzen, on the other hand, the allies had dug in beforehand, the objectives were defined and what was required was a good plan and exacting and intelligent performance in order to decide the entire campaign.

There is no question that Napoleon's operational plan at Bautzen was excellent and perfectly suited to the basic conditions of the coming battle: varied ground conditions, the fact that the allies had had more than a week to make their preparations, and relative infantry strengths giving the French a big edge. The creativity of the plan showed that the emperor's military thinking was still fresh and productive. All the moves were aimed at assuring that the battle would be decisive. The tactical moves were intended to upset the balance the allies had tried to achieve in their dispositions. And all this in harmony with the best of the Napoleonic military tradition. If this is the case, what went wrong on 21 May, and why?

In the criticisms and commentaries on the battle there is of course a good deal of the wisdom of hindsight, but this is the way of students of military history. At Bautzen it might have been expected that Napoleon would garner all his spiritual and mental resources, and even outdo himself, as a decision would radically alter his destiny and was even close at hand. His actions during the fighting do not indicate that he truly girded his loins. During these two days he showed a certain measure of sloth, of haughtiness, of showy leadership. Fuller said that like Lützen, Bautzen was another Pyrrhic victory, as the Allies were not hamstrung for future action. On the contrary, they felt that the battle confirmed their improvement and presaged future gains.

Ney is the principal villain in the criticism of the French in the battle of Bautzen. His delay before taking Preititz, sending in just one division to carry out this important task, and his incorrect reading of the last phase of the battle when the enemy collapsed in his sector – all this justifies placing the blame on Ney, who not only failed to read the battle properly but also did not understand his assignment. But where was the emperor? Why did he not gallop early in the morning to Klix, which was so close, to brief the marshal face to face? Perhaps he would have done better to set up his headquarters near Ney's right from the start in order to keep a close eye on things. The advantage was clear; the disadvantage was that when the allies identified the emperor on this wing they would have immediately understood that the main effort was going to come from there and would have responded accordingly at an earlier stage. It is certainly possible that the emperor believed that the double enclosure of his wings was so effective that it was unnecessary to transfer his headquarters to the site of the secondary effort, though it was here that the stratagem that was the key to the battle was being carried out. It is also possible that Napoleon himself should have commanded the group of corps under Ney, attaching himself to it when it was approaching its objective. The combination of the emperor and the marshal operating together at Bautzen fires the imagination: Napoleon crossing the Spree north of the huge Bautzen perimeter and sending Ney down to strike Blücher with the right timing and the right order of battle. This might have been a masterpiece.

The manner in which the Prussians extracted themselves from this sector has surprised military historians who have analysed it no less than it surprised Napoleon. It signalled a tactical flexibility and mobility that had been unknown except among the French.

Criticism has also been levelled against the very choice of Ney for independent command, which demanded quick, flexible and innovative thinking, with such candidates as the marshals Marmont, Davout, Soult and Gouvion Saint Cyr being held up as better commanders for this kind of operation. Napoleon knew his officers well and knew that Ney was a man's man, brave and dogged. But he also knew that Ney was both rash and as stubborn as a mule. One thing is certain: if the choice fell on him, and the emperor did not feel the need to be at his side, then at least he should have made sure that his orders to him were as clear and detailed as possible. And we have already seen that this was not the case. Napoleon therefore bears no small part in Ney's guilt.

When Count Yorck described the events at Preititz in his book on Napoleon he took time out for the reflection demanded by Ney's failure, writing the following: 'There is a system of command which absolutely precludes any attempt at disobedience or any idea of deviating from the letter of the order. The gift of authority has always characterised great leaders, and the Emperor possessed it in a very high degree. But he who adopts this system of command claims infallibility for himself and kills in his subordinates the spirit of independent action. This also was in a high degree the case with Napoleon and it explains the fact that the greatest leaders have never had great pupils. Napoleon curtailed all strategical thought in his subordinate officers, and trained them to utter dependence on himself, since he always claimed to guide everything and be responsible for everything.'

A chapter no less important in the criticism of Napoleon and his lieutenants concerns the use of troops. The original sin in this matter was the overly adventurous thinking in relation to Bülow and Berlin, which deprived Ney of the use of Victor's II Corps in the battle and caused Reynier to arrive too late to have any effect on its course. It is easy to imagine what would have happened if a huge force of two corps had joined the attack on the allied right flank, particularly against Barclay's weak force.

Another distinguished contributor to the failure in the use of forces was Bertrand, who did not succeed in getting all his men across the Spree on 20 May because of the resistance, albeit stubborn, of a very small Prussian force. Had he attacked Blücher at 11 a.m., when Ney was at Preititz, Blücher would of course not have sent reinforcements to Barclay and would have been pushed back earlier. It is reasonable to assume that in this case Ney could have sent out two divisions to cut off the line of retreat of the Prussians instead of sending them to Preititz because of Souham's failure there.

And finally, the Imperial Guard, the elite unit, the heart and soul of Napoleon's war machine, which he liked to keep close to the anticipated point of decision and send in with perfect timing. That was what had happened at Lützen just 20 days before. At Bautzen it was a matter of too little and mostly too late when it came to the Guard and Latour-Maubourg. The breaking point was the right time to deliver the crushing blow, but the enemy had been broken beforehand and when the Guard and the cavalry arrived on the scene the allied forces were already in retreat. In his final place of exile, at St Helena, Napoleon made a wise remark which undoubtedly derived from one of the basic lessons he had learned. Had he applied it at Bautzen at the right time with his Guard and cavalry reserve, it would of course have changed everything: 'There is a moment in engagements when the least manoeuvre is decisive and gives victory. It is the one drop of water which makes the vessel run over.'

Bautzen might have been one of Napoleon's greatest military triumphs, with far-reaching political consequences. Instead it was one of his greatest lost opportunities and exemplified everything he had said so long ago in Warsaw about the distance between the sublime and the ridiculous.

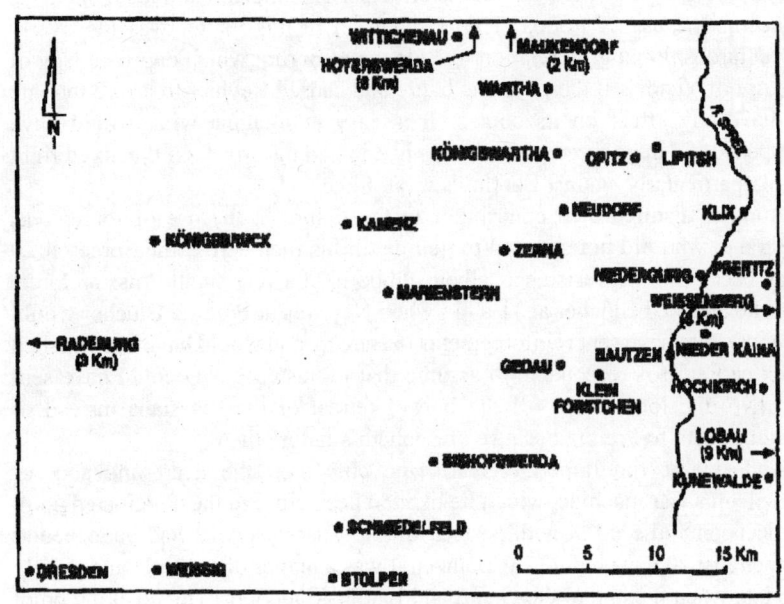

Map 7   March to Bautzen

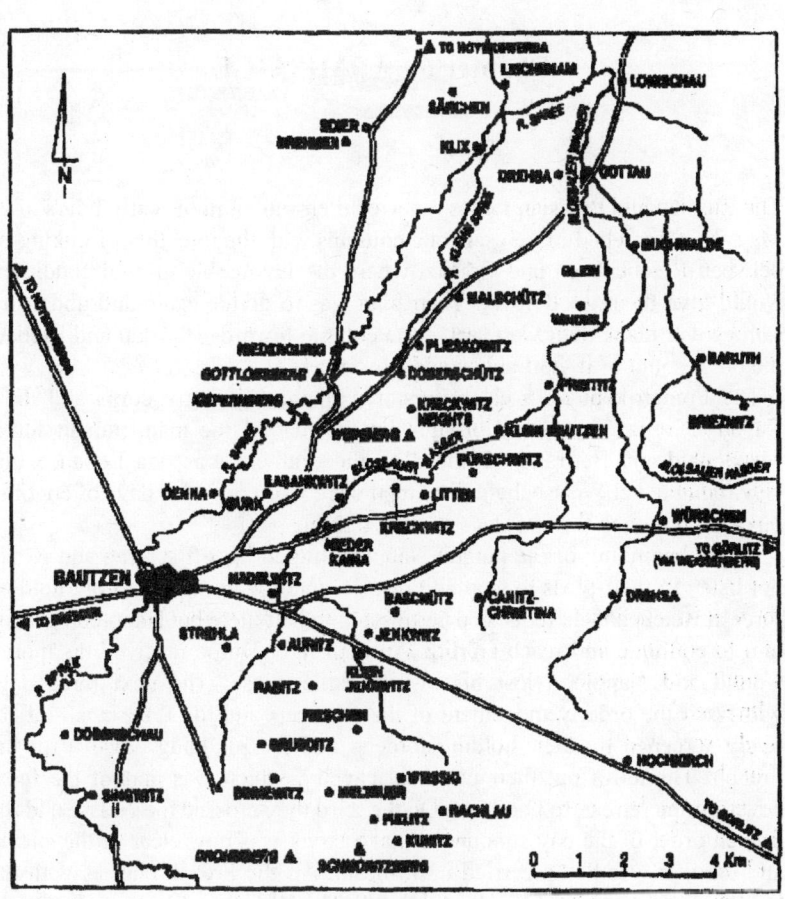

Map 8   Battle of Bautzen

Chapter 6 - ARMISTICE

The Russian and Prussian forces renewed their retreat in the early hours of 22 May. They marched in two separate columns with the intention of linking up between Reichenbach and Görlitz, where the favourable ground conditions would give them good cover. Their plan was to divide again and under this same cover make their way east – one column towards Bunzlau and Hainau, the other south of it via Lauban and Löwenberg.

The French kept up a close pursuit with three infantry corps and the I Cavalry Corps. The Guard brought up the rear of the main pursuit force. Macdonald and Bertrand advanced on the southern axis, via Lobau, while Ney remained at Weissenberg. The men were worn out after days of continuous marching and the two days of hard fighting.

At the beginning of the pursuit Napoleon urged his officers on and would not listen to their pleas to stop and rest. Reynier, who ran into a big holding force at Reichenbach, requested permission to halt there but Napoleon pushed him to continue and reach Görlitz. An hour later Duroc received his mortal wound and Napoleon lost his taste for the chase. The next three days witnessed the orderly movement of the Russians and the Prussians – effectively screened by their holding force – and the plodding advance of the French. The allies put their powerful cavalry, which was part of the force covering the retreat, to good use. On the 23rd they crossed the Neisse and the French order of the day announced that Saxony was now clear of the enemy and the war was being carried into Silesia. All the French clashes with the holding force were hard fought and costly. The XI Corps, for example, fought all day on the 25th against a Russian force the size of a division which only broke off contact late in the evening after Bertrand's advance units came to its assistance.

A more serious incident took place in the afternoon of the 26th. One of the divisions of Lauriston's V Corps was advancing carelessly along the axis leading to Liegnitz by way of Hainau, with no real guard on its flanks. Just as the men were getting ready to go into camp for the night, their officers assuming that the day's march had ended, a battery of horse artillery materialised on the nearby ridge and opened fire. In another moment thousands of Prussian cavalry charged the French, scattering them in every direction. Blücher, the tireless old general, had struck again, proving that he was not one of those officers who content themselves with set battles on chosen ground using well-practised tactics. He was a believer in night raids and surprise ambushes. The French did not have time to get into close order to defend themselves and the Prussians cut them down, taking hundreds of prisoners and a number of field pieces. Had units from other divisions not arrived on the scene, the results would have been even more disastrous.

These incidents as well as others clouded the atmosphere in the French camp. The absence of cavalry at such a critical stage of the war and the uncompromising fighting spirit of the enemy heightened the feeling of frustration among the French marshals. Ney had a falling out with Marmont, who was then under his command. The dispute arose from their different assessments of enemy dispositions and intentions. The hot-headed Ney even went so far as to tender his resignation to the emperor (it was not accepted). On one point there was no disagreement in the French camp: the enemy was far from being broken and was operating with considerable strength.

The deliberations in the allied command were also not calm and collected. The commander-in-chief, Wittgenstein, was fed up with the tsar's way of doing things, such as his habit of issuing instructions behind his back, and resigned. The tsar named Barclay in his stead on 26 May, with Wittgenstein now placed at the head of just the Russian forces alongside Blücher commanding the Prussians. Barclay, whose thinking was not substantially different from his predecessor's, was not inclined to fight another battle at this stage and recommended continuing the retreat and reaching Poland. This meant abandoning Silesia. He argued stubbornly that the troops needed six weeks to get re-organised and re-equipped. The Prussians, on the other hand, of course wanted to remain in Silesia, as near as possible to Austria. Frederick William was afraid to divide the armies. The tsar suggested a compromise – the retreat would be carried out in a south-easterly direction, to Schweidnitz. The upshot of this proposal, which the Prussians were willing to accept, though without much enthusiasm, was that a certain presence would be maintained in Silesia and contact would be made with Austria, whose participation in the anti-Napoleonic Coalition was the ardent desire of both the Russians and the Prussians. The weakness of the proposal was that it allowed the French to cut off the line of retreat to Poland and push the allies back on Austria, which had not yet completed its military preparations.

Napoleon could have seen the allied movement toward the Bohemian border as, on the one hand, exposing Prussia to his army and, on the other, as one more proof of the political and military agreements between the allies and Austria. Until then he had been convinced that the retreat would be in the direction of Breslau along the familiar allied lines of communication. But when it became apparent that this was not the case, the possibility opened before him of delivering an immediate blow on the flank, and Cathcart even testified that such a blow was expected by the allied command and awaited with foreboding. He was even convinced that Napoleon had missed a great opportunity, which might have been decisive, by not mounting the requisite attack.

It happened that Napoleon's thoughts had again turned to Berlin. He was concerned that Bülow would threaten his lines of communication, as he received reports that the Prussian general was carrying out disturbing movements south of Wittenberg. On 24 May he ordered Oudinot, who was still at Bautzen licking his battle wounds, to move to Hoyerswerda and stand ready to advance from there to Berlin. He would be required to encircle Bülow's force and keep him from stirring things up in the French rear. Victor's II Corps was given the assignment of reaching Sprottau on the Bober River, about 40 kilometres north of the main body of the army, and being ready to join Oudinot and attack Bülow from the rear. Bülow had about 30,000 troops, mostly militiamen, to defend the capital.

Before we continue to describe the events in the main theatre, let us pause to describe the events in this sector. Bülow was very active at the time. He believed – erroneously – that Napoleon had sent a not particularly large force against him and on the 28th attacked the XII Corps at Hoyerswerda. Oudinot drove the Prussian attackers back and Bülow, who had meanwhile learned of Victor's advance from the east, quickly broke off contact and spread his forces along a front of dozens of kilometres to secure the roads to the capital. Oudinot, who had been given a golden opportunity to race north, to Luckau, responded lethargically, as was the custom among his colleagues in those waning days of May, and when he finally got there on 6 June, Bülow was waiting for him with a large force. Oudinot hastened to attack, got himself chewed up and lost 2,000 men.

Success came to the French in the lower Elbe sector, where Davout continued his efforts to take Hamburg, cautiously, as was his way, and reinforced by a large Danish contingent that had joined him after the disappointment of the Danes with Bernadotte and the Prussians at the beginning of the month. The commander of the city, who had waited vainly to the last moment for assistance from the Swedes, abandoned it and on 30 May it fell into French hands. The town of Lübeck, north-east of Hamburg, was taken on 1 June. From every point of view it could be said that the roads to the sealed-up towns on the Oder and to Danzig were open to the French.

The activities of the armies in the last days of May were in keeping with the intentions conceived by the commands in this period: the allies aimed to reach Schweidnitz in an orderly, well-covered movement and the French advanced to the Oder River.

On the 26th the allies crossed the Katzbach River in the sector between Liegnitz and Goldberg. The Katzbach ran down from the Bohemian mountains and emptied into the Oder midway between Breslau and Glogau. On the 27th the allies changed their line of march, turning south-east and moving towards Schweidnitz. They got there on the 29th, but saw that the place was not suited for halting and setting up a line of defence, as the fortifications there had not been repaired since the war of 1807. The decision taken was to cut east, to the Oder, and avoid the danger that Napoleon, who was advancing on Breslau, would block their approach to the river. It is not surprising that the Prussians saw in this decision a return to the Russian idea of retreating to Poland. Consequently Blücher and Yorck recommended to Frederick William that if this was what actually happened the Prussian army should part ways with the Russians and keep to the mountain area.

The French movement on the heels of the allies was conducted in line with a basic aim that can be summed up in two words: Breslau and the Oder. The French were a day behind their enemies and between the main bodies the rearguards of the retreating forces operated with no little success. Napoleon, who had six corps with him on this front, wanted to pin down the allies in the Goldberg–Jauer sector with Macdonald and Bertrand and reach Breslau with the rest. This was a typical Napoleonic manoeuvre. In the next stage he planned to move up the Oder, pushing back the allies to the Bohemian mountains and destroying them there.

But the French emperor ran into difficulties in implementing the plan. The nature of French military activity at this stage of the campaign revealed some of the operational problems the emperor faced. One was connected with the poor fighting spirit of the troops, which was a result of the weak leadership of the senior officers in the army.

The French reached the Katzbach on 27 May and crossed it on the 28th. Macdonald, who on the previous day had run into a strong Russian rearguard force near Goldberg, had extricated himself by the skin of his teeth. His own men had deserted him during one of the assaults and other troops saved the day. On the 29th, Lauriston's and Reynier's corps neared Neumarkt along with the Guard. Reynier asked the emperor to relieve him of command of the advance guard so that he might attend to his wounds. On the 30th, Macdonald was about to leave Jauer but stopped in his tracks when he heard that the enemy had begun to retreat to Schweidnitz. He and Bertrand were ordered to advance to Striegau on the road to Schweidnitz but did not do so, sending off exaggerated reports of the strength of the enemy's holding units. Baron Fain, secretary of Napoleon's cabinet, said of these marshals: 'The turn of the wheel of fortune had ravaged these souls of iron.' In his memoirs Macdonald passed over this embarrassing stage of the campaign in total silence, not mentioning his personal experiences at all and contenting himself with a short general statement: 'We had done enough to retrieve the honour of our arms after the terrible misfortunes of the preceding campaign. France and the army earnestly longed for peace.'

Thus the pursuit of the allies lacked determination. As a result Napoleon was prevented from turning it into a springboard for important offensive action bringing to bear the numerical superiority he still enjoyed, and from exploiting the fact that he had prevailed on the battlefield less than ten days previously. On 1 June he knew beyond the shadow of a doubt that the allies were retreating towards Bohemia and arrayed his forces in the area between Jauer and Breslau – six corps in all, looking east and south.

Out of fairness to Napoleon's marshals and generals as well as to his soldiers, let us see why he himself did not do everything he could to exploit his military advantage to achieve his political ends. His critics argue that in the days after his victory at Bautzen promising opportunities had arisen with regard to Silesia and Berlin. To a large extent they are right, but the claim that his troops did not 'deliver the goods', even if partially true, is not the central issue. It should be added that after Bautzen, Napoleon began thinking more and more of an armistice that would lead to a peace agreement. It is conceivable that he understood that under the prevailing circumstances he had no chance of winning the war, for if not at Bautzen, then where?

The emperor not only considered an armistice, he was the first to signal to the allies that he was interested in a ceasefire and in a long-term armistice that would make peace talks possible. It was Caulaincourt who was sent to negotiate the truce. On 26 May, Napoleon spelled out his basic conditions for him: the armistice would remain in effect as long as talks continued, or alternatively it would last at least three months, until 1 September. Or as a final alternative, it was possible to agree to two months, but with 5-day prior notice of its termination at the end of the two months. Somewhat weak language coming from someone who had conducted such tough negotiations a few weeks before. Foreign Minister Maret instructed Caulaincourt: 'An armistice which is not at least two and one-half months is of no service to the Emperor, as that is the time needed to re-establish his cavalry.'

On 29 May, Caulaincourt met the Russian General Schowalov and the Prussian General Kleist between the lines under flags of truce. It was agreed to cease immediately all hostile acts for a period of 36 hours. The headquarters of the two armies hastened to draft the appropriate orders. Afterwards the two sides reached a number of agreements, which were set forth in a final document signed at Pläswitz on 4 June by Barclay and Berthier. The document stipulated that hostilities would cease until 20 July (in effect, until the 26th, as six days' prior notice had to be given of the termination of the armistice). The ceasefire lines would extend from the Bohemian mountains to the Oder River with a buffer zone between them that included Breslau. These lines forced the French to withdraw across the Katzbach. The lower Elbe was fixed as the demarcation line between Davout's French forces and Prussia. The armies would occupy the areas allotted to them on the two sides of the lines by 12 June. Somewhat later a third armistice was agreed on, which was supposed to remain in force until 10 August (actually the 16th). Thus the armistice began on 2 June and lasted until 16 August. During this time, according to the agreement, a peace congress was to be convened at Prague.

What caused Napoleon so stubbornly to seek an arrangement which many are convinced was the biggest mistake of his career as a military commander and ruler? He himself avowed, in exile on St Helena, that he erred when he took the lead in stopping the fighting. Why then did he take this step? Here is the letter he wrote on 2 June to his minister of war: 'We are negotiating an armistice. It would be possible that it is signed today or tomorrow. This armistice arrests the tide of my victories. I decided upon it for two reasons: my lack of cavalry, which prevents me striking heavy blows, and the hostile attitude of Austria.' Napoleon added that he hoped to concentrate another 150,000 troops during the month of July and deploy them against Austria. Napoleon hoped that the armistice would enable him strengthen himself considerably and went on to say in the letter that he would wait until September and then strike hard at his enemies in order to destroy them.

It should be emphasised that the allies too were undoubtedly interested in the cessation of the fighting, but they were able to hide it behind the French emperor's initiative. The continuing retreat, which had brought their armies back almost to their starting point in the campaign, was demoralising the troops. Add to this the continuous fighting and poor supply and you have a certain formula for the undermining of discipline in the face of the enemy. The allies needed time to rest and get re-organised no less than the French, and maybe more. After Bautzen they knew for certain that without Austria they had no chance of defeating Napoleon, and Austria would not be ready for a number of weeks.

Count Yorck wrote that he doubted if the reasons set forth in the letter to the minister of war, Clarke, were sufficient to explain Napoleon's steps, which he thought were a mistake. Jomini was convinced that this was the most serious mistake in the emperor's entire life. Fuller called the decision 'astonishing'. Yorck could understand Napoleon's political considerations, but argued that he erred militarily. He pointed to the seriously exposed position caused by the allied retreat towards Schweidnitz and argued that this had created an extremely favourable strategic situation for Napoleon, perhaps the best opportunity he had had in all his campaigns.

Other reasons that led Napoleon to seek an armistice, leaving his own remarks aside and turning to the various studies on the subject, are the following: the demoralisation that had spread through the ranks and which he could not ignore; the unwillingness of his senior officers to take action, which undoubtedly had its effect on the willingness of the soldiers to fight; the high number of casualties he had sustained until then; the high number of officers among the casualties, which affected the level of command in the army; the growing problem of desertion (the deserters were roaming the countryside). To all this can be added the numerous raids of Cossacks and local partisans, which played havoc with dispositions in the French rear and their lines of communication and most certainly added to the frustration of all the troops. One should also not dismiss the severe logistic problems that Napoleon faced as he advanced farther into Silesia, and there is no question that they had a great effect on his enthusiasm for the fray and on his willingness to continue the campaign without pulling up and trying to improve his situation. It is difficult to plan offensive operations when basic conditions are unfavourable, when there is a shortage of ammunition and food and when morale and discipline among the soldiers are at a low point. It is a fact that none of the French commanders and general staff officers tried to dissuade Napoleon from seeking an armistice.

An additional factor was the pressure being exerted on the emperor from France. Numerous communications that reached him from there expressed the ardent desire of the capital for an end to the war and the achievement of peace. Napoleon felt that at this stage of his rule he could not afford to ignore public opinion at home. Here, for example, is an impatient letter he wrote to his minister of police, General Savary: 'The tone of your correspondence displeases me; you are always worrying me about the need for peace. I know more about the situation of my empire than you do. I want peace, and am more concerned to get it than anyone else, but I shall never conclude a dishonourable peace, nor one that would mean another even more bitter war in six months. Do not reply! These matters do not concern you. Do not interfere in them.' To the president of the Senate, Cambacérès, who had an influence on the emperor, he wrote: 'I do not make of war my occupation and nobody is more pacific than I am.'

Fuller summed up the subject of the armistice as follows: 'In spite of the deplorable strategical position of the allies, Napoleon's momentum was exhausted, and like Pyrrhus he had to abandon his campaign.'* It is certainly possible to justify Napoleon's desire for the breathing space necessary to replenish his strength in men and materiel and raise the morale of his officers and troops, but it would also seem that Napoleon hoped that his numerical superiority would grow. He was convinced that if this were to happen, his passing up of the opportunity presented to him at the end of May would ultimately justify itself in creating the possibility of achieving a clear-cut military decision at the end of the armistice period and perhaps even peace on the appropriate terms.

If Napoleon really thought it was possible to improve relative strengths in his favour, it was a forlorn hope, unless he managed to neutralise Austria and keep it from joining the allies. It is reasonable to suppose that he refrained from advancing in the direction of Schweidnitz after he learned that the main body of the allied army was concentrating there because he did not wish to appear to be threatening Austria and push it into swinging to the Coalition. It appears that he also assumed that the allies allowed themselves to neglect their main line of operations, running along the road passing through Breslau on its way to Poland and Russia, only after reaching an agreement with Austria permitting them to retreat into its territory if Napoleon got their backs against the wall. If such an agreement did indeed exist, it served to weaken considerably the effectiveness of French offensive action on the Bohemian border.

Again and again we see how much Austria was a factor in Napoleon's actions. We shall also see in what is to come all the good his caution did him. Perhaps then we may address ourselves to the question that interests historians so much: what would have happened if Napoleon had actually attacked in the beginning of June 1813. Jomini, for example, maintained that if Napoleon had attacked at Schweidnitz and won, Austria would not have dared to join the Coalition against him after a third defeat of the allies, even if not decisive, like the previous two. 'Fear of Austria?' Yorck exclaimed in consternation. 'The man who fought Austerlitz, when Austria was in a position, and almost resolved, to fall upon his rear; the man who advanced into Poland and Eastern Prussia, when Austria might have played the same part?' Count Yorck concluded that at this stage of his military career Napoleon took into account factors whose disregard in the past was the reason for his success.

On 2 June, Napoleon wrote to Maret: 'We must gain time, and gain time without displeasing Austria, we must use the same language we have used for the last six months – that we can do everything if Austria is our ally... Work on this, beat about the bush and gain time... You can embroider on this canvas for the next two months, and find matter for sending 20 couriers.'

Analysis of the armistice therefore brings to light a good many reasons justifying, on the one hand, the wish for it and questioning, on the other, the good or the harm it did. The questioning is necessarily a result of making judgements after the fact, for Napoleon's hopes would be disappointed, and his judges know this, unlike Napoleon when he had to make his decisions. These considerations and decisions of his are unlike the ones that preceded the war in Russia a year before. The war of 1812 had no chance because of its very nature, but this is not the case with the armistice.

One interesting question still remains to be asked: what was Napoleon aiming at in the beginning of June – the creation of a better infrastructure for the renewal of war or a stable peace? An instructive document, which belongs to the effort to conclude the armistice agreement, deals with allied demands to include Breslau in the neutral zone, a demand which would of course have required the French to withdraw from the town, where Napoleon himself had taken up residence and was managing the affairs of the army and the empire. The document in question is to a letter written by Napoleon to Caulaincourt on 3 June: 'We must not dissimulate that this armistice is not honourable for me. It is I who abandon everything... Thus the enemy wish to humiliate me in chasing me by an armistice from the town into which I have entered as a result of the battle. Tell them then, that it was with the sole desire of peace that I consented to so disadvantageous an armistice, and that by pure cajolery I consented to abandon the capital of Silesia.'

The 4 June agreement created the following alignment of forces: the French were to array themselves behind the line extending from the Bohemian border to the Elbe and passing through Lahn, the Katzbach, the Oder and the northern border of Saxony. The demarcation line for the allies also commenced at the Bohemian border, running through Landshut and continuing along the Striegau-Wasser River until Kanth and from there to the Oder, excluding Breslau. Between the two lines there was a demilitarised zone 30 kilometres wide.

The French army took up its positions on 5 June in conformity with the following deployment order: II Corps (Victor) at Sagan; III Corps (Ney) at Liegnitz and Goldberg; IV Corps (Bertrand) at Sprottau; V Corps (Lauriston) at Goldberg; VI Corps (Marmont) at Bunzlau; VII Corps (Reynier) at Görlitz; VIII Corps (Poniatowski) – the Polish force stuck with the Austrians since Schwarzenberg's defection in January and now permitted to join the French army – at Zittau; XI Corps (Macdonald) at Löwenberg; XII Corps (Oudinot) at Baruth. The I Corps was at Hamburg and in the lower Elbe area.

The two cavalry corps were stationed at Sagan (Latour-Maubourg's I Corps) and at Steinau (Sebastiani's II Corps). Napoleon ordered General Arrighi to organise a third cavalry corps at Leipzig and station it at Wittenberg and Magdeburg. Mortier was positioned at Glogau with the Young Guard. Napoleon's headquarters were set up at Liegnitz.

The French army was thus deployed in three concentrations: the main body in the Bohemian foothills between the Bober and the Oder; the second body on the Bober, in the Sagan–Sprottau sector; the third downstream on the Elbe from Wittenberg to Hamburg.

When the armistice began the Russian and Prussian armies were concentrated in the Schweidnitz area.

On 5 June, a day after the signing, Napoleon returned to Dresden. He designated the Saxon capital as the place where he would work and devoted most of his time to building new units and re-organising the army. His instincts told him that the war would be renewed, despite the fact that he was shortly due to enter into peace talks. But Dresden was Dresden and the emperor had no intention of doing without his accustomed entertainment. On 8 June he wrote to Cambacerés in Paris after having asked that theatre players be sent to Dresden from the French capital: 'I would like this to be talked about in Paris, as it would have a good effect in London and Spain, by making them think we are amusing ourselves in Dresden.' According to the evidence, his artistic tastes had undergone a change and he now preferred comedy to tragedy.

The period of the ceasefire and armistice was exploited by both sides for reflection and practical preparations in view of the good possibility that the war would be renewed. The main subject that occupied the rival powers was Austria. At this stage Austria was busy acting in the capacity it had claimed for itself in the past months and even assumed the title of mediator, in the most active sense. Metternich, who played the principal role in the Austrian charade, was a foreign minister of the creative variety, and, more than carrying out the policy of his indecisive master, shaped it himself. Austria desired a situation whereby both Russia and France would modify their political and territorial ambitions and satisfy themselves with their natural borders. As will be remembered, Austria was not particularly enamoured of the idea of pan-Germanic unification under Prussian leadership, desiring rather a federation of German states under its own hegemony. It attached importance to maintaining its firm foothold in northern Italy and wanted to get back the Illyrian provinces. It may be assumed that Emperor Francis and Minister Metternich would have been happy to see these designs fulfilled without going to war. None the less, it was clear to them as well that the chances that the war would be renewed with Austria playing a decisive part in it were greater than the chances that peace would be attained, and therefore Metternich did everything in his power to ensure that the feverish diplomatic contacts he was maintaining would continue until his country completed its military preparations. Austria had successfully manoeuvred itself into the position of being able to tip the scales in the European balance of power, but at the same time remembered well that militarily it had always had a problem with France.

The Austrian envoys chosen to represent their country's positions, which were well enough known, were again Stadion and Bubna. Stadion was all for Austria's joining the war on the side of the allies, and to them he was sent. Bubna, a pleasant-mannered, peace-loving count, was sent to Napoleon's headquarters in Dresden. Metternich equipped the two with a list of Austria's conditions meant to serve as a basis for mediation and getting the sides closer together. This list was enumerated in a document which he drafted on 7 June, and contained the following: abolition of the Grand Duchy of Warsaw; restoration of Prussia and inclusion within it of Danzig; return of the Illyrian provinces to Austria; renewal of the independence of the towns of the Hanseatic League lost in 1810; dismemberment of the Confederation of the Rhine. In addition, a demand was set forth in the document that its framers knew Napoleon would not agree to – evacuation of all the Polish and Prussian fortresses held by the French.

These basic conditions to a large extent repeated what had been discussed with the Austrians after Lützen. The allied rulers were not taken aback by Austria's positions, which were more moderate than their own, and for a moment even suspected that Austria was trying to make fools of them, leaving its co-operation against France in doubt. Stadion was taken aback by their response and tried hard to appease them. He wrote to Metternich: 'These people are beaten owing to our faults, our half wishes, our half measures, and presently they will get out of the scrape and leave us to pay the price.' Metternich apparently sympathised with Stadion's view of things but, as mentioned, preferred for the time being to conceal this sympathy by presenting conditions that, even if not immediately acceptable to everyone, would serve as a logical basis for future negotiations and political discussions.

Metternich, who began to travel back and forth between headquarters to talk to the rulers, met Tsar Alexander on 17 June and succeeded in allaying his doubts and suspicions completely To the tsar's question of what would happen if Napoleon agreed to Austria's conditions for mediation, he replied that discussions with him would surely prove that Napoleon was neither wise nor fair and therefore little faith could be put in what appeared to be his agreement. Then the truce would come to an end and Austria would join the allies. This argument persuaded the tsar and Frederick William to consent to the Austrian conditions and on 27 June, while the French emperor and the

Austrian foreign minister were holding talks which will be described further on, a secret agreement was signed between the allies and Austria.

Great Britain participated in the talks that took place before the Metternich–Napoleon meeting and were concluded on the 24th. Russia undertook to provide the allies with 160,000 troops and also garrison forces. Prussia promised 80,000 men. Austria promised to become an active ally of Russia and Prussia if Napoleon rejected Metternich's 7 June document and in the meantime to continue its mediation efforts. Britain undertook to supply funds to finance the struggle. It promised Russia and Prussia £7,000,000 in grants and loans. Its only conditions were the restoration of Prussia and that no separate peace should be made with France. In an annex to the agreement Britain agreed to transfer £500,000 to Austria the moment it joined the alliance. These commitments on the part of Britain were an important aspect of Castlereagh's policy – the creation of a solid bloc of all France's enemies.

One of the serious criticisms levelled against Napoleon by those convinced that after Bautzen his path was strewn with error was that the very fact of his recognising Austria as an official mediator gave it a feeling of power far exceeding its real power. Napoleon should have exploited Austria's indecision to apply leverage and get it to back down with the threat of his nearby army. For Austria had been defeated time and again during the years of Napoleon's rule and he should have taken this factor into account in his relations with it. This he did not do. The fact that he had married Francis's beloved daughter had not brought the Austrian emperor closer to him, the latter seeing in Napoleon a bearer of the ideas of the French Revolution. Francis wished to see France return to its natural size and this desire was much stronger than the temptation of seeing Marie Louise, the kaiser's daughter, receive the crown of the French empire. Narbonne, the French ambassador in Vienna, whom Napoleon greatly esteemed, had warned the emperor already in April against according Austria the status of official mediator. He was convinced that at first its conditions would appear moderate, but then they would become tougher. Was it not Metternich who had said that Austria could not fight alongside France so that the Confederation of the Rhine would remain loyal to it? And this was just one example.

Now, with Austria having such an important position in European affairs, Napoleon could not get out of the trap he was in. If he refused to negotiate with the Austrians he would be represented to the world by Metternich as a warmonger unwilling to accept the peace being extended to him on such reasonable terms. However, it was fixed in Napoleon's mind that it was impossible for him to agree even to some of the conditions presented to him, which he believed would mean the end of his empire and a dramatic weakening of France. As he himself put it: 'These extravagant propositions were made that they might be rejected. Even had I consented to them, what would it have benefited France? I should have humbled myself for nothing, and furnished Austria with the means of making further demands, and opposing me with greater advantage. One concession granted would have led to the enforcement of new ones, till, step by step, I should have been driven back to the Tuileries whence the French people, enraged at my weakness and considering me the cause of the disasters, would have justly banished me for yielding them a prey to foreigners.' In his meeting with Metternich, Napoleon would remark in this context: 'Your sovereigns born to the throne can suffer defeat 20 times and yet each time return to their capital. But I am a child of fortune; I shall have ceased to reign on the day when I have ceased to command respect.'

This stormy and famous meeting took place on 26 June in the Marcolini Palace in Dresden. It lasted nine hours. The emperor was tense and lost his composure a number of times during the discussions. It is worth quoting the sometimes colourful account of the secretary of his cabinet, Baron Fain, which is full of interest and tells us something about the style of diplomacy in those days:

'"There you are, Metternich," said Napoleon, when he saw him. "Be welcome, but if you desire peace, why have you come so late? ... I have won two battles; my weakened enemies are losing their illusions. You come in among us ... and everything is embroiled. Without your unlucky intervention, peace between the allies and me would be made today... Agree with me. Since Austria has taken the title of mediator, she is no longer on my side, she is no longer impartial, she is my enemy... Today your 200,000 men are ready; Schwarzenberg commands them, he assembles them at this moment nearby, there behind the curtain of the mountains of Bohemia, and because you believe yourself in condition to dictate the law, you come to find me ... I have seen through you, Metternich. Your cabinet wishes to profit by my embarrassment... The great question for you is to know whether you can buy me off without fighting, or if you are to find yourself positively in the ranks of my enemies ... and you perhaps come here only to get better light on the question. Well, let us see; let us treat. I consent. What do you want?"' The emperor, in his biting style, made it clear to his negotiating partner right from the start that

Austria's intentions were clear to him and that he had no illusions that Austria would act the way he wished it to.

'This attack was lively; Monsieur de Metternich threw himself into the breach with the complete equipment of diplomatic phrases... "Speak more clearly," said the emperor, interrupting him, "and come to the point, but do not forget that I am a soldier, who better knows how to break than bend. I have offered you Illyria to remain neutral; does that suit you? My army is quite sufficient to bring the Russians and Prussians to reason, and your neutrality is all I ask."

'"Ah, sire," Monsieur de Metternich replied quickly, "why should Your Majesty remain alone in this struggle; why not double your forces? You can do so, sire, for it only depends on you to entirely dispose of ours. Yes, things are at such a point that we can no longer remain neutral. We must be for or against you."

'At these words the tone of the conversation quieted. The emperor led Metternich into the chart-room. After a rather long interval, the emperor's voice again rose: "Why, not only Illyria, but half of Italy, and the return of the pope to Rome and Poland, and abandoning Spain and Holland, and the Confederation of the Rhine and Switzerland; that is, then, what you call the spirit of moderation that animates you. You are thinking only of making profit out of the chances. You are busy only in transporting your alliance from one camp to another, so as always to be on the side where things are divided... In fact, you want Italy, Russia wants Poland, Sweden wants Norway, Prussia wants Saxony, and England wants Holland and Belgium. In a word, peace is only a pretext. You all aspire only to the dismemberment of the French empire. And to crown such an enterprise, Austria thinks it is sufficient to declare herself... And I am obediently to evacuate Europe ... and deliver myself like a fool to my enemies ... and this while my flags yet float at the mouths of the Vistula and on the borders of the Oder, when my triumphant army is at the gates of Berlin and Breslau, when I am personally here at the head of 300,000 men, it is that Austria, without a blow, without even drawing a sword, flatters herself to make me subscribe such conditions... Oh, Metternich, how much did England give you to decide you to play this role against me?" ... Metternich changed colour. A profound silence succeeded. Each walked rapidly up and down. The emperor's hat fell on the ground. Metternich did not even bother bending down and retrieving it. The emperor picked it up himself. Napoleon resumed the conversation with more coolness, and declared that he did not yet despair of peace, if Austria would listen to her veritable interests. He insisted that the Congress should assemble and should continue, even if hostilities were resumed ... "so that this door should at least remain open". In sending away Metternich, the emperor was careful to tell him that the cession of Illyria was not the last word.'

The meeting in Dresden represented not only a clash between two rival powers but also between two individuals whose backgrounds were completely different. Napoleon was a proud soldier, a ruler who believed he was on a great mission with justice always on his side. His diplomacy had a bullying manner but at the same time friendship and family connections played a part. During the stormy meeting he did not neglect to mention that his father-in-law, the emperor of Austria, was mistaken if he believed that a weakened imperial throne would be able to protect his daughter and grandson. Metternich belonged to the German nobility, coming from the Rhine district. The French Revolution had stripped his family of its property and represented for him evil incarnate. 'Robespierre made war on the nobility,' he was in the habit of saying, 'and Napoleon made war on all of Europe. The danger is the same, but on a much larger scale.' He was an extraordinary statesman and diplomat, silver-tongued and as shrewd as they come. Incidentally, according to another version of the story, Napoleon simply flung his hat across the room in anger – that was how much the Austrian fox had unnerved him. At the same time, it is said that at the end of the meeting Napoleon entreated him in somewhat conciliatory tones: 'You certainly will not make war on me.' This remark, quoted by Fain, also shows that Napoleon did not wish to shut the door entirely.

Another interesting facet of the meeting shows the extent of the arrogance that had grown up in Napoleon the dictator, an arrogance that is characteristic of the leadership of autocratic rulers prosecuting total war. The emperor told Metternich that for someone like him losing a million men did not matter one way or the other. Metternich, according to his own version, replied that he had better open all the doors and windows so that all of Europe could hear his words. Napoleon added that only ten per cent of the dead in Russia had been Frenchmen and that he had sacrificed mainly Poles and Germans. Metternich replied: 'Your Majesty, you forget that you speak to a German.'

Napoleon had hoped to terrorise his negotiating partner and send him away fearful and frightened. There can be no question that he was disappointed entirely in this aim. He had also wished to guarantee the convening of the peace congress in Prague, which he indeed succeeded in doing. Metternich managed to get across all of his and his partners' message in the talks. He observed that the French emperor was tense and nervous. He permitted himself to comment drily that the emperor's army was composed largely of untried boys. When he went out, Berthier was waiting for him there, accompanying him to his carriage and asking him if he was satisfied with the meeting with the emperor. 'Yes,' Metternich said, 'he has explained every-thing to me; it is all over with the man.'

A day after the meeting, Napoleon wrote to Eugene that the probability of war was quite great. Metternich remained in Dresden another three days and held talks mainly with Maret, at the end of which a paper was signed, again agreeing that Austria would have the status of mediator and confirming the holding of the Prague congress, under Metternich's chairmanship. Napoleon approved the document. On 30 June he wrote his father-in-law a letter cool to the point of threat: 'I desire peace. If the Russians are as moderate as I am, it will promptly be made. If, on the contrary, they wish to carry me to conces-sions repulsive to my honour and the interests of my allies, they will gain nothing. They will succeed in nothing. Your Majesty knows the sentiments I bear you. I hope you will not be drawn into a war which will cause the unhap-piness of your states and increase the evils of the world.'

During those very same days Napoleon received word of the defeat of his army in Spain, which confounded still further his thinking and consequently his plans. He knew that the defeat on the Iberian Peninsula would bolster the confidence of his enemies and their eagerness to defeat him. Ever since Soult had left Spain and joined the army in Germany, the French army in Spain had been without leadership. Moreover the Spaniards were regularly disrupting its communications with France, their small-scale fighting continuing to cause it losses and supply was bad. And Joseph was incapable of overcoming all these difficulties. He insisted to his brother the emperor that the root of the evil was the conduct of the French conquerors and the hostility it engendered in the populace. He also claimed that he could not be two things at once – king of Spain and general in the French army. The senior French commanders were on bad terms with one another and disorder was rampant in the French camp. Wellington's offensive had been mounted in June. His plan was brilliant, involving continuous frontal pressure and a wide flanking movement pushing back the French from one river to the next until they retreated across the Ebro. On 21 June Wellington attacked at Vittoria north of the river and defeated the French, sending them back towards their border with enormous quantities of arms and equipment left behind. Now, for the first time in the history of the empire, France itself was in danger. This was a disastrous defeat, and from Napoleon's standpoint – at a time when he had to display the threat of strength and could not afford to reveal any weak points in the complex tangle of his rule – the timing was less than propitious.

The next item on the agenda allowing the two sides to organise themselves and even giving peace a chance, however slight, was the Peace Congress due to be convened in Prague on 12 July. Napoleon's representative at the congress was Ambassador Narbonne, with Caulaincourt joining him on the 28th. On 26 July, at Neumarkt, all the sides agreed to a final extension of the armistice. Caulaincourt received instructions 'to conclude a solid peace that would be glorious'. At St Helena, Napoleon claimed that this was what he sincerely meant. But Caulaincourt's feeling was that his master was indeed ready to conclude a peace with the Russians, but no more than this.

Descriptions of the deliberations at the congress employ adjectives varying from 'barren' to 'ridiculous'. Metternich was heard to remark to his colleagues that the war was unavoidable and that he regarded the congress as a means of persuading Kaiser Francis that there was no chance of achieving a lasting peace. It was his feeling that Napoleon had no intention of promoting peace. Even the French foreign minister, Maret, referred cynically to the letter of accreditation he sent to Narbonne, writing in an accompanying note: 'I send you more powers than power, you will have your hands tied, but your legs and mouth free so that you may walk about and dine.'

Suspicion was rife, with no side trusting the others. The allied delegates saw every objection of the French as an attempt to buy time, principally to outfit and train their new cavalry units. Everyone was convinced that in the end Napoleon would accuse everybody of delays which he himself had caused and present some kind of ultimatum, which would lead to the renewal of the war. The feeling among these delegates was that at best the peace Napoleon would be willing to make was one whose conditions he could dictate 'with his foot on our neck'. Metternich wished to step up the pressure on the emperor and asked Stadion to give Cathcart a message for Wellington. The British general would be requested to take the bold step of threatening the south of France. It is small wonder that Napoleon attributed the stubbornness of his rivals to the situation in Spain and the intrigues of the British. He told Caulaincourt in one of the preliminary conversations he had with him that 'it is not blood which flows in the veins of these people, but cold policy'.

Among the allies too there was no lack of suspicion. Their delegates did not present political and military positions in the discussions themselves but submitted them in writing, through Austria. Metternich preferred this arrangement to make sure that no secret agreements were reached with France behind his back. The allies preferred it because they saw Austria as the only party with a serious chance of arriving at a compromise with Napoleon.

Quickly enough Caulaincourt realised that he had no chance of achieving what his chief had hoped to achieve. He felt that there was no point in his being in Prague and that the idea of making a separate peace with the Russians was illusory. In the first days of August the war atmosphere was heightened and hostility to France reached its peak. Narbonne's secretary wrote in his memoirs: 'We could no longer cross the street without being insulted.' The biggest French gain at Prague was in intelligence. They succeeded in getting their hands on secret documents setting out the order of battle of the Austrian army. These documents caused Napoleon to instruct Caulaincourt to contact Metternich secretly and again clarify how Austria saw the peace and what would happen if he accepted its terms – if it would join him, or at least remain neutral. This question and the fact that time was running out resulted in the end in its being Austria that presented France with an ultimatum, as will be seen further on. On 4 August, Napoleon wrote to Ney that nothing was happening in Prague. The British were complicating everything. The allies would terminate the armistice on the 10th. To Caulaincourt he wrote in the same vein, for this was how he saw things.

While the Prague talks were going on, Napoleon was busy preparing for the next stage of the war. He frequently toured the probable theatre of war, from the Elbe to Silesia and Bohemia. These preliminary reconnaissances were preceded by much thought and enormous staff work under the emperor's direction. For a full month he and his people busied themselves thinking out the continuation of the campaign, at the same time handling the tremendous workload of imperial affairs. During this period Napoleon stayed in Dresden, in the luxurious Marcolini Palace in the Friedrichstadt quarter, built in the baroque style. On 9 July, Napoleon left Dresden, remaining absent until the end of the armistice. During this time he also stayed in Mainz, meeting his wife there in an effort to enlist her in the effort to get the Austrian emperor to do his bidding. During his reconnaissances he went into the smallest details and instructed his people not to give him plans but only information: 'The engineer should not use the word "enemy". He is to reconnoitre the roads, their character, the hills, defiles, obstacles, decide whether vehicles can pass, and absolutely refrain from plans of campaign.'

One of the basic tenets in Napoleon's planning was resistance to the temptation to shorten lines of communication by retreating far to the west. This idea was liable to occur to his staff, since it was clear that France was in fact facing the combined power of all of Europe. With the addition of Austria to his enemies, Napoleon would be ranged against an unbroken concentration of forces in the form of an arc extending from Brandenburg in the north down to the northern border of Bohemia via Silesia. If he wished to array himself against this disposition with all his strength, in maximum concentration and with manoeuvrability permitting him to move forces to vital points, he would have to 'keep the mastery of the course of this river – the Elbe', as Count Yorck put it. His forward line would rest on the Elbe, where his army controlled all the important fortresses along its length – Magdeburg, Wittenberg and Torgau. It would be desirable to strengthen still further his foothold there, mainly with additional fortification at selected points. Had he withdrawn to the Rhine, he would in fact have been acceding to the demands of his foes with regard to his rule in Germany, his threat to Prussia and even his possession of Italy. Furthermore he would have turned the next phase of the war into a large-scale defence of France rather than continuing to fight for Germany. He wrote to Saint-Cyr (Marshal Gouvion Saint-Cyr, who had been seriously wounded in his leg in October 1812, served as Eugene's adviser at the beginning of the year and was now governor of Dresden): 'What is important to me, is not to be cut off from Dresden and the Elbe; I care little for being cut off from France.' His main area of manoeuvre would be between the Elbe and the Oder. He also commanded vital points along the Oder and the allied armies in fact had no solid foothold along either of the rivers.

Napoleon's offensive-minded thinking again focused on the northern part of the theatre. He wanted Davout to come out of Hamburg and draw most of the enemy forces around Berlin to the lower Elbe. Or conversely, if this was not possible, to link up with Victor and Oudinot, who were respectively not far from the Oder and the Elbe, and together with them attack along the lower reaches of the Oder. The objective was therefore the occupation of Berlin and command of the northern sector of the Oder up to Stettin. Napoleon was certain that the enemy would offer very weak resistance to such an attack. At this stage of the offensive the main army would be under Napoleon's command in a strong defensive posture anchored on Görlitz and Bautzen. Thus it would be impossible to cut him off from his supply bases in Dresden or from the Elbe. He would be in a good position to respond to the moves of the enemy. If defeated, he could retreat to Dresden, which would form part of the planned holding line.

On the basis of the partial intelligence at his disposal Napoleon believed that Austria was capable of concentrating in Bohemia for direct and active fighting against him an army of 100,000 men at the most, since the rest of Austria's army would be pinned down holding off the French forces arrayed against it. He figured that the Austrians would operate against him from the direction of the mountain region and mount their attack from Zittau. He also thought that it was the main body of the Allied army that had retreated to Silesia and that it would only be able to field 200,000 men against him. As will be seen, he was mistaken in his calculations.

The French plan took shape slowly, actually right up to the last moment. The armistice was scheduled to end on 16 August and the emperor's written instructions to Ney and Marmont on the 12th were still not unequivocal: 'Hostilities will recommence the 17th. This is the plan of operation which it is possible that I shall decide on definitely before midnight.' *Possibly decide*, said the emperor a few days before the renewal of fighting. This is not the young conqueror of Marengo, remarked one of the commentators – that one would have acted differently. Everyone – the generals on the eve of battle and the commentators in retrospect – expected Napoleon to strike a crushing blow in the direction of Bohemia and finish off the Austrian army there now that its participation in the war seemed certain.

Napoleon asked his commanders to raise any objections they might have to his plans. This unusual request is in itself proof of his misgivings. A few of them did. Marmont argued that in dividing his forces over such a great distance Napoleon was losing the advantage that came from his standing at the head of his troops on the battlefield. Saint-Cyr, who was now command-ing a recently formed corps, objected to the effort aimed at taking Berlin and said that Napoleon was underestimating the Swedish expeditionary force of Bernadotte, which was responsible for defending this sector. Marmont summed up his feelings by saying: 'I fear greatly, sire, lest on the day on which your Majesty has gained a victory and believe you have won a decisive battle, you may learn that you have lost two.' A glance at the way the allies were organised and their order of battle reveals the logic of these almost prophetic remarks. In his memoirs Marmont would argue that what motivated the emperor was his eagerness to avenge himself on Prussia and hit it hard on the renewal of hostilities.

The agreements reached at Reichenbach among the allies, with the underpinning of England's substantial financial aid, produced full co-ordination among them from the standpoint of planning and operations. On 7 July Bernadotte entered into talks with them and after all the problems were ironed out joined the coalition. The faith of Russia and Prussia in the young Swedish crown prince had been shaken somewhat by his refusal to help the Prussians resist the French attack on Hamburg. Bernadotte, for his part, was angered that Tsar Alexander had not stood by his word and strengthened his forces so that he would not be exposed to a Danish attack in the Norwegian dispute. The disagreements were overcome in a conference held at Trachenberg castle, north of Breslau.

At Trachenberg the principles of the fighting and co-operation against France were formulated. There the basis was established for the climax of the total war that all of Europe was involved in and the armistice could not prevent. Austria took part in the formulation of the war plan, though its official participation and declaration of war was not to come till the termination of the armistice. On 12 July the participants determined that their forces would be concentrated against the main body of Napoleon's army and not parts of it. This meant that the main effort would be aimed at total military victory without regard to the interests of any particular party. It was agreed that the Bohemian salient would be the principal base from which the attack on the main body of the French army would be launched. The forces operating on the flanks would direct their efforts towards cutting the French lines of communication. The first two of these decisions were framed in such a way as to satisfy Austria. The Austrian chief of staff, Radetzky, laid out the main lines of his country's military thinking – exhaustion of the French army through a series of manoeuvres and deliverance of the blow only when the concentration of forces in the chosen area was complete. The aim of the third decision was to force Sweden to concentrate its forces for the good of the common effort and to stop thinking incessantly about the defeat of Denmark.

Two important principles which were decided on accorded with previous decisions and were a result of lessons learned in the campaign. The first was that if Napoleon concentrated his forces against one of the armies, it would break off contact while the others advanced to meet the threat. The other principle had as its aim the neutralisation of Napoleon's charismatic effect on his troops: wherever the emperor was identified on the battlefield no attack was to be made there and contact immediately broken off until until a suitable force could be organised. A framework of operational plans at army level was agreed on.

Upon Austria's declaration of war, 100,000 Russians and Prussians would march from Silesia towards the Bohemian mountains and from there move clandestinely west, joining the Austrian army and operating against French lines of communication and the French rear on the Elbe, whose centre was at Dresden. This force – to become the Army of Bohemia – would number more than 200,000 men. Its commander was to be Schwarzenberg and his deputies were to be Wittgenstein, Barclay and Kleist, in addition to the commanders of the Austrian corps. In this planning stage it was called the Great Army or the Army of the Sovereigns, with Alexander and Frederick William joining it.

The Army of Silesia, under Blücher's command, would comprise 80,000 men, Russians and Prussians, and would be responsible for defending Silesia and securing the main operational axis linking the theatre to Russia and passing through Poland. Russian reinforcements regularly moved along this axis. This army would also threaten the French in Saxony. If possible, it would make a junction with Bernadotte, and if not, with the Army of Bohemia. The Russians, in fact, believed that it was better to post Blücher in Bohemia to cover the movement of the main force into Saxony and defend Prague. However, the Austrians rejected this idea, as it did not wish to turn Bohemia into a battleground where two foreign armies would be feeling each other out. The Prussians too rejected the idea. They wanted Blücher to be able to help defend their land if Napoleon attacked them.

The Army of the North consisted of the Swedish expeditionary force, Prussian reservists and Russians. Under Bernadotte's command, it would number 80,000 men. Its main task would be to defend Berlin and threaten Hamburg, but if the Army of Bohemia succeeded in carrying the fighting to the western side of the Elbe, the Army of the North would move south, cross over to the left bank of the Elbe in the sector between Torgau and Wittenberg and sweep down on the enemy's left flank. Its final objective would be Leipzig.

In terms of the campaign as a whole, the allies were planning a co-ordinated offensive on the two flanks of the French army – the Army of Bohemia against the right flank and the Army of the North against the left flank, with the Army of Silesia harassing in the centre. The Russians would concentrate a large reserve under Bennigsen that would march from Kalisch to Glogau and defend Poland. Bennigsen would join the general offensive if circumstances permitted. The division of the armies and their assignments also suited the status of the personalities involved. Alexander and Frederick William with their headquarters would be opposite Napoleon's right while Bernadotte, who also had the status of a ruler, would be opposite his left. Bernadotte had pretensions to be commander-in-chief and had vainly tried to get the appointment during the convention. His pretensions most likely derived from the fact that he had once been a French marshal.

It is not hard to see the great changes that had taken place in the thinking of Napoleon's foes. No longer narrow interests and direction of the war to theatres that would serve these interests alone – from now on the aim would be to defeat Napoleon and put a different France on the European map, within its natural borders and as a vital but more modest factor in the Continental balance of power. Militarily, considerations promoting the concentration of forces were the main ones and co-operation between the armies was geared to serving the main goal. It was also decided, clearly and explicitly, that no battle was to be initiated without clear-cut numerical superiority. The principle of concentration of forces also expressed itself in the decision that if the enemy attacked in strength at a given point, the defending force would retreat while the other forces advanced rapidly, putting heavy pressure on the enemy's flanks and threatening his lines of communication. This way of thinking constituted a suitable response to Napoleon's style of fighting, which was abetted as far as possible by interior lines. In the face of such a strategy, it was best to aim at pincer movements with large, numerically superior forces. The emphasis in thinking was shifted from the idea of victory in a particular place to the idea of annihilating the enemy physically.

The new disposition of forces, exploiting the topographical conditions of Bohemia and weighted towards the southern flank of the theatre, tipped the scales in favour of Austria, whose status in the coalition would exceed substantially its contribution in human and material resources. Allied commanders attached double-edged importance to Bohemia: they assumed that in the first stage Napoleon would attack Austria and consequently the Army of Bohemia; and Bohemia would also serve as a very convenient springboard for an attack on the French in Saxony.

While the sterile talks in Prague continued, the two sides were energetically building up their forces. The efforts of the coalition partners were more impressive – the number of men mobilised was so large that when the figures reached Napoleon's ears he refused to believe them, insisting they had been exaggerated to deceive him. He underestimated Austria's ability to release large numbers of men to fight against him, thinking that his forces on the Inn River and in northern Italy would pin many of them down.

The Russians received reinforcements numbering 100,000 men, including the wounded of 1812 returning from the hospitals and draftees of the same year completing their training and being organised into units. Russian conscription methods had improved considerably along with the means of getting troops to the front. There can be no question that the Russian army of August 1813 was far superior to the one that had faced Napoleon only a year before.

The Prussians increased their forces to 250,000 men – the result of previous years' drafts supplying trained soldiers by the first half of 1813. On 12 July, Gneisenau wrote to Stein: 'We now have an army such as Prussia never had before, even in her most glorious days.'

Great Britain did its share in shoring up allied forces as promised, mainly with money, but also with armaments, including cannon. Its unique contribution to the war was the supply of rocket units. This weapon had been developed by a royal artillery officer named William Congreve, who had completed his work in 1808. Wellington, however, had not been impressed by the advantages of the rockets; but the allies eagerly attached the units to their forces.

The allied force was not yet complete, as Austria had not yet officially joined it and its army was not at its disposal. On 7 August the Austrian cabinet met to discuss peace conditions, namely the conditions that would keep Austria from joining the war if France accepted them. In effect, the discussion was solely tactical, its aim being to justify Austria's position, since France's probable response had been mapped out by the emperor as well as by his representatives at Prague. The cabinet decided to represent once more to Napoleon the principles and conditions of peace, but this time as an ultimatum, saying: if they are not accepted by the end of the termination date of the armistice, and if the acceptance does not reach Prague by midnight of 10 August, Austria will declare its participation in the war against France. The emphasis in the ultimatum was on the restoration of Prussia to its previous status and the dissolution of the Confederation of the Rhine.

In his reply, handed to Count Bubna in Dresden on 9 August, Napoleon set forth his own conditions, including his agreement to give up the idea of a Grand Duchy of Warsaw, on the condition that Danzig be demilitarised and turned into a free town and that Saxony be compensated for damage caused to it by this concession. He also agreed to hand the Illyrian provinces back to

Austria, excluding Trieste. On the other hand, he demanded that the Confederation of the Rhine be expanded up to the Oder and that Norway be given to Denmark. This document only reached Metternich in Prague on the 11th. On the same morning Austria officially announced the cancellation of its pact with France and its alliance with the allies.

Napoleon's reply to Austria's ultimatum, though containing nothing new, reveals a certain hesitancy and perhaps even a trace of his hope to prevent the renewal of hostilities. Among the pressures he faced during those same days, mainly due to the planning decisions he had to make, were those from home, which intensified the closer they got to the end of the armistice. Caulaincourt, too, who was one of the few people who had Napoleon's ear and was very much involved in the recent contacts with the Austrians, pleaded desperately with him: 'I beg you, sire, weigh all the perils of war against the advantages of peace; pray heed the heart's cry, consider what will happen in Germany after Austria declares war, France's exhaustion, the devotion and nobility shown by the sacrifices in the Russian disaster...' Napoleon recoiled from the various ideas proposed to him to get out of the war, some of which struck him as clearly defeatist. 'Good God!' he exclaimed. 'Ten lost battles could not bring me so low as you would have me stoop; and that too, when I command so many strong places on the Elbe and Oder. The enemy cannot force me back on the Rhine till they have gained ten battles; but allow me one victory and I will march on their capitals of Berlin and Breslau, relieve my garrisons on the Vistula and Oder, and force the allies to such a peace as shall leave my glory untarnished.'

On the 12th, Austria's announcement of the previous day was handed to the French ambassador in Vienna, Narbonne, and it was clarified to him that beyond what was implied there concerning Franco–Austrian relations, the emperor should understand that Austria's policy was to strip him of all his conquests in Europe. Caulaincourt knew that his master, to put it mildly, was not at his best in handling the contacts with the Austrians. He wrote to Maret: 'The reason for our disappointment stems from our refusal to make temporary concessions and all this will end in our utter destruction.'

On 15 August, Austria completed its diplomatic moves by declaring war on France. The armistice was over. Austria won the appointment of commander-in-chief of all the allied armies despite the fact that its material contribution fell short of the contribution of its two senior partners. Many were convinced that the Austrian officer best suited to contend with a commander of

179

Napoleon's stature was Archduke Charles, the kaiser's brother. Charles was two years younger than Napoleon and had gained a good deal of military experience in the wars against France since 1792. He was responsible for the rebuilding of the army after Austerlitz. It was true that Charles had been defeated by Napoleon in the principal battles he conducted afterwards, but he was considered one of Napoleon's toughest and most talented rivals. However, the choice fell on Prince Schwarzenberg; it is just conceivable that the Austrian emperor did not wish to see his brother win all the expected glory and therefore chose the less talented of the two. In addition to having a military reputation, Schwarzenberg also possessed the qualities necessary for the commander-in-chief of an army comprising a number of nations. He had also impressed Napoleon in the short time he was in Paris, and this too was seen as important at the time of the appointment. The appointment was important to Austria not only for the influence and prestige it gave her but also because the first stage of the war was going to take place next to its territory, which served as a very important base of operations and administration.

The three rulers, Alexander, Frederick William and Francis, intended to stay at Schwarzenberg's headquarters, which would allow them to follow the conduct of the war from close up and delegate extra authority to their chosen commander-in-chief. The continuous presence of the sovereigns and their advisers was not always convenient and more than once made things difficult for Schwarzenberg. Once he complained: 'What I have to put up with is inhuman. I am surrounded by weak-minded people, instigators, blabber-mouths and gratuitous critics.' It may be assumed that he was referring to the entourages of the sovereigns in this biting diatribe, but sometimes the presence of the rulers themselves at the headquarters of the commander-in-chief was insufferable. Four years later, at some ceremony, Blücher toasted Schwarzenberg in the following words: 'To the hero who led us to victory despite the presence of the three rulers.' The cynicism of army people in relation to politicians did not begin with the Second World War.

Before the fighting was renewed, the allied general staff was strengthened professionally by the addition of Moreau and Jomini. General Jean Moreau, who will be remembered as a senior French officer commanding an army in the Revolutionary wars of the 1890s, had been a bitter rival of Napoleon within the army. In 1804 he was exiled to the United States on Napoleon's orders after being suspected of subversion and co-operation with royalists. Now his appearance at allied headquarters made him a candidate for the position of chief of staff to the commander-in-chief. Moreau preferred to serve on the Russian tsar's staff and was appointed his adviser. Baron Antoine Jomini was an army man of Swiss origins who had served in the French army in different capacities. As will be remembered, he was still Marshal Ney's chief of staff in the previous battle, at Bautzen. Jomini was not only a talented staff officer, he was also a talented military theoretician. Ney had recommended him for command of a division, but Berthier had voted down the idea, probably out of jealousy of his talents and achievements. During the armistice Jomini apparently thought things out and in the end went over to the other side, joining the enemy's army and serving as the tsar's personal aide. Napoleon was extremely upset when these two pieces of information came to him. He did not think much of Jomini as a soldier but praised his ability as a military analyst and his writings. Allied thinking thus received a big boost, as both the defecting generals, along with Bernadotte, knew the opposing army well and, more importantly, its leader and his style of command. It was Moreau who said to the Russian tsar: 'Expect a defeat whenever the emperor attacks in person. Attack and fight his lieutenants whenever you can. Once they are beaten, assemble all your forces against Napoleon and give him no respite.' This advice, it will be remembered, became a principle of fighting.

There is no agreement about the exact number of men in the allied order of battle before the termination of the armistice. There are big discrepancies among the various calculations, deriving from the desire to prove that the allies had succeeded in putting together an enormous force or the interest of a few writers to underscore the success of the military strategy of the allies and their determination without recourse to the claim of overwhelming numerical superiority. None the less, each set of figures has some basis and the differences between versions can be laid mainly to different definitions of the components in the order of battle.

The highest estimate of allied forces puts the number at over 900,000 – a mighty army in terms of size. Three armies alone numbered half a million men, though a month previously, at Trachenberg, it was decided that they would have 360,000 men. The remainder included reserves, garrisons, militiamen and siege forces:

Field forces (in three armies)	500,000
Anticipated Russian reinforcements and Russian reserve	100,000

Militia, garrisons and siege forces   300,000
                                       900,000

Allied artillery numbered 1,400 guns. There can be no question that these figures, though based on official reports, are exaggerated at least with regard to the number of troops available for fighting. If we deduct troops stationed outside the theatre of action who never reached it, though taken into account in case of dire need, the total number will come to around 500,000. Even in this case the allies show a numerical superiority they did not have previously. It is thus possible to break down the field forces present for duty on the battlefield as follows:

Division by armies:
Army of Bohemia (Army of the Sovereigns)   250,000
Army of Silesia   105,000
Army of the North   145,000

      500,000

Division by nations:
Russia   180,000
Prussia   160,000
Austria   130,000
Sweden   30,000

      500,000

Napoleon, too, on the other side of the hill, did not mark time in the respite that had been given him. While making his political and diplomatic moves he also took steps to strengthen his forces and fortify their positions. He put his engineers to work hard on strengthening the important passages on the Elbe and did much logistically, mainly in the way of accumulating large stores of supplies along the river. He devoted much attention to Dresden and its environs, as well as to Hamburg, which, though it was far removed from the main theatre of action, he saw as vital in that by commanding it he could sever the direct link between the allies and England and cover Denmark. He explained to Davout how much importance he attached to his ability to defend Hamburg: 'The possession of Hamburg is of the greatest political importance and I shall never feel assured until Hamburg can be looked on as a stronghold provisioned for several months and prepared in every way for a long defence.'

Before the termination of the armistice the French army numbered around 530,000 men, 450,000 in the field and the rest in garrisons. A great effort had been made to augment the number of cavalry units and before the armistice ended three cavalry corps had been added to the French force. Artillery, too, had been augmented considerably.

The disposition of the Grand Army before the renewal of fighting suited the strategy that had taken shape in Napoleon's mind. He had concentrated a large army to go up against two enemy armies and designated another force, numbering four corps, for independent operation to fulfil the design that kept cropping up during the campaign – the conquest of Berlin and control of northern Germany. The forces were thus deployed as follows:

On the Katzbach, on the front facing east: the III Corps (Ney) and the V Corps (Lauriston) and the II Cavalry Corps (Sebastiani), a total of 80,000 troops; behind it, along a second line on the Bober, the VI Corps (Marmont) and the XI Corps (Macdonald), over 50,000 men; the reserve in the Görlitz–Sagan–Glogau–Liegnitz area, numbering around 100,000 men and including the Imperial Guard, the II Corps (Victor) and the I Cavalry Corps (Latour–Maubourg); at Bautzen – the I Corps (now commanded by General Vandamme and which had arrived at Bautzen from the lower Elbe on 17 August) and the IV Cavalry Corps (Kellermann), a total of 40,000 men; at Dresden, Pirna and Königstein – the XIV Corps (Saint-Cyr), the V Cavalry Corps (L'Heritier) and garrison units, altogether 35,000 men; on the southern flank at Zittau – the VIII Corps (Poniatowski) with fewer than 10,000 men. These forces were in effect an army under the direct command of Napoleon.

In the northern sector, opposite Berlin, were stationed forces planned to operate under the command of Oudinot, with the assistance of Davout: the IV Corps (Bertrand), the VII Corps (Reynier) and the XII Corps (Oudinot), as well as the III Cavalry Corps (Arrighi), concentrated in the Luckau sector, a total of 65,000 men; two divisions between Luckau and Wittenberg – around 15,000 men. The XIII Corps (Davout) was in the Hamburg area and numbered 40,000 French and Danish troops. This was the force that remained with Davout after Vandamme had been taken from him with the I Corps and attached to the army under Napoleon's direct command. Oudinot's task was to take Berlin by 22 August while Davout marched on the capital from

Hamburg and cut communications between Berlin and Stettin. After Berlin was taken, Davout would take command of all the forces in this theatre.

The French forces included around 65,000 cavalrymen and 1,300 artillery pieces. Most of the additional cavalry had arrived from Spain. Another force, under Augereau's command, which was based on Bavarian conscripts, was still getting organised in the rear and was scheduled to join the army shortly. Napoleon was pleased with the size of the army and the means of warfare at its disposal. On 18 August he wrote with satisfaction to his minister of war: 'I have here 365,000 rounds for my artillery, all horsed, which is the equivalent of three battles like Wagram, and 18 million cartridges.' He felt that his quantity of arms permitted him to conduct large-scale battles.

The army planned to operate under Napoleon's direct command was deployed in three strike forces in the area between the Elbe and the Oder. One strong force rested on the Oder and the Katzbach, another was in the Dresden–Bautzen sector and the third upstream on the Elbe in a southerly direction. A strong reserve was deployed between the advance strike force and the two rear ones. A small but well-positioned force was designated to defend the mountain passes in the Zittau area. Napoleon planned to attack each enemy army in turn and destroy it and it was very important to him to begin with the Austrians. The allies were arrayed against this powerful alignment of his from two directions and a large force was deployed in the north. They commanded the axes leading to Dresden from Bohemia and Silesia.

In his assessment of his defensive alignment, Napoleon assumed that the deployment of his forces and the size of the corps guaranteed that any allied attack could be withstood. If the Austrians attacked along the Elbe, from south to north, Saint-Cyr, Vandamme and the Guard could deal with them, together or individually. If they attacked in the direction of Zittau, they would quickly find themselves facing Poniatowski, Victor and the Guard. If such an attack by the Austrians were to be accompanied by an attack by Blücher in a westerly direction, the Army of Silesia would run into the corps on the Katzbach, which would make their way to the Bober, link up with the garrison forces there and constitute a very large force that could be further reinforced from the reserves.

Thus, despite his misgivings up to the very last moment, Napoleon felt that his decisions on the deployment of his army accorded well with the basic conditions dictated by terrain and what he knew about enemy forces and that he was capable of responding effectively to most of the military options open to the allies. The main body of his army was arrayed opposite the main body of the enemy, his forces were well concentrated and he had the advantage of operating on interior lines and the ability to go over from the defensive to the offensive. On 12 August he wrote to Ney: 'It seems to me that to bring about a decisive and brilliant result, the best way is to keep on a close formation and allow the enemy to approach.' This feeling permitted the emperor to stick to his parallel plan of an offensive in the Berlin sector and northern Germany against the Army of the North under the command of Bernadotte.

Thus passed the ten weeks of the armistice and the armies were once more ready for war. The aims of the war were now clear in the minds of the allies, sharply formulated and deriving with simple logic from the supreme aim that united them – ridding Europe of the French empire, an alien concept in the traditional Continental balance of power. The operational plans that had been formulated were based on agreed rules, without involving narrow interests, and most importantly were the product of the lessons of the May battles and a deeper understanding of the French emperor's personality and military thinking. The allied plans still lacked creativity, for their forces were arrayed in a kind of half-circle opposite the French, a deployment suitable for offensive pressure and even a pincer attack. But we find no mention in these plans of any variation on the pincer theme. The partial use of three armies when it is clear that the situation of any one of them will be inferior is the way of caution and betokens an absence of the requisite boldness. The French emperor still terrified his foes and their fear of him was no small factor in their thinking.

The French indeed had an advantage over their foes in their unity of command and the homogeneity of their men, but what motivated their supreme commander derived largely from indecision, from a lack of the fervour that was so vital during those same summer days, from the mix of a desire for peace and resistance to anything that would undermine the status of France and of himself, from a desire for vengeance against individuals and countries. His frustration at losing the chance for a decision in May, which had been without a doubt attainable, caused a loss of self-confidence and such a loss always affects the quality of decision-making and planning.

Giving up from the start the idea, with its good chance of success, of transferring the theatre of war to Bohemia is indicative more than anything else of the change Napoleon had undergone, a change for the worse. Had he concentrated a large force at the foot of the mountains and opposite its passes, like the one he stationed opposite Zittau – which was in fact small – he would have created a threat to northern Bohemia, including Prague, that could not be ignored. Had he done so he would have had a good chance of neutralising the advantage the allies had gained for themselves by arraying three armies in such a way that Napoleon had to keep his eyes peeled in every direction despite being deployed on interior lines, a deployment that was essential in such a situation. Had he been able to control parts of Bohemia he would have improved his sources of supply significantly, as these areas had not been stripped for military needs, unlike Saxony, which had to sustain the masses of soldiers stationed there. Of course, one can defend not conquering Bohemia on the grounds, very logical in themselves, that had Napoleon conquered northern Bohemia he would have exposed himself to a major attack by Blücher and Bernadotte against the weak forces that the French would probably have left behind to defend Saxony. What emerges from this analysis therefore relates more to Napoleon's state of mind than to a strategic alternative that he might have chosen. There is no evidence that he considered the alternative outlined above and rejected it for the reason mentioned.

A large-scale defensive alignment like the one the French set up in August was also unprecedented in Napoleon's military thinking. But this change in mentality is worthy of every praise, as such a concentrated defensive posture was the only answer to the increase in allied forces and the way they were deployed, whether Napoleon had the precise figures or not. There is no question that this new thinking of his was perfectly attuned to the changes in the military thinking of his foes and that his response was one of analysis and intuition more than a response to anything he might have known as to the decisions reached in the various councils of the allied commanders in their many deliberations. When all was said and done, the defensive posture did not eliminate the possibility of attack, for it was possible to strike enemy forces approaching from their outer ring.

With regard to Napoleon's offensive strategy in the next stage of the war, a great deal of strong criticism has been levelled against it and, as we have seen, those of his officers whom he consulted voiced their objections too. It is hard to understand the stubbornness with which Napoleon clung to the idea of isolating and taking Berlin, an idea he kept coming back to all the time. Berlin had no military value and even its political value and the lift in morale capturing it might produce were doubtful. For Prussia identified completely with the higher strategy of its Coalition partners – the crushing of Napoleon – and also believed that the loss of Berlin would only be temporary if the allies stuck to their aims. Napoleon should have been disturbed by the fact that this plan pinned down a French army of a few corps, which diminished the superior strength Napoleon would have been able to bring to bear in the presence of the main body of the allied army. In any event, the defeat of Bernadotte could not have been decisive, since even if the Army of the North had been annihilated the main enemy force would not have been defeated. Critics of the French emperor are convinced that the choice of Marshal Oudinot to command the army charged with the offensive was not a good one, for Oudinot did not have the special talents required of an officer commanding a force consisting of more than one corps.

Be that as it may, in August 1813 Europe witnessed the final preparations for a great war that would range over a vast theatre, between foes who knew one another well and well knew that the results would be fateful to themselves and to the entire Continent. The die was cast.

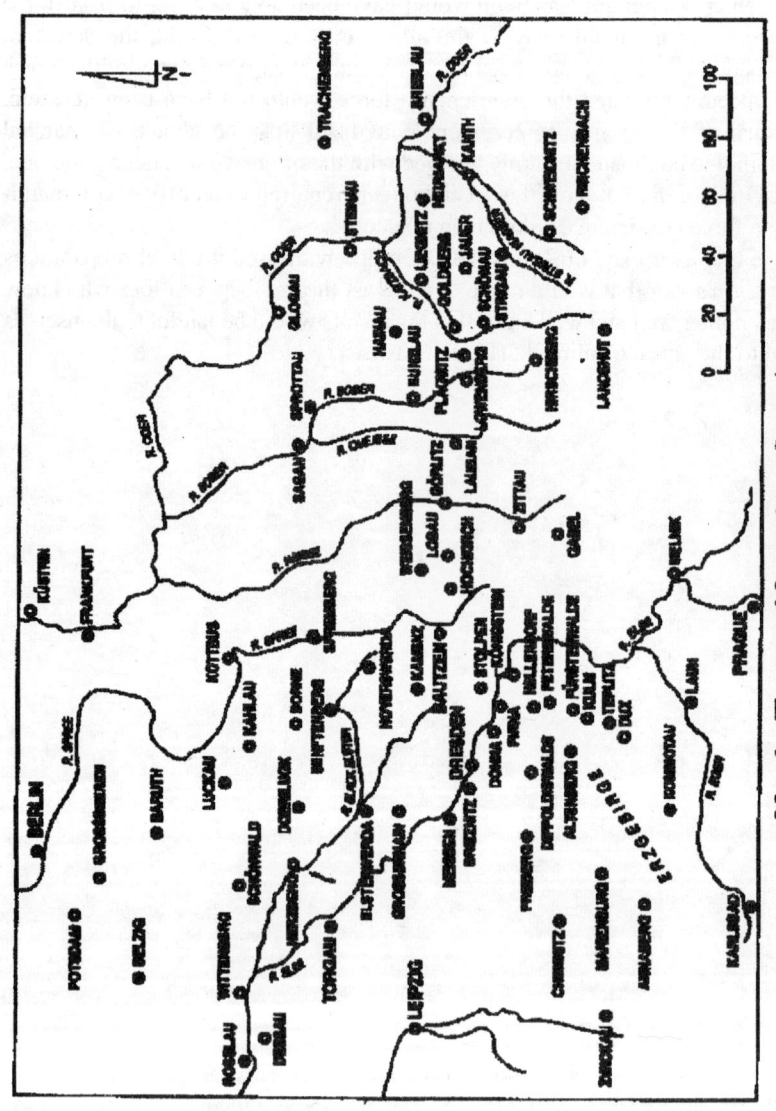

Map 9 Theatre of Operations: June–August

Chapter 7 - AUGUST

'Finally we know exactly where we stand' – this was how Napoleon reacted to Austria's official announcement that it was an active participant in the conflict. The announcement was expected and put an end to Napoleon's indecision, if indeed he was still troubled by it. His fighting spirit returned, and with greater strength, and he felt that he was ready to continue the war. 'I have allowed for everything,' he told his intimates. 'The rest depends on fortune.' During those same days, on 15 August, he celebrated his forty-fourth birthday, certainly a young enough age for someone still intending to stand at the head of his armies in the field and knowing very well that the war would decide the fate of his empire as well as his own. It seems that the parades and celebrations in his honour were pushed back a few days, as the emperor anticipated that he would already be busy with the war on his birthday and his mind would not be on such trivial matters.

On 14 August the king of Naples, Joachim Murat, joined the French army at Dresden. The man who had abandoned the army in Russia, which he had commanded after Napoleon returned to Paris, was again dragged back to his chief's side, grumbling and cursing. Murat was convinced that the end of Napoleon's rule was in sight and in the previous months had been courting Metternich to ensure the preservation of his kingdom, which his master and brother-in-law the emperor had given him. None the less he had obeyed Napoleon's summons, the latter writing to him a few weeks before: 'I assume you are not one of those who believes the lion is dead ... because if you do, you will soon find out that you have been very much mistaken.' The language of the letter shows that the faith Napoleon placed in one of the best commanders he had had in the past was not great, but apparently he very much wanted him at his side. In any event, the barbed letter succeeded in getting the marshal back in the army and he was named commander of the cavalry reserve.

The allies were already occupied from 12 August with the movements that would complete the troop dispositions they had decided on at Trachenberg. Barclay marched to Bohemia at the head of more than 100,000 Russian troops to link up with Schwarzenberg's army. Blücher violated the terms of the armistice and entered the Breslau demilitarised zone on his way to the Katzbach. His objective was basically to draw Napoleon into Silesia. With the termination of the armistice the allied armies were arrayed as follows: Schwarzenberg in northern Bohemia, not far from Melnik and behind mountains which were to conceal from the French the direction of his advance in the coming days; Blücher in the Striegau area with most of his force; the Army of the North in place, defending Berlin.

This is the first time we are seeing the new Austrian army and it is worth giving its order of battle and dispositions in this initial stage of the war. Its main body was assembled north-east of Prague in the Laun area on the Eger River. It included three infantry corps (seven divisions): the I Corps commanded by Count Colloredo; the II Corps commanded by Marquis Chasteller; the III Corps commanded by Count Giulay; cavalry units under the command of Prince Lichtenstein and Count Bubna and a cavalry reserve under Count Nöstitz. A fourth infantry corps, composed of young Bohemian conscripts, was being formed under General Klenau. The Austrian army was thus an army commanded by noblemen whose titles were attached to their names militarily as well.

Napoleon left Dresden on the afternoon of 15 August and went to Bautzen, where he remained for two days. While he was there, the news of the Russian movement from Silesia to Bohemia reached him and he ordered Victor's II Corps, which was part of the main reserve, to be sent to Zittau. He wanted to be certain that the Russians really got to Bohemia, figuring that Blücher would reach Bunzlau, and then, as he wrote Macdonald on the 16th, the army in Bohemia would advance to Zwickau or Dresden, engage Blücher and destroy his army. 'This is a situation that gives me great hope,' he declared. 'It appears to me that the enemy is exposing himself to heavy blows.' He planned to meet the threat to Dresden with the I and XIV Corps under the command of Vandamme and Saint-Cyr.

On the 19th, Napoleon rode to Zittau to keep a closer watch on developments. He reconnoitred in the area with Poniatowski as far away as Gabel south of Zittau. He believed that there was little chance that the allied army would advance via the mountain region and his thoughts turned once again to the attack on the Army of Silesia. Blücher, whose nickname among his men was Marshal Forward (Marschal Vorwärts), had been busy for three days clearing the French out of the Katzbach area. He ordered that attacks be made in every possible place and that every opportunity be exploited but to avoid fighting against superior forces. On the 20th he pushed Ney and Lauriston back from the Katzbach area to the left bank of the Bober in the Löwenberg–Bunzlau sector. On the same day Napoleon arrived at this front and decided the time had come to attack. 'The great thing at this moment is for us to concentrate and then march against the enemy,' he said and ordered that preparations be made to cross the Bober on the 21st.

The attack against Blücher was disappointing. Löwenberg was taken easily and the bridge on the Bober, which was partially destroyed, quickly repaired, but the French crossing it discovered that Blücher, true to the strategy developed by the Coalition partners, had retreated and broken off contact. Blücher had no difficulty discerning the presence of the French emperor on the battlefield, not the least from the cries of *Vive l'Empereur!* that rang out from every direction. In truth, he himself had planned to cross the Bober and thus had his forces very close to the place of the crossing, in the valley beyond the bank of the river. Consequently, had Napoleon attacked him immediately after the crossing, Blücher would have found it difficult to extricate himself. The frustrated Napoleon interpreted the Prussian general's move as indicative of a lack of confidence in the fighting ability of his troops, but also discerned a lack of enthusiasm in his own generals. 'What is most regrettable,' he wrote to Maret, 'is the little confidence which the generals have in themselves; wherever I am not personally present, the enemy's forces appear to them considerable.'

On the 23rd, after a few skirmishes – the most serious one being at Goldberg – the French forced Blücher to continue his retreat across the Katzbach. However, Napoleon's thoughts were now focused on Dresden, as he received messages from there warning of an enemy advance in this sector. Before leaving for Görlitz, Napoleon ordered his commanders to forestall the advance of Blücher from Silesia in any direction where French forces were deployed. The direction of the drive had to be Jauer, with special attention to keeping the enemy from advancing on Dresden. He appointed Macdonald commander of all the forces in the eastern sector and christened them 'the Army of the Bober'. He told his staff to summon Ney, transferring command of his corps to Souham. With a number of options now open to him, each stirring his mind, he wanted his boldest marshal at his side.

At this stage the emperor intended to march to Pirna by way of Königstein at the head of 100,000 troops. If the enemy moved on the Peterswalde–Dresden axis he could strike him in his rear. If he moved towards Leipzig the pressure on Dresden would be removed and Saint-Cyr could attack. Then the emperor might march into Bohemia. Along the Elbe in this area, cavalry units would be scattered to convince the enemy that the French were holding Dresden with large forces. The plan was therefore to cut off the enemy columns if they marched on Dresden, or to turn towards Prague if the enemy moved on Leipzig. Count Yorck praised this line of thinking and said that Napoleon's judgement was true, as Schwarzenberg's initial plan had indeed been to march on Leipzig. But Napoleon quickly gave up the idea of a flanking movement via Königstein and decided to focus on Dresden. Before taking leave of Macdonald, he told him: 'If I march on Bohemia, I can be in Prague in three days, but I prefer a more prudent method of debouching through Dresden, with the intention of launching a powerful attack against the army that arrives there.'

The news that Napoleon had left Dresden on the 15th and was heading for Silesia reached Prague, where the allied rulers were staying – the Russian tsar, the Austrian emperor and the king of Prussia. The war council decided to send in the Army of Bohemia immediately to relieve the anticipated French pressure on Blücher. Dresden was a natural objective because of its strategic importance and also because the council had a feeling that the force defending it was not large. The great fear of the allied leaders was that, while their army was moving into Saxony, Napoleon would create a diversion on the Elbe, advance towards Prague and cut of their lines of retreat. This was a calculated risk that the allies had to take.

On 19 August the sovereigns left Prague for Schwarzenberg's headquarters. On the 22nd, the army began its advance into Saxony in four columns through the four passes of the Erz Mountains in the heavily wooded area separating Bohemia from Saxony: the Peterswalde pass, leading to the Teplitz–Dresden highway, was used by Wittgenstein and Kleist; the Altenberg pass by Barclay's Russian column; the pass leading from Kommotau to the main road to Leipzig in the direction of Chemnitz by the main body of the Austrians; the Annaberg pass by Klenau's newly formed Austrian force, moving from Karlsbad on the Zwickau axis. The Army of Bohemia therefore bypassed the French from the south, on the Zittau–Görlitz axis, which was manned by Poniatowski and Victor.

Already on the 22nd the Russians moving on the right-hand axis ran into the advance force of Saint-Cyr's corps and drove it out of its positions. On the 24th they assaulted the French line at Pirna and captured it. Saint-Cyr had to give up his outposts and concentrate his entire force in Dresden, leaving one division at Königstein. The temptation for the allies to advance to the west of Dresden and take Leipzig was great, but still greater was the fear that Napoleon would strike from the Dresden area, hitting the advancing columns on the flank and gaining the victory in a decisive battle of annihilation. Though a Leipzig offensive was apt to lead to an effective junction with Bernadotte, cut off Oudinot's army and constitute a real threat to Napoleon, the fear overcame the temptation. Dresden remained the objective of the Army of the Sovereigns.

On 25 August, Klenau, Wittgenstein and Kleist reached the edge of the open area forming a half-circle to the south of Dresden. Towards evening Alexander, Frederick William and Schwarzenberg viewed the pleasant scenery spread out before them from one of the hills near Rocknitz, a landscape just a few kilometres removed from the town and destined to become a battlefield in just one day. The bolder spirits at allied headquarters were convinced that an immediate attack should be made. They asserted that the French would not be able to withstand an attack by such superior forces and that the ground overwhelmingly favoured the allies, because of the commanding position of the hill regions to the south and west. Moreau, on the other hand, thought they should wait until the army reached its maximum strength, otherwise they would 'get their noses broken'. The tsar's position was that the first condition of any decision was the preservation of the Army of Bohemia – it was better to avoid a battle that would wear down the army with heavy losses and instead threaten the vital axes of the French. The Prussian king happened to favour an attack and expressed his apprehensions that the avoidance of battle and breaking off of contact would have a bad effect on the morale of the troops.

Schwarzenberg, who had now made up his mind to attack Dresden as the main objective and given up once and for all the Leipzig idea, insisted on waiting for the Austrian units. His plan was to concentrate the three columns advancing from the south in the Dippoldiswalde area and have Klenau make a wide flanking movement on the left from Freiberg via Chemnitz. Barclay, too, who was very close to the southern part of the town, did not show much enthusiasm for attacking that night. In view of the fact that the French defence that day was based only on the XIV Corps and on the reduced V Cavalry

Corps, it would appear that the reluctance of Schwarzenberg and Barclay resulted in the loss of a good opportunity.

In any event, on 25 August the commanders of the two sides definitely pinpointed their objectives. Both sides were now thinking only about Dresden. On the same day Napoleon, who was at Stolpen, learned of Oudinot's defeat in the north and it is possible that this news too led him to put any other idea out of his mind and to concentrate on getting out orders for a stubborn defence of his positions in the Dresden area. He sent one of his officers there to see what was going on and on his return was told that the situation demanded very urgent action. Saint-Cyr was sending him a stream of messages concerning the enemy advance and the contact that had been made. The emperor instructed him to hold on to the last extremity and promised to send Vandamme immediately to the sector south of Dresden. In addition, he ordered the reserve – the corps of Victor and Latour–Maubourg along with the Imperial Guard – to move rapidly to the area of the anticipated battle, throwing in Marmont's corps as well. Napoleon pushed his engineering units to complete their preparations and fortifications in the town and its environs. He told Saint-Cyr and the chief engineer officer that right after taking care of Dresden he intended to move south towards Bohemia.

Oudinot had begun advancing on Berlin on 18 August. As will be remembered, he had under his command three infantry corps (IV, VII and XII) and the III Cavalry Corps. In his memoirs, Oudinot cautions the reader not to be unduly impressed by the strength implied by his order of battle, as half his forces were composed of Italians and Saxons whose fighting spirit could not be relied on. The assembly point of the army was in the Baruth–Luckenwalde sector, from which three parallel routes led north, straight to Berlin.

Before 23 August, Oudinot ordered his forces to deploy on a broad front whose centre was at Grossbeeren, about 25 kilometres south of Berlin. The area the French were moving in was heavily wooded and full of swamps and watercourses, which made the movement of gun carriages difficult and ruled out any attempt of the three corps to support one another. The absence of connecting roads between the lines of march made things even more difficult. Under these conditions, individual units of the same corps also found it difficult to co-operate, not to speak of such a large force. From the start, Oudinot found it difficult to keep his colleagues, the commanders of the other corps, in hand.

The Prussians were deployed on the left flank of Bernadotte's army with the assignment of blocking the way to Berlin with two corps -- one under Bülow and the other under Tauenzien. The fighting began on the morning of the 23rd. Bertrand attacked along the right-hand line of advance, at Blankenfeld. Tauenzien used his forces – numerically inferior to those of the French – very wisely and Bertrand's hesitant attack continued until 2 p.m. before petering out.

At approximately the same hour, Reynier attacked at Grossbeeren. The Prussians did not attempt to stop his advance. He captured the village fairly easily and began to make preparations to go into camp for the night, believing that the fighting had ended for the day. He did not bother to designate forces to pursue the retreating enemy and lost contact with him. Reynier was not aware of the fact that he was in fact planted opposite the entire Army of the North, excluding Tauenzien's corps. Bülow had been advancing since the morning along the road leading from Berlin to Grossbeeren. Bernadotte understood very well that the disposition of the French offered him a golden opportunity to destroy their middle column – the VII Corps – without the other corps having the possibility of intervening. But he hesitated, only acceding to the pleas of the Prussians to allow them to lead an immediate attack, even without the support of the rest of the army. Bülow wanted to make contact with the French. He met soldiers coming back from the area of the fighting and, from their reports on the situation of the French, concluded that it was possible to attack immediately. The heavy rain that had been falling most of the day kept Reynier's men from discerning the movement of the Prussians towards them and they were hit in the midst of preparing their suppers. A close-range artillery duel commenced and the Prussians began to flank the French to the east of the latter's position, over heavily wooded ground. Towards evening the Prussians attacked from the north and east and Bülow led a cavalry charge that broke the backs of the French units still fighting. Reynier tried to organise a counter-attack, but it was carried out feebly. At this point, Reynier decided that there was no point in further decimating his forces and that it would be best to withdraw. The French retreat to the south was a panic-stricken flight. In the morning Reynier reached Löwenbruch.

Oudinot, who had been advancing on the left on the 23rd, heard the sounds of battle from the direction of Grossbeeren at six o'clock in the evening, when he was at Ahrensdorf, moving toward Potsdam. He dispatched cavalry to the area of the fighting, which arrived two hours later. A wild, confused battle ensued and in the end the forces broke off contact without reaching any decision. Oudinot and Reynier met in the night and Reynier convinced his superior that his corps was incapable of continuing to fight. Oudinot decided to retrace his steps and ordered the forces under his command to retire to their starting point on the Elbe. The pursuit of the French was feeble, as the Prussians were worn out from the previous day's effort, but in the following days the French retreat to the Elbe was marked by continual fighting.

Bernadotte too was afraid to advance too far, lest he be greeted by a French attack in his front and on his right flank. And a French division under Girard was in fact advancing towards his right flank, having begun to move from Magdeburg towards Belzig on 21 August. All along the way it skirmished and clashed with the enemy but, on the 27th, the Prussian corps responsible for covering the right flank of the Army of the North mounted an attack against it. The battle, known also as the battle of Hagelberg, lasted all day and ended in complete victory for the Prussians. What was new here, and a bad sign for the French, was that the Prussian corps was second rate from both the standpoint of the quality of the new troops that filled its ranks and the quality of its commanders, while the French division was battle-hardened and far more experienced. The French also had a numerical advantage in every department. After this series of battles, Bernadotte advanced on the Elbe from north of Wittenberg, deploying there at the end of the month.

So much for France's first real effort to attack Berlin in the campaign. Historians and analysts are convinced that entrusting the Berlin mission to Oudinot was a big mistake. He had accepted the assignment with a singular lack of enthusiasm. He had represented his misgivings to the emperor: the corps under his command did not constitute a well-meshed force, they were numerically inferior to the enemy, the terrain was difficult, etc., etc. Given the emperor's shrug of his shoulders, Oudinot accepted 'with much self-denial ... the accomplishment of my difficult task, whose unfortunate result I all too well foresaw'. Analysts writing about the command of Oudinot's army are convinced that Davout, who was operating in a marginal sector in the northern part of the lower Elbe, would have been much more successful and they find it hard to understand why Napoleon preferred Oudinot over him. It is possible that the reason is tied to Berthier's bad relations with Davout, or to his bad relations with Ney, going back to the Russian campaign. In any event, Davout, who had been quite active in the first days of the renewed fighting, sealed himself up in Hamburg with his small force the moment he heard the results of the fighting in the Berlin area.

Let us return to Dresden, to the observation point south of the town where the allied rulers looked out across the next day's battlefield. It was the evening of 25 August, a hot summer day. Opposite them was the Old Town (Altstadt) of Dresden, already known by that name. It nestled on the left bank of the Elbe, south of the big bend in the river twisting to the north-west. A big stone bridge at the royal palace of the Old Town connected it with the New Town (Neustadt), also known by this name at the time. The New Town was well defended with engineering works, which had been strengthened and augmented since the arrival of the French in the town after Lützen. They had also improved the defence of the Old Town during the armistice, as the expected participation of Austria in the war made imperative the fortification of this bank of the river as well. With the need to strengthen this sector, the French emplaced five batteries around the outer ring of the Old Town. These commanded a flat, unobstructed field of fire. About a kilometre north of the river bend the Weisseritz River emptied into the Elbe, flowing down from the south-west and bordering the Friedrichstadt quarter. This quarter was completely undefended and the nearby riverbanks were unfortified. Near the Old Town, south-east of it, in an area measuring one by two kilometres, was a park called the Grosser Garten with a palace in its centre. This area was vital for the defence of the outer eastern sector, which was a broad, open area. The high hill region commanding the plateau south of the river extended in a semicircle from Tschernitz to Brieznitz.

The allied rulers had indeed missed an opportunity to strike at the close of day on the 25th or even early the next morning. On the morning of the 26th, two French infantry corps, one cavalry corps and the Guard were moving rapidly towards Dresden from the east. Napoleon himself reached the town during the morning and mainly examined the progress of the engineering work. Right behind him came the reinforcements, exhausted from the rapid march and pouring into the town without a stop. Vandamme's corps occupied the Pirna–Königstein sector. Napoleon, who at first had planned to attack in strength from Vandamme's direction, had to give up this alluring plan because of the pressure already being brought to bear against Dresden. He left the attack from the direction of Königstein by one corps only to Vandamme's discretion. Saint-Cyr's corps, less a division stationed at Königstein, and another few thousand troops from such French satellites as Westphalia and Holland, arrayed themselves in a still thin defence line blocking the passages through the town and its suburbs.

The allies strengthened their forces all through the night and with the break of day on the 26th were in a threatening position, extending from Bläsewitz on the Elbe, east of Dresden, to Plauen on the Weisseritz, a few kilometres south-west of the Old Town. The Russians held the right, up to Grüna, as well as Göstritz on the high ground of the centre of the line. The Prussians were to the left of the Russians, in the hill region up to Ostra, and the Austrians completed the line on the left flank, up to Plauen. A reduced corps, consisting of a cavalry division and elite units under the command of Miloradowitz, was still in the Dippoldiswalde area and Klenau was in the Freiberg area.

Schwarzenberg's attack orders for the morning of the 26th were halting, calling for 'preparatory reconnaissance in force, from several directions'. Such orders are odd for an army as large as the one massed before Dresden. The Russians and Prussians went into action at 7 a.m., attacking in the direction Grosser Garten. The fighting lasted a few hours with the French holding the line without losing any important positions in this sector. The Austrians began their attack in the Plauen sector at approximately the same hour with more or less the same results.

In the afternoon, when the fighting died down a little, the allies were somewhat nearer to the French redoubts but had not succeeded in really penetrating them. At this hour Napoleon was occupied directing the troops arriving in the town to their designated positions and giving orders to his artillery to fire on enemy units still in contact with the French forces.

At around noon, the Russian tsar and the Prussian king had again stationed themselves at the observation point where they had stood the previous day and observed the French reinforcements streaming into the town. Jomini felt there was no point in continuing the fighting here and suggested withdrawing to Dippoldiswalde. After a protracted discussion, Schwarzenberg ordered that the continuation of the attack planned for the afternoon be cancelled. 'The emperor is in Dresden!' he declared. 'It is impossible to doubt it!' For unknown reasons the cancellation order did not reach the troops and the signal to renew the attack – three cannon shots – was given.

The afternoon's fighting began at four o'clock and continued till dark. The Russians continued to attack on the right flank, from the Elbe to Grosser Garten, under heavy and continuous French artillery fire from the walls of the town and from behind their redoubts. The Russians managed to get even closer to the redoubts but not to capture them. The Prussians, operating mainly in the Grosser Garten sector, tried to overrun the French positions in co-ordination with the Russians on their right, but without success. The fiercest fighting took place on the left flank, where the Austrians assaulted the redoubts again and again but were unable to withstand the heavy fire of the defenders and retired from most points.

In another sector, far from the Saxon capital, to the south-east, Vandamme grappled with the challenge laid down by the emperor. The decision was indeed his, but the note he had received from the emperor on the morning of the 26th was phrased in such a way that few possibilities were left open to him if his honour as a soldier meant anything to him: 'It is more probable that the forces against you are quite inconsiderable. Debouch as quickly as possible and seize the plateau. Master of the extremity of this plateau, you will be so of the town of Pirna. This operation will carry terror to the enemy and may bring about a great result.' Vandamme therefore sallied forth from the Königstein area in the afternoon, crossed the Elbe and attacked the forces covering the route leading from the Erz Mountains to Dresden. The Russians held on until dark and when they could no longer withstand the pressure retired to the plateau along this route, abandoning Pirna. The defeat of the Russians mainly affected communications, as the Pirna route led from the mountain region and the supply depots for this flank of the allies.

All this time Napoleon was busy hurrying along the reinforcements. Before 6 p.m. he felt he had a large enough force at his disposal to mount a successful counter-attack. The rapid concentration of forces was an achievement in itself, which Count Yorck sums up as follows: 'How was this accomplished? By the fact that the emperor did not march in our modern marching columns, but on a broad front, and thus crowded together numerous forces in a short column, corps side by side with corps, corps close behind corps.' At this hour the strength of the allied attack had passed its peak and this had always represented the opportune moment for Napoleon to strike. He ordered the attack and himself rode to the suburbs south-east of the left bank to observe developments. He came up very close to the Russian forces and a few of the officers in his party were hit as a result. He had a good feeling and was sure of victory. He remarked that the enemy had indeed started out well but was now operating mistakenly and this could cost him the entire campaign.

The Young Guard, under the command of Mortier, was posted on the extreme left of the French and engaged in a fierce battle with the Russians, whose assault took them by surprise. By 8 p.m. Mortier had pushed the enemy back to Bläsewitz and Striesen. Other Guard units attacked the Prussians at Grosser Garten and there too a fierce fight developed. By nightfall, half the park area was in French hands and only the avenue running down the centre separated the two sides. Still other Guard units, including cavalry, carried out a determined counter-attack against the Austrians on the allied left. Murat led the attack and here too the French got the better of the fighting. A force patched together from Ney's nearby corps attacked on both sides of the Weisseritz and the Austrians were pushed back even further.

The fighting of the 26th waned, night descended and a hard rain began to fall. Fires had broken out in many parts of the town and the French ran wild in the streets. Napoleon visited his troops and praised their officers; he was quite pleased with the results of the fighting. The success of the French resulted from their determined stand in the face of allied pressure at the outset of the battle and the well-co-ordinated counterblow levelled in the second phase of the fighting. The result was even more striking in view of the fact that the French attack had been made mainly by units of the Guard, with the infantry corps not really getting into the fighting.

In contrast, morale among the allied forces fell sharply and the feeling at headquarters was of having missed out on an opportunity as a result of the hesitancy of the high command. Not only had the chance been missed to capture Dresden before the French forces arrived from the east but the attack orders for the same day had been equivocal and objectives had not been set forth clearly. In the view of the allies the battle of the 26th lacked importance, as it had ended with the two sides more or less occupying the same positions as at the start, but the fighting had exposed weaknesses in the system, particularly at the level of command. Losses amounted to 6,000, including 2,000 prisoners. The supply situation had been very bad, owing to the poor roads leading from the mountains to the battlefield area, but mainly because of the loss of control of the Pirna axis as a result of Vandamme's success. Having been pushed back by the French, the allied forces – as before the battle – took up the Elbe line, from the right, deploying along the ridge running to the Weisseritz and beyond. This line ran parallel to the Elbe, at a distance of five or six kilometres from it. Giulay's corps was in the rear, at Gittersee, waiting to make a junction with Klenau, which was expected to occur on the morning of 27 August. At allied headquarters it was believed that the French would attack first, the following morning, and allied forces were ordered to hold themselves ready.

By midnight the French had completed their night-time dispositions, arrayed in an arc paralleling the enemy line, but in the plain, nearer to the town. In the meantime the corps of Victor and Marmont had completed their junction with the forces at Dresden. On the right flank the French forces under Murat were superior in number, owing largely to Klenau's delay. Now these forces included the corps of Victor and Latour-Maubourg. In the centre, from Plauen to Strehlen, which was opposite Grosser Garten, the allies had the edge over the corps stationed there, those of Marmont and Saint-Cyr. The left flank, held by the Guard and other units, was under the command of Ney and here the French had a big advantage.

The heavy rains continued all that night and on the morning of 27 August the whole area was blanketed by a thick fog. The 27th was also a very rainy day, stormy and foggy. Napoleon looked out across the battlefield from the belfry of one of the churches and took note of enemy dispositions. He discerned the weakness of the allies on the flanks, mainly of Giulay, who was separated from the rest of the army, and decided to pin down the centre – as opposed to his usual practice – and attack the two flanks in strength, hitting the weaker left hardest. He wanted to destroy the forces on this flank before Klenau's arrival. The French deployed for attack early in the morning behind their redoubts and fortifications, which concealed their movements. During the morning an artillery barrage was unleashed preparatory to the attack. Murat came out of the Friedrichstadt quarter at 7 a.m. and attacked the Austrians west of the Weisseritz. He had a big advantage in cavalry. The weather considerably reduced the value of infantry, who had trouble firing their weapons effectively. Murat himself, at the head of two columns of cavalry, made a flanking movement and succeeded in attacking the Austrians in their rear. One after another, the Austrian positions were taken and Murat extended his hold south of the Elbe for a distance of more than ten kilometres from the river. On this flank the French cleared enemy forces out of their front completely. Thousands of Austrians laid down their arms. Among the many prisoners were senior officers.

In the centre the French were deployed as follows: Marmont on the right, Saint-Cyr to the left and two divisions of the Guard west of the Dippoldiswalde road. The French forces in this sector carried out their assignment – pinning down and blocking the enemy forces opposite them – driving back the assaulting Austrians and Prussians and keeping them under continuous artillery fire. Saint-Cyr even made an attack of his own before noon, capturing the Strehlen heights with a bayonet charge and emplacing artillery batteries there which did good work pinning down the enemy.

On the left flank, Ney and Mortier attacked the Russians furiously. Already in the first stage Mortier gained complete control of Grosser Garten. Ney arrived from the Grüna area and despite the stubborn resistance of Wittgenstein's troops drove them back to the Pirna axis and beyond. Because of the continuous downpour it was almost impossible to fire muskets, making it a battle of bayonets, lances and cannon. The allies tried to mount a large-scale counter-attack under Barclay, including Miloradowitz's reserve, but it was carried out weakly and achieved no results. In fact, Barclay did not act in the spirit of his orders at all, merely moving forces back and forth. He explained to Jomini that headquarters had sent him an attack order that could not succeed given the numerical superiority of enemy forces and if it were carried out on the large scale demanded and ended in failure, there would be a danger that their lines of retreat would be cut.

While the fighting at Dresden continued, Vandamme continued to press forward and, after a lengthy battle with the Russians under the command of Osterman-Tolstoy, gained complete control of the Pirna area. Effectively, the allies now remained with just one secure line of retreat – the Dippoldiswalde road – as the approaches to the Freiberg axis were now entirely in the hands of Murat, though Vandamme had not succeeded in cutting the road to Peterswalde completely.

Napoleon himself was very active during the fighting on this day. From six in the morning he had been riding from unit to unit. Before noon he was with the forces on his left flank and urged his troops to the attack under the difficult weather conditions. In the afternoon he arrived in Saint-Cyr's sector, near the village of Leubnitz, and issued orders even down to the level of the artillery batteries. One of them he ordered to silence an Austrian battery. Nearby were some horsemen who looked to be a group of dignitaries. The emperor's order was carried out, but he had no way of knowing at that moment how much reason he had to be satisfied with it. A shell hit General Moreau, who was among the group. He was seriously wounded and both his legs had to be amputated. A few days later he was dead. Before dying he managed to say to the tsar, who had come to visit him: 'How good it is to die for a good cause, under the eyes of so great a monarch.' A wartime story relates that the French caught a dog with a tag hanging from his neck that said, 'I belong to General Moreau.' The tag was brought to the emperor, who was curious to know who was hit among the top brass he had observed.

Assessing the situation, Schwarzenberg decided on a general retreat owing to the blows his forces had received in the various sectors, the bad weather, the depletion of ammunition, which was becoming more serious – particularly for the artillery – and above all the serious threat of being completely cut off from his lines of retreat. Alexander and Frederick William were against a retreat but, in the discussion they all had, Schwarzenberg was insistent. He ordered the retreat in three columns: the left on the Freiberg axis, the centre on Dippoldiswalde, the right on Hellendorf–Peterswalde. The retreat was scheduled to begin on 28 August, early in the morning, covered by fast-moving Cossack units and other irregular forces.

At Dresden, Napoleon won one of his greatest victories. He ploughed into a big army, manoeuvring brilliantly on both flanks, taking a large amount of spoils and many prisoners. His aim had been to push the Army of Bohemia out of the Dresden area and towards the mountains in order to shift the centre of gravity of the southern theatre to Bohemia. This was accomplished after two days of fighting when the enemy began to retreat, battered, worn out and abandoning large numbers of their wounded and much booty. In this battle, Napoleon was at his best, demonstrating impressive leadership and tactical resourcefulness in the style of his finest hours. He also took advantage of the weakness in allied military leadership during the battle as well as the tactical errors made on the 27th – particularly the disregard of the weakness of the left flank, which fell victim to the determination of the forces under Murat. This weakness resulted from the battle of Dresden along the outmoded lines they had vowed to free themselves from during the armistice. The fact that within a day Napoleon had forced them into a defensive posture despite their intention at the outset to attack is evidence of their failure in the conduct of the war. In Schwarzenberg's defence, his problem both as commander-in-chief and army commander should be noted – having the sovereigns underfoot. We have already mentioned that their presence not only created confusion in planning but also made it possible for any general dissatisfied with the Austrian commander's decisions to go directly to his master and protest. The size of the Dresden battlefield gave the French an immediate advantage and Napoleon knew how to exploit it to the full by attacking on the flanks while only pinning down and blocking the enemy in the centre: the two armies had been aligned along the segments of a circle with a common chord, the Elbe, but the arc of allied deployment had been twice as long as the French. Furthermore, the French had the town with its fortifications at their back and could easily conceal their movements to the front and use it as an excellent cover for riflemen and artillery. The allied command erred in not sending in the cavalry in the central sector. This was because of the difficult terrain, which the bad weather made even worse, and because the battle-ground was bristling with artillery, endangering the cavalry units. However, in addition to all these causes which are, so to speak, obvious, the allied failure indicates a deficiency in the level of operational command.

As mentioned, until 23 August Napoleon had been in the eastern sector with the corps pitted against the Army of Silesia. On that same day he turned over command of the army concentrated there to Macdonald and left for Dresden. The V, III and XI Corps were deployed in the Goldberg–Liegnitz sector, on both sides of the Katzbach. On the 25th, Blücher sent out forces to try to make contact with the French in the terrain compartment between the Katzbach and the river called the Wuthende Neisse (Raging Neisse), an indication of its sometimes turbulent character. These forces moved as far south as the Jauer area. The ground between the two rivers is not particularly rough but east of the Wuthende Neisse climbs to form imposing heights, making the right bank quite steep.

Before taking leave of Macdonald, Napoleon had told him that Blücher would probably try to attack him in the Bober sector while he was moving in columns. Therefore Macdonald was to lie in wait for him there, confronting him with a massed force and attacking while Blücher was still on the march. Macdonald saw his mission as a large-scale diversion. He was to divert the enemy's attention from Bohemia and threaten Breslau – that is to say, Silesia. According to him, that was what his commander told him when he explained the significance of the composition of the corps under his command.

No doubt the emperor's early departure for Dresden played into Blücher's hands after he had avoided coming into contact with the French wherever Napoleon was to be found. There was confusion connected with Napoleon's departure from the Bober theatre when he sent Ney instructions to join him. The latter thought his entire corps was meant and thus the III Corps started moving west. Macdonald waited two days to make a junction with this corps again, which Souham was now commanding. On the 26th Macdonald made up his mind to attack the Army of Silesia and move towards Jauer. However, Blücher also decided to attack that day and ordered that contact be made with the French in their positions in the Goldberg–Liegnitz sector. Incidentally, he too was informed of the order sent to Ney and also believed that it signified the imminent departure of the French III Corps from his sector. He imagined that Schwarzenberg's threat worried the French emperor a good deal and consequently was encouraged to renew his attack.

After the fighting along the Bober the Army of Silesia was not in too good a shape. The men were exhausted and supplies were not coming in. Blücher was afraid he was going to lose his army through a slow process of attrition and concluded that he had to move to the attack immediately to forestall such a sorry occurrence. But before he drafted his final attack orders, and while his forces were moving towards the expected point of contact, a clash occurred between Prussian and French forces.

Macdonald had planned his attack as follows: the III Corps (Souham) to cross the Katzbach at Kroitzsch and take the road connecting Liegnitz and Jauer; the XI Corps, now commanded by Gerard, and the II Cavalry Corps (Sebastiani) also to make their crossing at Kroitzsch and to march to the Wuthende Neisse, crossing it too and moving on Jauer to the right of Souham; the V Corps (Lauriston) to march from Goldberg to Jauer with the Wuthende Neisse to its left. The attack on the Jauer front was scheduled for 27 August and planned to be carried out with divided forces over a very wide area, as opposed to Napoleon's instructions. In fact, the French were moving on a more than 20-kilometre front, extending from Liegnitz to the north of Schönau. Furthermore, Macdonald went too far with his division of forces, taking two divisions from Lauriston and Gerard and sending them south into the mountain region.

On the 26th, before noon, the opposing forces were moving towards one another: Langeron, at the head of the Russian force, opposite Lauriston on the left bank of the Wuthende Neisse, at Hennersdorf, with superior numbers; Yorck and Sacken opposite the other three French corps – which outnumbered them but were divided – in the plateau on the right bank of the Wuthende Neisse, not far from the point where it emptied into the Katzbach. Blücher observed the French crossing the Wuthende Neisse under very difficult conditions because of the heavy rain and ordered that they be allowed to complete their crossing so that they could be attacked when soaking wet and in disordered ranks. The first troops to cross began moving towards the plateau in the Janowitz–Weinberg hills sector, infantry and cavalry mixed together, at around 2 p.m., with the Prussians and Russians awaiting them impatiently. An hour later Yorck and Sacken opened with a spirited assault, though the rain ruled out effective musket fire almost completely. They attacked Gerard and Sebastiani under the cover of heavy artillery fire while Souham's men were still struggling to get up the slope leading from the Wuthende Neisse to the plateau.

Battle conditions dictated the almost exclusive use of the bayonet and this was Blücher's finest hour as he urged his men to abandon their ordered ranks and cut down the French before they regrouped. 'I have enough French over here,' the old general complained. Disorganised hand-to-hand fighting broke out, a murderous battle in which the Prussians and Russians began to get the upper hand. Souham, who heard the sound of battle, made a supreme effort to bring his men forward in support, but his presence on the southern part of the battlefield, in the Nieder Krain area, only increased the crowding and disorder among the French, who were being pushed back further and further on the river, with heavy losses in casualties, prisoners and drowned. As mentioned, Macdonald and Souham were separated and Macdonald could not brief the commander of the III Corps. He could not even be sure that his orders had reached Souham. He claimed that even if they had been handed to him, Souham did not act in accordance with them. Now Blücher was ploughing into the rear of the retreating French and upsetting still further their movements in the sector stretching north to Dohnau on the Katzbach.

At the same time, less than five kilometres away, fighting broke out between Lauriston and Langeron, who ran into each other near Hennersdorf. At first, Langeron mistakenly believed that he was outnumbered and prepared to return to Jauer. Lauriston attacked and even achieved some success. Because of his position, had he been able to rout Langeron, he could have attacked Blücher from the flank and rear and decided the entire battle. But Langeron regrouped, making a determined counter-attack and recovering by evening all the ground he had lost in the initial stage of the battle. Lauriston had to abandon the battlefield and began to withdraw in the direction of Goldberg. The next day he was attacked there by Langeron and had to retreat further to Löwenberg, turning north to Bunzlau from there, crossing the Bober and calling a halt west of it. Macdonald withdrew Gerard, Souham and Sebastiani across the Katzbach, completing the movement on the 27th. It will be remembered that for some unaccountable reason he had sent two divisions south to the source of the Bober in the Hirschberg area. One of them, belonging to the XI Corps, retired before engaging in battle when word reached it that Macdonald had been routed. But the fate of the other one, belonging to the V Corps and under the command of Puthod, was bitter. Puthod tried to carry out his assignment and engaged a number of enemy units, but on the 29th, in the morning, he realised that he was surrounded and decided to try to escape. The division marched north along the Bober, but between Plägwitz and Löwenberg, Langeron's pursuing force caught up with it and it was forced to surrender after a fierce fight.

Napoleon, who during those very same days was achieving his victory at Dresden, was conceivably reminded of Marmont's warning that he might find himself winning a victory in one battle and learning that he had lost two. The defeats of Oudinot and Macdonald wiped away his own victory. He must naturally have gritted his teeth when he learned the details of Macdonald's fight on the Katzbach. For he himself had clearly defined the tasks of the Army of the Bober – to block the Army of Silesia and keep it from coming to the assistance of the two other armies by making a junction with them. He had strongly advised concentrating forces and not dividing them. Macdonald did the opposite. The weather was indeed bad, but it was bad for both sides. Macdonald did not have the slightest idea how to contend with the enemy's superiority in cavalry, the solution to which problem lay in occupying better positions. Jomini said that if he had followed the emperor's instructions and the latter had exploited his advantage, 'there is no question that his operational plan ... would have achieved the most brilliant success'. The very selection of Macdonald to command an army seems strange, as it should have been known from the first, through acquaintance with him, that he was not fit to command such a large force. He was a slave to detail, tactically limited and lacking broad military vision. He himself blamed his subordinates: Souham was too slow and Sebastiani manoeuvred poorly on the muddy plateau as did the artillery units.

Blücher achieved all the goals he had set himself for the latter days of August. He had won a victory in battle and driven the French from the Katzbach to the Bober and then from the Bober to the Queisse. His direction of the battle on the Katzbach had not been flawless, the most serious of his errors being his not exploiting his superior cavalry for gathering intelligence and fighting. Consequently the fighting had been largely unrestrained and disorganised, but Blücher had won, and that was what was important to him. His prestige among the coalition partners as someone capable of standing up to Napoleon rose considerably. The battle won him the title of prince. On 1 September he could report that Silesia was clear of the French.

The retreat of the allies into Bohemia had already commenced on the night between the 27th and 28th, in pouring rain and on poor roads. The units marched in tight formations and the troops were exhausted, hungry and almost barefoot. Morale was at a low. Had the French pursued them immediately, they would have been in serious trouble. But Napoleon had not imagined that the allies would retreat. On the contrary, he was certain that another day of fighting lay ahead of him, as can be seen clearly from the orders he drafted in the night preceding the 28th. Whoever compares the orders for following up the success at Austerlitz with the orders Napoleon dictated after Dresden has to conclude that a great change had come over the nature of the emperor's military leadership. On the evening of the 27th he wrote to Ney that 'the enemy is not in retreat and he regards the affair as an attack that had failed... Everything leads to the belief there will be a great battle tomorrow.' He wrote to Murat in the same spirit, expressing doubts as to the intention of the enemy to retreat. Later in the night he received a message from Marmont reporting that he heard sounds suggesting a retreat. Napoleon ordered him to follow the enemy along the Dippoldiswalde road and occupy commanding ground.

The next morning the emperor went out to the battlefield and observed the columns of the enemy being swallowed up in the valleys leading to the central Dippoliswalde axis. He ordered Murat to cut the Freiberg axis and Vandamme to prevent the retreat to Teplitz and cause maximum damage to the enemy's supply convoys. Saint-Cyr and Mortier were made responsible for the pursuit in the Dohna–Pirna sector and for mopping up the Elbe plateau. Marmont was ordered to keep after the central column. The pursuit was not conducted purposefully. Conceivably, the French were not aware of the disorganised retreat of the Army of Bohemia. As mention, in Napoleon's strategic concept the southern flank of the theatre of war was seen as defensive and therefore the victory at Dresden was also seen as part of the defence effort. In the meantime, the bad news from Berlin and the Katzbach reached him and if there had been any enthusiasm in him for the idea of striking into Bohemia it was considerably dampened by what he heard.

The retreat was carried out laboriously but with perseverance, up the mountains and through the few passes on the way. The Austrians took the Altenberg route and reached Dux, south of Teplitz, on 29 August. Klenau, who had not appeared on the battlefield at all and who was about to be cut off by Murat at any moment, bypassed the road to Freiberg and took a difficult route to Marienberg, arriving there on the 30th.

Barclay led the Russian–Prussian column that had operated on the right flank of the army at Dresden and was supposed to withdraw to Teplitz via the Peterswalde route. He justly feared that if he marched the entire column by this route he might find himself between Vandamme's corps to the south and the French forces pursuing him from Dresden. If that happened, he was lost. Consequently he veered to the right to the Dippoldiswalde axis, in a march that was a terrible nightmare for his soldiers, and made for Fürstenwalde, the main body arriving on the 29th. Kleist was forced to take to the hills, abandoning the crowded road with its men and wagons, in order to forge ahead.

On the morning of the 28th, the allied forces that had fought two days previously against Vandamme, under the command of Prince Eugen von Würtemberg and Osterman-Tolstoy, were south of Pirna, at which time a courier arrived with news of the rout at Dresden and the retreat to Bohemia. The two commanders fell to arguing: the Russian wanted to get to the road taken by Barclay in order to cover his movement and save the Russian Guard under his command; the Prussian insisted on staying where they were, on the Peterswalde road, so as not to give it up to Vandamme's Frenchmen. The Prussian prevailed, but not before confirming in writing that he was personally responsible for the decision. The two corps marched south, here and there cutting their way through with the bayonet and taking heavy tosses. On the evening of the 28th they reached Hellendorf and Peterswalde with the French right behind them.

A few hours before this, Napoleon had dictated an order to Vandamme from Dresden: he was to concentrate the forces operating in his sector – the I Corps and other units – and march to Peterswalde. From there he was to continue into Bohemia, striking whatever forces stood in his way and destroying as much equipment as possible. In terms of the French army as a whole, with the exception of Vandamme, the story of the pursuit and the exploitation of the success at Dresden ended on the 28th, in the night; Vandamme operated in the Bohemian theatre from 29 August. An order written out by Berthier at Napoleon's dictation gives Annaberg as the enemy's probable destination. In other words, the emperor believed that, in order to avoid contact with his forces along the routes rising into the mountains, the allies would bypass this area from the south-west with a huge flank movement. If that was what occurred, Vandamme would have a golden opportunity to do almost anything he liked in the area under his control: 'The enemy, whom we have defeated, appears to be retiring on Annaberg. His majesty thinks that you could arrive before him on his communications, and there take all his carriage, ambulances, baggage, in fine everything which marches behind an army.' Vandamme replied that he had around 6,000 Russians in front of him and was going to attack them on the 29th, at the crack of dawn.

On the morning of the 29th, Osterman-Tolstoy moved up the Peterswalde axis while his rearguard fought grinding holding actions along the way, up through Nollendorf, Kulm and Priesten. He sent a message to Teplitz intended for the tsar saying that he could not hold out against Vandamme and was continuing to retreat in the direction of the Eger River. The tsar was not at Teplitz, but Frederick William was and his reply to Osterman avowed that this retreat of his was endangering the entire army, and the life of the tsar as well. These arguments, particularly, it would seem, in regard to the tsar, persuaded Osterman to halt at Priesten and fight. Frederick William made great efforts to send him reinforcements. The tsar, too, having arrived in the meantime, succeeded in organising troops to aid Osterman.

In the afternoon the Russian Guard deployed along the line extending from Straden on the left to Karwitz on the right, with Priesten in the centre. This force, numbering around 20,000 men by evening after being reinforced, occupied a front of about five kilometres. From noon to evening Priesten changed hands a number of times in fierce fighting. Vandamme, who was assaulted by cavalry from the flank while advancing for the last time on the enemy position, decided to call off his attack until he concentrated more forces. He expected reinforcements from the Guard and from Saint-Cyr's corps, which were due to arrive during the night. During the evening the Russian tsar, the king of Prussia, Schwarzenberg and Barclay met in Priesten. It was clear to the four of them that they would have to continue holding off Vandamme if they wished the whole army to move into the interior of the country from the Erz Mountains. This seemed possible given their relative strengths, on the condition that Napoleon did not reinforce Vandamme during the night. On the 30th, at dawn, Kleist was scheduled to reach the front, marching now through the mountain region by irregular routes. Another concern of the allied leaders was that the French and Bavarian forces, under Augereau on the Inn River in Austria, would advance into Bohemia to make a junction with the rest of the army. A courier was sent to Blücher with an order instructing him to march to Bohemia immediately.

The battlefield of 29 and 30 August was an equilateral triangle whose vertices were at Tellnitz, Priesten and Striesowitz and whose sides were about five kilometres long. This terrain compartment stretched to the upper and very steep level of the southern part of the Erz Mountains. The village of Kulm was located in a valley commanded by a wooded ridge sloping down into the valley and affording an excellent view of the entire area.

Until the morning of the 30th the Army of Bohemia concentrated large forces in the sector, giving it a considerable edge in numbers. These forces consisted mainly of the Russian Guard, the troops of Prince Eugen von Würtemberg, Colloredo's Austrian corps and Kleist's corps, which was due to arrive before noon. The battle opened at 7 a.m. Vandamme attacked from the right and the Russians stopped him. Barclay, too, attacked from the right, in order to push the enemy back to the hills. Vandamme's situation became so perilous that he himself began to doubt whether he could continue to hold the Kulm sector. At around noon Kleist's lead troops, advancing from Nollendorf, charged out of Tellnitz and in their first assault scattered the French in their front.

With the progress of the battle the situation of the French worsened. Night fell, but the pressure on them did not abate and, at 10.30 p.m., Kleist's artillery, emplaced on the ridge line, bombarded the valley stretched out beneath it. Vandamme was tempted to believe that the sound of the cannonade presaged the arrival of the promised reinforcements, perhaps with the emperor at their head. When he understood that this was not the case he was already surrounded by all the allied forces that had taken part in the fighting and had no choice but to order a retreat. His idea was to flank Kleist's corps and break through there. The French forced their way between the enemy's infantrymen and overran a few batteries in the process. A number of units filtered through the wooded area. The breakout was accompanied by wild and confused fighting. French cannon and a good deal of equipment remained behind and many of the men were captured. Without a secure line of retreat the French scattered in every direction. Vandamme himself remained in Kulm until the last moment and was captured while trying to escape. He was taken with due respect to the tsar and a few days later sent to Russia, where he was imprisoned for a number of months, afterwards returning to France in time to fight one more time at Napoleon's side.

Vandamme's corps, the I Corps, was in effect destroyed at Kulm. In the middle of August it had numbered 35,000 men and after the battle mustered fewer than 10,000. It had lost all its guns and means of transportation. The emperor appointed a new commander to the corps, General Mouton, the count of Lobau. Lobau was one of Napoleon's intimates. He had done outstanding service as one of the commanders of the Imperial Guard in the 1809 campaign and was one of the few men chosen to accompany Napoleon on his journey from Smorgoni. He immediately got down to the job of rebuilding the unfortunate corps and within a few weeks managed to get it back on active service with the Grand Army.

The battle of Kulm, though not involving the main bodies of the rival armies, was none the less a turning point in the campaign as a whole. Saint-Cyr said of the defeat at Kulm: 'On that day we lost the fruits of the victory at Dresden. The enemy gained self-confidence and unity returned to its ranks. Napoleon lost the advantage of being the attacker, the enthusiasm of his soldiers waned and most of all – fear entered his heart.' And Cathcart, a writer with perhaps a vested interest, said: 'The fortunate victory at Kulm conferred advantages that are beyond all calculations. It was more than a compensation for the disasters of the army at Dresden and in the retreat. It raised the spirits of the disappointed soldiers and the confidence of their commanders, exactly at the right moment and in the right place.' The rout at Kulm was seen as demonstrating such ineptitude that, in trying to understand it, historians have latched on to an explanation that seems quite doubtful – that the bad weather caused Napoleon, who had caught a cold running around in the rain during the battle of Dresden, to stay indoors at the Dresden palace so as to avoid getting wet. All find it hard to explain why Napoleon did not exploit his success of 27 August properly, having conducted the battle with such skill, and are agreed that had he done so he would have been able to destroy the allies' biggest army.

There is no doubt that the weather was a major factor in the events of 28–30 August. The stormy night between the 27th and 28th was the reason that information about enemy movements was not gathered. Napoleon was sure that the enemy was regrouping for a continuation of the battle and that one more day of fighting lay ahead. He did in fact rise early on the 28th and reconnoitre the area at dawn as was his custom, but it was still difficult to predict the movements of the enemy to the point of reaching definite conclusions and changing plans. The terrain also contributed to the concealment of allied forces. Only later in the morning, when he rode with Marmont to the hills overlooking the Elbe plateau and saw what was happening behind them, could the emperor get a real impression of things as they were.

A real justification for his decision not to carry out a general movement with the army that had fought at Dresden, meaning a deep penetration into Bohemia, can be found in the news that reached him about the defeat of his marshals at Grossbeeren and on the Katzbach. The significance of these defeats was, among other things, that if he were to move south from Dresden he would run the risk of leaving Saxony at the mercy of the two victorious allied armies. This was a valid consideration, but only in part, for he still had forces facing these armies that were capable of fighting. He also did not have to march to Bohemia with all the corps at Dresden, given the sorry state of the enemy forces retreating before him and the fact that Vandamme was blocking their way with a large force. In any event, there is nothing in these strategic considerations to justify the weak and nonchalant pursuit on the night between the 27th and 28th. The crushing victory at Dresden demanded that the retreat be turned into a rout.

Napoleon thus gave up the idea of an invasion of Bohemia and at the same time also reached a strange conclusion about the direction of retreat of the Army of Bohemia. At a certain point on 28 August he was convinced that the direction of the retreat was to the west (Annaberg!) and this conviction also determined the nature of the assignment he gave Vandamme: not as a force intended for all-out fighting in its sector, which would have demanded serious reinforcement from the nearest corps – Saint-Cyr and Mortier and perhaps even Marmont – but as a kind of raiding force intended to stir things up behind the lines. And for his part Vandamme acted in the spirit of his instructions, believing that while he was engaged his comrades would push back the enemy in the other sector and together they would achieve an overwhelming victory. This line of thinking sat very well with the emperor's method of pinning down the main body of the enemy with part of his army while the other part undertook a large-scale manoeuvre leading to decision. Napoleon expected Vandamme to destroy Eugen von Würtemberg's force, which was much smaller than his. He did not anticipate that Eugen and Osterman-Tolstoy would recover and make a fight of it and that the allies would be able to reinforce them with some of the retreating troops and even get Kleist to the battlefield in a move that in retrospect is seen to have been decisive. And most seriously of all, Napoleon did not bother to inform Vandamme of his decision not to send him reinforcements, leaving him in the lurch. This is how Vandamme's command, not reinforced properly, was converted from a force capable of carrying out a brilliant operation and destroying the Army of Bohemia in the mountain passes into an ineffective force and the victim of a military disaster. An illuminating note sent by Napoleon to Saint-Cyr on 1 September reveals the extent of Napoleon's surprise when he understood from the reports what the battle of Kulm had looked like: 'The unhappy Vandamme, who appears to have killed himself, had not left a sentinel on the mountains, or a reserve anywhere; he threw himself into a gulf without reconnoitring in any way. If he had only four battalions and four guns in reserve on the heights, all this disaster would not have occurred. I gave him positive orders to entrench himself on the heights and only to send isolated parties of men to disturb the enemy and collect news.' There is no other documentation for an order of this kind and it would seem that this is an attempt at self-justification of the variety typical after military disasters suggesting in some way the failure of the supreme commander. The emperor did not attempt to hide his bitter disappointment and his contempt for Vandamme. One of his officers mourning the loss of the corps said it was one of the best corps in the army. Napoleon replied: 'Yes, with respect to numbers, but with respect to their military qualifications, they were louts, like all the rest.' Vandamme's biographer, on the other hand, blamed the emperor and even accused him of destroying evidence of his responsibility for the defeat of the I Corps, believing that Vandamme was no longer among the living.

Another strategic consideration attributed to Napoleon's decision not to leave Saxony has to do with his view of Austria. From this angle, he believed that if he did not invade Bohemia he would win the heart of the Austrian emperor, who would be ever grateful to him and perhaps even abandon the crumbling anti-Napoleonic Coalition. Given the blow the Austrians received at Dresden, where they were the principal victims of the defeat, there was some logic in this line of reasoning.

The events of August 1813 presaged the beginning of the end of Napoleon's glory. He had won one battle where he himself had been in command and was defeated in three battles under the direction of three of his senior commanders. Indeed he had still managed to teach his rivals a harsh lesson, but at the end of August they had learned that it was possible to defeat the French emperor and that they could achieve their aims. They knew that they still had to improve the co-operation in command between them and other basic factors involved in conducting a war, but they had the positive feeling that they were moving in the right direction.

Napoleon, ill and tired, summed up the lessons of August with the usual fine aphorism. This time it was another variation on a subject that had troubled him for a number of months because of his failures and he spoke it to Murat: 'This is the fate of war, exalted in the morning, low enough before night. There is but one step between triumph and ruin.' In a story there is no reason to doubt Napoleon is said at that moment to have picked up the map of Germany lying permanently by his bedside, looked at it and mumbled the words of the poet Corneille:

I have served, commanded, conquered forty years.
Of the world, in my hands, I have seen the destinies
And I have always known, that in each event,
The destiny of states depended on a single moment.

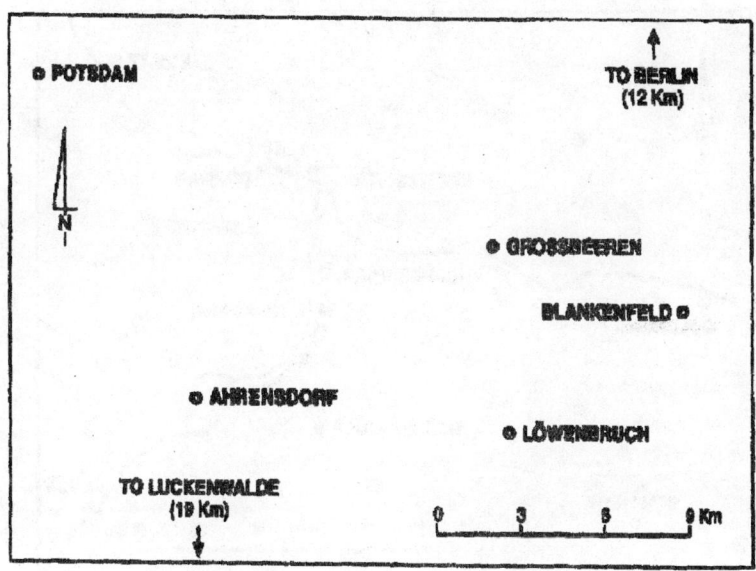

Map 10   Battle of Grossbeeren

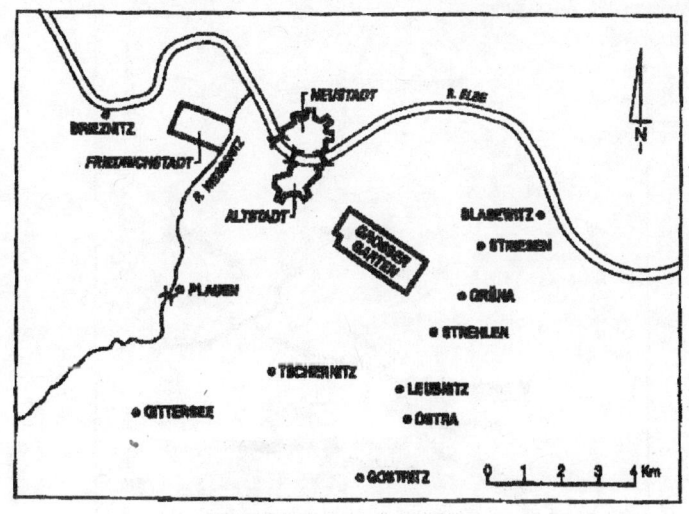

Map 11   Battle of Dresden

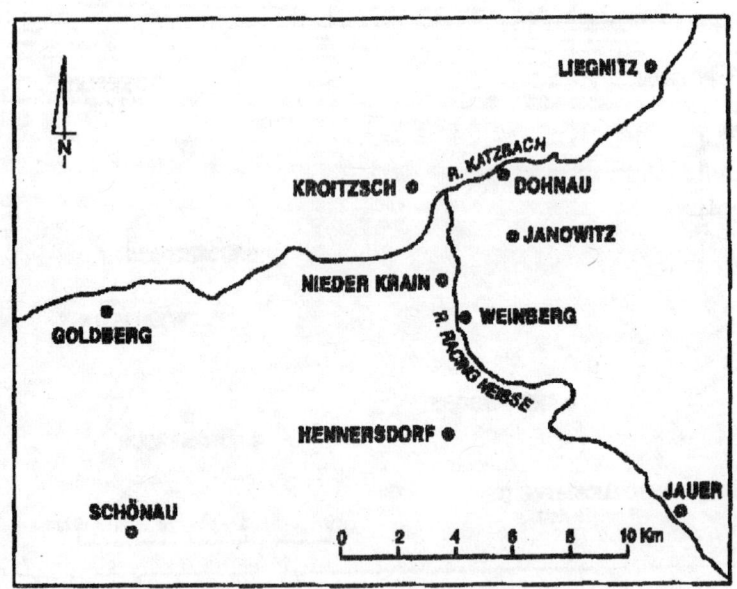

Map 12   Battle of the Katzbach

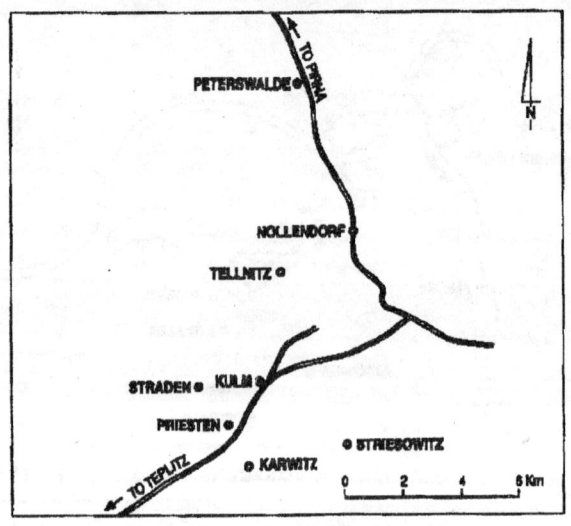

Map 13   Battle of Kulm

Chapter 8 - SEPTEMBER INTERLUDE

Three armies had been ranged against Napoleon in three sectors. Two had defeated his forces, whose commanders had made tactical mistakes and carried out their plans with little success. In the battle which he himself had directed the success was not inconsiderable but the sting had gone out of it because of indecision and lack of follow-up. Now he had to decide on his next steps and it had to be clear to him that the allies had no intention of giving up. On the contrary, they had gained confidence and felt that it was within their power to achieve their political aims by conducting a military campaign against their ancient enemy. The basic decision Napoleon had to make was where to direct the main effort of the army.

Logic dictated that it should be directed against the Army of Bohemia. This was the principal force of the enemy. The main body of the French army was facing it and it had to defend territory important to the weak partner in the Coalition fighting the French emperor. If he continued attacking this army he would not lose the initiative. Furthermore, opposite the other two allied armies he had considerable forces capable of pinning them down, thus isolating the sector where he was operating against Schwarzenberg's troops.

At the beginning of September, Napoleon decided to make his main effort – incredibly – against Berlin. He replaced Oudinot with Marshal Ney – proof that he no longer trusted Oudinot with a force larger than a corps. On St Helena, where he reflected on his actions again and again, he was more forgiving and attributed a measure of success to him at Grossbeeren, because he 'drew the enemy from his lines, dragged Bernadotte towards Wittenberg and left open the line from Dresden to Berlin'. Now Napoleon planned to put together a force including two infantry corps, the Imperial Guard and cavalry. All these, under his command, would render assistance to Ney. He instructed Ney to be at Baruth by 6 September and attack Berlin no later than the 10th.

On 30 August, Napoleon produced an enlightening document summing up his estimate of the situation and his thoughts about the next phase of the war. In essence, the document – called 'Notes on the General Situation of My Affairs' – brought him to the conclusion that a campaign aiming at the capture of Prague would not be wise. If he were led into it, his lines of operation would be dangerously over-extended, from Bohemia to northern Germany, and he would be vulnerable to attack. He himself would be at the far end of the line and would not be able to make his presence felt if a crisis erupted somewhere else. The chances that he would take Prague were slim, since the enemy would reach it first and it was well fortified.

An operation against Berlin was much more logical, justifying his breaking off contact with the army he had fought at Dresden. In fact, he would not really be breaking off contact. He would leave Murat, who would remain at Dresden, the corps of Saint-Cyr, Vandamme (he was as yet unaware of the defeat at Kulm), Marmont and Victor. Such a force could pin down and even block Schwarzenberg. Macdonald would pin down Blücher and hold Bautzen and Hoyerswerda. He debated whether to withdraw Poniatowski from his position at Zittau, where he was covering Macdonald's flank, and bring him to Hoyerswerda, where he could secure Ney's rear and join him in a four-day march.

Napoleon thus remained in thrall to his old obsession. He would capture Berlin and operate along the Oder. If he appeared before Stettin with a large army the Russians would not be able to remain indifferent and would send troops into the sector. The Prussians too would undoubtedly lose all interest in Bohemia when their capital was in danger. Thus he would bring about a sharp clash of interests among his foes. He would also be able to hit Blücher in his rear in the second stage. If he marched to Berlin he would be operating in the centre of his line of operations linking Hamburg and Dresden, just five days' march from either end. He would create dilemmas and threats disturbing the Russians and Prussians and in this way 'I should be menacing Prague without going there'. The Austrians would be isolated and have to return to Dresden under the pressure of their partners and 'if they recommence their foolishness, I should be back in Dresden with an assembled army; great events, a great battle, would terminate the campaign and the war'.

Napoleon concluded: 'The Prague project. I must go there personally.' For such an operation he could only earmark those corps that were in the area in any case. The rest of the army would be greatly over-extended: Davout in Hamburg, Oudinot at Wittenberg and Magdeburg with three corps and Macdonald in the Bautzen area. In a word, a defensive alignment. 'I am threatening nothing. The offensive is the enemy's. On the other hand, if I carried my headquarters to Luckau, I should be two days from Torgau, three days from Dresden, four from Görlitz. I should then be in a central position abreast of choosing my course, either to throw all that I desire on Berlin, or go there personally.'

These lines of thought run counter to the logic that had always guided Napoleon. He was in the habit of rejecting ideas that focused on geographical localities and not on military forces. He always aimed at defeating the main enemy army facing him 'and the others will fall by themselves'. No longer. He would be transporting himself to distant sectors and believed that from there he would be able to influence the principal front. He had not adapted himself to the new reality, which was foreign to him, a reality in which countries joined in a coalition against him were determined to defeat him and prepared to disregard narrow interests, even if it cost one or two of them the temporary loss of territories, important towns or prestige, so long as the final aim would be achieved at the end of the process.

Soon enough the facts hit him. Macdonald, who had retreated from Blücher after the defeat on the Katzbach, had withdrawn all the way to Bautzen, from the Katzbach and the Bober to the Spree. Blücher's men did not pursue them hard, breaking off the chase on 2 September, but he pushed his forces to march rapidly by the southern flank to the Spree.

Napoleon did in fact send Ney to replace Oudinot on 2 September, but he himself left for Bautzen on the 4th to be at Macdonald's side and stop Blücher, with the idea of setting out for Berlin only afterwards. He sent Macdonald an urgent message to concentrate his army in anticipation of the expected attack. 'I desire to be able to ride in half an hour along the whole front of the army.'

Napoleon indeed acted with determination when he joined Macdonald. On his way there he ran into numerous stragglers from the XI Corps and his temper flared. He went wild with rage, galloping back and forth and haranguing the men. At Bautzen he met Macdonald and Sebastiani, went over their recent operations with them and ordered them to be ready to mount an immediate attack. Already on 5 September he went into action, attacking units of the advance guard of the Army of Silesia near Hochkirch and driving Blücher across the Neisse. The Prussian general discerned immediately that the emperor was on the front and acted post-haste in accordance with the Trachenberg doctrine, that is, he broke off contact and avoided battle. Though Blücher had avoided battle intentionally, he declared to his staff that if the

French moved out of this sector for Zittau in order to drive their way into Bohemia he would go out after them.

As Napoleon was about to leave for Hoyerswerda, bad news arrived from Dresden: the enemy was sweeping down from the mountains and threatening to reach the Pirna axis. The emperor dispatched Latour-Maubourg there and hastened to go himself, once again postponing his departure for the north to be at Ney's side.

Schwarzenberg had again sallied forth from the mountains of Bohemia to renew contact with the French, but this time with the involvement of the Army of Silesia as well as his own. Consequently he sent a strong advance guard under General Ziethen towards Dresden, on the Pirna axis, while he himself led a big Austrian force towards Rumburg and Zittau. The second movement, carried out on the other side of the Elbe, was intended to create a threat on the flank of the French forces fighting against Blücher. Schwarzenberg hoped that Napoleon would be drawn to Dresden and concentrate most of his forces there, making it easier for Blücher to destroy those still facing him.

Barclay remained in Bohemia with the Russian and Prussian troops and two Austrian divisions. The allied plans for him were that if Napoleon turned on him in strength from Dresden he would avoid battle and retire. If outnumbered, he was even authorised to cross the Eger River to the area south of it. The Austrian movement on Zittau would indeed create a threat useful to the Army of Silesia, but it would also serve as part of the alignment for the defence of Bohemia if Napoleon attempted an invasion from the direction of Zittau. That is to say, the allied command was very much concerned that the French would capture Prague, though we have seen that Napoleon gave up on this idea in favour of the offensive against Berlin.

Saint-Cyr, who had the responsibility of defending Dresden on the Pirna axis, occupied his designated line on 7 September. On the same day he met the emperor, who remarked that he had erred in not going to Vandamme's assistance but did not respond to Saint-Cyr's reply that now he had another chance to strike Schwarzenberg. Apparently he did not wish to be distracted from his plans for the Army of the North. On 8 September, in the afternoon, Saint-Cyr attacked in his sector and Barclay's forces retreated on the Peterswalde axis. On the 9th, Saint-Cyr advanced on the old Teplitz road passing through Fürstenwalde to head off the enemy retiring on the parallel road and attack him in the rear. Napoleon joined him.

Schwarzenberg, who received reports of the French movement and Napoleon's presence quickly called back the forces he had sent to the Zittau sector and ordered the Austrians at Chemnitz and Freiberg to assemble in the anticipated battle area. On the morning of the 10th the French were in a position overlooking the site of Vandamme's battlefield in the Kulm area. The emperor looked down into the valley and saw the Russians and Prussians streaming towards him. The Austrians had not yet arrived. Saint-Cyr began making preparations to sweep down the slope and charge the enemy, but Napoleon thought better of it and ordered him not to engage his forces but only to observe enemy movement from his hilltop position. Saint-Cyr was surprised. The emperor already knew what had befallen Ney a few days previously and this may have influenced his thinking. It was possible that he was afraid that if he became engaged here he would remain absent from Saxony and if Bernadotte neared Leipzig it would greatly endanger his positions there.

The following days saw some skirmishing in the rough ground between Pirna and Nollendorf, clashes without any defined purpose indicating that at this stage of the campaign Napoleon, who was present in the sector all through the period, did not intend to make any move of strategic significance – not in Bohemia, but also not in Berlin. On the 12th he ordered his main force to come out of the mountain region and return to Saxony. He himself started back to Dresden. The turn of events served Schwarzenberg's purpose – to keep the French from descending into the valley and threatening Prague. His Russian and Austrian forces had time and again stopped all such attempts, even causing the French heavy losses in men and equipment.

At this point the two sides avoided making any far-reaching operational decisions and committing their main forces to a large-scale offensive. On the 16th Napoleon was still convinced that he could prevent Schwarzenberg from leaving the valley for Saxony and this was also his principal aim. Schwarzenberg himself saw in Napoleon's movements preparations for a large-scale invasion of Bohemia. The emperor guessed his intentions, saying: 'I cannot believe that the enemy is going to attack in earnest; if he is getting ready, it is merely because he expects to be attacked. I shall be content with this game of moving hither and thither, and wait for an opportunity.'

Ney reached the Wittenberg area on 3 September and reviewed the French troops, which numbered about 60,000 men. He found the condition of the troops unsatisfactory and also failed to receive satisfactory intelligence as to the condition of Bernadotte's army, including its location. These two facts kept him from launching an immediate attack, but he still remained faithful to Napoleon's orders and attacked on 5 September, in the direction of Juterbog on the northbound road from the Elbe to Berlin. He pushed back Tauenzien's Prussians after striking them at Zahna. Bülow, who was to the west, had to come to his colleague's aid during the night and approached the French positions without being seen. On the morning of the 6th the two Prussian generals met and co-ordinated their operations. Ney, who did not make previous reconnaissances, was surprised to discover that the enemy was arrayed for battle on the high ground above Dennewitz.

In his briefing to Ney before setting out, the emperor had estimated that his appearance alone would result in the withdrawal of Bernadotte's forces towards Berlin. He had not understood from the battle at Grossbeeren that the enemy's performance had reached a satisfactory level and that it was therefore desirable to proceed with caution. The result was that Ney dispersed the corps under his command instead of keeping them together in a single concentration. On the eve of 6 September, Bertrand's IV Corps was south of Juterbog with the task, among other things, of covering the left flank in the general movement in the direction of Berlin. The VII Corps was at Zahna preparing to move in the direction of Dennewitz. The XII Corps was north of Sayda. Ney's army also included the III Cavalry Corps, which was arrayed in the rear of the infantry, and Dombrowski's Polish division.

Dennewitz is located on the road from Wittenberg to Berlin, which passes through Juterbog. The surrounding area is flat and open, spreading out between low-lying and gently sloping hills. The plain is bisected by the Agerbach creek, running from the east to the west. The banks of the creek were quite marshy and it was thus possible to cross it only via the bridges at Dennewitz and Rohrbach. The area was suitable for the deployment of both infantry and artillery.

Now, with the Prussians arrayed before him, Ney only had Bertrand's IV Corps at his immediate disposal; Reynier and Oudinot were still on the march in the rear, at intervals of two hours from one another. The march was difficult because of the sandy ground. Quickly, most of the Army of the North assembled in the area. Its aim was to catch the French in a kind of ambush. However, in the first stage of the battle one of Bertrand's divisions clashed with Tauenzien's force. At first it seemed that the French had the upper hand, but the two sides waited for the arrival of Bülow's corps – Tauenzien in order to make a junction with him and seize the initiative and the French in order not to expose their flank to him while assaulting Tauenzien.

Bülow arrived at Nieder Gorsdorf early in the afternoon and attacked Bertrand from the flank. A seesaw battle developed, but by the end of the day the Prussians had the better of it and cleared the enemy out of the area north of Dennewitz. The late arrival of Reynier's corps with Oudinot's in tow did not do any good. Oudinot remained near Sayda until the afternoon, though he could hear the sound of the cannons very well. He only began to move when an urgent order from Ney reached him, but marched at an ordinary pace and showed no eagerness to rush to his colleague's aid. Reynier displayed no more enthusiasm than Oudinot. The two corps became engaged at 1 p.m., fighting side by side, but the lack of co-ordination between them as well as with Bertrand's corps deprived Marshal Ney of the victory. He himself stayed with the IV Corps instead of directing the entire battle from a central position. French losses reached 10,000 men while Bernadotte lost fewer than half that number.

Ney was forced to order a retreat. The French were seized by panic and by evening the retreat had become a rout. The retreating troops overtook the supply wagons and chaos ensued. Ney tried to restore order, but in vain. Reynier and Oudinot marched towards Torgau. Ney and Bertrand made for Dahme but ran into Prussian forces there and had to engage them. After extricating himself, Ney came to the conclusion that his force was too small and set out for Torgau as well. Not stopping there, he crossed the Elbe and some of his units fled as far west as Düben to pick up their pieces and reorganise.

Ney's defeat at Dennewitz was no less serious than Oudinot's at Grossbeeren and Macdonald's on the Katzbach. Ney failed completely as commander of an army of four corps. The army was dispersed and its full strength was not felt during any stage of the battle. Ney did not prepare a clear, single-minded battle plan and was personally involved in the fighting instead of directing it. Oudinot's lack of enthusiasm, which bordered on a breach of discipline and indifference, played no small part in the disaster. Morale in the Army of the North got a huge boost while plummeting among the French. Again Napoleon was not without blame: in choosing the commander, in his vague briefing and in the hopes he aroused, including his unfulfilled promise to be present himself in the theatre of action.

The battered Ney wrote immediately to the emperor, hiding nothing: 'I have been totally beaten, and still do not know whether my army has reassembled.' He offered his resignation and asked to serve as a simple soldier. The news reached Napoleon on the evening of 8 September, when he was dining with Saint-Cyr. He reacted quietly, without any of the outbursts of past occasions. According to Saint-Cyr, he fell once again to philosophising about the changing fortunes of war and referred to the Dennewitz disaster 'with all the coolness he could have brought to a discussion of events in China in the preceding century'. On the 14th he wrote to Bertrand: 'I see with pleasure that your corps behaved well, but I have seen with pain the bad issue of the battle, which seems to me to have been ill engaged. I shall soon take the command of the three corps, to strive to procure you your revenge.'

On 10 September, Napoleon instructed Berthier to order Ney to take up positions in the Torgau front. If the Army of the North marched on Leipzig or Dresden he was to impede its movement. Thus the French emperor's plan to capture Berlin was laid to rest for good. Bernadotte hastened to exploit his success, sending Bülow to lay siege to Wittenberg and his engineering units put up bridges at different points along the Elbe.

Count Yorck saw Napoleon's idea for a northern movement in a positive light despite the defeats. An offensive movement on Berlin would have expanded the theatre of war to the left, making possible control of the lower Oder area and over-extending the Army of the North. Yorck believed that these results would have given the French advantages and that their chances of success were good, 'taking into account Bernadotte's qualities, which were well known to the emperor'. Had the operation failed, it would have been possible to make an orderly retreat via Wittenberg and Magdeburg. One should not be enticed into drawing incorrect conclusions by 'the failures at Grossbeeren and Dennewitz, as it was impossible to foresee these defeats and the emperor had every reason to expect entirely different results'.

Jomini, on the other hand, criticised Napoleon's strategy after Dresden: 'Had he pursued the enemy into Bohemia after his victory at Dresden he would have spared himself the disaster at Kulm. He would have threatened Prague and perhaps would have been able to dismember the Coalition. To this error, another one may be added, no less serious – the battles he fought without massing his forces.' Clausewitz too felt that Napoleon would have done better to march on Prague (or in his words: 'To Vienna via Prague!'). One of the results of such a move would have been that Blücher would not have been able to remain in Saxony and would have had to come to the aid of the army in Bohemia.

The situation of the French army was not encouraging. Though the allies were still trying – successfully – to avoid fighting Napoleon personally, they had routed and humiliated his marshals. In the major battle at Dresden, which the emperor had directed, he had indeed prevailed, but the French had known the bitter taste of humiliation on the Katzbach, at Kulm, at Grossbeeren and at Dennewitz. The legend of the undefeated Grand Army suffered a ringing reversal and such a deflation of the myth had enormous significance in terms of the quest for decisive victory. The allies could rightfully tell themselves that the principle of avoiding battle against Napoleon had justified itself and that the moment was approaching when they might concentrate their efforts in order to smash an enemy that had lost much of his self-confidence. There are those who liken the battles of August and the early days of September to a bullfight, with each of the allied armies acting as a picador egging the bull on, wounding and weakening him more and more.

The picadors had almost finished their work and now the time was coming for the honing of swords and the coup de grâce. Bernadotte's army constituted a real threat, expected to arrive in Saxony almost without any opposition. Blücher was eager to operate from Silesia and the lower reaches of the Elbe. The French had suffered their defeats in a circle whose centre Napoleon occupied. This circle was getting narrower and narrower, constricting the emperor more and more. The advantage the French had derived from operating on interior lines had suddenly become a disadvantage because of the forces closing in on them.

In the French camp morale hit rock bottom. Many, it seemed, had lost their taste for the war, particularly among the officers, whose mood greatly affected the entire army. The frustrated Napoleon told Marmont: 'The chess board is very confused: it is only I who can know where I am.'

Another indication of the ever-tightening circle of operations and manoeuvres closing in around Napoleon was the difficult situation of his logistic set-up in the rear. Here partisans and irregular forces operated with considerable freedom and aggressiveness. Senior allied officers serving as communications officers with the Army of the North realised that the French rear was entirely exposed and reported this to general headquarters. The latter dispatched Cossack and other forces there who raided the bases on the Saale, sowing death among the French and taking thousands of prisoners as well as pillaging the rear artillery units and depots. The damage was so great and the disruption so distressing that Napoleon decided to create a special unit of infantry and cavalry to deal with the problem, under the command of Lefebvre-

Desnoettes. The unit, whose task was to secure the entire area west of the Elbe, began operating on 14 September. On the 17th, Augereau was ordered to transfer his IX Corps from Würzburg to the Saale in order to secure the passages on the river.

The war in the rear was something new and unknown in European warfare. It was rooted, among other things, in the nationalistic character of the campaign of 1813. The populace throughout Germany, which was extremely hostile to the French, came to the aid of the many raiding parties operating in the French rear, supplying them with food, forage and information on the French units.

Napoleon was aware of his weak points in maintenance and in discipline, whose decline was spreading through the army, and gave these problems much attention. Here, for example, is an order published on the subject: 'Every officer and sub-officer, who, being on grand-guard, shall neglect the precaution prescribed by military regulations; every commander, whoever he may be, of light troops sent on reconnaissance, or detached without infantry on scout duty, who shall neglect to take the prescribed precautions, every cavalry general who, flanking the position of the army, shall neglect to place his grand-guard as required by military regulations, and shall expose the army to a surprise of the enemy, shall be sent before a military commission and condemned to death.'

Saxony had been stripped almost completely clean and was incapable of supporting the French forces operating there and living off it. The problem of supply in the French army kept getting worse. Napoleon was well aware of all this and did not delude himself: 'The army is no longer being fed. It would be an illusion to take any other view of it.' At the end of September it was necessary provide forces on the scale of a corps to protect the supply convoys. Napoleon could also not count on reinforcements joining him. In fact, Augereau's corps, with fewer than 20,000 men, was the only fresh force reaching him in September. The XII Corps was dismantled and two of its divisions attached to Reynier's corps. Oudinot received two divisions of the Young Guard in his command. The allies, on the other hand, received a reinforcement of Russians under Bennigsen's command which had been earmarked when manpower needs were mapped out during the armistice and numbered more than 50,000 well-equipped men.

Napoleon had completely lost the initiative, which had enabled him to control events to one extent or another. The negative consequences of his loss of initiative did not escape his notice, causing him growing concern. He himself had said that there was no substitute for lost time in war. On 21 September he published an order whose main aim was to consolidate his forces and set out their tasks for the near future, which would predictably be characterised by offensive-minded allied initiatives, the ball now being in their court. The order was prefaced by the somewhat self-justifying remark that the bad weather necessarily limited movement. This was not a factor that played an important part in Napoleon's orders and planning, but it was mentioned time and again in those waning September days. 'Why hurry?' he said to Berthier on the 20th in a tone that students take to be a sign of his depleted energy. 'We have time enough, what cannot be done today will be done tomorrow.' He instructed his chief of staff to inform Murat, Marmont, Macdonald and Poniatowski that 'the wretched weather today renders every movement out of the question and if the weather is not better tomorrow, we cannot be ready to move, until the day after.' Yorck, who discussed this matter, quoted him as having said: 'The moment we let slip today, no eternity can restore.' He argued that in 1805 Napoleon's way of thinking had been entirely different: 'It is raining heavily, but that will not delay the forced marches of the Grand Army.'

In accordance with the order of the 21st the French army was mainly deployed on the left bank of the Elbe, between Magdeburg and Königstein. The centre of gravity of the Elbe line was around Dresden and south-west to its rear. Ney was given command of the Magdeburg–Torgau sector, with the emphasis on Wittenberg at its centre. Under his command were the III, IV and VII Corps. It followed that this force would be the one to face the Army of the North, which was expected to advance along the Berlin–Leipzig line of operations. Saint-Cyr was responsible for the Pilnitz–Königstein sector upstream on the Elbe, with the V, I and XIV Corps under his command and the assignment of defending the river line and blocking the Army of Bohemia if it came out of the Erz Mountains in the Königstein–Freiberg sector. The defence of the Dresden holding line up to Pirna was given to the XI Corps and the Imperial Guard. The II Corps was deployed at Chemnitz facing south to forestall a possible attack by Schwarzenberg in the sector extending from Freiberg to the Saale. The VIII Corps was stationed at Stolpen, about 20 kilometres east of Dresden, in a forward position, one eye on Bohemia and the other on Blücher on the Bautzen–Dresden axis. The VI Corps was also earmarked for Freiberg but if it became apparent within a few days that the enemy was approaching the Elbe in the Dessau area – and there were rumours to this effect stemming from the movements of the Army of the North mentioned above – it was to hasten to the Torgau–Wittenberg sector. After distributing the order of 21 September, Napoleon again thought things over and decided to put the emphasis on placing forces opposite the main passages of the Elbe, in accordance with the plan outlined in his previous order One can discern here a continuation of the unavoidable process of retrenchment that had set in since the stormy events of August.

Before the end of September, a month of 'indecision on both sides', as Von Cäemmerer put it, Napoleon made a diplomatic move whose aim was to try to end the war. On the 25th he sent a letter to Bubna, who was now serving as an Austrian general in the Army of Silesia. Napoleon claimed that he was truly and sincerely interested in peace and prepared to make far-reaching concessions to Austria and Prussia 'if they will only listen to me'. But the Austrian emperor did not deign to listen as, in the meantime, his military support of Russia and Prussia had become a real alliance and he felt considerable commitment to them. In addition, he was about to reach an agreement with England on the increase of its financial aid and with Bavaria on its official inclusion in the coalition. These anticipated agreements served to toughen his stance as well as bolstering his confidence in the approaching military victory.

Now, when the initiative was entirely in the hands of the allies, they were uncertain what to do. They weighed a large-scale offensive, with ideas revolving around the main objective and the grouping of forces. It was clear to them that the main effort had to be based on the Army of Bohemia, not only because of its strength relative to their other armies and the armies of the enemy but also because of its position given the centre of gravity of the French forces. It was also clear to them that they would have to use the Army of the North as a hammer pounding away on Schwarzenberg's anvil. Accordingly, the Army of Silesia was the 'secret move' in the game of chess that had developed in the second half of September. At first it appeared desirable to attach Blücher's army to Schwarzenberg's and he would therefore have to move to the mountainous Zittau and Rumburg passages. At Schwarzenberg's headquarters, wild ideas were sounded too, such as having the Army of Bohemia move under cover of the mountains and south of them towards Bayreuth, bypassing Saxony and threatening the routes back to France. In the end, good sense prevailed and Saxony remained the main objective, to be approached in the normal way, via the Erz Mountains, with the direction not

Dresden but Leipzig. The allied command was afraid that if the attack were directed against Dresden, Napoleon would quickly break off contact, and if that were to be the case it was preferable to attack Leipzig. These ideas were interesting and in keeping with the military situation that had been created but there is little question that Schwarzenberg was lacking in boldness in September, his activities being random and more in the way of responses to French movements than the product of clear and determined planning.

Because of the decision to see Leipzig as the main objective, Blücher's army was now planned to link up with Bernadotte. Blücher himself had not been keen on the idea of serving under Schwarzenberg and preferred co-operating with the Swedish crown prince. He believed that Bernadotte needed his help and since he was responsible for the sector that included the capital of Prussia, this was the sector where Blücher wished to operate and not in Bohemia. He also probably believed that if he operated alongside the neighbouring army, it would cause Bernadotte to be more active, for after Dennewitz Bernadotte had preferred 'to build bridges and remove them when he felt that the enemy was coming', in Von Cäemmerer's words, instead of riding the wave of success and rapidly crossing the Elbe and advancing.

Bennigsen was scheduled to arrive in Bohemia at the head of the Russian reinforcements to strengthen the army there. At the end of the month the allies were deployed as follows: in Bohemia – at the foot of the mountains, from the Aussig area to the passages leading to Chemnitz (Schwarzenberg); in the Bautzen area and to the right of the Elbe – for the purpose of the junction between Blücher and Bernadotte; in the very broad area from Jessen on the Elbe to Barby near the confluence of the Saale and the Elbe (Bernadotte). The plan of operations was that Bernadotte would cross the Elbe in the Wittenberg area, Blücher would cross in the Torgau area and Schwarzenberg, reinforced by Bennigsen, would invade Saxony. The wedge whose long side was along the Elbe and whose short side was at the base of the mountains was to become a tightening ring.

The decision to deploy opposite the Elbe passages led to a number of adjustments and before the end of the month French deployment looked like this: on the Elbe, between Torgau and Wittenberg – Ney with the IV and VII Corps; on the Elbe, between Dresden and Torgau – the III and VI Corps along with the I Cavalry Corps; in the Dresden area (including Pirna) – the XI and XIV Corps and the Guard; along the road from Dresden to Leipzig – the V and VIII Corps; at Freiberg – the II Corps; the IX Corps, under Augereau's command, was on the way to Jena.

Count Yorck criticised Napoleon for his hesitation in September, and rightfully so. Though he did in fact achieve what he set out to do, it was for a limited time. He pinned down the enemy in Bohemia, commanded the mountain passes and lay in wait for Schwarzenberg along his lines of advance. But Schwarzenberg too achieved what he set out to do, both as commander of an army and commander-in-chief of all the allied forces. He held his ground without retiring into Bohemia and the fact that the French arrayed themselves in his front relieved Blücher of pressure and allowed him to move in very close to the main theatre of events. Yorck asserted with justice that the advantages gained by each side cancelled out those of the other but, when all is said and done, it was Napoleon who lost time. He gave his opponents the time to think, 'to bring harmony to their plans and to join their forces. He will assuredly be crushed by their superior forces united.'

September constituted an interlude in the campaign of 1813. After the great drama of May, after the armistice with its frenzied diplomatic activity and the military preparations during the summer and before the final battle of October – an intermezzo in September. The events that transpired during the month, as unexciting as they were, served as a vital and unavoidable phase in this all-European war. Napoleon's dilemma was complicated – whether to fight on German soil, seeking one great battle, or to abandon the country, retiring to the west and defending France. The allies, on the other hand, knew exactly what they wanted – to drive Napoleon out of Germany and chase him all the way back to France.

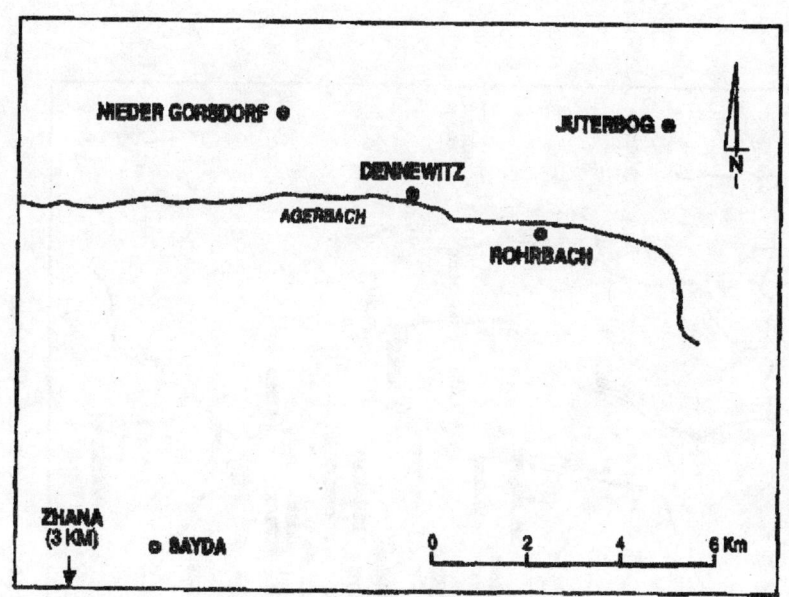

Map 14   Battle of Dennewitz

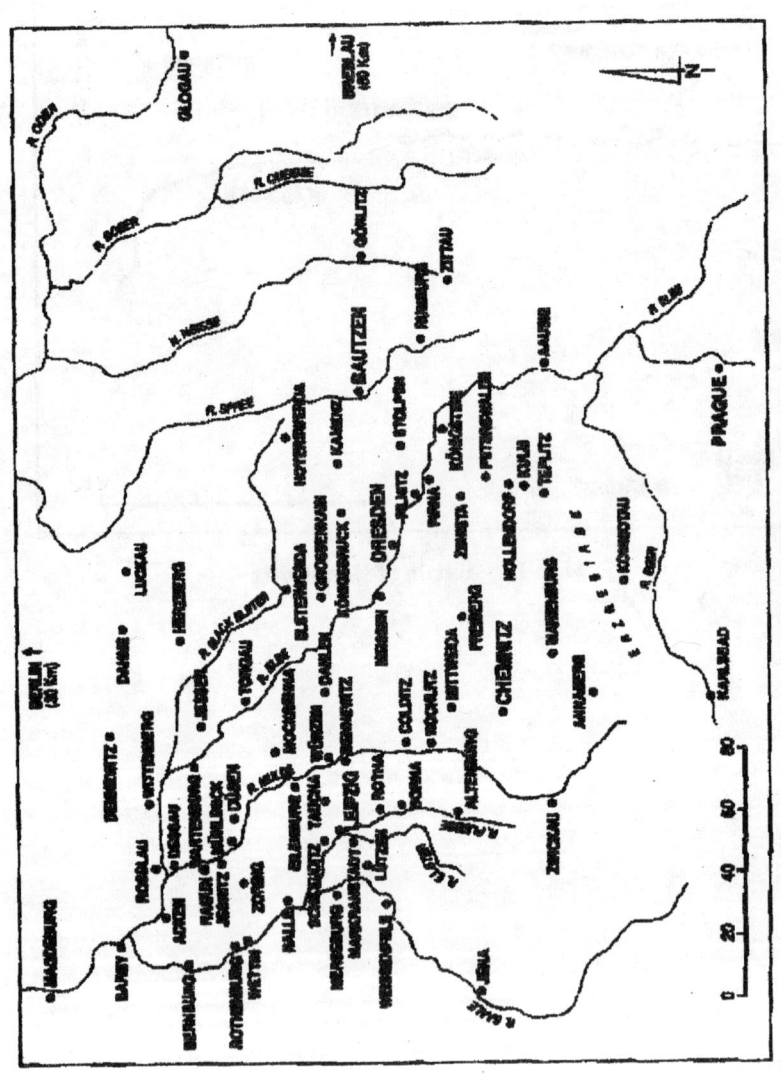

Map 15   Theatre of Operations: September–October

Chapter 9 - TOWARDS DECISION

Allied operations in the last days of September discomfited the French emperor to no small extent. On the distant western flank enemy raids were carried out against Lefebvre-Desnoèttes's units. On 26 September there was a raid on Altenburg on the Pleisse. The French general responsible for defending the rear withdrew his forces all the way back to the Saale. Napoleon concluded from this action that the Army of Bohemia was going to cross the western part of the Erz Mountains and invade Saxony from there and consequently he moved forces into the Leipzig zone. Blücher's movement towards the Schwarze Elster deceived Napoleon into believing that the Army of Silesia would attack Dresden from the north without having to cross the Elbe. But the Prussian general had planned to take the Kamenz–Königsbruck–Elsterwerda route and cross the Elbe at its confluence with the Schwarze Elster. On 4 October, Napoleon ordered Macdonald to carry out a reconnaissance in force towards Grossenhain and in other directions to seek out Blücher's forces and ascertain their intentions. In the same communication Napoleon asked his corps commander if he knew where Blücher's army was.

But Blücher did not leave the French in the dark for long, hastening to act. He left a Russian force of 20,000 men at Bautzen to defend the approaches to Silesia and nearer to Dresden an Austrian force of 10,000 (under our old friend Count Bubna). With the rest of his army he crossed the Elbe far from where the French were looking for him on the night of 2–3 October. When he tried to take Wartenburg he ran into stiff resistance from Bertrand. The terrain posed problems for Yorck's Prussians but after a day of fighting and after Blücher himself appeared on the battlefield Bertrand retreated to the south with his corps. (A year later the battle won for Yorck the title he is known by – Von Wartenburg.)

Bernadotte crossed the river at Rosslau and Acken on 4 October and pushed back Reynier's corps, which made no real resistance. On 5 October the energetic Blücher was already at Düben on the Mulde after dispatching troops to lay siege to Wittenberg and keep an eye on Torgau. Thus Marshal Ney found himself squeezed in between two armies, on the right and left, with the Mulde between them. Ney had the corps of Bertrand and Reynier under his command but could take no offensive action as he was outnumbered and the enemy armies could support one another if need be.

The allies were now in the midst of a large-scale movement. On 27 September, Schwarzenberg had begun moving from the lower reaches of the Eger to Saxony, from Kommotau towards Chemnitz and from Karlsbad towards Annaberg and Zwickau. On 5 October he was in the Marienberg area. Napoleon tried to head off the Army of Bohemia, without knowing exactly what it was up to. He put the II, V and VIII Corps and the V Cavalry Corps under Murat's command and ordered him to block the forces coming out of the Erz Mountains.

Had Napoleon had a clear picture of the allied advance from the beginning, a glance at the map would have told him where they were heading – to Leipzig. This conclusion would have forced him to shift the centre of gravity of his forces from Dresden and the area held for its defence to the space that had been created between the two arms of the allied armies. Concentration of the main part of the French army there would have enabled Napoleon to engage one arm while blocking the other. Information on the situation of the enemy and the engagement between Blücher and Bertrand began coming into French headquarters on 5 October. The emperor was greatly surprised. The allied command even believed that he had fallen into a certain apathy. He had failed to take account of the initiative of the old Prussian general. Napoleon wavered, changing his plans a number of times. On the night between the 6th and the 7th he formulated his new deployment orders, made necessary by his understanding of the enemy's intentions. The main idea was to base himself on the Mulde River, in the Würzen area, as a jumping-off point for making contact with Blücher's and Bernadotte's armies in order to strike them and afterwards link up with Murat, who would have blocked Schwarzenberg, and hit the Army of Bohemia.

In this document, Napoleon is again seen at his best, though it was drafted after much hesitation and indecision by someone who, in the past, had known how to act in such situations and get the most out of circumstances. In addition to ideas for an offensive he also mentions the possibility of deploying west of the Saale: 'As a result of this movement [to the Mulde], I shall be able to do what I choose. From Würzen I can go to Torgau against the enemy, debouching from Wittenberg, or turn my whole army on Leipzig for a general battle, or repass the Saale.' Shifting the centre of gravity from Dresden to the Mulde would enable him to strike any forces crossing the Elbe and drive them back. Afterwards he would be able to link up with Murat again and deal with Schwarzenberg. Napoleon relied on his ability to extricate himself from doubtful situations like the present one by simply giving battle. What the mind could not work out the sword could.

The estimate of the situation at allied headquarters, from the standpoint of the enemy's best course of action, was that Napoleon would do well at this point to concentrate all his forces and take up defensive positions across the Saale in order to command the main route to the Rhine and France. In such a case the allies would bring up troops from the rear to guard the rear and flanks of the forces advancing towards him; he would then have a strong and excellent line of defence and could begin a new phase of the war with a defensive battle that held good prospects for him. His decision to concentrate in the northern sector struck the pundits at allied headquarters as tantamount to playing into their hands.

On 7 October, at the end of the day, the French army was deployed at Dresden (I and XIV Corps under the command of Saint-Cyr), Meissen (XI Corps, Sebastiani's cavalry corps and the Imperial Guard) and Torgau (III Corps and Latour-Maubourg's cavalry corps). This large force, anchored on Dresden and the Elbe, shows that at this stage Napoleon had not yet understood – or perhaps it would be better to say decided – that this sector had completely lost its importance and that the centre of gravity of the war had shifted westward. Consequently the two corps stationed at Dresden would be absent in the next stage of the offensive. Some analysts are convinced that the real reason for staying close to Dresden was a matter of prestige: how could the protector of the Confederation of the Rhine abandon the capital of his most faithful ally, the king of Saxony? Or in the words of Count Yorck: 'He, the successful soldier on the throne, could not, though in a military sense it was better, retreat with impunity, give up countries he had once occupied, and retire to his own frontiers.'

In the Mulde sector, facing Blücher and Bernadotte, Ney had the IV and VII Corps at Bennewitz near Würzen and to the west, at Taucha, the VI Corps. These three corps were Napoleon's immediate answer to the threat against Leipzig posed by the Armies of Silesia and the North. The Elbe line made

235

possible relatively rapid reinforcement of the Mulde line, as the distance between them was less than a two days' march. Opposite the Army of Bohemia, between Dresden and Leipzig, in the Chemnitz area, the large force of Marshal of Cavalry Murat was deployed.

At the end of the day the northern dispositions of the allies were as follows: Blücher on the Mulde from Düben to Eilenburg with 60,000 men; Bernadotte at Dessau and Zorbig, in the zone west of the Mulde, with 70,000. Blücher believed that given the relative positions of the sides the right move was to place the Army of the North opposite the Saale, in the Merseburg sector, while the Army of Silesia manoeuvred between the Mulde and the Saale. This would remove the two armies from the French line on the Elbe and allow them to support each other in the face of any possible enemy movement. Bernadotte reminded Blücher that their task was to block the enemy until the Army of Bohemia came up and attacked on the flank and in the rear. Because of the movements of the French he suggested retiring behind the Elbe.

Bernadotte's suggestion is indicative of his fear of facing Napoleon and his attempt to postpone any fight until Schwarzenberg arrived. From Blücher's point of view, on the other hand, this was a very dangerous idea, since his force might be hit while crossing the river. Blücher also remembered what Bernadotte perhaps chose to forget with Napoleon nearby – that the junction of the three armies was to be made in the Leipzig area and that he and Bernadotte were supposed to make their way there from the Halle area. He therefore favoured a different solution – that the two armies move to the west bank of the Saale. He knew that Bernadotte would not like this solution, so he promised him that the Prussians would march rapidly and cover their own rear as much as possible. Blücher did not put too much faith in the Swedish crown prince, who took no initiatives of his own and left everything to his Prussian colleague while seeking above all to keep his army intact. In any event, Blücher ordered his forces to cross the Mulde between Düben and Jessnitz on the 9th.

Napoleon figured that he would have a two and a half to one advantage over Blücher in the Mulde sector. On the eve of 9 October he decided to attack Blücher the next day at Düben and move immediately on Wittenberg, which was under siege. From there he would not have any difficulty gaining control of the bridges at Dessau and Wartenburg. If possible, he would destroy them, the enemy would be held up a number of days and he – Napoleon – could march on Schwarzenberg and defeat him. His plan was to concentrate more than 120,000 men at Eilenburg and Mockrehna – the III, VII and IV Corps and the II Cavalry Corps, all under the command of Ney – and to send the VI Corps, the I Cavalry Corps and the Guard cavalry toward Düben; the emperor himself would reach Eilenburg before noon and stand at the head of the army that would attack Blücher in the Düben area in the evening. The XI Corps, which had already arrived at Dahlen, would follow Bertrand and come to his assistance if necessary.

The approach march of the French forces went off out without a hitch. The push against Düben started in the afternoon with the Prussians forced back to the north-west along the river. They crossed the Mulde in the broad sector between Mühlbeck and Ragun on 10 October, late in the morning. Bernadotte's and Blücher's armies linked up on the same day in the Zorbig area. It can be assumed that the Prussian general was more pleased than his colleague with the site of the junction. Napoleon only succeeded partially in achieving his aim. Blücher stayed faithful to the principle of avoiding battle when the French emperor was personally present, until the great day of reckoning came, and in any case had intended to cross over to the left bank of the Mulde that very same day.

The real meaning, militarily, of Blücher's adherence to the Trachenberg principle and the junction of the two allied armies was that they were getting very close to the decisive stage they had aimed at, in the theatre of their choosing – Leipzig. The intention was to the town and its satellites and the many surrounding villages in the heart of a fertile valley – Leipzig the inter-section of numerous roads leading in every direction. Leipzig was a suitable objective, as the concentration of all allied forces in its environs was apt to serve the strategic aim of this stage of the war – command of the roads west, leading to France. To achieve this aim it was possible to disregard to a certain extent the roads leading east, to Poland and Russia. Now the two allied armies were arrayed between the Mulde and the Saale in a single strike force and it was doubtful if Napoleon would expect such a turn of events. As early as the 7th he had shared his thoughts with Murat, telling him to hold on until he reached him. He was to prevent the enemy from approaching Leipzig and rest on that part of the Mulde in his sector. If he did as ordered, 'we may all close in on Leipzig together, to retard the enemy's advance towards it, so that we shall hold the enemy at a distance, or if necessary, fight a pitched battle'.

When Napoleon joined his forces on the Mulde, with all his thoughts focused on defeating the enemy in this sector, the Army of Bohemia was marching through Saxony on two main axes: Bennigsen and Colloredo were on the Teplitz–Dresden road, with their advance units at Zehista and Pirna by 8 October; Bennigsen left a large force opposite Saint-Cyr and then moved towards Leipzig on the Colditz road. The rest of the army was to the west and before the 10th approaching Altenburg on the Pleisse, about 40 kilometres south of Leipzig. Schwarzenberg's headquarters were already set up at Chemnitz on 8 October. Wittgenstein, Kleist and Klenau were at Borna on the 11th.

Murat, who faced the allied forces as they came out of the mountains in the Mittweida–Rochlitz sector, engaged them on the 8th and 9th. When he understood that enemy forces were heading for Borna he retired to the Pleisse line at a distance of less than ten kilometres from Leipzig – the Wachau–Liebertwolkwitz line. Augereau's IX Corps had joined Murat's forces on 12 October after a long march from Bavaria on which enemy units operating on its line of advance from Jena to the north caused serious problems in accordance with the allied policy of harassment.

Schwarzenberg tarried and allowed Murat to get organised without facing any pressure. He preferred to wait for the two other armies rather than getting drawn into a battle alone. His advance from Bohemia to Leipzig was characterised by excessive caution and a snail's pace. In the space of two weeks he advanced just 110 kilometres at the head of a large army that easily outnumbered the enemy forces waiting in its front. Much criticism has been levelled at Schwarzenberg for his timidity in the fighting of 8 and 9 October. He knew that the French in his front were fewer in number than he and that Blücher was under great pressure. None the less he did not attack in strength on the 10th. Had he done so the momentum of the attack might have carried him all the way to Leipzig. Von Cäemmerer said that his generalship was a sorry affair and that his operations were not carried out in the spirit of the prior agreements among the allies.

On 10 October, in the afternoon, Napoleon arrived at Düben, a small town on the bank of the Mulde, midway between Wittenberg and Leipzig. He stayed at a castle surrounded by water and buried himself in work as was his habit on those days when he was not running around on a battlefield or riding with the Imperial Guard on its way to the heat of the fighting. He was disappointed that he had again been deprived of the opportunity to strike a blow. This time the advantage in his favour was so great and the movement to contact so perfectly carried out that he had had no doubts about the outcome of a clash with the enemy. And despite all this the enemy was making him run around in circles without being able to force a decisive battle. He was restless, surrounded by maps, couriers coming and going while for the most part he wrote out instructions and directives and doodled big Gothic letters, a sure sign of inner turmoil and doubts. The days he spent at Düben were among the most fateful for him since he had become ruler of France. Here and now the fate of his empire would be decided.

The information that arrived from Murat worried the emperor a good deal. He wrote to his foreign minister, Maret, who was at Würzen with the king of Saxony, that if Murat was forced to abandon Leipzig he would attack Blücher and Bernadotte, force them to retire across the Elbe and destroy them systematically. The plethora of communications dictated by Napoleon on the 10th and 11th bear witness to his perplexity with regard to the intentions of his enemies. On the 11th he was convinced that they were to be found around the northern passages of the Mulde with a large concentration at Dessau, only learning at the end of the day their forces at these places were very small. He again toyed with the idea of bringing the war to Prussia while his staff pleaded with him to get off the subject and hasten to Leipzig, where the real danger was to be found. Though he was inclined to agree with them, he tried to find some ingenious solution: he would operate against the nearby enemy as he had proposed to Maret and afterwards march on Schwarzenberg from the direction of Torgau and attack him in his rear near Leipzig.

It was clear that Napoleon wished to hold Blücher and Bernadotte on the Elbe and make them leave Schwarzenberg to his fate. But the former kept to their assignments, not seeing any reason to change the direction of their advance. Blücher marched toward Halle, arriving there on 12 October. On the same day he also entered Merseburg. Bernadotte only reached Rothenburg on the 12th and to be on the safe side left behind forces at Dessau to secure the bridges.

Blücher's direction of movement was reported to Napoleon on 12 October, at dawn. At 10 a.m. he gave instructions for the preparation of orders that would concentrate forces at Taucha, less than ten kilometres north-east of Leipzig, on Partha Creek. Napoleon believed that this was where the great battle would take place, and if not, Taucha would serve as a convenient jumping-off point to any area where the fighting developed. In these instructions, routes and timetables for the various corps were delineated in excessive detail. The concentration of forces would be accomplished between 13 and 15 October.

In this radical change of plans one may see the waverings of a commander who had lost his self-confidence and the determination he was so famous for. But it is also possible to see it as a lightning-fast adaptation to changing circumstances as the activities of the enemy became clear. Here is how F. L. Petre, one of the important historians of the war of 1813, describes the decline in Napoleon's decision-making ability: 'On the 10th he proposes to go to the right bank of the Elbe if Murat could not keep Leipzig; the same afternoon he talks only of driving Blücher and Bernadotte over the Elbe and keeping them there by destroying their bridges. Then he would return to Leipzig. On the 11th he is in great uncertainty as to Blücher's and Bernadotte's whereabouts, and reverts to the idea of going to the right bank and leaving them stranded on the left. Then he finds out that they are not, as he had fancied, towards Dessau, but towards Halle. On the 12th he has changed his plans entirely, and proposes fighting a great battle at Taucha. All this is very different from the quick grasp of the situation and the immediate decision as to his course of action which characterise his earlier campaigns.'

Petre does a good job of describing what appears to be the emperor's fickle thinking, though he is also a little too hard on him. More than confusion there is great uncertainty here deriving from the lack of current information on the situation of the enemy. Napoleon did not know where the enemy was and could only guess at his intentions. His suppositions and responses are as interesting as ever. He knew that the basic circumstances of the coming battle constituted a new reality for him and his people and his thinking represents an almost desperate attempt to contend with it.

Marmont, with whom the emperor spent five hours engaged in what was perhaps more of a monologue than a conversation, lasting till the morning of the 12th, sums up his feelings as follows: 'One fails to recognise the old Napoleon again during this campaign.' During the conversation Napoleon likened the situation to a tangled ball of twine that only he could unravel, and with great difficulty. One thing is certain – the Düben order of 12 October is a masterpiece of military organisation. When Napoleon translated his thoughts into operational orders, whatever the state of his mind and his misgivings might be, his organisational ability was superb, as always.

While Berthier laboured away drafting and distributing the order, Napoleon again mulled over its components. In the afternoon he wrote to Murat: 'Can you without compromising yourself hold the entire day of tomorrow, the 13th, your position and Leipzig?... You will be increased by 80,000 men whom I will bring up, and the 14th all the rest of the army. We shall have in the morning of the 15th 200,000 men... It is of great importance to hold Leipzig...

They say that towards Schkeuditz is a good position to take against an army coming from Halle; have the ground reconnoitred.' Napoleon was still assuming that Bernadotte had withdrawn to the Elbe, on the basis of reports reaching him from Ney which did not interpret correctly what had been observed: the forces securing the bridges in the Dessau area and convoys of equipment moving north. Napoleon thought he would have 40,000 fewer enemy troops to contend with in the battle he believed would be fought on the 15th or 16th. It would appear that until the very last moment he was unaware that the allies were closing in on him with a single, determined aim in mind – to annihilate him in one great battle, his army against theirs, head to head.

The main problem troubling Napoleon was Blücher's stance. All thoughts of retreat repelled him, he hated the French emperor and could not stomach Bernadotte. Without any doubt it was Blücher's stubbornness and valour that had brought Napoleon to a pass previously unknown to him. He had not been able to prevent the allies from achieving their principal operational aim in the preliminary stages of the coming October campaign – concentration of all their forces on the vital flanks of the anticipated theatre of war. Furthermore, in a brilliant rolling movement they had managed to place themselves on the main line of retreat of the French, opposite the solid anvil coming up from Bohemia with the mountains to its back and the great plain before it. Now the main allied lines of retreat were open and secure. Despite the perfect organisation of his movements, Napoleon had not been able to attack Schwarzenberg before his colleagues linked up with him. Although the junction was not yet complete, for all practical purposes Napoleon had to assume it as a fact in making his calculations. The allied forces were in the process of becoming a single large army capable of mounting co-ordinated attacks from several directions.

On 13 October the French army set out for Leipzig. This was a day of bad tidings. It turned out that Bernadotte had not returned to the Elbe and was already at Bernburg on the Saale. A captured courier revealed that Bavaria, France's old and faithful ally, had decided to turn its back and go over to the allies. The agreement between Bavaria and Austria placed over 30,000 men at the disposal of the allies in return for guaranteeing the throne of the Bavarian king. What is more, the Austrian force facing the Bavarians on the Inn River was relieved of its task and made available to the allies. All this did not cause real damage, but it did have a demoralising effect. In another two days Napoleon would exploit this turn of events for propaganda purposes.

But there was more. The emperor's brother, Jerome king of Westphalia, whom the Westphalians dubbed the Merry King (*König Lustig*), lost his crown when he fled a Russian force raiding his capital. Jerome had reigned in Westphalia over six years under the Treaty of Tilsit. He was married to a German princess, Catherine of Würtemberg. With his deposition all of Germany was united against Napoleon. The French lines of retreat and communication leading from the theatre of operations back to the Rhine and to France no longer ran through secure and friendly territory.

Napoleon left Düben on the morning of the 14th after revising his orders about the routes and timetables of the various corps. The last order he drafted was for Macdonald, who was due to arrive in Düben that same day, adding at the end: 'There can be no doubt that tomorrow, the 15th, we shall be attacked by the Army of Bohemia and by the Army of Silesia. March then in all haste, and if you hear a cannonade, march to its fire.'

The emperor reached the neighbourhood of Leipzig in the afternoon, accompanied by the king of Saxony and his wife. The royal couple entered the town and the emperor continued on to Wachau to Murat's headquarters. He was convinced that Murat was using his troops, especially the cavalry, carelessly and ineffectively, and was not happy with what he saw.

The fighting on 14 October took place about seven kilometres south of Leipzig. The Army of Bohemia was looking to capture ground at the approaches to the town in order to command the plain to the south. The day before, in the light of Schwarzenberg's and Bernadotte's hesitation, Blücher had written to the sovereigns: 'The three armies are now so close together that a simultaneous attack, on the point where the enemy has concentrated his forces, might be undertaken.' Consequently Tsar Alexander demanded that Wittgenstein make a reconnaissance in force with his cavalry in the southern sector of Leipzig.

The battles of the 14th mainly involved cavalry with neither of the two sides fighting well. Murat commanded the Liebertwolkwitz–Wachau ridge line, which was the main objective of the allies, and would have done well to use his infantry instead of wasting his cavalry. He himself took part in the fighting from time to time, standing out in his strikingly colourful uniform and consequently almost being taken prisoner. His opponents used too small fighting units. Though the day saw the biggest cavalry battles in the entire war, units were sent in piecemeal. The result was that at the end of the day no change had taken place in the positions of the two sides.

Napoleon passed the night in a modest dwelling in the village of Reudnitz and met a few of his marshals there. He greeted them coolly and criticised them. When he told Augereau, one of his oldest commanders, that he was not the Augereau of the Italian campaign, the latter replied heatedly: 'Give me back the old soldiers of Italy, and I will show you that I am.' It is doubtful if Napoleon himself was the Napoleon of old, even of Dresden.

In the Bulletin of the Grand Army from before the great battle, from 15 October, we read: 'After having thus seized all the enemy's bridges, the emperor's project was to pass the Elbe to manoeuvre on the right bank from Hamburg to Dresden, to menace Potsdam and Berlin, and to take for centre of operations Magdeburg, which with this view had been provisioned in munitions of war and food. But on the 13th the emperor learned at Düben that the Bavarian army had joined the Austrian army and menaced the lower Rhine. This inconceivable defection led him to foresee the defection of other princes, and made the emperor adopt the part of falling back to the Rhine, an annoying change, because everything had been prepared to operate on Magdeburg. But it would have necessitated remaining separate from and without communication to France for a month. This had no difficulties at the moment when the emperor had determined his project; it was no longer the same when Austria was going to have two fresh disposable armies: the Bavarian army and the army opposed to Bavaria. The emperor then changed with these unforeseen circumstances, and carried his headquarters to Leipzig.'

Thus the emperor blamed the defection of the Bavarians for the change of his plans, though an intelligent estimate of the situation would have been reason enough. It should be remembered that his orders for the movement to Leipzig were drafted on the 12th and he only found out about the defection on the 13th, though rumours to that effect had been reaching him before this. The document itself, the Bulletin, was aimed first and foremost at Paris and there is a broad hint that the French army might find itself marching back to the homeland.

There was little fighting on the 15th. In the morning hours Murat showed up at general headquarters to report on the previous day's events. He had a long talk with the emperor and afterwards they went out to reconnoitre. The emperor stayed a few hours on the forward Liebertwolkwitz line and then visited Poniatowski's VIII Corps, which was camped slightly to the rear. He studied the terrain in this sector because of its proximity to the Pleisse. All the while reports kept reaching him about the movements of Bernadotte and Blücher and he sent various messages to the corps commanders, especially Marmont, who was in the Lindenthal area north-west of Leipzig and commanded the road to Halle. In one of these messages he informed him that Bernadotte was expected to arrive from the direction of Merseburg with Blücher and that the two would not arrive on separate roads. He was sure that this would make things easier for Marmont and also prove advantageous in terms of general operations as it would lengthen the enemy march and make it possible to take Schwarzenberg in detail. Two hours later Napoleon informed Marmont that there were signs that the enemy was moving away towards Weissenfels and thus their junction with the Army of Bohemia would be made to the south and there was no longer any danger of attack from two directions. There was another possibility – that Blücher would come from Weissenfels and Bernadotte from Merseburg – but in any case an approach by the Halle route was not anticipated.

In actual fact the situation of the allied forces was different. Blücher had indeed taken the road leading from Halle to Leipzig and had already reached Schkeuditz. Marmont had reported this in reply to the information sent by the emperor. Bernadotte was very far from Merseburg. He was covering the entire movement in the Zorbig–Wettin sector, about 30 kilometres north of Merseburg. The information that the enemy might arrive from Weissenfels, a point quite far to the south relative to the theatre of action, was based on the observation of camp fires that seemed to be burning there. These camp fires had deceived those who saw them, as often happens in the night. They were coming from the extreme left of the Army of Bohemia, which extended almost to Lützen. The line of deployment of this army stretched east to the Dresden axis and beyond via Cröbern and Guldengossa. The total number of soldiers that these armies – including the Russian and Austrian forces approaching from Dresden – were capable of concentrating at Leipzig was 340,000, equipped with 1,400 guns.

The French were deployed around Leipzig at nightfall on 15 October defending the area in every direction: in the northern sector the line rested on Partha Creek – Macdonald (XI Corps) at Taucha and Sebastiani with his cavalry on their way there; Souham (III Corps) was at Mockau and on the Düben axis; Bertrand (IV Corps) at Eutritzsch; Marmont (VI Corps) at Lindenthal facing the Saale opposite Halle; Latour-Maubourg and his cavalry between the Würzen axis and the Dresden highway at Zweinaundorf; cavalry units at Holzausen; Augereau (IX Corps) at Zückelhausen; Lauriston (V Corps) between the Dresden road and the Pleisse, at Liebertwolkwitz; Victor (II Corps) at Wachau; Poniatowski (VIII Corps) at Dosen and Markkleeberg;

the Imperial Guard at Reudnitz and Krottendorf as a general reserve. Reynier (VII Corps) was still at Düben. All these forces numbered around 200,000 men and included about 700 guns. Thus there had been a complete turnabout in relative strengths, in men and artillery.

Exactly six months had passed since Napoleon had left Paris on his way to Germany. On the next day, 16 October, the curtain was due to rise on the last act of the last campaign Napoleon was to initiate. History has called this clash the Battle of the Nations. As in a well-written play, things had come to an inevitable pass, through an inner logic that it was impossible to escape, though pundits may know how to demonstrate how things might have been different. The number of errors attributed to Napoleon over a period of less than two weeks could fill a biography covering years in the life of any other ruler. Had he decided to abandon Saxony and withdrawn to the Rhine in time, at the end of September, he could have struck the allies at a time and place of his own choosing. Had he done this, it may be supposed that the rulers of the powers aligned against him would have taken it as a sign that he was ready to relinquish his conquests and consequently stop the war and make peace with him. Had he not concentrated large forces in the lower reaches of the Mulde and waited for the Army of Bohemia, he could have struck it before the two other armies arrived and changed the relative strengths to his disadvantage. Had he given up Dresden, whose occupation was pointless, he could have had two more corps at Leipzig and they would have increased his chances. Already on the 14th he could have broken off contact with Schwarzenberg on his southern flank, marched to the nearby Saale, ploughed into Blücher and Bernadotte and rekindled the possibility of fighting another successful battle or ending the war.

These are only a few examples of the endless stream of strong criticism, suppositions, suggestions and commentaries that has poured forth over the more than 150 years that have passed since the curtain fell on the drama of Saxony. But not a single one of these ideas represents a real alternative to what actually occurred. Whether historical events are predetermined or it is given to our heroes to change them, what was going to happen to Napoleon Bonaparte at Leipzig starting on 16 October was sealed the day he decided to defend his great empire instead of being satisfied with a large and secure France. The verdict of history was to be carried out by Tsar Alexander and General Vorwärts, Blücher, who would not rest, come what may, until he was removed from the imperial throne.

Four watercourses define the ground that was to constitute the Leipzig battlefield. The two main ones, the Weisse Elster and the Pleisse, meet within the bounds of the town. The area between them as they near one another south of Leipzig was very marshy, crisscrossed by many water channels and wooded. Luppe Creek branches off from the Elster near Lindenau, flowing parallel to it and creating still another marshland. North of the town, near the small village of Pfaffendorf, Partha Creek empties into the Pleisse. One gets the impression that the creek was created just for the purpose of marking off the eastern end of the battlefield. It twists north-east from Pfaffendorf and then arches south.

Leipzig is a major road junction. Three roads run through its western sector leading to the towns of the Saale – Halle, Merseburg and Weissenfels. The ground in this sector is flat and plainlike, but from Märkranstadt to the river it is rougher. The northern sector, which is also in the nature of a plain, but drier, is bisected by the road to Düben. The principal sector is the one bounded by the Partha and the Pleisse, where the roads to Würzen and Dresden (via Chemnitz) and secondary roads to the bigger villages in the area are to be found. The area is still plainlike but it has ridges and two low-lying hills overlooking the neighbourhood – the Galgenberg and Kolmberg. The sector south of the town was suited to both infantry and cavalry fighting. The rolling nature of the ground gave the advantage to the defenders.

Leipzig was surrounded by a wall enclosing an area of one square kilometre, its gates opening towards the neighbouring towns to which the roads mentioned above led. The wall was not in good repair, but the gates had been reinforced and strong fortifications had been built alongside them. The town also spread beyond the walls and was surrounded by suburbs, mainly on three sides. The southern side was more thinly populated. The French engineering units had thrown up earthworks and obstacles in different places near the town wall as well as in the suburb of Lindenau, through which the only two lines of retreat to the west passed and were intended to serve the French. By order of the emperor most of the bridges across the Pleisse and the Elster had been destroyed.

Allied headquarters were busy on the 15th formulating operational plans for the 16th. The decision to bring on the main battle on the 16th had been reached the day before. Bennigsen and Colloredo, marching from the direction of Dresden, were indeed scheduled to arrive with all their forces only on the 17th, but it was decided not to delay any longer, even if this meant deciding the battle in two consecutive stages instead of one. Communications with Bernadotte and Blücher were poor and Schwarzenberg had to guess for the most part at their location and movements. The first plan to be proposed aroused strong opposition at headquarters and the Russian tsar vetoed it. It envisaged four lines of attack: Wittgenstein, Kleist and Klenau to attack from the south, in the area east of the Pleisse, pushing the enemy back on Leipzig; the Austrian General Meerveldt with an Austrian–Russian force of over 50,000 men to move on Leipzig from the area between the Pleisse and the Elster; Blücher to attack Leipzig from the north-west, along the Merseburg axis, with Giulay under his command as well and attacking Lindenau from the direction of Märkranstadt. The opposition to the plan stemmed from the fact that the attack was directed at the French strong points and that part of the forces would have to operate over difficult terrain making passage problematic. The idea of advancing between the Pleisse and the Elster aroused not only opposition but amazement as well. The tsar, influenced by his senior advisers, did not approve the plan, but given the insistence of his commander-in-chief decided that the Russians and Prussians would operate according to a different plan but that Schwarzenberg could use his Austrians as he wished.

Finally, the following plan was agreed upon: Meerveldt would attack according to Schwarzenberg's original plan, but his force would include just 30,000 Austrians; Wittgenstein, Kleist and Klenau would also attack along the lines of the first plan, on a broad front from the south, in the Markkleeberg–Liebertwolkwitz sector; the Russian Guard detached from Meerveldt would be held in reserve in the rear, at Rotha on the Pleisse. In the secondary effort, Blücher would operate from north of the Elster and move on Leipzig from the north; Giulay would attack Lindenau. The two would attack from the direction of Schkeuditz and Märkranstadt, respectively.

At midnight two white flares were fired from the south and answered by two blue flares and a red one from the direction of Blücher. The Prussian general had confirmed that he stood ready for tomorrow's battle.

Before morning on the 16th the French made a few changes in their dispositions, mainly on the southern front. Macdonald and Sebastiani extended from Taucha to Holzhausen; most of the reserve was moved from the eastern approaches of Leipzig to Probstheide and thus became in fact part of the operational southern line; Poniatowski stretched his sector towards Kunnewitz along the east bank of the Pleisse. Napoleon's attention was naturally directed to the vital southern area, where most of the enemy forces were concentrated opposite him in threatening proximity. He gave Ney command of the secondary front north of Leipzig. Under his command were the III,.IV and VI Corps.

Napoleon did not appear to be deceiving himself, given the superior strength being brought to bear by the allies. This could be seen after 10 October when he changed his plans so rapidly. According the Caulaincourt, the emperor said to him on the eve of the battle that in the end numbers would tell: 'There are no scientific combinations which can compensate, on this point, for the thinness of our squares. We shall be overpowered by mere numbers.' The desperate tone of these words struck Caulaincourt as a death sentence. Whether they actually had this conversation or Caulaincourt invented it to accommodate his memoirs, it reflected the mood projected by the emperor in his immediate surroundings. During the evening he visited some of his units, distributed new battle flags and pledged his soldiers to prefer death to defeat. He passed the night at Probstheide, among his veteran troops. Alexander and Frederick William also spent the night near their forward units, at Wachtberg.

Chapter 10 - THE BATTLE OF THE NATIONS: 16-19 OCTOBER

The evening of 15 October was a wet and wintry Friday evening. Field Marshal Schwarzenberg, the commander-in-chief of the allied armies, wrote a long letter to his wife, Countess Marie Anne, or Nanny as he called her. 'If God is with us,' he wrote, 'the enemy will receive his just deserts from us. God knows I would happily turn my back on everything, but giving up at this point would have tragic results. The battle will necessarily last several days, because the situation is unique and the result will have infinite consequences. When I look out my window and see the many camp fires of the Guard and when I think that I am facing the greatest military commander of our age and one of the greatest of all time, a true imperial warrior, I must confess, my dear Nanny, that I feel my shoulders are too slender to bear this enormous weight.' Further on in the letter Schwarzenberg cast the burden onto an omnipotent God, though he might have been satisfied with his superior numbers. He also wrote that he had been interrupted 'by a messenger from the brave Blücher, who announced that he would be ready as planned and appear at the agreed time'. The first favourable sign from a Divine Providence.

The order of the day produced by allied headquarters was Napoleonic in spirit and bristling with exclamation points: 'Brave soldiers! The most important epoch of this holy war is at hand. The decisive hour is striking. Prepare yourselves for battle! The bond which unites the mighty nations in one great enterprise will be drawn closer and tighter on the battlefield. Russians! Prussians! Austrians! You fight for a cause! You fight for the independence of Europe, for the freedom of your sons, for the immortality of your name! All for one! One for all! Victory is yours!'

The Battle of the Nations began on 16 October at nine o'clock in the morning, south of Leipzig. Fighting also took place to the north and the west of the town, but the principal events occurred in the sector of the Army of Bohemia. Napoleon wished to isolate this sector and destroy the army. In the morning he met Murat on the Galgenberg ridge and the two rode along the front line. The weather had not changed from the previous day, with a heavy fog reducing visibility. From what he could see, the emperor was able to conclude that the enemy attack would preempt any offensive move that he himself might make. Odeleben has described what happened at 9 a.m.: 'Three cannon fired in regular intervals, announcing the opening of the Allied attack. Next followed a terrific cannonade on both sides.' Many wrote in their journals that the cannonade was unlike any they had ever heard.

The allied army in the southern sector had been in the assembly areas from six in the morning. Barclay de Tolly was in command of the attack in this sector. The troops marched on their objectives in five columns: Klenau and Gortchakow to Liebertwolkwitz from the east and the south, respectively; Eugen von Würtemberg to Wachau from the south east; Kleist to the Wachau–Markkleeberg sector; a column of cavalry under Pahlen operated between Eugen and Gortchakow. The width of the attack front was around ten kilometres and the number of men in the allied force over 65,000. The poor visibility ruled out an attack co-ordinated by eye contact.

Napoleon tried to observe the area in his front. The wind dispersed the fog somewhat. A fierce fight had broken out on his right. Kleist charged the Markkleeberg position and captured it but had trouble holding it before being reinforced by Austrian cavalry and infantry units. Eugen captured the village of Wachau. Heavy artillery fire in his front kept him from advancing farther and a hot fight developed with the position changing hands a number of times. Battle-scarred French veterans swore they had never witnessed such concentrated artillery fire. Kleist tried to render assistance from the flank but took heavy casualties. Two hours after the start of the fighting the cool-headed Eugen was driven back to the south but stubbornly held on along a dip in the ground because he had the feeling that if he was routed and retreated the whole offensive would collapse.

Napoleon was in full command of the defensive battle. He reinforced the artillery with the guns of the Guard, which punched holes in the enemy forces. Gortchakow, operating without co-ordination with Klenau, was pushed back under the pressure of the murderous artillery fire and a dangerous gap was opened between himself and Eugen. Klenau, operating on the right flank, climbed the Kolmberg ridge and saw that a large French force was advancing rapidly from the north-west. These were the reinforcements Macdonald had sent at the emperor's orders to assist Lauriston, whose corps was facing a double-pronged attack on the Liebertwolkwitz position.

On the extreme left flank Meerveldt ran into trouble as anticipated. The waterlogged area between the Pleisse and the Elster slowed down his advance and made the movement of artillery difficult. His troops tried to make their way between the numerous swamps and water channels. All they could accomplish until the end of the day was to capture the position east of the Pleisse at Dohlitz. The fight against Poniatowski's Poles cost them heavy losses and every effort to continue the attack in the direction of Kunnewitz broke down. Schwarzenberg, whose command post was advancing with Meerveldt's Austrians, was dismayed at what he was seeing and perhaps already regretted insisting on the line of attack he had chosen for Meerveldt. Kunnewitz was an important link in the plan of attack, as its capture would block a certain line of retreat of the French. But meantime the latter showed no signs of retreating. On the contrary, during the day Napoleon dispatched Augereau, who was at Zückelhausen, to reinforce Poniatowski against the Austrians wallowing in the swamps of the Pleisse. The reinforcement was sent mainly to serve as a basis for an expected counter-attack.

The Russian tsar observed the action near the village of Guldengossa and took cognizance of the mounting difficulties in that sector. It was obvious to him that the attack was piecemeal and unco-ordinated and that French resistance was very strong. He ordered the units of the Russian Guard to the battlefield, on the broken ground between Cröbern and Auenhain. He also sent a message to Schwarzenberg telling him to send in the Austrian reserve immediately.

At around 11 a.m. it was clear to everyone that the allied attack had lost its momentum and that the time had arrived for the French counterblow. From Napoleon's viewpoint this attack represented an irritating delay in his plan of destroying the enemy. From the early morning hours he had been sending forces forward. He believed that no special problems were to be expected during the day from the Saale. He was convinced that Blücher was near Märkranstadt and therefore ordered Marmont to move his corps to the southern sector and position himself midway between Leipzig and Liebertwolkwitz. As will be remembered, the VI Corps was covering the road to Halle and had fortified itself in a very strong position between Lindenthal and Mockern. The emperor felt that Marmont's new position would make possible the more effective use of the corps against the Army of Bohemia, but that if he were unfortunately mistaken in his calculations he could also send it against Blücher. Marmont knew that his commander was making a mistake, as he had seen the camp fires of the Army of Silesia in the Schkeuditz area during the night, Nevertheless, at 10 a.m., he started on his way. At the same time Blücher's advance units ran into the French outposts at Radefeld on the road to Magdeburg, at Stahmeln and at Wahren between the Halle road and the Elster. Marmont halted his marching columns at once.

Napoleon therefore waited in vain for Marmont to reinforce him. He also ordered Souham to send him two divisions from his III Corps. At around 11 a.m. he positioned a very strong artillery force, 150 guns, between Liebertwolkwitz and Wachau, between Lauriston and Victor. Macdonald was ordered to attack Klenau with the support of Souham's divisions when they arrived. He was to assault Kolmberg Hill and then turn east to Seifertshain and roll up the right flank of the enemy. Murat, commanding a powerful con-centration of cavalry, would break through the centre towards Guldengossa as soon as the artillery softened up the enemy, in a movement that was intended to decide the battle. After the cavalry charge the entire force, moving across a broad front, would destroy everything that lay in its path.

A short while after 2 p.m. all the allied forces that had been operating east of the Pleisse since the morning were pushed back to their original staging area, with the exception of the force at Guldengossa, which was still holding its ground. Napoleon directed the battle from the position he had occupied all day, on the Galgenberg ridge. Victor moved on the farmhouses of Auenhain with the support of two divisions of the Young Guard under Oudinot. The Old Guard mopped up Wachau and its environs. Augereau, supported by Poniatowski, attacked Kleist in the Markkleeberg sector and drove him back on Cröbern according to plan. Lauriston pushed the Austrians from Liebertwolkwitz to Gross Posna parallel to the Chemnitz–Leipzig axis. Macdonald operated on a broad front, moving on the enemy positions east of Partha–Kolmberg, Siefertshain and Klein Posna. The fierce fighting there see-sawed back and forth. In the end, Klenau's troops retreated as well as Gortchakow's, pushed back to the wooded area south of Liebertwolkwitz known as University Woods. The whole offensive was accompanied by dense artillery fire from the concentration of batteries placed in the centre, some of which were afterwards moved forward to the slopes of Galgenberg Hill.

At about 3 p.m. the time arrived for the movement dictated by Napoleon's time-honoured tactical doctrine. And indeed Murat and his cavalry with Latour-Maubourg's I Cavalry Corps at their head were committed to the battle. The charge was directed toward Guldengossa and Cröbern and it was magnificent. The French galloped down the muddy slopes towards the artillery batteries and cavalry awaiting them; but they could not force the issue as Napoleon had wished. Latour-Maubourg lost a leg to a shell; the tsar sent in the Russian cavalry units guarding him to drive back the enemy; the French were not determined enough to gain a decision and had mounted their attack in a formation lacking sufficient depth. Murat was almost taken prisoner towards evening. He abandoned the field and his forces retreated behind Wachau in utter disarray.

Napoleon was stricken – or pretended to be – by a premature feeling of great victory. From where he stood overlooking the battlefield he issued instructions for the broadcast of his success – the ringing of the church bells of Leipzig and announcement of his victory to the king of Saxony. But as stated, all this was premature. After 5 p.m. the tsar, his headquarters at Wachtberg almost having been swept away by the French cavalry, sent in his last reserves. The allied recovery caused Las Cases, one of the senior members of Napoleon's entourage, to assert in his memoirs that 'the allies had such vast numbers that when their troops were fatigued they were regularly relieved as at parade'. The battle of Wachau, as the engagement of 16 October in the southern sector would be called, was still not over. The French were forced to give up the positions they had taken in their counter-attack – Victor at Auenhain, Macdonald at Seifertshain and Mortier in the southern part of University Woods. Now Poniatowski got into unexpected trouble on the right flank of the French. At 5.30 p.m Meerveldt finally managed to extricate himself from the Pleisse marshland and moved east towards Markkleeberg and Dohlitz, forcing the French to send over nearby forces to support the VIII Corps. Poniatowski finally got out of his bind after a sharp clash but the events in his sector also had an adverse effect on the development of the afternoon attack launched by the French. The unlucky Meerveldt, who did not achieve a single one of his objectives, also erred in identifying troops he ran into and was taken prisoner.

With the onset of darkness the shooting stopped. The battle of Wachau was a drawn battle from every point of view and its results were of no importance in the overall accounting of the Battle of the Nations. The forwardmost position of the allies had been in the area of Markkleeberg (Dohlitz was retaken by the French during the evening) and of the French, in the northern part of University Woods. Napoleon's desire to fight a decisive battle in the 1813 campaign had been foiled again, for the nth time, but in this instance the preliminary conditions necessary for a decisive victory had not been created. All day Napoleon had waited for Marmont, who had been entangled in his own battle. The biggest mistake of the allies on 16 October had been the pointless movement of the Austrians between the Pleisse and the Elster, which deprived them of a large force in the see-saw battles of the day. Whoever had eyes to see could have predicted the poor results of the Austrian force in this sector. It may be that Schwarzenberg insisted on carrying out this movement because he wanted a purely Austrian achievement and saw in his mind's eye a move that might surprise just because it was improbable.

At the height of Murat's and Latour-Maubourg's splendid charge a muffled sound was heard from the direction of Leipzig. Napoleon understood at once that this was the sound of cannon (Berthier thought he was actually hearing thunder) and also understood its significance. Some historians assert that he immediately mounted his horse and galloped north, but there is not enough evidence to bear this out. These historians send Napoleon racing to every place where gunfire was heard. In their version of things, Napoleon was absent from the battle of Wachau in its critical phase, providing another logical explanation for his failure to win. However, as stated, it is almost certain that the emperor remained on the Galgenberg ridge. In any event, at that moment it was Blücher who was attacking Marmont.

The VI Corps was one of the best in the French army. It had many veteran soldiers in its ranks, being in this respect the exception. Marmont had made a major effort to fortify his position, which extended between the Magdeburg and Halle roads. He was supported by artillery of an unconventional kind – 40 naval guns adapted for field use. Until the 16th he was supremely confident of his ability to withstand an attack by one of the two armies moving down from the north or even by both. Souham's and Bertrand's corps were right behind him and able to come to his aid fairly quickly. On the evening of the 15th, looking out from the steeple of the Lindenthal church, he saw the distant camp fires and knew that his meeting with the enemy was close at hand. However, the emperor's orders, based on an erroneous assessment of the possibility of Blücher's arrival, yanked Marmont's corps out of its position on the morning of the 16th. With the emperor's error a given fact, Marmont had no choice but to deploy somewhat hastily in the Mockern area. He reported to Ney, who commanded this entire sector. The latter mulled things over and considered which forces he had available to close the gap that had been created.

Blücher's army had been ready to move to the attack from the morning hours of the 16th. The Prussian general knew that he could not expect help from Bernadotte, who had informed him that he could only count on him from the 17th. None the less, he was determined to attack the French on that same day. He was not one to sit still when his comrades were fighting tooth and nail. His left wing would attack along the Magdeburg axis and the right, under Yorck, along the Halle axis almost up to Stahmeln and from there to Lindenthal. By 3 p.m. both axes were clear of the enemy up to Breitenfeld and the environs of Mockern. Lindenthal was captured. At the same hour Marmont was already deployed from Mockern to Eutritzsch and Wiederitzsch along a narrow, swampy stream – the Rietzschke. The deployment of forces and the nature of the ground dictated the probable point of contact between the two armies – Mockern – and there the hero of the day might prove to be Yorck, whose commander, Blücher, had said of him a few days previously: 'It's very hard to lead him into the line of fire, but once he's there, no one is better.' Blücher himself, who was afraid of the French forces moving from Düben, attached himself to Yorck's left, because he was convinced that this was where the real action would take place.

In the initial hours one of the fiercest battles in the entire war took place at Mockern. The village passed from hand to hand a number of times. After 5 p.m. a fresh Prussian reserve joined the battle and assaulted the French furiously, but the latter fought courageously, driving the Prussians back and even routing them. Marmont ordered the Saxon General Norman to pursue the retreating forces with his cavalry, but Norman carried out the order hesitantly and half-heartedly (two days later, on the 18th, he would betray the French and defect to the allies). Yorck then committed his last reserves, which came out to attack from the centre of the village. He was heard shouting at the commander of his cavalry unit: 'If the cavalry doesn't do something now, all is lost. You must attack!' A terrible battle ensued in which the French were in the end decisively beaten and retreated in total confusion, leaving behind many prisoners and spoils, including dozens of guns. Yorck was grateful to the commander of the cavalry reserve and according to the same witness told him at the end of the battle: 'To you and only to you do I owe the victory today and I shall never forget you and your noble regiment.'

While the main fighting was going on at Mockern, a Polish division sent by Ney to assist the VI Corps and secure Marmont's far-off right flank at Wiederitzsch was attacked. The position was essential to cover the road to Düben, on which French supply convoys were still moving as well as

Reynier's corps, which still had not arrived at the front. There too a bloody battle developed, with the advantage shifting from side to side, but in the end the Poles along with the reinforcements sent to them by the French (a division from the III Corps) had to retreat across the Partha in the Eutritzsch area. Marmont, who had been wounded in the battle, camped his mauled right wing between the Partha and the Rietzschke, north of Leipzig. The two remaining divisions of the III Corps, which had marched south in the morning to reinforce Napoleon, did little good there and were sorely missed north of Leipzig.

Right after the battle began, Blücher, who wished to establish for himself a decisive advantage all along the front, asked the messenger who had brought him the news that the Army of the North would only arrive the next day to go back and get his chief to hurry up, so as 'not to be the only leader left out of the battle'. The messenger was Sir Charles Stuart, who was attached to Bernadotte's headquarters and had kept urging him to advance together with Blücher. The Swedish crown prince did not show any inclination to do so and found numerous excuses not to. It was obvious that he intended to remain in the Prussian general's rear and avoid fighting in the first stage. Stuart's return message did not help either and he followed it up with an angry note to Bernadotte on the evening of the 16th.

On the afternoon of the 17th, when the Army of the North finally arrived at Breitenfeld, it was the corps of the Prussian Bülow and the Russian Winzingerode and not the Swedes that marched at the head of the army. Cathcart, who discussed this extraordinary sight, offered a number of explanations for Bernadotte's disgraceful conduct: his desire to protect his soldiers, whom he might need back home to secure his rule; his fear of losing support in Sweden when lists of the dead and wounded arrived there; and possibly his hopes of patching things up with his former comrades in arms, the French. One should also mention a letter sent by Bernadotte to General Moreau at the end of August, saying among other things: 'I shall not expose myself to the deadly blows that Napoleon so often succeeds in striking. I shall exhaust him with manoeuvres... Despite his ability, his might and his fame, it is still possible to defeat him in the end.' He made no secret of his intentions and his methods.

The third front planned by allied headquarters for 16 October was in the neighbourhood of Lindenau, a village lying at the confluence of the Luppe and the Elster. As mentioned, the French attached supreme importance to the bridge there, which gave on to two roads to the Saale – to Merseburg and Weissenfels – that might serve as vital lines of retreat and extrication. Stationed at Lindenau were some units of Arrighi's cavalry corps. Austrian occupation of Lindenau could place Leipzig itself in immediate danger. It could constitute the junction point between Schwarzenberg's left flank and Blücher as well as establishing a continuous front of all the allied forces.

Giulay left Märkranstadt at 8 a.m. after receiving reports from his observation post that there were signs of an impending battle south of Leipzig. He mopped up the area ahead of him along a broad front south and north of the Lindenau road. After 10 a.m., while the Austrian corps was on the march, the concerned Arrighi alerted Bertrand to what was occurring near this vital position. Bertrand immediately headed in that direction. The two commanders recalled Napoleon's briefing emphasising the importance of Lindenau and the necessity of holding it at all costs.

During the afternoon hours Giulay, who still outnumbered the French, occupied Plägwitz and Leutsch on either side of Lindenau. None the less, all his attempts to break through to the central objective ended in failure. At this point in the battle, Bertrand threw everything he had at the Austrians and pushed them back, though failing to retake the previously lost outposts. Until evening mostly artillery exchanges took place and at the end of the day Giulay retired with his main force to Märkranstadt. Bertrand remained where he was.

At the end of this hectic day Napoleon left his hilltop command post, where he had spent most of the day, and transferred his headquarters to a field north of Probstheide, where he intended to pass the night, surrounded by his Old Guard. He had not achieved the results he had wished for. In ordinary, objective terms the results had been drawn, though the French maintained a slight advantage from both the tactical point of view and in terms of losses. However, Napoleon knew that even if he insisted on claiming the victory, it would be an empty one and the new day did not augur well. He only had the prospect of being augmented by one additional fighting force – Reynier's VII Corps – while the enemy was about to receive a huge reinforcement of over 150,000 men. The Army of the North would appear on the morrow and the forces of Bennigsen and Colloredo would arrive at around the same time. He could only regret the pointless disposition of the I and XIV Corps, stuck at Dresden by his own decision. The superior numbers of the allies were going to decide the issue. Their fighting spirit, their discipline and morale were infinitely superior to those of the French.

The exhausted emperor could again reflect on the factors that had kept cropping up in the battles since the beginning of the war. Something had gone wrong with his sense of timing, just as it had with his reading of changing circumstances on the battlefield. These poor assessments of the developing situation had inspired him again and again to move parts of his forces unwisely. That was what had happened on this day with Marmont because of his mistaken view of Blücher's location and options. That was what had happened, more pointedly, with Souham's corps, where two divisions had run around all day without contributing anything significant to the fighting. Had they taken part in the afternoon attack the results would undoubtedly have been better and perhaps victory too would have been theirs. Since they were not there, the French would have been better off mounting their counter-attack much earlier, at 11 a.m. for example. At the same time, one cannot accept the standard criticism that Napoleon could have diverted a large part of the forces fighting Giulay and Blücher to himself at Wachau. This would have exposed his rear and strategic lines of retreat to great danger.

The allies too were not free from grave errors. As will be remembered, only Alexander's intervention kept the poor planning that had sent Meerveldt on his way from being even more serious. The start of the attack at Wachau was piecemeal and unco-ordinated. Blücher erred in not concentrating a larger force on his right flank, at Mockern, out of fear of a French attack on the Düben axis. Giulay did not exploit his decisive advantage on the Weissenfels axis in time and lost the opportunity to occupy the important Lindenau crossroads and perhaps even penetrate into Leipzig.

What good could come out of a continuation of the fighting from the French emperor's viewpoint? What chance did he have to turn the tables? There can be no doubt that on the night of the 16th he recognised the pointlessness of continued fighting and seriously considered a general retreat which would end in redeployment along the Rhine. He sent preliminary orders to Bertrand to be ready to secure a number of vital passages across the Saale. He could have ordered Saint-Cyr to move down the right bank of the Elbe and link up with him. He could also have ordered Davout to do the same from the north. There was another possibility, more creative – to withdraw with all his forces to Torgau, link up with Saint-Cyr, make a junction with Davout at Magdeburg and get to the Rhine with all this formidable mass of men. Had he chosen any one of these options on this night there is no question that he would have been able to save his army from the bitter fate that awaited it and avoid the pointless deaths of thousands of men. But the Emperor Napoleon could not reconcile himself to what General Bonaparte understood so well. He drafted his preliminary orders to Bertrand and readied himself for another superfluous battle. He acted like an obsessive gambler who decides to stop but wants to try his luck one more time.

Napoleon asked that Meerveldt be sent to him. He knew him well. It was Meerveldt who had come to him after two of Austria's defeats to request an armistice, once at Lauban in 1796 and the other time at Austerlitz in 1805. The Austrian general came and Napoleon praised him as was customary on his fighting that day and afterwards proposed that he take a message to allied headquarters setting forth his conditions for an armistice. He went overboard, as was usual for him, and spoke once again as a statesman whereas just a few moments before he had been entirely immersed in the business of fighting the war. He complained about Austria's position and about the deaf ear England had turned to him ('They wish to bind me not to build more than 30 ships of the line in my ports.' Just 30!) He proposed solutions to the problems connected with Holland, Spain, the Confederation of the Rhine and the Hanseatic towns. Why, he asked, should a peace not be arranged along these lines after the armistice: 'I will retire, if desired, beyond the Saale; let the Russians and Prussians retire behind the Elbe, you Austrians to Bohemia, and let poor Saxony be neutral.' Napoleon returned Meerveldt's sword to him and sent him to his emperor. Some are convinced that Napoleon was trying to buy a little more time with this move, but it must be said that there is no certainty that this conversation took place on the night of the 16th. That is the French version. Meerveldt himself claims that it took place on 17 October. The development of the story and its logic favour the earlier time. Anyone who reads the memoirs of generals knows that they are full of errors. A young officer accompanied the captured general to the advance lines and when he returned told his comrades what Meerveldt had said to him when they parted: 'My heart weeps for you, my good Frenchmen. You are caught as if in a mousetrap.' Napoleon waited in vain for an answer from the allied sovereigns.

Early on the morning of the 17th Murat arrived at the emperor's headquarters to cheer him up. He told him again and again that the enemy had sustained heavy losses in the previous day's battle. The two had a long talk. Napoleon held Murat in high esteem as an army man and liked to share his thoughts with him. When they were through he returned to his headquarters tent and remained there most of the day. Murat rode back to his troops. Reynier's corps was scheduled to come up during the day and complete the French order of battle. Napoleon decided to take up the Partha line and deploy behind it. He would shorten his lines and carve out a sector on the Leipzig perimeter while preparing for a general retreat. He did not expect anything of importance to occur that day as both sides were licking their wounds and relieving troops. He was greatly concerned about ammunition and was not sure he had enough for another day of fighting. The movement of troops towards the city would take place in the night, after midnight. More bridges would be put up at Lindenau or at least passages would be prepared there to cross the Elster. The road from Leipzig to Lützen and Weissenfels passed through swampy country crisscrossed by a number of branches of the Elster. Headquarters were transferred to a tobacco plant at Stotteritz about three kilometres south-east of Leipzig.

At Blücher's headquarters the words of the chief of staff, Gneisenau, back in September, may have been recalled: 'Gentlemen, we'll be eating grapes on the banks of the Rhine this year still. And understand me correctly, these will be the last grapes still on the vine, in November.' The Rhine had been the right answer for the French emperor as early as September and the aim of the allies all through the campaign. However, between the warring parties and the Rhine there still stood the city of Leipzig, where the god of war was not ready to pass up the spectacle awaiting him. The long-suffering residents of the city also wished to see the French turn west battered and beaten. Of the hard times they had lived through there is no lack of written evidence – of the destructiveness and pillaging of the French soldiers and of the terrible crowding as endless refugees clustered in the centre of the city. The residents of the suburbs and the many outlying villages had been turned into cannon fodder.

On 17 October in the afternoon, the allied war council met at Schwarzenberg's headquarters at Guldengossa. On the subject of forces it was reported that Bennigsen's Russian reserve was behind schedule and would only arrive in the evening (Bennigsen himself took part in the discussion). Colloredo would arrive a few hours before. As for Bernadotte, nothing was known about when he would arrive. The night before preparatory orders had been issued for an attack on the left flank of the French in the afternoon. In the morning Wachau had been placed under observation in the presence of the tsar, the king of Prussia and the commander-in-chief, Schwarzenberg. A few enemy infantry concentrations were observed and a long line of cavalry under arms, but it was clear that they were not deployed for attack but rather in an ordinary defensive posture. The commander-in-chief immediately ordered a cessation of all activities that might provoke the enemy to attack. In view of the expected times of juncture and the absence of aggressive movement by the French it was decided to postpone the scheduled afternoon attack till the morning of the 18th. It was also decided to allow the troops to recover from the previous day's fighting, to attend to the wounded and regroup. Because of the heavy rains the ground had turned into a huge quagmire, making it easier to decide on the postponement of the attack. On that same morning (or perhaps the next morning?) the tsar received Meerveldt, who told him of the mission the French emperor had forced him to undertake. The tsar shrugged his shoulders.

Military activity on the 17th was thus very slight. None the less, one note-worthy attack took place. Not surprisingly, it occurred in the sector of the busy Blücher. He had been impatiently awaiting the agreed signal to commence the general offensive planned for that day. When it failed to come he adjusted his lines along the Rietzschke in the Gohlis area and along the Partha near Pfaffendorf. In both these places Marmont's men were to be found. 'If I still commanded my old Hussar regiment,' Blücher said to a Russian general standing next to him, 'I would attack those infantrymen from the front and take their guns from the flank.' The Russian responded to the challenge. 'With your permission, sir, I'll try it with my Hussars.' He took the French by surprise and pushed them back to the suburbs of Leipzig.

During the night Napoleon met Ney at Reudnitz and talked to him about what could be expected on the morrow. Afterwards he rode over to Lindenau, reviewed the situation there and ordered Bertrand to carry out the previous day's instructions, namely to march to Weissenfels and secure the Saale passages to allow easy movement towards Naumburg and from there on to Erfurt. During the early morning hours Napoleon reached his new headquarters and his troops moved into their new positions in the Leipzig sector, between the Partha and the Pleisse. Mortier, at the head of the Young Guard, was directed to Lindenau to relieve Bertrand. The forces within this vast perimeter were arrayed as follows: Dombrowski's Polish division, which had fought at Wiederitzsch on the 16th, was stationed at Pfaffendorf; Marmont at Schönfeld; Reynier, who had just now arrived, at Paunsdorf on the road to Würzen with a forward unit to the north east at Taucha; Macdonald in the Zückelhausen–Holzhausen sector; north of him and slightly to the rear

Lauriston and Sebastiani's cavalry corps; Victor at Probstheide and the enormous artillery concentration emplaced the day before alongside him; Augereau and Poniatowski defended the Pleisse sector, narrowed down somewhat since the previous day to between Dohlitz and Kunnewitz; the improvised force of Oudinot and Kellermann's cavalry corps was to the rear of Victor and Augereau; behind Victor the cavalry of the wounded Latour-Maubourg's corps was also posted; the general reserve included Souham, Arrighi's cavalry, stationed at Leipzig, and the Old Guard, stationed at Thonberg, south of the city. An entire army – 160,000 men – in a vast defensive alignment, but with the morale of men on the run.

Napoleon was not feeling well and was completely exhausted. Caulaincourt has written in his memoirs of the emperor's sorry physical state on the eve of the great battle at Leipzig. His words to the troops he visited on the 17th were few and commonplace with none of the eloquence he was famous for. But he did not pass up the opportunity to make a gesture of recognition towards one of his outstanding commanders: on the same day he raised the commander of the VIII Corps, Prince Poniatowski, to the rank of marshal. Marmont writes in his memoirs: 'The 17th passed quietly, the enemy was awaiting reinforcements. We, on our part, were busy in restoring order among our troops. Yet we ought to have begun our retreat on the instant, or at least made preparations for it so as to effect it when night came on. But a certain carelessness on the part of Napoleon, which cannot be explained and only with difficulty be described, filled the cup of our woes.' A closer look at things leads one to suspect that Napoleon simply did not believe he could extricate his army to the west without a fight. But while he did not stand much of a chance it was possibly better to have made the attempt.

Schwarzenberg's plans for 18 October were based on three troop concentrations simultaneously attacking in the southern sector under Murat's command: Bennigsen with his own corps and Klenau's Austrian corps as well as additional Austrian and Russian forces would attack the left flank (Macdonald, Lauriston and Sebastiani) from Seifertshain and Gross Posna towards Holzhausen and in the end form a junction with the Army of the North; Barclay with the Russian and Prussian troops under the command of Wittgenstein, Kleist and others would attack Murat's centre (Victor, Augereau and the cavalry units in the sector) from the Guldengossa area towards Wachau; an Austrian force including Colloredo's corps under the command of Prince Hesse-Homburg would attack Poniatowski and part of Augereau's corps along the right bank of the Pleisse; Meerveldt's Austrian corps, under the command of General Lederer, would advance along the left bank of the Pleisse towards Kunnewitz.

As for the northern sector, the allied plan covered the entire French defensive alignment there with the added aim of forming the junction between the Army of the North and the right wing of the forces attacking from the south (Bennigsen). In accordance with his demand, Bernadotte would be reinforced by a few of Blücher's divisions and his mission would be to cross the Partha between Schönfeld and Taucha and attack Leipzig from the north-east. Blücher, at the head of his reduced army, would attack Leipzig from the northwest, breaking into the city through the Halle gate. Giulay would attack Lindenau along the Elster, from south to north.

Allied forces now numbered 300,000 men. Their advantage over the French was clear-cut, with more than twice as many guns as well. Napoleon arrayed his forces in a convex alignment, which enabled him to defend his position and quickly bring to bear his reserves as well as to pull out troops for the inevitable general retreat, which of course depended on keeping his lines to the west open. Unfortunately, in the absence of other bridges, Napoleon could only rely on the Lindenau route. The concave, overlapping offensive disposition of the allied forces, whose effectiveness derived mainly from their numerical superiority, created a difficult problem for the French in addition to the problem of being closed in on three sides by rivers and, as stated, being dependent on one main line of retreat.

The allied left began to advance along the Pleisse early on the morning of October 18. The sun came out at approximately 8 a.m. and the skies cleared. Hard fighting developed, during which the Austrians took Dohlitz and Dosen. The two places passed back and forth and at 2 p.m. the French even mounted a spirited counter-attack, but in the end – on Monday evening – the two villages were in Austrian hands. Prince Hesse-Homburg was wounded during the battle and Colloredo took command. He succeeded in capturing Lösnig too. Lederer, on the other hand, did not succeed in gaining control of the important position of Kunnewitz, which Poniatowski defended stubbornly till evening.

Barclay, who attacked in the centre, discovered that his front, including Wachau, was undefended. He arrived before Probstheide fairly quickly but had to wait for the Austrians on the left and Bennigsen on the right to come up and form their line of battle on him. Alexander and Frederick William watched the action in this sector from a vantage point right behind Barclay's force. The delay irritated the tsar and he urged Barclay to attack. The village of Probstheide, large and well fortified, was clearly a key position and there was good reason to hope that with its capture the entire French line would collapse. Napoleon himself had been present there since the afternoon encouraging the forces holding it. Victor's corps fought tooth and nail and all attempts to take the village failed. At 5 p.m. Napoleon sent in Lauriston to reinforce Victor, whose men were sorely battered. Another of Barclay's attacks was beaten back and the offensive against the village was broken off, having also become redundant as good news came from the right concerning the attack on Murat. The tsar too accepted the idea that at this point it would be better to await results in other sectors and not 'bang their heads against the wall' here of all places. The order was given to stop the fighting and not allow the French to come out of their positions.

Bennigsen had already been on the move at 3 a.m. He sent forces north along the Partha to establish contact with Bernadotte's units. When they reached Hirschfeld they surprised Macdonald's supply column on their way to the positions occupied by the corps. Bennigsen had to cross the Partha in order to reach his objective. He made the crossing in the morning on a broad front, putting heavy pressure on the French in the sector between Liebertwolkwitz and Holzhausen. The French retired step by step, their counter-attacks failing to turn things around. The withdrawal was carried out in a kind of fanlike movement with the left wing brushing the Würzen axis where Reynier's corps made a stubborn defence in its first appearance in the battle of Leipzig. In the afternoon the French still held Zweinaundorf and Paunsdorf. All of Bennigsen's attempts to establish contact with Bernadotte failed. There was no sign of the Swedish crown prince. Bennigsen brought his forces to a halt, as the plan called for him to attack Leipzig on the Würzen axis, shoulder to shoulder with the Army of the North.

Bernadotte too had intended to come up on the Würzen axis, in a fanlike movement sweeping across the area south of the Partha in his sector from the north-east to the south-west, with Taucha at his back. His movement was carried out slowly, concerned mainly with covering itself. Langeron, one of Blücher's commanders, sat in on one of Bernadotte's war councils at his headquarters on the 18th. His description of the discussion explains something of the slowness of the crown prince: 'I found the prince dictating the placement of his units to his generals. He spoke in French, maybe even Gascon, as he did not know a word of Swedish. What he said sounded very logical to me, though too detailed. He even specified the place of junior officers in the columns.' The crossing in the Plaussig area was made only at around 4 p.m.

At the same hour Bennigsen renewed his pressure and attacked with the support of the British rocket units, whose fire threw the French into a panic. The latter were gradually pushed west along the Leipzig axis. At this stage Norman's Saxon units, now under Reynier's command, went over to the allies. For a few days now it had been possible to discern that their hearts were not in fighting alongside the French, of which Reynier had warned Napoleon. The news that the expected had indeed occurred reached Napoleon quickly and he galloped from Probstheide to a meeting with Ney to examine the implications of the defection. A good deal of historical analysis deals with the betrayal of the Saxons and some have tried to see in it the main reason for the defeat of the French at Leipzig. This is of course quite an exaggeration. A few thousand Saxons did not change the outcome of the battle, which was decided before that.

A spirited attack was made on Stotteritz from Bennigsen's left flank, but the French withstood it, aided by engineering works and flank fire from their artillery to the south, from the direction of Probstheide. At nightfall Bennigsen was well deployed opposite Leipzig but his success until then had not been decisive.

Starting in the morning, Blücher attacked on two axes: one from Göhlis to the Halle gate, the other opposite Schönfeld. Until noon he got nowhere. Dombrowski's Poles on the right wing withstood the pressure being exerted against them very nicely. The attack on Schönfeld began after 2 p.m. Marmont's men held their ground for three hours and then had to retire from the village. Ney mounted a counter-attack with his reserves. The French retook the village but were again pushed out towards evening, retreating south toward the city and regrouping at Reudnitz.

Bertrand, who advanced from Lindenau to carry out his assignment, attacked a division of Giulay's with the kind of fury that is reserved for a breakout prior to a retreat, punishing them badly. He continued on to Lützen. From there he continued to Weissenfels, reaching it in the afternoon. Giulay was ordered to report on the French movements along the Lützen and Saale axes. He ordered an Austrian force stationed at Weissenfels to destroy the bridge there and retire from the place. Blücher, who understood during the evening that the French were carrying out the operations indicative of a general retreat, ordered Yorck to occupy the Saale passages at Halle and

Merseburg. At the same hour the French concentrated cavalry forces at commanding points around Lindenau along the road leading out of the town.

With the close of day Napoleon lost interest in the battle. It was clear to him that Leipzig could no longer be held. Before he recognised this the rival armies had had to bring their awful masses together on 18 October. Count Yorck put it just right: 'The retreat, which the monarch had refused to begin voluntarily on the 17th, the defeated general would be compelled to begin on the 19th.' He returned to his headquarters at Stotteritz and as on many occasions in the past when he knew that he faced a new and different stage in a war he was conducting he felt he must regain his strength for the night's work that lay ahead and went to sleep. A shell exploding nearby woke him from his troubled sleep and he rode over to the headquarters set up for him at Rossplatz, called together his aides and drafted his instructions for the retreat of the army. He did not neglect a single detail: part of the artillery was to be evacuated that night, and before dawn all the units of the Imperial Guard, Victor's and Augereau's corps and one cavalry corps. All the other corps would continue to defend Leipzig and cover the retreat. Instructions were written out for all the garrisons along the Elbe, the Oder and the Vistula. The emperor did not forget to send a message to the chief recruiting officer in Paris telling him not send any more reinforcements to Germany. The emperor worked all night and his orders went out post-haste to all units and covered every aspect of this complicated retreat from right under the enemy's nose as it were.

Towards evening most of the allied commanders met on the hill north of Galgenberg which had served the tsar and the Prussian king as an observation post all through the day. The Austrian emperor joined them and there was considerable excitement. According to one of the exaggerated accounts of the meeting on the evening of 18 October, the three monarchs knelt and recited a prayer of thanksgiving for the great victory against their satanic enemy. Apparently all this never took place, but as a legend it faithfully reflects the feeling that reigned on the hill.

Schwarzenberg busied himself with writing out orders for the continuation of the attack. It would have to conclude with the capture of the city of Leipzig, which would symbolise victory. The fighting would be renewed at dawn and all forces would advance on Leipzig aiming for its centre in the current order of their disposition. Five columns would attack, entering the city from three directions. The staff work done during the night, constantly fed by updated intelligence on French movements, refined the excited order prepared during the evening. There was no sense in entering Leipzig with such a large force, so Schwarzenberg gave the Austrians, who were in any case on the left flank, the task of taking up positions opposite the first French concentration expected after the first phase of the retreat, in the Weissenfels–Naumburg area. During the night this sensible order was cancelled for unknown reasons and just a relatively small Austrian force was dispatched to carry out the original intention only partially – seizure of the area to be used by the French for retreat and regrouping.

At 2 a.m. the French began evacuating their positions in the northern sector and along the Pleisse and withdrawing towards Leipzig. They left behind burning fires in their camps and rearguards, making it difficult for the allies to guess their intentions. Only at daylight could the allied morning patrols along the previous day's battle line report on the retreat.

All the French cavalry corps made their way out of the big Leipzig front during the night. For defensive action and to cover the retreat the following forces and assignments were designated: Reynier's VII Corps in the Halle suburb; Marmont's VI Corps, reinforced by a division from the III Corps, from the Partha to the Grimma gate; the encirclement of the city up to the Pleisse was carried out by the rest of the corps in the following order: the III (Souham), V (Lauriston), XI (Macdonald), and VIII (Poniatowski). The rearguard, covering the retreat, would include the VII, VIII and XI Corps under the command of Macdonald and would be required to delay the enemy for 24 hours to allow as orderly a retreat as possible. All the others would start out according to circumstances.

As mentioned, orders went out on the same night from the emperor dealing with the organisation of the rest of the retreat west and the first steps in the defence of France. Bertrand was ordered to lay out the line of retreat to Erfurt and turn the town into a supply depot for the forces coming in from Leipzig. The order sent to Saint-Cyr at Dresden was to withdraw under the best conditions possible, including confirmation of the surrender of Torgau and Wittenberg, guaranteeing free passage of troops and the evacuation of the wounded. Napoleon suggested to the king of Saxony that he accompany him and guaranteed his safety, but the king preferred to await the allied sovereigns. And in fact he dispatched a letter of surrender to the tsar on that same day. The tsar's reply was quite cool.

The movement of the troops into Leipzig during the night created chaos with units and wagons getting all tangled up. The streets were filled with the wounded and with stragglers, who were rushed beneath the hoofs of horses and the wagons pushing through. The organisation of the defence also involved great destruction. Soldiers gathered materials from wherever they found any to improve their positions. The method of designating forces for defence – according to which those that had been in close contact with the enemy on the 18th were the ones to man the widest circle in the defensive alignment – left little time for regrouping as the contact between the opposing sides remained quite close.

On 19 October, a warm, sunlit autumn day, at 7 a.m., the allies commenced their attack on Leipzig. The approach was carried out as planned – from every direction except the west, which remained open – Blücher from the north, Bernadotte from the east, Bennigsen from the south-east, Barclay from the south and Colloredo along the Pleisse. By 10 a.m. the last of the French had been driven out of the suburbs north and east of the city. At 10 the tsar announced a truce to allow the French to surrender and spare the further shedding of blood and the pointless sacrifice of further victims on the two sides. Napoleon took advantage of the involved ceasefire procedure to buy time. When he discovered that the allies had done nothing on the western flank to cut his line of retreat or impede the retreat itself he breathed a sigh of relief. After leaving the Saxon king he was swallowed up together with his entourage in the stream of people leaving the city and at 11 o'clock reached Lindenau.

The fighting was renewed at 11 a.m. The confusion and the slaughter were terrible. The units fighting against the allies were those whose escape route was cut off owing to the crowding and they fought for their lives. An officer put in charge of the bridge leading out of Leipzig, near Lindenau, was ordered to blow it up after the departure of the last French unit. Because of the chaos it was impossible to identify this unit and the officer in charge set out to find it. A corporal who remained at the bridge and was put in charge there set off the explosives when he thought no Frenchmen were left to the east of him. When the smoke and dust settled it became clear that thousands of French soldiers had not got to the bridge and could not break out of the encirclement. They had little choice but to try to swim the river if they did not wish to surrender and be taken captive. Thousands surrendered. Many jumped into the water, some drowning in the foaming waters of the Elster, including the newly appointed Marshal Poniatowski, who tried to swim across with his horse. Five days later a local fisherman pulled his body out of the river.

Among the many senior officers taken captive were two corps commanders, Lauriston and Reynier.

At 1 p.m. the battle ended. Alexander, Frederich William, Schwarzenberg and their entourages entered the city through the Grimma gate. Bernadotte and the senior generals also arrived. They all made for the market square. As they passed through the streets the crowds went wild with joy. All the hardships and suffering of the past weeks seemed to be forgotten. The tsar passed the house where the king of Saxony was staying. The latter stood in the entrance with a few of his courtiers. The tsar rode on without glancing at the king, who was in effect a prisoner now (afterwards he was taken to Berlin and Stein was appointed high commissioner of Saxony). When he was in the square the captured French corps commanders were brought to him and he greeted them cheerfully. He was particularly cordial towards Lauriston, who had once served in the Russian capital. Lauriston was wearing a simple, roughly made coat over his magnificent uniform. Apparently he had hoped to be swallowed up in the crowd and perhaps escape from the city without being identified. Bernadotte requested to be excused so that he might return to his army and review the Swedish troops. The tsar granted his wish and took the opportunity to appoint him governor of the city of Leipzig. The sovereigns, now including the Austrian emperor as well, left the market square and went to the houses taken over for their use.

Losses were astronomical: 60,000 dead and wounded for the allies and 40,000 for the French with another 30,000 prisoners taken on the last day of fighting. The French left behind considerable spoils – hundreds of guns, many wagons and enormous quantities of arms and ammunition.

The nature of the fighting on 18 and 19 October makes it seem amazing that Napoleon decided to postpone the general retreat for a day. In actual fact no organised fighting took place on these days. The work of the French general staff in this period also deserves severe censure. Despite the emperor's detailed instructions no effort was made at headquarters to co-ordinate troop movements to and from the city. Marmont has commented on the subject as follows: 'Everyone assumed that officers had been appointed to supervise the transfer of the artillery during the night as well as the orderly transfer of equipment. Nothing like this happened and no one made sure that it did.' The general staff also failed to provide for artillery ammunition and a serious shortage developed. The French fired over 240,000 rounds in the first two days of fighting! Someone had to translate this figure into terms of the ability to continue fighting the next day. Macdonald was furious about the way the last two days of fighting had been managed, writing: 'I do not yet know by what name to call this criminal indifference; whether incapability, cowardice, or absence of all feeling, of all regret at this sacrifice of so many lives.'

As for the allies, they acted as if they were still afraid that the emperor might pull some mysterious rabbit out his magic hat. The impression created was that everything done in the last two days of the battle ended with the preparation of the victory ceremony in the city of Leipzig and that little thought was given to the next phase of the war, which might have consisted in energetically pursuing the enemy towards the Rhine and France and exploiting success. Had they broken through to Leipzig along one axis while earlier blocking the single line of retreat open to the French and pursued them immediately, giant strides would have been made towards putting the French army out of commission. Such a course of action would have turned the battle of Leipzig into a really decisive victory. The only commander who was for pursuit already on the evening of the 18th was of course Blücher. It will be remembered that he ordered Yorck to advance towards the Saale – to Halle and Merseburg – but he was alone in taking such an step.

The allies had allowed true glory to slip out of their hands first because they had been typically drunk with victory and because all tension had dissolved. It is not hard to imagine what the heads of the Coalition must have felt when they saw their arch-rival escaping by the skin of his teeth. It can be assumed that the troops were exhausted after three continuous days of fighting and incapable of summoning the physical and spiritual strength for one more strenuous effort. To this general falling off of energy three more possible reasons can be added: the absence of sufficient leadership at the command level, deriving from Schwarzenberg's qualities as a commander; the poor performance of the Army of the North during the critical days of the Battle of the Nations, which was a direct continuation of Bernadotte's contribution to the war against Napoleon; the desire to leave the French a way out and enable them to get back to France, for the good of future European political relations. Even if the latter reason were actual, it would not have been calculated. This way of thinking was deeply rooted in the political tradition of modern Europe and did not require discussion in councils of war.

The concluding Imperial Bulletin published on 24 October blamed the events of Leipzig on the serious shortage of artillery ammunition, the defection of the Saxon units and the hasty action of the wretched corporal who blew up the bridge. 'When the corporal, a man without intelligence and ill understanding his mission, heard the shots fired from the town ramparts, he lighted the match and blew the bridge.' Quite unbelievable. And another proof that the Imperial Bulletins were meant for the salons of Paris and not to document and clarify events honestly. Blaming the fiasco on such an insignificant figure was wicked beyond words. Unlike the retreat from Russia, where Napoleon personally directed the heroic crossing of the Berezina, here he was not present at the most sensitive spot, the spot where his presence was desperately needed. Hinging the entire retreat on a single bridge was a very serious error and one that could have been avoided. Over 100,000 men struggling to break off contact with the enemy within the walls of the city had to beat a path through a single gateway, cross two rivers and march over difficult swamp land.

The Battle of the Nations was over and with it in fact the whole war of 1813. It was destined to be the battle of the century and only in the war of 1914 did we see greater ones. Over 550,000 men had fought in it and around 2,300 guns had spat their fire. The sad end is nowhere better expressed than in Macdonald's deeply felt words describing the flight from Leipzig: 'Our unhappy troops were crowded together on the river bank; whole platoons plunged into the water and were carried away; cries of despair rose from all sides. The men perceived me. Despite the noise and the tumult, I distinctly heard these words: "Monsieur le Maréchal, save your men!" I could do nothing for them! Overcome by rage, indignation, fury, I wept!' Jomini tells of a French general who passed by the Lindenau bridge and saw 'a man of peculiar dress and with only a small retinue; he was whistling the air of *Malbrouk s'en va-t-en guerre* [Malbrouk goes off to war], although he was deeply lost in thought. The general thought he was a burgher and was on the point of approaching him to ask a question... It was the emperor.'

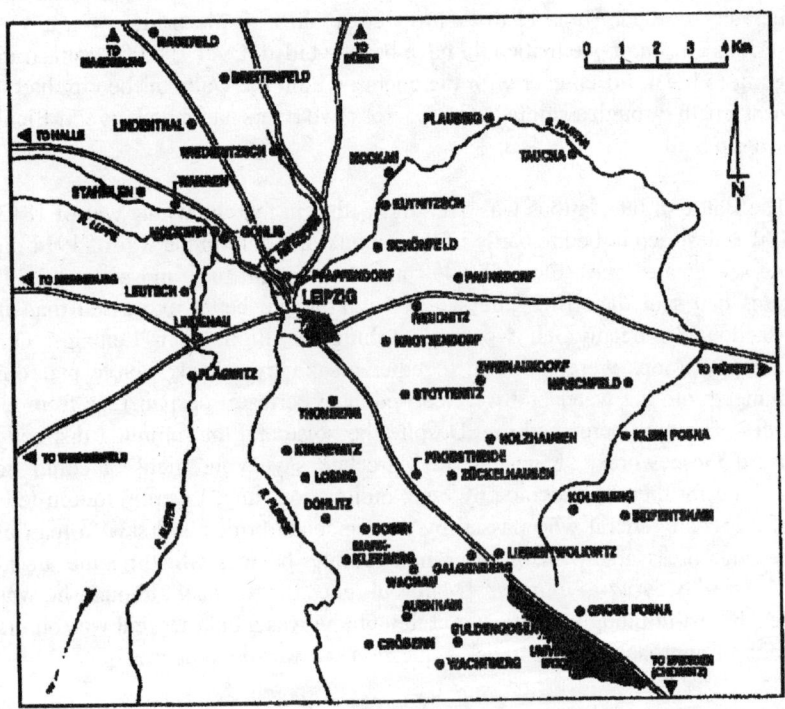

Map 16   Battle of the Nations

Chapter 11 - AFTERMATH

The residents of Leipzig were now busy removing the signs of the great battle that had taken place within its walls, the aftermath of which consisted of the expulsion of the French army from its environs and back to France and the beginning of the end of the great Bonapartist empire. First, the many wounded had to be attended to. In one of the city's squares, opposite a church, there was a big pile of bodies. Charred corpses were lying everywhere and beside them the wounded, dying or racked by hunger. The French had emptied the warehouses in the city of food and it was impossible to supply the conquering forces gathering there. The various headquarters had located themselves in the city precincts and hundreds of senior officers along with countless junior ones had to be fed. Thousands of French prisoners increased the congestion, which was great even without them. For want of provisions, their principal food was the remains of the dead horses strewn in the streets.

The French army that had escaped Leipzig numbered around 100,000 men, a not inconsiderable force in military terms. But it should be remembered that on 20 October 1813, this was a severely beaten army. Cathcart has written that if a formula had to be elaborated for undermining the army's strength and destroying it one could do no better than devising the one evacuation route leading from Leipzig to Lindenau – a web of redoubts rising above a waterlogged swamp five kilometres long and bisected by five streams. It was wet and cold there. The allies figured that the French would not be able to stop and fight at Erfurt or anywhere else in Germany. It should also be remembered that the whole country was imbued with the spirit of German nationalism and a hatred of the French and their emperor and that news of the French defeat had spread quickly and stirred up feelings even more.

Napoleon left Märkranstadt on the morning of the 20th, escorted by the Old Guard. On arriving at Lützen he ran into units of the army. His impression of their appearance was very bad. Disorder was rampant. Murat, who was in the same coach with him, had to get down and straighten things out so that the emperor could pass. Napoleon did not have to concern himself with a close pursuit of his army. The rearguard covering the retreat had destroyed all the bridges on the Lindenau ramparts. The Austrian forces, who were closest at hand, showed no great enthusiasm for the chase, both because of their weakness and because of the determination Bertrand had displayed in pushing them aside on his way to Weissenfels. Yorck, whom Blücher had sent to the Saale as far back as the 18th to block the possible lines of retreat of the French, could not arrive in time, as he was taking a roundabout route via Halle. He did however succeed in hitting the French rear units at Freiburg, causing them losses and freeing thousands of Austrian prisoners marching with them.

The allied plan was to follow the French in two columns: Schwarzenberg on the Zeitz–Jena–Weimar axis, Blücher on the Weissenfels–Freiburg axis. Bernadotte, reinforced by Bennigsen's corps, was supposed to follow Blücher, but the idea was abandoned and it was decided to dispatch the reinforced Bernadotte to Hamburg. This division of forces was mainly a result of the allocation of routes, the aim being to concentrate at Erfurt before 25 October.

Napoleon arrived at Erfurt on the 23rd. The first thing he thought of was to regroup there over the space of a few days. He summoned Macdonald. The marshal's recollection of their meeting gives a good indication of the mood prevailing among Napoleon's marshals at the time: 'We had been there for some hours when the emperor sent for me. I went to the castle, and first saw the king of Naples [Murat], who cautioned me that the emperor's intention was to find a strong defensive position, where he could remain for five or six days. "You had better find a weak one," added Murat with an oath, "or he will not rest till he has ruined himself and us too." "Never fear," I replied. "Even if the position be excellent, I will tell him my mind about our situation." I was ushered in. The emperor gave me the commission of which Murat had warned me. "It is out of the question to make a reconnaissance at this moment," I said. "But," I continued, "are you in earnest in talking of remaining here?" "The men are tired," said the emperor, "and the enemy pursuing slowly. We must give them a rest." "No doubt that would be advisable, or even necessary under other circumstances," I replied; "but in our present state of demoralisation, as I may call things by their proper names, you will gain nothing by it. We must get to the Rhine as fast as possible. The majority of the men are already in disorder, and making their way thither.'" It was easier to talk this way to the emperor in a book of memoirs than in his intimidating presence and it would be inadvisable to take Macdonald's description literally but, as stated, it is indicative of the rupture and the heavy atmosphere.

In the end the emperor gave up on the idea of the reconnaissance and the defensive posture and ordered the march to continue to the south-west. The ranks were being thinned out every day. Some deserted, some straggled because of hunger or severe illness and some organised themselves into bands of brigands seizing whatever came to hand.

At Erfurt, Murat made contact with the allies. He did not have to be a prophet to understand that Napoleon's protection was not going to do him much good any more. He wished to assure the continuation of his reign at Naples with the blessing of the victors. He undertook to abandon the emperor and remain loyal to them. Napoleon gallantly allowed him to resign from the army – Murat claimed that the affairs of Naples demanded that he return there immediately – and Murat returned to Naples. In the end it turned out to be a bad bargain for Murat. At the beginning of 1814, after he kept Eugene from leaving for France at the head of an armed force to help his stepfather, the allies reneged on their promises and refused to guarantee his crown. He escaped to France, tried to regain his kingdom by force, and was apprehended. This wayward figure, the greatest cavalryman of his time, was executed before a firing squad in October 1815.

Quickly enough it became clear to Napoleon that the allies were indeed pursuing him along his escape routes and that a threat had materialised in his rear that might have been expected in the light of the defection of the Bavarians. They and the Austrians who had confronted them on the Inn River before the defection joined forces under the Bavarian General Wrede. This individual, who had fought alongside Napoleon from 1805 on and whom Napoleon had advanced, was now given the task of advancing to the Main River and cutting the French line of retreat if it passed through Frankfort and Mainz. He concentrated a force of more than 30,000 men at Hanau, less than 20 kilometres east of Frankfort. Wrede arrived there after marching north from the Danube via Donauworth and Würzburg. He estimated that most of the French army was moving north of him. He deployed his forces unwisely, which led Napoleon to remark to his circle afterwards that while he had awarded him the title of count he had not accorded him the rank of general (in the Bavarian army Wrede was made a field marshal!).

The principal fighting at Hanau took place on 30 October. The French had half as many men as the force facing them. Napoleon personally commanded the troops, which included Victor's corps and part of Macdonald's, using his artillery most imaginatively. After thrashing Wrede soundly with many losses, he sent in Sebastiani's cavalry, which cut him to pieces, sowing disorder and continuing the killing. The emperor thought of the battle as a minor disturbance and did not bother to exploit his success, simply earmarking troops to pin down the enemy and cover the rest of the movement. The road to Frankfort, and from there to Mainz, was open and secure and Napoleon ordered the march to the Rhine to continue. In his later memoirs, dictated in exile, Napoleon did not complain about the defection of the Bavarians, attributing it to weakness and inability to withstand the pressure being exerted on them by the allies.

The crossing of the Rhine began on 2 November and lasted three days. Most of the operation was carried out at Mainz. Schwarzenberg only arrived at Frankfort on the 5th, when most of the French were already on the other side of the river. The last military action of the 1813 campaign took place at Hochheim, near Mainz, on 9 November. Schwarzenberg himself commanded the Austrian force that moved out to drive back Bertrand. Units of the IV Corps had remained there as a covering force. The Austrians numbered a few thousand troops and succeeded in carrying out their mission. Bertrand's force vanished into the nearby woods.

On the same day, the 9th, Napoleon reached his residence at St Cloud. Of the enormous army that had fought in Germany, only around 80,000 men returned home. Thiers, who wrote the history of the empire in 20 volumes, gives a good description of the mood in Paris after the withdrawal of the army across the Rhine. The mood was one of disappointment and despair. Nor could the police, despite its efforts, do anything to prevent it from spreading or dispel its outward signs. The public did not forgive the emperor for missing out on a chance for peace after the victories at Lützen and Bautzen. He was also thought to have failed in the contacts during the armistice and his excuses were unacceptable. Now his ambition was seen as cruel in its cost to mankind and fatal for France.

Let us now examine the fate of the French forces that remained in the rear of the main body of the army and had to contend, each alone, with the superior forces closing in on them and seeking their defeat.

Bernadotte had remained for a while at Hannover and then came out at the head of his Swedish troops to fight Davout. Davout barricaded himself in Hamburg with the French units under his command. His Danish allies had remained in the Holstein district, easy prey for the Swedes, who swarmed over them in superior numbers. In the end, under the dictates of circumstance, an agreement was signed in January 1814 with the king of Denmark, who conceded Norway to the Swedes and contented himself with Pomerania. Denmark also undertook to provide the allies with an army of 40,000 men. Davout remained in Hamburg until the fall of Napoleon in 1814. Until then he was under siege, showed no signs of breaking though he had absolutely no chance. In the last stage of the siege Bennigsen's Russian corps faced him.

At Dresden, Saint-Cyr made many efforts to break the siege which the I and XIV Corps were under, but in vain. He had wanted to link up with the French forces still garrisoned on the Elbe. On 11 November, suffering from lack of food and the pressure of the siege, he signed an agreement with Klenau allowing him to return to France with all his troops on the condition that he undertook not to fight again against the allies. Saint-Cyr had already reached Altenburg on his way to the Rhine and to France when he was stopped, for Schwarzenberg had refused to approve the agreement. It was proposed that he return to Dresden and the situation as it was before the signing of the agreement, but he preferred to surrender and be taken captive to Bohemia. Lobau, the commander of the I Corps, joined him.

Danzig, on the Vistula, was occupied for many months by General Rapp's X Corps, which surrendered on 30 November, its soldiers being taken back to Russia as prisoners. Stettin, on the Oder, had already surrendered on the 21st. Torgau, on the Elbe, surrendered on 26 December. One by one all the rest of the French garrison towns fell, until the surrender of the last French stronghold in Europe.

We have already mentioned Eugene, who had been sent to Italy in May. He managed to raise an army of 50,000 men and in August, after the Austrians joined the war against France, marched on their forces at the head of his troops in order to pin them down and keep them from joining the fighting on the main front. He carried out his mission to the best of his ability, fighting against an Austrian force that numbered only 30,000 men under Hiller. As Eugene was married to the daughter of the king of Bavaria he was able to go there after the fall of his stepfather in 1814.

Another chain of events whose aftermath should be traced was the one unfolding in Spain. When last visited, Wellington had gained his victory at Vittoria, in June. At this point there was a real danger of an invasion of France from the south, from the Pyrenèes. Wellington raced north to San Sebastian, fearing that the war in Europe would end in an amenable settlement that would allow Napoleon to transfer all his forces to the Iberian Peninsula. After the rout at Vittoria, Napoleon had sent Soult, who was with him in Germany, to Spain with the task of organising the army and stopping an invasion of France. At the end of July, Soult mounted a counter-attack in the border region between Spain and France. His plan was a good one, holding much promise and surprising Wellington. Had things turned out better the British would have been driven from France. But luck was against Soult. Because of the foggy weather and the stubborn resistance of the British and the Spaniards, the fight for the Pyrenèes ended in failure for the French and withdrawal of Soult's forces to France. Simultaneously a French attack in Catalonia under Marshal Suchet petered out and Wellington was able to direct all his efforts to the north. He tightened the siege of San Sebastian, which fell into his hands at the beginning of September. In October, the battles were already taking place on French soil, in the Bayonne area. Soult made enormous and desperate efforts to stop the British advance but at the beginning of 1814 was already in retreat – though slow – into the interior of the country. The Spanish soldiers attached to the invasion force took their revenge and their uncontrolled rampaging led Wellington to send them back home.

Thus Napoleon found himself forced to defend the eastern and southern border of his country simultaneously in the face of the expanded Coalition that had begun to organise itself against him a year before. The Peninsular War came to an end in April, but not before a big battle was fought at Toulouse in southern France in which Soult was defeated for the last time by Wellington.

Another fruit of the allied victory in the war, which was part and parcel of the reorganisation of Europe in line with the interests of the anti-Napoleonic Coalition, was plucked in Holland. First the populace rose up against the French, expelling them from the capital and proclaiming the prince of Orange governor. The prince, who was domiciled in England, arrived in the country on 2 December and entered The Hague escorted by British troops. Winzingerode and Bülow, belonging to the Army of the North, moved into Holland and gained control of the entire country. Another tier of the French empire had collapsed.

Cathcart summed up the situation at the end of 1813 from the standpoint of the allies: 'Germany had indeed been liberated, but it was evident that the tranquillity of Europe could not be established upon a safe and permanent basis, until the disturber of the peace of nations, who had been hunted up to his stronghold, but not subdued, should be brought by force of arms, or by negotiations, carried on at the head of formidable armies, to submit to restrictions much more binding than any he had yet been disposed to endure. But although the work of retribution was not yet completed, the necessity of restoring the ranks (after the losses incidental to the severe contest at Leipzig, and the continual forced marches which had followed, as well as the precaution, no less indispensable, of providing supplies and means of support for a winter campaign in an enemy's country), placed it out of the power of the allies to pursue their advantage any further in that campaign. For two months they allowed themselves an interval of repose, intending to take to the field again in the month of January 1814, to cross the Rhine at the head of the armies amounting to more than 200,000 men, and with renewed vigour to carry the war into the enemy's country.' The licking of wounds, the taste for revenge and preparations for the renewal of the war were all mixed together.

At the end of 1813 Napoleon faced a situation very similar to the one he had faced at the end of 1812, though under different circumstances and for different reasons. In December 1812 he had returned to Paris full of energy and plans. In November 1813 his energy level was considerably lower and his ability to act much more limited, though the Napoleonic spark and pretensions were as prominent as ever. As early as 25 October he wrote to the president of the French Senate, his friend Cambacerés, in Paris: 'I am writing to the minister of war on the subject of a levy of 80,000 to 100,000 men which I need. With the whole of Europe under arms ... France is lost unless she does the same.' And on 3 November, he added: 'Say a word to the pusillanimous councillors of state and senators. I am told on all sides that they show great fear and little character. Be well persuaded that my infantry, artillery and cavalry have such superiority over those of the enemy that there is nothing to fear ... I am sorry that I am not in Paris. They would see me more tranquil and more calm than in any other circumstances of my life.'

It is appropriate to complete the story of the year 1813 with a synopsis of the events constituting the final chapter of the political and military biography of Napoleon Bonaparte. In November the allied rulers had still not decided what their final goal was: to content themselves with keeping Napoleon where they wanted him, with nothing remaining but for him to accept the current status of his country, which was no longer the heart of a great empire, or to aim at deposing him. The identity of interests of the members of the coalition was somewhat shaken. The king of Prussia was in no hurry to continue the war. His primary concern was to keep his army intact, though Blücher remained watchful, urging the continuation of the war until final victory. Austria believed that total victory over France would serve the interests of Russia and Prussia more than its own. It had gained a great deal since joining the allies. It had regained territories in Italy and had established a distinguished position for its diplomacy on the Continent. Among the Russians there were those who were against continuing to be involved in a war so far from home, arguing that Russia would gain very little from it. The tsar, on the other hand, wanted to see the complete downfall of the French emperor. He wanted to avenge himself for the conquest of Moscow by conquering Paris in an operation in which the Russians would play a prominent role. Alexander contended that the active participation of Russia in the continuation of the war would win for it a position so strong that it would have no difficulty taking a big chunk out of Poland as part of the final settlement in Europe. Needless to say, Austria and Prussia had little reason to be enthusiastic about this possibility. Bernadotte, born French, strongly opposed an invasion of France, his participation in which would have aroused much feeling against him in France. There were signs that he had his eye on the French throne. The British government was anti-French. After years on the Iberian Peninsula, Wellington was now fighting in the south of France and from his government's point of view there was no reason not to rake in the dividends of this investment.

The representatives of the Powers, the allies, convened at Frankfort to discuss various plans. The conflict of interests quickly became apparent; the solution was to make overtures to Napoleon, the leader so recently defeated. Metternich was the leading figure in these deliberations, engineering a joint appeal to Napoleon which would be seen as a final attempt to prevent war. In a message sent from Frankfort in November, it was proposed to Napoleon that he agree to the confinement of France to its natural boundaries: the Pyrenées, the Alps and the Rhine. The designation of the Rhine as a natural boundary was a kind of confirmation of Napoleon's declaration at his coronation that he would preserve the integrity of his country within its borders at the time. If he agreed to this proposal, the message read, it would be possible to arrive at a comprehensive European peace agreement. It was the old scenario. Napoleon saw the proposal as a sign of weakness and sought to buy time to rebuild his army. When he finally replied, after two weeks, it was too late. The allies had withdrawn their proposal.

In fairness it should be said that the proposal drafted by Metternich was more of a declaration for purposes of negotiation than a 'take it or leave it' proposition. Had Napoleon replied favourably a peace congress would have been convened with the participation of England, and Napoleon had no illusions as to the chances of a congress of this kind. At Frankfort the allies made a distinction for the first time between France and its emperor. 'We do not make war on France,' read an appeal to the French nation, 'but are casting off the yoke which your government imposed on our countries. We hoped to have found peace before touching your soil. We go to find it there.'

The allies crossed the Rhine. The battle for France had begun – in France. The agreed aim was to end the emperor's rule and the agreed final objective was Paris. The French army was very small and overwhelmingly outnumbered. Its troops were the survivors of the German campaign and new recruits, mere children. Arms and ammunition were in short supply. Consequently Napoleon concentrated his army along the lower Rhine at the cost of defending the upper Rhine and the border between France and Switzerland. The allies had over 400,000 men arrayed along the border: Blücher on the right with 80,000 troops, Schwarzenberg in the centre with 200,000, an Austro-Italian army numbering over 50,000 men on the left and Wellington in the south with 80,000 men. As noted, most of the Army of the North, under the command of Bülow, had been directed to the Low Countries.

The campaign lasted around four months, from the end of December to April 1814. In the first two months Napoleon scored impressive successes, striking the enemy again and again. He was again at the peak of his powers as a leader and organiser. He positioned most of his force opposite the allied centre and operated in accordance with his tried and proven fighting principles. In this phase of the war he conducted a brilliant campaign, but one that was fruitless. Though Schwarzenberg was forced into a long retreat at the end of February, Blücher kept on fighting and pushed back the French.

Napoleon tried to give the struggle the 'do or die' patina of the Revolutionary wars. The allies recalled that in the 1890s, after the French had expelled the invading armies from its borders, they had kept up the pursuit. This memory steeled their wills, as the last thing they wanted to see was France recovering and again striking into the heart of the Continent. They thought things out, did not take the bait Napoleon dangled before them as to the direction of his movement (to deflect their advance on the capital), reconcentrated their forces and saw their pressure begin to bear fruit.

The capital was divided and riven by intrigue. The hated Bourbon dynasty was the hero of the hour and Talleyrand orchestrated the designs against the emperor on its behalf. The commanders of the army tried to prevent the support of the allies for the restoration of the Ancien Regime, but at the same time most of them turned their backs on Napoleon. Paris offered no real military resistance, making a stand only for form's sake. Marmont and Mortier surrendered on 30 March and Paris fell. The next day Alexander and Frederick William rode through the main streets of the city at the head of their forces in a victory parade witnessed by thousands of downhearted and apprehensive residents. The tsar had fulfilled his dream and was also the sovereign who was going to determine the new regime in France.

Napoleon, who was at Fontainebleau, outside the capital, could still count on a few thousand loyal soldiers, but his important marshals had abandoned him. The marshals Ney and Berthier urged him to resign and leave the country. In the argument that ensued Napoleon insisted that the army was loyal to him and would obey his orders and the excited Ney replied: 'Sire! the army obeys its generals!' Marie Louise and the emperor's son had escaped from Paris and gone to Vienna and Napoleon would never see them again. He realised that the end had come and left a letter of abdication with his intimates. Ney, Macdonald, Marmont and Caulaincourt delivered the document to the tsar. On 11 April the Treaty of Fontainebleau was signed, according to which Napoleon was to be exiled to the tiny island of Elba in the Tyrrhenian Sea off the western shore of Italy. He was granted sovereignty over the island and he and his family would receive a generous yearly pension. He tried to commit suicide but failed in the attempt, and some say that he saw in this failure a sign from on high that further adventures were in store for him. A few days later he set out with a few hundred volunteers from among the Old Guard who were permitted to join him. They reached Elba on 4 May.

The new sovereign of France was Louis XVIII, who had claimed the throne ever since his brother, Louis XVI, was executed. His appointment was settled by the Treaty of Paris, signed in May, which fixed the question of the monarchy and the principles for determining the borders of France. The Senate confirmed Louis on the throne but decreed that the French monarchy would be constitutional. The pre-Revolutionary government institutions were not revived, the Bonapartist ones being retained instead. As for relations with Europe, Talleyrand aspired to reach an agreement with the allies focusing on fixing the borders of France. The man said to flourish in crises or at congresses wisely exploited the conflict of interests among the Coalition partners. The Powers mulled over the fate of Europe at a congress convened at Vienna in November 1814 and whose deliberations lasted until June 1815. The parties quickly got bogged down in disagreements threatening to put an end to the cordial relations that had prevailed when Napoleon was their common enemy. The leading actors were Talleyrand and Metternich, for whom the Congress provided a fine stage for the display of their varied talents for diplomacy and intrigue. In the end the sides were able to draw up a map of Europe acceptable to everyone, along the lines set out in the Treaty of Paris. The history of the nineteenth and twentieth centuries bears witness to the fact that the Vienna accords were far from settling the basic issues, a fact confirmed by the ensuing wars.

Napoleon devoted his undiminished energy to administering his tiny island. As was his habit, he went into the smallest details. He improved the fruit orchard economy, opened up fields to irrigation and supported the local fishing business. But he did not forget France and stayed abreast of what was going on there. He knew of the hostility that had developed towards Louis XVIII, mainly because the public was afraid that the achievements of the Revolution would be swept away. He also knew that a scheme was being hatched to banish him to some remote place, far removed from the Continent. All this inspired him to make a move that astounded France and all of Europe. The historian Herbert Fisher has called it the most marvellous adventure in the world's history. On 1 March 1815, Napoleon landed in the south of France with the small Guard unit that had been with him on Elba. On his way to Paris he met with resistance, but also with enthusiasm. When Marshal Ney joined him, after some hesitation – having in fact been sent to stop him and even promising to bring him back 'in an iron cage' – nothing stood between him and Paris. When he reached the capital, on 20 March, in the midst of growing popular support, Louis XVIII fled the country and Napoleon again seized power.

In the Hundred Days of Napoleon's revived rule, he seemed to have been interested in producing a new constitution and confining himself to ruling France within its recognised borders. He talked peace and preached civil liberty. On the international front he tried to drive a wedge between the Coalition partners and again promote French-Austrian relations as well as personal relations with Kaiser Francis. However, his traditional enemies were not willing to give him a second chance. His return to France reunited them. They proclaimed him 'the enemy and disturber of the peace of the world' and placed him outside the law. They were determined to get him out of France.

The army that arrayed itself against him this time was mainly composed of British and Prussian troops, with Wellington and Blücher at their head. This army planned to invade France once more, by the shortest route, via Belgium. Napoleon went out to meet it there at the head of an army composed mainly of veteran troops. His enemy had a clear-cut advantage in relative strength, which Napoleon sought to overcome by mounting a lightning attack and driving a wedge between the two parts of the allied army. And indeed his sudden appearance before their outposts on 15 astonished the two commanders, his old enemies. The curtain had risen on the last act in the military drama of Napoleon Bonaparte and its final scene was destined to be one of the most famous battles in history.

On the 16th Napoleon was able to catch Blücher alone and defeated him at Ligny. He made a brilliant tactical move – an attack along two axes – and might have destroyed the Prussians but for a lack of co-ordination between forces causing a delay of a few vital hours in delivering the decisive blow with the Imperial Guard. When it came, in the evening hours, Blücher himself stood at the head of his troops to prevent a rout. Gneisenau, the Prussian chief of staff, organised as orderly a retreat as possible. Because the French failed to exploit their success to the full, he was able to regroup all the Prussian units north of the battleground and within supporting distance of Wellington in what was to be the decisive battle two days hence. This very important movement confounded Napoleon's estimate that the Prussians would retire to Namur, to the south-east. The battle of Ligny saw the participation of Vandamme, who had recently returned from his Russian captivity.

About ten kilometres north-west of Namur, Marshal Ney was supposed to gain control of the axes linking the two concentrations of the allied army, of the British and of the Prussians. Ney took his time, reaching his objective, the town of Quatre Bras on the Brussels highway, on the afternoon of the 16th.

He was astounded to discover that he was missing 20,000 men, who were moving in a different direction. This was the force that had caused the failure of co-ordination at Ligny. Ney attacked furiously and destroyed a British regiment, but did not gain a decisive victory in the battle. Wellington attacked in great strength in the evening and regained most of the ground he had lost. The next day he slipped away and redeployed on a ridge south of Waterloo, about 15 kilometres to the north. Blücher too completed his withdrawal and in the evening hours the two parts of the allied army were less than 20 kilometres apart, the Prussians east of the British.

On the 18th Ney ordered Grouchy, commanding a corps of over 30,000 men, to establish contact with the Prussians and engage them wherever they were to be found along his line of advance. He himself linked up with Napoleon's right and the two of them advanced towards Wellington. Blücher left one corps, under Thielmann, where he had been the previous day and marched west with three corps to reinforce the British. Wellington agreed to open the battle where he stood only because he counted on Blücher to come to his support by evening. Napoleon was aiming to reach Brussels by nightfall. The night before there had been a heavy rain and the emperor postponed his attack until the ground dried a bit. This delay played into the hands of Wellington. He placed most of his units on the reverse slope and thus spared them the French cannonade that opened the attack at 11.30 in the morning.

Ney directed the main effort, attacking the left of the enemy centre in force. The battle plan was simple: a four-division infantry assault with cavalry and infantry pouring into the gap created and pounding their way to Brussels. All this while, faithful to the original orders he had received, Grouchy remained in contact with Thielmann's unimportant rearguard instead of joining Napoleon, though he clearly heard the sounds of battle. Grouchy was a general with mediocre talents. He did not take part in the 1813 campaign because of poor health but had fought in the 1814 battles on French soil and had only received the rank of marshal two months previously. The officers under him pleaded with him to break off contact with Thielmann and reinforce Napoleon, but in vain. Meanwhile the main French assault was not going well and Napoleon already knew of the coming junction of the two parts of the enemy army. He dispatched Lobau's corps to block Blücher and ordered Grouchy to join him quickly (the order only reached Grouchy at 5 p.m.).

Now Ney sent in most of his cavalry and attacked the right of the enemy centre, but the British held their ground and repulsed the French attack, though with heavy losses. At 6 p.m. Napoleon sent in his last reserves in one sector while Ney mounted a co-ordinated attack in the other, taking an important enemy position. He implored the emperor to send him the Guard in order to decide the battle, but the Guard was already engaged. This was the critical moment for both sides. After an hour the Guard succeeded in concentrating its forces and attacking, but the British held fast. Then came the Prussian moment of glory. Arriving on the scene, they decided the battle. Wellington had withstood the French attacks all through the day, taking advantage of the ground and closing every gap in his line caused by the French pressure. The tenacity of his infantry was extraordinary. Grouchy did not reach the battlefield at all and retreated in perfect order the next morning. Napoleon extricated himself by the skin of his teeth and arrived in Paris three days later.

The Prussians would have had Napoleon executed, had it been up to Blücher. Fortunately for him, his fate was determined by the British, to whom he surrendered on 15 July. Admirers of Napoleon's grand gestures will find much to enjoy and capture their attention in his letter of surrender: 'Exposed to the factions which divide my country, and to the hostility of the principal powers of Europe, I have terminated my political career, and I come, like Themistocles, to sit at the hearth of the British people. I place myself under the protection of their laws, as the most powerful, the most constant and the most generous of my enemies.' The former emperor, who always found his analogies in history, had chosen as an example the Athenian leader who gave himself up to the Persians out of fear of the Spartans. The British hesitated, consulted their partners and replied to the appeal of General Bonaparte (as he was now being called) as follows: to prevent definitively the possibility of another disruption of the European peace he was to be exiled to a place from which it would be very difficult to engineer a second escape. This was the island of St Helena, in the South Atlantic Ocean. Napoleon protested the decision, arguing that it smelled of tyranny and violated international law, since he had surrendered of his own free will and thus spared Europe the prolongation of hostilities. The British shut their ears to the arguments of the French Cossack who was finally being robbed himself, so to speak, and on the instructions of the prime minister, Lord Liverpool, their prisoner set sail on 7 August, 1815, aboard His Majesty's ship the *Northumberland*, on a ten-week journey. Accompanying him were a few members of his circle who had fought with him and served him in his days of glory, among them our old friend from the IV Corps, General Henri Bertrand.

On St Helena, Napoleon settled his endless accounts, fulminating against his enemies and his many critics – all of which was dictated to his circle and eventually saw light as his memoirs. In his final years he suffered from a stomach ailment – ulcers or cancer – which killed him. He died on 5 May 1821, bitter and humiliated.

Some people are of the opinion that a hero of history like Napoleon should end his life in tragic wretchedness rather than in his bed in a splendid palace or even in battle. In this way he may gain a measure of the sympathy and pity that would certainly have been denied to him had his deeds been judged by the suffering he had caused to entire nations, and by this alone.

Chapter 12 - THE FIRST WORLD WAR

'One good battle' would solve all his problems and convince all of Europe that there was no point resisting his hegemony – that was what Napoleon believed on the eve of his Russian campaign when he considered his relations with Russia and reflected on the upheaval that threatened to unite the Continent against him. Underlying the campaign were misconceived notions and judgements and it failed for an entire range of reasons, but the great sin can be summed up in the thinking that expressed itself in those same three words. Napoleon refused to understand that the age of one good battle had passed, in a process that had worked itself out at the beginning of the century. He could not read what Clausewitz was to write in a book published in the 1830s, namely that the days had passed when disputes between nations were settled when one of them lay helpless on the battlefield after being defeated in that seemingly one good battle. Clausewitz concluded his discussion of the subject with a singular statement: 'In Napoleon's day, war came close to its true nature, its absolute perfection.' The true nature of perfect war is that it is decided by rules totally different from the rules of the 'one battle'.

The soldier-emperor who returned from the snowy bloodstained wastelands of Russia had undergone a terrible experience in the 224 days that he had been absent from Paris. Within 84 days of his return he had devised a master plan for a new campaign, laid out in the paper of 11 March 1813. The thinking that underlay the plan was already worthy of war that 'came close to its true nature' and showed that its creator had understood very well that as a commander he would soon have to adopt lines of strategic thinking much different from the old ones, though we have seen that to a large extent he still remained faithful to his fixed concepts. The plan was ahead of its time, mainly in relation to the means required for its implementation; its principal importance lies in its being a milestone on the road to total war.

We have seen that Napoleon built an enormous army from the bottom up, mobilising the nation and the economy for total war, and everything while 'in motion'. He concentrated the new army in big assembly and staging areas at the edge of the theatre of operations at the same time that he carried out holding and delaying actions with the remnants of his old army. He succeeded in stopping a tentative enemy, lacking an overall plan, just where he wanted to and commenced his advance in a mammoth offensive formation. The direction of the advance was the result of a strategic parallelogram of forces, a poor compromise between his desire to operate on a broad front and circumstances dictating its constriction. This time he was absent from his capital 209 days and conducted a campaign whose end result was more than a quarter of a million in killed and wounded. In May he fought two great battles and it was of all things his superior numbers that came back to haunt him. So much blood spilled and no prisoners, no spoils, no captured flags. In these two battles – at Lützen and Bautzen – his generalship was at its peak for the last time. But these two battles were on the borderline between the one good battle and components of only secondary importance in the intricate web of total war.

We have already seen that his enemies built up a total strength that was the real sum of its parts, and that they too, while 'in motion', became a worthy opponent in this new kind of war, learning lessons quickly and adopting ideas and principles that were a logical consequence of the precise formulation of their goals. They came out of the two battles in which the enemy still held the advantage with the feeling that there was a definite formula for success and that they were on the brink of grasping it and acting on it. Fuller, who said that at Jena Napoleon destroyed the last vestiges of feudalism and that out of the ashes rose the new national army, added: 'On the corpse-strewn fields by the Elster, present-day Europe writhed out of its medieval shell.' (Fuller, J. F. C.: *The Decisive Battles of the Western World*).

Subsequently the war of 1813 was fought in accordance with a scenario that could not be altered. One commander attempted to go a fixed route though it led him into the whirlwind. He relied on his understanding, on his experience, on his leadership, tried one remedy, then another, chasing his armies from one end of the theatre to the other, erring in his choice of objectives, erring in his choice of commanders and the division of forces. The opposing commanders were caught up in a process of trial and error, still pulling in different directions, speaking different languages and shaped by different traditions. However, in a single conference in the middle of the war they managed to formulate the guidelines that saw them through the remainder of the struggle and the formula they were seeking came into being.

Napoleon found himself at the centre of a tightening circle. The repeated failures of his secondary forces – he won one battle while they were routed in two – led to their forced entry into the centre of the circle while the allied forces closed in on the Grand Army, linking up in every direction on a vast killing field. The battle of Leipzig, said the German historian Lenz, was a battle the likes of which Europe had not seen since the days of Attila. The portents of total war were already to be seen in 1809. Europe – from the Rhine to the Vistula – lay conquered and cowering beneath the feet of the French emperor, but still the idea of throwing off the yoke was in the air. In the east, the Russians spun their expansionist designs at the expense of the Poles and the Ottomans, waiting apprehensively for the next crisis in their relations with France. They had been defeated, but lost no territory, and were officially still in alliance with France – the shaky Erfurt alliance. In the west an injured and angry Britain incited all the parties to rebel against Napoleon and attack him, offering its money and its resources. Sweden sought support for its aspirations in Scandinavia and northern Germany in return for support and even participation in the coming struggle. In Spain a real war against France had entered its second year. The world was unwittingly primed for an all-out war and when the 'thousand shots' were fired all of Europe would hear them.

And who was the first to act in this seething cauldron? None other than Austria, which was not exactly the bold, hot-blooded nation you would expect to stand up alone to the victorious Grand Army. But Austria had good reasons to dare all: it was surrounded by political entities completely controlled by Napoleon; French forces, or forces that answered to France and were stationed near Austria's borders, threatened it; it feared the winds of revolution that might be wafted in the direction of its empire under French inspiration. To survive, as well as to preserve its influential position in Europe, it had to act. Austria felt that its time had come, for Napoleon was bogged down in Spain, England had promised substantial aid and it had a big army and a feeling of strength and capability.

The war of 1809 was fought in more than one theatre of operations, taking place in Germany (and spreading from there to Austria) and Italy, but the latter was an entirely secondary front and the fighting there was not within the framework of a strategic plan integrated with the fighting in the other theatre. There was even a further theatre, Poland, but the effort made there by Austria against France's client was minor in the extreme and not very successful either. Mobilisation for the war was not comprehensive, though the armies that clashed were very large and the Austrian conscription campaign was the greatest in the history of the empire. The war was between just two armies and Austria's potential partners only stood on the side and watched. This was therefore a large-scale war with budding signs of total war.

The Russian campaign represented a magnification of the previous one in terms of geographic scale and the application of force. From the standpoint of methods of fighting and operational considerations it was unique. Its principal battles were head-on collisions almost entirely devoid of tactical sophistication – pulverisation in the name of pulverisation inspired by fury. The troops never stopped marching. The French wanted to penetrate into the interior of the country on their eastward swing and made desperate efforts to get out on their way back west. The Russians retreated to avoid battle and draw the enemy on and then advanced to trap and destroy him. The battle of Borodino was perhaps the only one calculated to serve the original aims of the war. All the other battles were a product of circumstance. The campaign was marked by skirmishes and raids carried out by Russian units specially designated for those purposes and not taking part in regular operations. This phenomenon was unique to the war, as was the enlistment of the local populace in active fighting and harassment. The main quality that French generals were called upon to exhibit was exemplary leadership, as well as resourcefulness and endurance. This was indeed a unique campaign, and at the same time one more stage in the evolution of large-scale, all-embracing war.

The 1813 campaign saw the participation of all the states that had stood on the sidelines and tested the waters. Massive war preparations and convoluted diplomatic activity gave way to the real thing. The campaign was a continuation of the previous one, but by different means, and was not a two-sided struggle but one that involved many parties. It played itself out mainly on German soil, but this is only a geographic definition. Militarily, it was fought in many theatres – Silesia, Saxony, the Bohemian mountains; Greater Berlin; and the lower Elbe. All the theatres of war were guided by a single strategy and a single operational concept, aiming at mutual interaction between them. Victory in one theatre was apt to contribute to victory in another. This was the first appearance of the idea of a 'second front'. Simultaneously large-scale siege operations were carried out on the Vistula and the Oder with the beleaguered towns constituting a strategic objective in the thinking of the two sides: the French were trying to link up with them and add the large forces bottled up there to their orders of battle in the theatres of operation; the allies were trying to pin down these troops and frustrate the French hopes of getting them into the fighting. The one strategy and one design had been formulated by Napoleon while still in Paris and remained in force despite the many changes wrought by the war. The allies devised their strategy and operational plans gradually in a process unfolding on the field of battle. Within six months, from February to August, the garb of hypocrisy and political self-interest was shed till another time. This was a striking demonstration of the will to victory and the creation of the appropriate means. The Trachenberg conference and the subsequent high-level war councils, up to the end of the armistice, represented the peak of this process, a unique event in the history of practical military thinking, dealing with the enlistment of different nations in a single common cause.

Liddell-Hart was of the opinion that the main contribution to the evolution of great wars was made by the system of mass compulsory conscription: 'Conscription precipitated war in 1914. Mobilisation of conscript armies disrupted national life ... confirming the warning "mobilisation means war".' (Liddell-Hart, B. H.: Why Don't We Learn from History?) The compulsory conscription instituted by the Revolutionary regime was rooted in the spirit of popular volunteerism that swept the French nation, but the vast scale the system assumed from 1812 on was a result of its compulsory basis. The connection between the military apparatus and civilian systems became tighter and more closely co-ordinated. Conscription was carried out on the basis of regional quotas and on the responsibility of the provincial governors, who had been appointed as part of Napoleon's nationwide administrative reform in the first years of his rule. The supply of manpower needs and the organisation of the economy for the war effort were carried out under the direction and control of the civilian ministry of war, in accordance with military demands formulated in Napoleon's behalf. In a study of the manpower supplied to the army, it has been determined that between 1800 and 1813 around 2.5 million Frenchmen were called to the flag, most of them in the last two years. More than a million were drafted for the 1813 campaign alone. In the first decade of the century annual call-ups ran into no more than the tens of thousands.

Napoleon's downfall was the result of the many mistakes he made, and first and foremost his mistaken overall aim, an aim that could not be realised. There is no point in once again reviewing the operational and tactical errors he made in the latter years of his reign, as we determined from the start that the moment he entered into a total war his fate would be sealed, and therefore an analysis of these mistakes is not to the point. What is of interest in approaching the question of 'why he fell' is to be derived from a summation of his way of thinking, his way of doing things, his relations with others and his character. A somewhat oversimplified remark of Fuller's sums up the 'mistaken aim' thesis thus: 'Napoleon had aimed at establishing a universal empire and had followed in the footsteps of the great conquerors of the past. But times had changed ... and Europe was now a mass of crystallising nations.' (Fuller, J. F. C.: The Decisive Battles of the Western World). But despite the basic truth of this observation, we would do well to treat the subject in greater depth.

'Within five years, I shall be master of the world. Russia alone remains, and I am about to crush her.' This is one among many of Napoleon's statements before he embarked on the hopeless campaign of conquest of 1812. Was his motivating force really the idea of being ruler of the world? Was all the suffering and destruction and loss of life endured by the nations of Europe the price of the unrestrained and pathological ambition of a single individual? We might settle for such a view of things were it not so simplistic and self-evident, for even if his motives were to reveal no signs of self-service or self-aggrandisement, they would still be seen to have contained a certain measure of ambition. A look at the sources documenting his various remarks on the subject, or at the views of others, will make for a less circular discussion. For before leaving for Russia, Napoleon also said the following: 'I'm going to finish what is so far only on the drawing-board. We want a European legal code, a European appeals court, a single currency, a single system of weights and measures. I shall make the European nations into one nation and Paris the world capital.' On St Helena, his place of exile, he again remarked that he had aspired to stand at the head of a united Europe. It would not be unreasonable to assume that he dreamed of a world empire as the object of his personal ambition and, judging by the character of his rule in France, a universal regime bearing the stamp of 'enlightened despotism' rather than repressive tyranny. Napoleon had a marked inclination 'to impose order' and with his sense of a fateful and progressively self-fulfilling mission it is not surprising that this inclination developed into all-embracing ambition.

One of his critics, Quinet, examined the roots of this ambition in his book *La Revolution* (1865). He attributed it to Napoleon's Italian origin, finding there the tendency to impose order. 'His ideal was the empire of Constantine and Theodosius. He inherited this tradition from his ancestors... When he dreams of the future, it is always of the submissive world as imaged by the medieval imperialist thinkers.' However, with a little goodwill it is also possible to discern in the imperial dream something of French patriotism. In 1809 he asserted that he had one desire and one desire only, just as he had just one mistress – France. The remark strikes one as sincere.

The combination of a vision of conquering power and the feeling of power deriving from conquest is one of the factors that kept Napoleon from realising that he had no chance of defeating the close-knit Coalition that finally succeeded in acting as a single body. He excelled in estimating the number of forces opposing him and assessing the significance of their quantity and quality. Nor did he fail to grasp the significance of the fact that in addition to the enormous front created in Germany he was involved in a difficult struggle in Spain. None the less he fell victim to the illusion – not completely lacking a logical basis – that he could divide and isolate the forces of his rivals in order to defeat them in detail. Had his monarchical ambitions been limited from the start to France itself and nevertheless he had set out for Russia, but had learned the real lesson of his defeat there (and not harboured the illusion that it was simply the weather that was his undoing), he might have used the army he built to secure France's new borders and rule over a vast and secure country – the object of his ambition. Had he done so he would have spared Europe the total 'world' war that it was plunged into in 1813.

It was imperative that Napoleon wind up his affairs on the Iberian Peninsula in the first months of 1813, when he was building his new army. He had a big, well-trained army and first-rate generals there and should have realised that he was fighting a pointless war. He should have broken off contact with British and Spanish forces, placed troops on the French-Spanish border, which was easy to defend, in order to block the enemy and sent the rest of the expeditionary force to Germany. Had he done so, not only would his infantry have received a big boost but he would have gained cavalry units he was so sorely lacking. For many see the lack of cavalry as a major reason for his failure in the campaign. At St Helena he confessed: 'After Russia, I should have made a deal in Spain. With that army, I would have become master of Germany.' It was already impossible to achieve anything in Spain and if he decided to continue fighting there it was for reasons of prestige and vanity.

The adventure on the Iberian Peninsula has its origins in another fateful mistake involving strategic considerations having a certain logic but on the one hand erroneous in the final analysis and on the other displaying the blindness of someone unwilling to admit his mistakes. Napoleon put up a stubborn but hopeless fight against Great Britain. The economic war he declared against Britain was a substitute for the invasion he was incapable of launching. The economic blockade hurt Britain to a certain extent, but it also hurt France, and hurt other European countries even more, who were unwilling to accept the damages. By persevering in this struggle Napoleon allowed Britain to wage an effective war against him on the edge of the main theatre, which was something it had avoided until then at any cost. The emperor's ill-advised involvement there had begun in 1806 and the truth is it is easier to level justifiable criticism against this involvement than to suggest ways to get out of it in 1813. It stands to reason that Napoleon would have liked to put an end to defuse the hostilities with Britain before embarking on the big war, but there was no chance of Britain's going along with any kind of intrigue other than a settlement acceptable to both itself and the allies, which Napoleon saw as surrender. It is interesting to note that Hitler too, when he was already at war with Britain and France and had conquered Poland, spoke publicly of his readiness to make immediate peace with Great Britain. There is no guarantee that this was not a ruse, but none the less it made sense.

A number of strategic errors connected with the art of war also contributed to the 1813 defeat. The battles of Lützen and Bautzen were fought along tried and proven lines and the mistakes that were made were made in most of the battles that Napoleon directed. The nature of great battles is such that mistakes are made in them, they have critical moments when everything hangs by a single thread. What matters is the final result – on the battlefield and in terms of overall aims. But after Bautzen it was as if Napoleon had lost some of the command qualities that were unique to him, or they were greatly diminished. The commander who always looked to continue striking, to attack without letting up, to control the rhythm of the battle and create new advantages in terms of ground and numbers, was a different man. The commander who maintained that his army was not limited in its ability to shift the centre of gravity of the fighting to wherever it wished no longer displayed the necessary leadership for this. Instead he secured an armistice, after which everything changed. The allies greatly strengthened themselves, their command procedures improved unrecognisably and Austria joined the fray, which might not have happened if a third great battle had been fought, even if the French did not gain a decisive victory.

In August, after the renewal of the fighting, Napoleon lost another advantage he had held in most of his past wars – the advantage of operating on interior lines. Jomini has defined these operational lines as those chosen by a commander to operate along in the face of the enemy while 'concentrating the masses and manoeuvring with his whole force in a shorter period of time than it would require for the enemy to oppose to them a greater force'. The loss of this advantage also resulted from the calculated strategy of the allies, which became more and more purposeful and consistent as the battle of the Nations (October) approached; but the failures of the French played no small part. After the armistice, allied forces were able to finesse the French into the centre of a noose by casting an ever-tightening circle around them which left wide open spaces to the rear for the shifting of troops and logistic organisation: Schwarzenberg in Bohemia and the mountain region, Blücher first in Silesia and then in north Germany alongside Bernadotte. Instead of trying to strike a blow in one place and break through to the spaces serving the enemy – and after the great battle of Dresden he had a golden opportunity to do this – Napoleon divided his fighting effort and within two weeks suffered four reverses which sealed his fate even before the decisive battle of Leipzig. These four battles were fought in the outside of the ring instead of having one battle directed outward from within while concentrating forces.

Many have written of the decline in Napoleon's command ability and leadership, and though one should not exaggerate the part played by these changes, it is impossible to discuss Napoleon's fall without considering them. Cathcart has said that when the events of May are examined it is impossible not to be deeply impressed by French military superiority, despite 'the disasters of 1812'. Maude has asserted that in 1813 Napoleon was 'at his best and his worst'. It may be that the frustrations of May suddenly sapped his strength and dampened his enthusiasm and he lost his enthusiasm and determination though aware that the campaign was a matter of life and death. Count Yorck turns much attention to the personal side of things and these are some of his thoughts: Napoleon was no longer true to himself and therefore erred; his military genius was paralysed, though not entirely, as some of his exploits in the 1813 campaign were equal to his greatest. But this genius was no longer consistent, for it lacked the energy of the past; he had lost the ability to form a picture of the battle on the basis of reports coming in from his commanders and measure it against his preconceived idea of how things would develop; he disparaged reports even if they were accurate. 'His imagination deteriorated into self-deceit.' Chandler believed that Napoleon was increasingly given to a fatalistic attitude, according to which everything was in any case predetermined, and that this mood came to dominate him to the extent of affecting his other talents. Chandler, who enumerated Napoleon's virtues, maintained that for every positive trait there was a negative counterpart that neutralised it, particularly in his latter days: he was endowed with an iron will, irresistible charm, incredible mental gifts, quickness in making decisions, amazing powers of concentration and great industry. But his genius had a grain of madness in it; he fell victim to wishful thinking, believed what he wished to believe and lost his power to judge what was possible, began to gamble and believe in miracles. As early as 1807, Marmont had said: 'He no longer believed the truth when it ran counter to his aspirations.'

Napoleon admitted at St Helena that in the last stages of his career as emperor he lost the self-confidence that had always characterised him, as well as his talent for prediction. He no longer had any luck, he said. 'I sensed within that something was lost to me.'

Napoleon would have done better to give rein to his fatalistic inclinations not only as a mystic force influencing his judgement but also when weighing his chances in the world war he embarked on in April 1813. There was no reason for him not to understand that he was facing a new kind of war. It was impossible for him not to have known that while he was mobilising all of France to realise his designs, his European enemies were doing the same thing. This understanding and this knowledge is the key to the alternative policy he might have pursued, for the formula for aggregate power – the sigma – yields the absolute certainty that France alone had no chance of winning the war.

This formula embraces all the basic factors characterising each of the parties, and not only territory, population, natural resources and civilisation, though these are of the first importance. Total war is more than war between armies; it is war between human societies, between cultures. Therefore one should add to the factors mentioned above, level of general education, national spirit, loyalties to the regime and so forth. In a word, when entire nations go to war, that combination of nations will emerge victorious when the multiple of whose power-enhancing factors yields the highest product. Since it is impossible to quantify many factors in the product, it is only possible to estimate their weight intuitively as a substitute for quantification. Napoleon, endowed with formidable intellectual and intuitive powers, might have calculated his chances and prevented his unavoidable downfall. Unfortunately for him he did not understand, or chose not to understand, what forces had been unleashed in Europe as a result of his conquests and his policies as a conqueror. He underestimated the capabilities inherent in this awakening. Given the new realities that had been created there was a measure of folly in his faith in one decisive battle. Thus any discussion of Napoleon's decline is all but pointless in the face of the one certain and undeniable fact: his real weakness at the most crucial moment of his life was that he did not understand the new circumstances and the new reality and the meaning of the great changes that had taken place in Europe.

Studies of the 1813 war in Germany are replete with the word 'if' in relation to the options open to Napoleon. If he had done this and that, if he had done this instead of that and if this or that marshal had acted differently, then everything – and naturally history as well – would have turned out differently. If Ney had not fallen down in his duty in the village rectangle on 2 May and if the emperor had sent in the Guard earlier on that some day, the French would have won a decisive victory at Lützen. If Ney – again Ney – had attacked at Preititz on 21 May at 10 a.m. instead of 11 a.m., Blücher would not have got away and the victory in the battle of Bautzen would have ended the war. If he had pursued the beaten, retreating enemy after the battle of Dresden on 27 August and not abandoned Vandamme at Kulm and if he had invaded Bohemia and undertaken a war of annihilation there, he would have destroyed the allies' largest army and captured Prague and the war would have been over. If he had appointed one of his three most talented marshals – Davout, Marmont or Saint-Cyr – as commander of an independent army instead of Macdonald, Ney or Oudinot, he would have been victorious on the Katzbach and Berlin fronts and probably won the entire war. And the biggest 'if' of all relates to his decision to seek an armistice in June instead of continuing to fight despite his weakness at the time. The wisdom of hindsight, after almost 200 years, is as empty as the air. If any of these views have a grain of truth in them, they are valid with respect to given military decisions as such and not the war as a whole. The result of the 1813 war in Germany was a foregone conclusion. Its fate was determined the moment it was born. Whether the war was born in the terrible nights of the retreat from Russia or in the sleigh ride from Smorgoni to Paris, the defeat too was born in that snowy wilderness or along that route which ran down the middle of Europe. So too was the fate of Germany sealed when Hitler made war on the combination of forces created in the years 1939–41, a combination that checked him in the western desert and at Stalingrad and moved in for the kill when the United States joined the war against him. It was that simple and straightforward.

The only doubt in this judgement revolves around the question of what would have happened if he had taken up the line of retreat open to him, leading to the Rhine, instead of making his stand at Leipzig. It may be assumed that if he had done so the allies would have left him in peace within the 'natural boundaries' of his country and Europe's balance of power would have been reconstituted without bloodshed. Then France might have participated in the Congress of Vienna and been active in designing Europe's new stability. The historian Sorel, on the other hand, believes that the war aim of the allies was to deny France its natural boundaries as well, which were a result of Revolutionary and early Napoleonic conquests. According to Sorel, the allies brooded on this ambition for 20 years and had this purpose in mind when they embarked on the war of 1813, which could not have been concluded from their point of view until France gave up the Rhineland and Belgium too. In this view, when Napoleon said that acceding to the demands made on him from the end of May to the renewal of hostilities in August would be injurious to France, he was not referring to the empire – this went without saying – but to the security of France itself.

We have seen that in preparing for total war the armies that were to fight against Napoleon adopted the approach and concepts that Napoleon himself fostered and utilised. We have also seen that the limits of the first total war were set mainly by the gap between technology and strategic and tactical thinking. These limits served to retard the process creating such wars until science and technology caught up. Thus, for this reason, if not only, or even mainly, for it, there was a 'retardation' of the process lasting exactly a hundred years. It would seem that the victorious powers were taken aback by the implications of the total nature of war such as it had just been fought, by the unforeseen effect of this kind of war on society and the economy. No method of fighting or more efficient organisation of forces and maintenance could equal the effect of the national element in the great army that had been created, which rested on a spirit and zeal whose end was unpredictable.

In that same period the world was also taken aback by what it had seen with its own eyes of the horrors of the new form of war. The wars of 1812 and 1813, which ranged over the entire European continent, left in their wake death and destruction such as had never before been seen. With the one who had brought it on no longer able to do any more harm there was a feeling that a long period of stability in international relations was about to set in. Most thoughts would now turn to achieving domestic tranquillity, lest the conservative regimes be undermined and undesirable ideas be imported. Total war was necessary for someone seeking sweeping results. The first and main result was a cutback in forces and a return to the old small professional base in place of mass compulsory conscription. This set off a chain reaction, as an army of this kind is physically removed from centres of civilian activity, takes a smaller bite out of the national product and has less of an influence on policy makers.

Military thinking in the period after Napoleon required theoreticians who would sum things up and devise doctrines of warfare that took into account what had been tested on the battlefield. Clausewitz and Jomini were among the most important of these theoreticians. Not only were they capable of composing masterpieces on the art of war through study and reflection, they also had behind them the real experience of serving in the great campaign. This was also a drawback, as they were not sufficiently far removed in time from the events, a necessary condition for fruitful study. This was especially true of Jomini, but Clausewitz too could not give full voice to the implications of everything he had experienced in his empirical studies. He was convinced that if the world did not wish to experience the horrors of the Napoleonic age again, it had to limit the aims of war, which are an extension of political aims. At the same time he expected that given the precedent of total war as an instrument for attaining all-encompassing goals, the model would be revived.

The return to old models had almost no effect on operational and tactical ideas as they had come to the fore in the last campaigns of the Napoleonic era – and not only because these two thinkers expressed them so clearly. The main reason for the continuity in operational and tactical thinking was the continuity of command in the various armies, as it was very difficult to uproot rules and principles that had been formulated and tried out on the battlefield and proven valid. Armies and commanders operate in accordance with the lessons of the past and changes in the means of warfare at their disposal. Consequently operations in the principal wars of the nineteenth century greatly resembled what had been seen on the battlegrounds of Germany and France in 1813 and 1814. As stated, almost the only differences were a function of technological progress. There was an improvement in the rate and accuracy of infantry fire because of the improvement of its basic weapon – the rifle. Artillery weapons were similarly improved. However, a real revolution occurred in the second half of the century in mobility and communications with the advent of the railway and the telegraph.

The adaptation of armies to these changes was incredibly slow. The great innovations were mainly effective in the opening phases of wars, but as soon as forces reached the battlefield no real differences were seen in deployment and assault formations. This is mainly true of the two great wars that took place after 1815: the Crimean War (1853–6) and the American Civil War (1861–5). But also in the two wars that Prussia took part in, against Austria (1866) and against France (1870–71), things were not really different. It should be emphasised that the revulsion from the all-encompassing nature of Napoleon's last campaigns did not affect Prussia, which clung to the concepts of total war developed in the first decade of the century. The armies that participated in the wars of 1866 and 1870–71 were extremely large, though of an order of magnitude similar to the one in 1813. They arrived at the front by railway, but this was only a difference in degree, though a very significant one with regard to mobility; logistic operations were aided by the railway and by telegraph communications, but these do not win wars, which are only decided on the battlefield. At the same time, the width of the front hardly changed. Unfortunately for the young soldiers battle formations remained almost identical, though weapons – including automatic weapons that were being used for the first time – were far more effective. Operationally, what decided the two Prussian wars were encircling and pincer movements, but these were also used at Leipzig in October 1813.

The world war that began in 1914 was monumental in every respect, global in terms of its participants, enlisting all the major economies in the world for its needs, seeing industry hit an incredible peak in the supply of weaponry and auxiliary means, becoming two-dimensional with the beginning of aerial warfare, and including unprecedented naval battles. Battlefields were bristling with troops, artillery and firepower. Senior army commanders and general staffs found it difficult to grasp the significance of the new means of warfare and an enormous gap was opened between capabilities and operational decisions. Consequently the great battles of this war basically resembled those of the nineteenth century, from 1813 on, though the fronts on which they were fought were much broader and the great spaces created were crammed with troops and weapons. The number of artillery shells fired in one day was at least ten times greater. Tactics, however, remained pretty much the same and many operations thus strike one as pure folly. Another development unknown in the past was trench warfare, which characterised the western front after the opening offensives got bogged down. This stalemate testifies to tactical impotence and the inability to exploit military capability to achieve operational decision. It marked a shift from mobile warfare utilising the new weaponry and means of transportation for large-scale manoeuvres to a vast war of attrition in which the opposing sides hoped to prevail by systematically destroying the enemy's means of warfare. Thus the war of 1914–18 was fundamentally a total war fought according to the basic model that had come into being at the end of the Napoleonic era, but with means that had not existed then. At the beginning of the nineteenth century there had been a gap between advanced theory and backward technology. At the beginning of the twentieth century there was a gap between advanced technology and backward thinking.

In the two world wars of the twentieth century, in their final phase, the losing side was able to prolong its death throes to the extent of giving the victorious armies a good scare. In 1918 the Germans launched a tremendous offensive in France and were a step away from victory. In 1944 Hitler unleashed a desperate major offensive in the Ardennes. In both cases the victors extricated themselves from their momentary discomfiture, for in world wars the die is irremediably cast. In 1813, too, a narrow escape route led Napoleon out of the closing ring to delay the end, regroup and stir things up again and maybe again, but twice was the limit.

The French general and theoretician Jacques Antoine Guibert, from whom Napoleon learned a thing or two, wrote in 1778 of the tactics of the future, adding these prophetic remarks: 'And then a man will arise, perhaps hitherto lost in the obscurity of the crowd ... that has been only conscious of his power while actually exercising it, one who has studied very little. He will seize hold of opinions, of circumstances, of chance, and will say to the great theoretician: "All that my rival tells you, I will carry out."' Liddell-Hart examined Napoleon's exploits with the eyes of an 'unromantic historian' and was unimpressed. To such an historian, he said, 'Napoleon is more of a knave than a hero,' and 'to the philosopher, he is even more a fool than a knave: his folly was shown in the ambition he conceived and the goal he pursued.' Clausewitz – like many in his time and subsequent to it – found it difficult to take an unequivocal stand. Napoleon belonged to that class of great conquerors whose main characteristic was that they were statesmen who dictated to military commanders – themselves – what moves to make. Clausewitz was greatly interested in the connection between statesmanship and war. He asserted, rightly, that such people should be judged solely by final results, the bottom line, otherwise we shall fall prey to the illusory charms of these heroes of history.

Thus it must be said that Napoleon was not the man Guibert was looking for. He was no Prometheus. He indeed languished in exile but he did not bring salvation to the world. He was also not a knave, and certainly not a fool. He was great, he wanted it all and got nothing. Standing beside Jean Jacques Rousseau's grave, he said that maybe it would be better if people like Rousseau and himself did not exist. Rousseau never harmed anyone (aside from his children) while Napoleon sacrificed hundreds of thousands of lives. Despite the difference, it may be assumed that what he meant was that in everything great there is the potential to do harm or at least create havoc. If we pause here and reflect we shall see that for most of its history the human race has been governed by men of flesh and blood like itself, making slow progress – with a step back now and then and changes in the cast – and little by little improving the human condition. Perhaps this is as it should be.

POSTSCRIPT

Marshal LOUIS NICOLAS DAVOUT, duke of Auerstädt and prince of Eckmühl. Exiled by order of King Louis XVIII, pardoned and restored to his previous titles. Died of tuberculosis in 1823.

Marshal CLAUDE VICTOR, duke of Belluno. Served the post-Napoleonic regime and was French minister of war, dying in his bed at a ripe old age in 1841.

Marshal MICHEL NEY, duke of Elchingen and prince of Moscow. The hot-blooded redhead who started out as a cooper returned to Paris from Waterloo wishing only to retire and rest his weary body, but was tried, convicted and sentenced to death before a firing squad. Requested and was allowed to give the command to fire himself (December 1815).

General HENRI BERTRAND, count. One of Napoleon's most loyal commanders, never rewarded with the rank of marshal but with him throughout all the stages of his downfall – in exile with him at Elba, looked after him to the day of his death on St Helena and even brought back his remains for reburial in Paris. Lived a distinguished life in Paris until his death in 1844.

Marshal JACQUES ALEXANDRE LAURISTON, count and even marquis. Last seen at Leipzig while still a general – trying in vain to avoid being captured – he was freed in 1814 and returned to France. Took an oath of loyalty to the king, which paid off, getting him the title of marquis and the rank of marshal. Was also minister. Died in 1828.

Marshal AUGUSTE FREDERIC LOUIS MARMONT, duke of Ragusa. Last seen raising the white flag in Paris, for which Napoleon did not forgive him. Exiled from France after the revolution of 1830, lived in Russia, Turkey and Egypt. His unforgiven betrayal gave birth to the French verb raguser as a synonym for treason. Died in Venice in 1852.

General JEAN LOUIS EBENEZER REYNIER, count. Also taken prisoner in Leipzig; freed after a few months and returned to Paris, but his strength failed him and he died of exhaustion a few weeks later (March 1814).

Marshal CHARLES PIERRE FRANCOIS AUGEREAU, duke of

Castiglione. A soldier from his youth, he abandoned Napoleon before he was deposed the first time but did not serve the king and died in 1816.

General JEAN RAPP, count. Contributed little to our story, being stuck in Danzig with an entire corps and being notable for his absence. Surrendered, went back to France and even joined Napoleon when he returned from Elba but was of no further use. Died of cancer in 1817.

Marshal JACQUES ETIENNE JOSEPH ALEXANDRE MACDONALD, duke of Tarantum. Turned his back on the emperor after the fall of Paris but also did not serve the king much. Called by Louis 'Mr Sincerity'. Retired to his estate and died a natural death there in 1840 at the age of 75.

Marshal NICOLAS CHARLES OUDINOT, duke of Reggio. Started out as an apprentice in his father's beer brewery. The most wounded marshal in the Grand Army. Abandoned Napoleon in 1814 and served the king as a commander in the army. Reached a ripe old age and died in his bed in 1847.

Marshal GOUVION SAINT-CYR, count. Studied engineering before serving in the army, joining us at Dresden, where he ended his army career. Served as King Louis's minister of war. Retired in 1819 to farm and write his memoirs. Died in 1830.

EUGENE BEAUHARNAIS, viceroy. Last seen departing for Bavaria to live under his father-in-law the king's protection after promising him to keep his fingers out of France. Dedicated the rest of his life to helping war veterans. Gathered to his fathers at the early age of 43 in 1824.

Marshal LOUIS ALEXANDRE BERTHIER, prince of Neuchatel and Wagram. Napoleon's old faithful chief of staff who knew his master so well and also knew much suffering on account of him. Turned his back on him out of loyalty to France and retired to his father-in-law's estate in Bamberg, Germany. One day, in June 1815, while watching allied soldiers marching off to the Belgian front from his balcony, doubled over, collapsed and died. Rumour had it that he committed suicide.

General ARMAND AUGUSTIN CAULAINCOURT, marquis (from birth), duke of Vicenza. Master of Horse, officer and diplomat and confidant of the emperor, and accompanying our story from beginning to end. Retired immediately after Waterloo and died in 1827.

Field Marshal GEBHARD VON BLÜCHER, prince of Wahlstadt. Spent the last years of his life, when not fighting, receiving honours, including an honorary doctorate at Oxford University (it cannot be said for sure that he read a single book in his life). Died in 1819 in Silesia at the age of 77, in full regalia.

General JOHANN DAVID LUDWIG YORCK, count of Wartenburg. Promoted to field marshal for his services and given a large estate. Died there in 1830.

General FRIEDRICH HEINRICH KLEIST, graf von Nollendorf. Continued to serve in Prussia as a field marshal until his death in 1823.

General AUGUST WILHELM GNEISENAU, graf von Neithard. Appointed governor of Berlin after Waterloo. Commanded the force that put down the Polish rebellion in 1831 and died there of cholera, also with the rank of field marshal.

General FRIEDRICH WILHELM VON BÜLOW, count of Dennewitz. Caused not inconsiderable damage to Napoleon at Grossbeeren, Leipzig and Waterloo, but did not live long enough to enjoy these memories, dying in 1816.

Prince MICHAEL BARCLAY DE TOLLY, field marshal. Received his exalted rank and title after Waterloo. Died in 1818.

Field Marshal LUDWIG ADOLF PETER, Prince WITTGENSTEIN. Sent to fight in Turkey in 1825, could not muster much enthusiasm and retired. Died in 1843.

Count (later Prince) CLEMENS LOTHAR METTERNICH. A diplomat and the son of a diplomat; responsible for making Austria such a major factor in Europe and hatching endless schemes. At the height of his influence during the Congress of Vienna and continued to be a leading figure until the 'spring-time of nations' (1848) when even his legendary powers of manipulation failed him and he was exiled from his country, living three years in Holland. Allowed to return to Austria, he lived quietly on his estate until his death in 1859 at 86, an aged repository of rich memories.

JEAN BAPTISTE BERNADOTTE, marshal of France and crown prince of Sweden. Hoped to reign in France after the fall of Napoleon but in the end became King Charles XIV of Sweden. Despite being a sly schemer, turned out to be a progressive ruler. Died of a stroke in 1844 at the age of 81.

FREDERICK WILLIAM III, king of Prussia. Had a difficult childhood and as king fell under the spell of Tsar Alexander and Metternich. Showed ingratitude to his people after they had responded enthusiastically to the call to the flag. Despite his promises did not grant them a constitution or even basic rights. However, because of his simple ways kept the affection of his people to his dying day, which came in 1840 when he was 70.

FRANZ I, emperor of Austria. Also a ruler of the reactionary type with rigid views but loved by his subjects, who called him 'our good Franz'. Died in 1835 at the age of 67.

ALEXANDER I, tsar of Russia. Napoleon's greatest enemy – a tragic Dostoyevskian figure – who, of all people, looked out for the interests of France after Napoleon's downfall. Despite what appeared to be good intentions, left a legacy of darkness and terror when he died in 1825.

NAPOLEON BONAPARTE (formerly Buonaparte), emperor of France. Asked in his last will that his remains be returned to France. In 1840 his request was granted and his coffin passed beneath the Arc de Triomphe in a splendid procession and was ceremoniously reinterred in the Invalides, as was fitting. In June 1940 another conqueror stood beside the marble monument, his moustache clipped and the straight hair falling across his forehead, stood and quietly reflected. Did he already know then that his fate was sealed?

BIBLIOGRAPHY

The following list includes books that helped me write the present work. I have avoided reproducing the comprehensive list that appears in any general study of Napoleon Bonaparte and his period. At the same time, the books listed here deal with subjects vital to a presentation of the basic characteristics of the great war that was fought in Europe in 1813.

Abbott, John S. C.: *The History of Napoleon Bonaparte*
Ben Jones, R.: *Napoleon Man and Myth*
Bergeron, Louis: *France under Napoleon*
Bowden, Scott: *Napoleon's Grande Armee of 1813*
Brett-James, Antony (ed.): *Europe Against Napoleon*
Bruun, Geoffrey: *Europe and the French Imperium 1799–1814*
Burghersh, Lord of: *Memoirs of the Operations of the Allied Armies, 1813–1814*
Cambridge Modern History VOL. IX Napoleon
Cathcart, George: *Commentaries on the War in Russia and Germany*
Caulaincourt, General de: *Memoirs 1812–1813*
Chandler, David G.: *The Campaigns of Napoleon*
Clausewitz, Carl Von: *On War*
Clough, S. B.: France. *A History of National Economics*
Correspondance de Napoleon Premier
Dard, Emile: *Napoleon and Talleyrand*
Delderfield, R. F.: *Napoleon's Marshals*
Dodge, Theodore A: *Napoleon. A History of the Art of War from Lützen to Waterloo*
Fain, Baron de: *Manuscrit de 1813*
Fisher, Herbert: *Napoleon*
Ford, Franklin L.: *Europe 1780–1830*
Fournier, August: *Napoleon The First. A Biography*
Freedman, Lawrence (ed.): *War*

Bibliography

Fuller, J. F. C.: *The Decisive Battles of the Western World*
Geyl, Pieter: Napoleon: *For and Against*
Guibert, J. A. H. de: *Essai General de Tactique*
Holtman, Robert B.: *The Napoleonic Revolution*
Horne, R. H.: *The History of Napoleon Bonaparte*
Howard, Michael: *War in European History*
Jomini, Baron Antoine Henri de: *Life of Napoleon*
— *The Art of War*
Jones, Archer: *The Art of War in the Western World*
Kemp, Tom: *Economic Forces in French History*
Kennedy, Paul: *The Rise and Fall of the Great Powers*
Kircheisen, F. M.: *Napoleon*
Lachouque, Henry: *The Anatomy of Glory. Napoleon and His Guard. A Study in Leadership*
Lefebvre, Georges: *Napoleon From Tilsit to Waterloo*
Lenz, Max Dr: *Napoleon. A Biographical Study*
Liddell-Hart, B. H.: *Why Don't We Learn From History?*
Macdonald, Marshal: *Recollections*
Macdonnel, A. G.: *Napoleon and His Marshals*
Markham, Felix: *Napoleon*
Maude, F. N.: *The Leipzig Campaign 1813*
Mowat, R. B.: *The Diplomacy of Napoleon*
Nafziger, George: *Lutzen & Baurzen: Napoleon's Spring Campaign of 1813*
— *Napoleon's Dresden Campaign: The Battles of August 1813*
Ney, Marshal: *Memoirs of Marshal Ney*
Nicolson, Nigel: *Napoleon 1812*
Odeleben, E. de: *Relation Circonstanciée de la Campagne de 1813 en Saxe*
Oudinot, Duc of Reggio: *Memoirs (Compiled From Souvenirs of the Duchess of Reggio)*
Petre, F. Loraine: *Napoleon's Last Campaign in Germany – 1813*
Quimby, Robert S.: *The Background of Napoleonic Warfare*
Quinet, Edgar: *La Revolution*
Rose, John Holland: *The Life of Napoleon*
Rothenberg, Gunther E.: *The Art of Warfare in the Age of Napoleon*
Seward, Desmond: *Napoleon and Hitler*
Sorel, Albert: *L'Europe el la Revolution Française*
Taylor, A. J. P.: *The Course of German History*
Tulard, Jean: *Napoleon the Myth of the Saviour*

Wallach, J. L.: *Krigstheorien*
Wilson, R. T. General: *Private Diary of Travels etc. in the Campaigns of 1812–14*
Yorck von Wartenburg, Count: *Napoleon as a General*